The
RECOVERY
of
MEANING

Anthropological Society of Washington

The RECOVERY *of* MEANING

HISTORICAL ARCHAEOLOGY
IN THE
EASTERN UNITED STATES

EDITED BY
MARK P. LEONE AND
PARKER B. POTTER, JR.

Smithsonian Institution Press
Washington and London

The Smithsonian Institution Press publishes a
series of significant volumes in anthropology
edited by the Anthropological Society of
Washington. The Society, the oldest continuously
functioning anthropological association in the
United States, was founded at the Smithsonian
Institution in 1879. Each volume in the series
collects essays written by leading scholars on
aspects of a central topic and originating in a
program of lectures sponsored by the Society.

Library of Congress
Cataloging-in-Publication Data

The Recovery of meaning.

(Anthropological Society of Washington series)
Bibliography: p.
1. Archaeology and history—Atlantic States.
2. Material culture—Atlantic States. 3. Industrial
archaeology—Atlantic States. 4. Atlantic States—
Antiquities. 5. Archaeology and history—Southern
States. 6. Archaeology and history—New England.
7. Southern States—Antiquities. 8. New
England—Antiquities.
I. Leone, Mark P. II. Potter, Parker B.
III. Series.
F106.R39   1988   974   87-26499
ISBN 0-87474-616-7 (cloth)
1-56098-422-8 (paper)
British Library Cataloging-in-Publication Data
is available.

∞The paper used in this publication meets the
minimum requirements of the American
National Standard for Permanence of Paper for
Printed Library Materials Z39.48-1984

Manufactured in the United States of America

The illustration on p. 270 is reprinted with
permission of the Royal Anthropological Institute
of Great Britain and Ireland.

This book was edited by Vicky Macintyre and
designed by Linda McKnight.

Contents

Contributors

Texas B. Anderson
Executive Director
Art League of Houston
Houston, TX 77006

Elise M. Brenner
Department of Philosophy and
   Anthropology
Bloomsburg University
Bloomsburg, PA 17815

Constance A. Crosby
Department of Anthropology
University of California
Berkeley, CA 94720

James F. Deetz
Lowie Museum of Anthropology
University of California
Berkeley, CA 94720

Mark P. Leone
Department of Anthropology
University of Maryland
College Park, MD 20742

Barbara J. Little
Department of Sociology and
   Anthropology
George Mason University
Fairfax, VA 22030

Randall H. McGuire
Department of Anthropology
State University of New York
Binghamton, NY 13901

Roger G. Moore
6621 Wharton Street
Moore Archaeological Consulting
Houston, TX 77055

Charles E. Orser, Jr.
Department of Geography and
   Anthropology
Louisiana State University
Baton Rouge, LA 70803-4105

Contributors

Ann M. Palkovich
Department of Sociology and
  Anthropology
George Mason University
Fairfax, VA 22030

Robert Paynter
Department of Anthropology
University of Massachusetts
Amherst, MA 01003

Parker B. Potter, Jr.
New Hampshire Division of
  Historical Resources
Concord, NH 03302-2043

Theresa A. Singleton
National Museum of American
  History
Smithsonian Institution
Washington, DC 20560

Stanley South
South Carolina Institute of
  Archaeology and Anthropology
University of South Carolina
Columbia, SC 29208-0071

David Hurst Thomas
Department of Anthropology
American Museum of Natural
  History
New York, NY 10024-5192

CHAPTER I

Introduction
Issues in Historical Archaeology

MARK P. LEONE AND PARKER B. POTTER, JR.

This volume began with a lecture series organized by Mark Leone and presented by the Anthropological Society of Washington during its 1984–85 season. The series was entitled "The Recovery of Meaning in Historical Archaeology." The lectures focused primarily on the use of archaeology and documents to investigate meaning and structure and secondarily on sites whose meanings were by and large religious or ideological.

Although we have organized the following essays chronologically, beginning with those dealing with the 16th century, our purpose is not to affirm culture history or cultural evolution. This book is neither an archaeologically based culture history of the historic Eastern United States nor is it, on the whole, informed by an evolutionary perspective. The danger, of course, in using evolution as an analogy for understanding long-term cultural change is that this perspective can make people appear passive and subject to change somehow beyond the realm of human agency (Leone, Potter, and Shackel 1987:292). Such a view would be particularly damaging to the essays in this volume because all of the contributors share the sense that people (not necessarily individuals) have an active role in conceiving, making, using, discarding, and thinking about the items of material culture that have become the historical archaeological record.

Despite the drawbacks of a chronological framework, our arrangement has the benefit of placing together essays that deal with similar data from different perspectives. Particularly interesting are the complementary pairs of essays by South and Thomas on 16th-century Spanish America, Brenner and Crosby on the 17th-century contact period in Southern New England, Deetz and Leone on the 18th century, and Singleton and Orser on 19th-century plantation slavery. We hope that this organizational strategy gives the book the feeling of a discussion, and one not yet completed, rather than the appearance of a set of final pronouncements on issues already solved.

The book is divided into five parts, each preceded by a brief introduction to the chapters that follow. In the rest of this chapter we draw on several of the essays to explore three issues that are relevant to many of the studies described in the book and to much of historical archaeology.

THREE ISSUES IN HISTORICAL ARCHAEOLOGY

We would like to begin by quoting Warwick Bray:

> One can recognize . . . a fairly standard cycle of events [in the development of archaeology]. A new movement emerges (generally based on ideas developed in another discipline, and often just as these are beginning to go out of fashion on their home ground), is accepted uncritically by its devotees, fails to deliver the promised goods, gradually loses its adherents and is in turn replaced by another "new wave." . . . The good (and there is always some) is retained and adopted into the mainstream of archaeology, and the sillinesses . . . fade away with maturity. (Bray 1986:784)

As Bray points out, archaeology is well known as a consumer of ideas from other disciplines, and historical archaeology is no exception. Of the two side issues raised by Bray—"paradigm lag" and the uncritical acceptance of ideas from outside archaeology—we find the latter to be quite significant. As long as archaeologists have ideas from which to create a method, the source of those ideas seems unimportant. What is important, however, is the way that ideas from other disciplines become archaeological ideas, a process that should be transformational and not simply uncritical acceptance.

In this essay we discuss three sets of ideas that historical archaeologists use to recover meaning. Each set is called upon to solve particular problems. First, functionalism has been used as a paradigm that produces meaning by creating systematic coherence in the object of study. For functionalism, and evolutionary theory, with which it is often allied, meaning is equated with religion or any of the other things labeled "ideology" under non-Marxist definitions of that term. Second, symbolic and structural analysis has been used to constitute meaning from the point of view of "the other" under study. In symbolic analysis, the definition of meaning is broad; meaning is considered to be the entirety of the native point of view. In structural analysis, meaning is found in the ways the mind works, creating, operating, and mediating structural oppositions. A cognitive approach finds meaning in native taxonomies distilled from the native point of view. Third, the most recent development among the methods detailed here is the use of Lewis Binford's middle-range theory (Binford 1981, 1983, 1987) to forge a more productive relationship between the archaeological record and the documentary record so as to recover the richest meaning possible from the combination of these two sources of knowledge about the past.

Functionalism: Coherence and Continuity

In chapters 2 and 3 we see senior, accomplished, experienced archaeologists Stanley South and David Thomas making two useful and productive assumptions: coherence and continuity. Coherence is made up of two parts, the basic functionalist assumption that the elements of a society can be fitted together to achieve a view of how that society works or worked, and the corollary assumption that societies achieve some functional end, like colonization through the missionization of Native Americans. South's and Thomas's second assumption, continuity, which is less clearly stated in their work, is that 16th-century Spanish nationalism, including its Roman Catholicism, are understandable be-cause, despite incremental changes within them, these phenomena still exist. Neither extinction nor dramatic alteration has created an unmendable cleavage between past and present.

The work of South and Thomas demonstrates the benefits of using the assumption of coherence, the most notable being the place it gives religion. Every author in this book, and probably every historical archaeologist, knows that religion was central to the society with which he or she works and thus religion needs a serious explanation. By considering religion in terms of its contributions to the overall goals of the Spanish colonial system, the functionalism of South and Thomas is a way of seeing Roman Catholic institution building and belief as significantly more than epiphenomenal. Part of the reason for South's and Thomas's successes in this area is that both scholars are probably more

3

influenced by world systems theory, by Braudel and Wallerstein, than they are, in any immediate way, by Radcliffe-Brown or Leslie White. This mix of functionalism and world systems theory has strengths beyond its crucial ability to deal with religion, but it also has some weaknesses.

There are at least three strengths. First, in historical archaeology, including that of Spanish America, the relevant systems were and can be reconstructed to be worldwide, or at least "half-a-world wide." This facilitates comparative analysis and is a strong hedge against particularism. Second, the colonization of the New World was explicitly oriented to aggrandizing power and profit; profit and wealth were produced by using ideas of rationality and efficiency. This makes obvious the value and appropriateness of functionalist models based on these same ideas, and in particular South's version of White's energy-flow model. Third, frontiers are an important part of colonization, nation building, conquest, and missionization. Culturally, frontiers mean loss, failure, poverty, struggle, barbarism, and the mix of armies and cultures. These cultural phenomena often produce strange archaeological residues, more military artifacts than is usual, more artifacts associated with "male" activities, more but selectively deposited native materials, and oddly impoverished yet richly skewed European materials. The value of a functionalist approach for understanding frontiers is that any notion of coherence contains ideas about boundaries, and thus frontiers have a clear place, analytically. These are some of the strengths of the assumptions made by those using the mix of functionalism and evolutionary theory now entering historical archaeology through world systems theory (Wallerstein 1974, 1980; Braudel 1981, 1982, 1984).

Largely missing in current applications of this body of theory in historical archaeology are the vulgar materialism, the dismissal of religious and other symbolic systems, the search for perfect correlations, and the overriding emphasis on subsistence efficiency characteristic of many applications of the same body of theory in prehistoric archaeology. Also missing is the active distancing of archaeologists from the objects of their study through the use of universalizing concepts of increasing complexity.

Despite its strengths, the world systems approach is not without flaws, three of which are particularly noteworthy. First, failure, irrationality, emotion, the cultural survival of the defeated and the cultural subversion of the conquering are all poorly grasped within this approach. Although these concerns are not dismissed as irrelevant issues, they are sometimes thought to be unamenable to testing with concrete data. However, a more fundamental problem is that this approach seldom employs a conceptual framework for describing phenomena that cannot be understood as having a clear and simple relationship to the systematic functioning of a society achieving, or not achieving, its goals. The cause of that tendency requires research and self-reflection. The question of how to deal with these phenomena, particularly failure, is a serious one. Evolutionary theory, even as practiced in prehistoric archaeology and paleoanthropology, rarely takes into account the matter of failure. The failures of Spanish missions, forts, colonies, ships, and armies are usually treated as historical episodes but not as an index to a weakness in the theory, nor as a chance to use another approach or to address weaknesses in the theory.

Second, the world systems approach provides only limited ways to achieve an appreciation of native meanings and cultures. This weakness, like several of its strengths, flows from the striking resemblance between functionalist theory and the phenomenon under study. This particular weakness is, in fact, the other side of the third strength just cited: Colonization of the New World left clearly marked frontiers, which functionalist approaches are good at locating; but many of the colonizers failed to understand the natives on the other sides of frontiers, and systems approaches are often unable to characterize what lies beyond boundaries. Like the 16th-century Spanish, many contemporary analysts have failed to learn from the failures of the Jesuits or the limited successes of the Franciscans that a systems-based frame of reference has a hard time finding a satisfactory place for "the other"; some even fail to see this as a problem. Not even an ethnohistorical approach touched by a Marxian view, like Trigger's (1980, 1986) or Orser's (with tenant farmers) in this volume, contains the assumptions or method needed to describe the experience of another culture.

The third flaw of the functionalist/world systems approach is the most complex. For the same reasons that this approach has trouble dealing with "the other" in the past, it has difficulty recognizing its own operation in the present. This dilemma is inherent in a universalizing perspective. It is particularly troublesome in light of the issue of continuity between past and present. Just as functionalist theory is probably continuous with the Western European capitalist ideology emergent in the time periods studied by historical archaeologists, so too is there continuity, between the present and the past under study, among the objects of study. Florida and coastal Georgia were settled by the Spanish in the 16th century, and parts of that colonized area are inhabited by Hispanic Americans today, although contemporary Hispanics are by no means members of a dominant culture in the way that they were in the 16th century. But it is not a coincidence that Hispanic sites are being excavated in several places in the coastal Southeast and that a celebration of the 500th anniversary of the Columbian voyages is occurring simultaneously with the first serious political action by Hispanic Americans in the United States. In fact, most American historical archaeology is conducted among the descendants of the societies under study, if we define the terms *descendant* broadly. The difficulty is that there are many different contemporary interests to be served, or that can be served, by the archaeology of a past continuous with the present. The danger is that historical scholarship could become dominated by presentism, held consciously or unconsciously, which casts the past in terms of the present without being explicit about how or why. Such inexplicit presentism can make the present seem inevitable and contemporary inequalities natural or appropriate while hindering the production of knowledge about the past that could be used to challenge the contemporary order. Archaeologists have suggested two ways to get around this. The first is to take the functionalist stance and place one's faith in the scientific method as a way of controlling or eliminating bias. The second way to control the use of the past—exemplified by Wylie (1985), who holds that the first way does not go far enough—is to understand contemporary interests and the ways in which contemporary social context acts on and can use the products of even the most bias-free historical scholarship.

Recognizing the use of the past is the easier part of the problem. To cite one example, many know that objects from the past have been used to foster social goals since the American preservation movement began in the 1870s (Wallace 1986). Chapter 3 provides another example. David Thomas discusses the "black legend"—the British-perpetuated idea that the Spanish were predisposed to inhumane actions against others—and tells how it became a powerful and durable piece of propaganda. An understanding of phenomena like this can lead one to ask whether seemingly neutral historical knowledge has contemporary social and political uses. The functionalist/world systems approach offers little assistance for those wishing to formulate such questions, since a part of the ability to form these questions derives from having the freedom to question and challenge analytical categories. But this freedom is lacking in an analytical framework that depends on universal, atemporal categories as the basis for global analysis spanning five hundred years.

There is little question that inappropriate categories have been invented by those who colonized and by those who have studied colonization. Indian leaders, chiefs, and heros were made up; Indian religion had to be distinguished from Native American economy and politics. Land had to be given value, and labor along with it. An entirely non-Western way of life had to be both ignored and reclassified before European expansion could happen. But world systems theory, so helpful in digesting European expansion, sometimes perpetuates those categories by pushing quite creatively right up to the boundaries of a profit-motivated system, without ultimately crossing them. This flaw is not readily acknowledged in the literature on how to conduct world systems analysis. Thus, not only is the perspective limited in its ability to handle other cultures, but it runs the risk of perpetuating the categories that created the modern world by using them for analytical purposes. It does this by necessity. Domination is perpetuated by using for analysis the categories of the dominant, a process Marxists term hegemony.

This discussion of the weaknesses of the functionalist approach to historical archaeology leads directly to the second major set of perspectives we wish to discuss: symbolic and structural analysis. These two methods have attempted to address the larger problems that characterize the functionalist approach.

Symbolic and Structural Approaches

Whereas the great advantage of functionalist approaches is that they enable us to see cultures as coherent and integrated, the principal benefit of symbolic and structural approaches is that they help us understand cultures in terms that approximate native meanings. A native point of view is one that represents people who have been disfranchised, destroyed, encompassed, colonized, or silenced in some way. Representing Native Americans (as Brenner and Crosby do) or black tenant farmers (as Orser is sometimes able to do) is not done simply, automatically, or without attention to relevant details. The world view of another people can be presented by two means: symbolic analysis and structural analysis. In this volume, Brenner and Crosby use the former, Deetz the latter, and the goal of all three is to arrive at a coherent sympathetic understanding of another way of thinking.

Symbolic and structural approaches are by no means the only ones interested in native meaning. Critical theory is concerned with ideology and attempts to understand systems of thought or systems of representation. Native meaning among capitalist and stratified societies is a concern, insofar as it is possible to specify the relationship between native meaning and social, political, and economic factors. This linkage is not necessarily limiting, particularly when it is coupled with a critique, such as McGuire's in chapter 14, that raises questions about the strength and the integrity of the dominant ideology. Like symbolic analysis, critical theory calls upon the analyst, in this case the archaeologist, to situate him or herself within his or her own culture.

SYMBOLIC ANALYSIS.   A symbolic approach to meaning has several strengths and weaknesses, but we cite the main two in each category.

One strength of the symbolic approach is that it presents native meaning coherently. When Crosby uses the concept of *manit*, drawn from native and English texts, she begins to present the coherence inside the Native American culture of 17th-century southeastern Massachusetts. She does not give a complete picture, but it is deeper than the one Trigger (1986) paints for the Huron and the Iroquois. Orser tries to analyze black tenant farm life, but Jones (1985) has the quotations, texture, and feeling. And even in these analyses the main organizing symbols are missing. But *manit*, as discussed by Crosby, is both symbol and metaphor and clearly acts metonymically. That is, things do not simply stand for the quasi supernatural; some things that possess *manit* actually are divine. Thus we can see not only native meanings for things, but also native ideas about meaning and coherence among meanings. Getting this far is hardly a triumph for an anthropologist, but getting this far is relatively new for archaeology.

The second strength of the symbolic approach is its value to archaeology, which can be explained best through an example. Brenner discusses red coats, traded by the English to Native Americans. From ethnohistorical sources we know that these coats played a particular social role in Native American culture. However, historical archaeologists as a rule do not dig up coats; they dig up the buttons that were sewn onto coats. The question is: How are buttons to be placed into a broader, coherent context? The functionalist choice, rooted in the categories of the dominant culture, might well turn to the European context of button manufacture and distribution, placing archaeologically recovered buttons into a ready-made typology based on chronology and/or material. This assumes that the folks who made and sold European goods had the last meaningful ideas about what buttons were and what they meant, a procedure that involves the imposition of categories that were very likely meaningless to the Native Americans buried in the red coats whose buttons we dig up. A symbolic approach would challenge these categories and attempt to restore native meaning. In this case, buttons become parts of coats, which is what they were to Native Americans, instead of evidence for the history of technology. Thus Brenner is able to use buttons as evidence of social status: To trade for a coat required particular skills, and red was a prized color because the visibility of a red coat could demonstrate at great distances the trading skills of its wearer.

These are the strengths of the symbolic approach: It enables the researcher to discover and present native meanings and systems of meaning and to move the analyst beyond the strictly archaeological record in ways that are sympathetic to the native point of view. The two weaknesses we discuss below are not so much demonstrated deficiencies as they are questions that have not yet been answered by those using this mode of analysis.

The first of these areas of concern is methodological. A symbolic analysis requires an enormous commitment to historical documents, anthropological theory, and patience. This is also the theoretical environment in which to see that historical archaeology is not necessarily privileged epistemologically because it has access to documents. Rather, the researcher has to develop a complex and sophisticated method in order to handle the inaccessibility of meanings characteristic of either documents or artifacts. Brenner, Crosby, and Orser, as well as others not represented in this volume, have had success in employing the documentary record, but methodologically such successes usually come across as specific and unique. What is missing in even the best work so far is a method that solves the problem of how to array the documentary and archaeological data against each other productively. One solution to this problem is proposed in the third section of this chapter.

The second drawback of symbolic analysis is a direct result of the depth of insight into other cultures that one can gain by using that approach. We criticized the functionalist approach because it has sometimes been used as a basis for dominating "the other." However, although the symbolic approach solves the immediate analytical problem of meaning, it does not explicitly address the larger political problem of domination. In fact, if one argues that knowledge is power, then the knowledge produced by symbolic analysis is likely to be dangerous to the objects of that knowledge. This point becomes even clearer when we consider the questions for which symbolic analysis has no built-in answers: Who has rights to the past of "the other?" What do we do with what we know? What are the obligations of white scholars using powerful techniques like symbolic analysis to gain access to Native American culture? Is anyone disfranchised by such scholarship? Is anyone overempowered? By posing these questions, we do not intend to suggest that there are any simple, clear-cut answers, only that the answers do not exist within symbolic analysis and remain to be worked out. Here is yet another important question: What about using sophisticated symbolic analysis, which is effective at opening Native American culture, as a way to open up areas of our own culture in which the notions of the past and cultural integrity were created and remain largely unexamined?

STRUCTURAL ANALYSIS.   In this chapter we have linked symbolic analysis with structuralist method and cognitive analysis. Deetz (1977, 1983) is the chief scholar here and virtually the only one in historical archaeology to use structuralism and cognitive anthropology effectively. And, of course, if his example had not been so powerful in its results, there would be little need to explore the strengths and weaknesses of the approach.

The signal strength of Deetz's structural approach is its ability to discover or create links between functionally different things. We all know that 18th-century people did not think using the categories in most of our site reports: ceramic thoughts here, faunal thoughts there, and so on. Further, many of us have wondered what houses, gravestones, and, say, plates all had that makes them seem, at some inexplicit level, comparable or alike. Deetz's answer, and the idea that has become his intellectual trademark for half a generation of historical archaeologists, is the mental image, template, or cognitive pattern that he calls bilateral symmetry and that he uses to characterize the (European) New England mind in the 18th century. The concept is intellectually elegant, has tremendous integrative power, and has led Deetz to a broadly satisfying understanding of 17th- and 18th-century Anglo-America. But like the approaches previously discussed, it too has certain weaknesses.

The first question one might ask is How do we know? Deetz's understanding of 18th-century Anglo-America, like that gained through any other structural analysis, is built on symbolic repetition of which natives do not have to be consciously aware. Native awareness is beside the point, and "the other" remains largely statistical, as in structuralist analyses in general. The structuralist method produces meanings that are rich but that rarely use native voices. The meanings recovered sometimes remain untied to the societies to which they are ascribed. For example, Deetz categorizes emotion but shows us none in his analyses. This foreclosure of an internal understanding of "the other" may be a form of disfranchisement and is the same flaw we noted in the functionalist perspective. The concept of mind used in structuralism is just as external to the native objects of analysis as functionalist notions of coherence and efficiency.

Another weakness of the structuralist approach is its treatment of history, particularly its handling of questions such as What makes Georgian ways of thinking appear and disappear? The answers are crucial because they determine whether we will be able to work with and use Deetz's picture of 17th- and 18th-century Anglo-America rather than simply admire it. Once we understand how this pattern of thought emerged we will be able to understand how it is connected to what is thought about. This knowledge will in turn allow us to examine that pattern of thought in other contexts. In his elaboration of the idea of mediation, Deetz is beginning to deal with the mechanisms of change. When fully developed to include notions of causality, it will enable us to examine local expressions of the Georgian order in a sophisticated way, and to ascribe meaning to deviations from the regionwide Georgian cultural norms. Such an understanding of change, causality, and context will in turn allow us to take an idea fitted to New England and use it to understand the Chesapeake, Charleston, or even South Africa without destroying local contextual meaning or denying the need for it. But both of these moves are yet to be developed.

To sum up, both symbolic and structural approaches to historical archaeology produce a richness of meaning beyond the reach of most functionalist analyses and the universalizing categories they typically employ. However, each has significant problems. For symbolic analysis the key questions concern the social responsibility that accompanies the deep insights that are possible. For structural analysis the central question is how to introduce chronology and change in a way that leads to an understanding of local variation and that enables us to apply adequately the idea of the Georgian Order to areas beyond New England.

Middle-Range Theory

Our discussion of middle-range theory, the third major issue of interest here, takes the form of a proposal rather than an appraisal of previous work. Our starting point is the relationship between the documentary record and the archaeological record, which is touched on to a greater or a lesser extent in every essay in this volume and is indeed a concern of all historical archaeologists. By highlighting this problem we do not mean to suggest that there have not been some creative and productive uses of documents and some intelligent integration of documentary and archaeological evidence within historical archaeology, only that such successes are specific to particular analyses and point to the need for a more broadly applicable method.

The problem is that there are currently only two ways to link the documentary record and the archaeological record, and neither adequately advances the growth of knowledge. With the first method, one excavates first and uses the documentary record to identify the archaeological finds as if the documentary record was some kind of time machine. With the second, one begins with a history based on documents, in order to provide context, and then excavates to fill in gaps or add detail. In both of these procedures the archaeological record and the documentary record are treated as if they are linked, with one a dependent version of the other. Rarely is this assumption made explicit or justified, but it leads the researcher to integrate documentary and archaeological materials in a single move, from one line of evidence to the other, and to do little more than search for extremely circumscribed information. Unexpected information is usually labeled an exception and thus is discarded, with the result that any hope of fresh insights is lost.

A tremendous improvement on this unsatisfactory pattern of research may be found in Binford's work on middle-range theory. We turn first to his advice to the ethnoarchaeologist:

> We must make decisions and design research strategies. We must therefore rationally consider and discuss ways that we can use our secure knowledge to tease our ignorance for new insights and ideas. One very important strategy is conducting middle range research. . . . One must be able to use the knowledge gained through such studies to design research procedures that will be likely to yield more provocative observations of relevance to the past. (Binford 1981:244)

More specifically, Binford writes of the

> tendency of Africanists to note the similarities among assemblages, presumably deriving from their all having been subjected to various destructive agents, and therefore dismiss the "unpatterned" variability remaining as "noise." . . . The point is that assemblages generally have multiple causes. We must use our knowledge of some causes linked to their diagnostic effects. . . . Given an unknown we must perform various tests with each, eliminating known elements or compounds from the unknown material. That is, we must continually break the unknown down into recognizable constituents. . . . The residue from our use of knowledge that should receive our research attention eventually appears. (Binford 1981:245–46)

In a more recent article, Binford (1987) is more precise about the methods of such research. He notes the importance of the difference between what would be predicted on the basis of ethnography and what is found archaeologically. Referring to the differences as "ambiguity," Binford points out that rather than being noise, or the result of a poor, discrediting, or irrelevant fit, the difference is a critical piece of knowledge. He suggests that such knowledge has substantial epistemological value, which stems from the assumption that each line of evidence is *independent*. This assumption makes it possible to move back and forth from one line to the other, rather than use one as a check on the other. In other words, the assumption of independence permits a dynamic, almost dialectical relationship between archaeological and ethnographic evidence, a relationship virtually precluded under the assumption of dependence, in which unexpected evidence is usually relegated to irreducible nondata residual categories like ignorance and error. Independence allows us to continue to expand our knowledge and enrich the meanings we recover.

Ambiguity cannot be identified without a precise system of description to facilitate meaningful comparisons between the ethnographic and archaeological records. In Binford's recent work with bones (Binford 1987), the concept of economic anatomy serves as the descriptive grid. In this case the grid is simply the mammal skeleton in a butchering context, and it serves as a frame of reference against which to compare samples of bones observed ethnographically and recovered archaeologically. Neither sample is considered correct and therefore superior to the other. The precision gained by comparing precisely one set of butchered bones with another by means of a descriptive grid is a great step forward with application of middle-range theory and makes it possible to identify ambiguity—namely, the differences between the sets of bones. It is by examining these differences that knowledge of the past is gained, Binford argues.

Still another important concept from middle-range theory is the idea of organizational behavior, which refers to the behavior of people using material culture. In the case of bones, butchering is the organizational behavior that must be considered by the ethnoarchaeologist. Frequently it is by referring to organizational behavior that the analyst is able to assign meaning to ambiguity.

In adapting Binford's middle-range theory from ethnoarchaeology to historical archaeology, we propose that the concept be used as an analogy, and that the documentary record be substituted for the ethnographic. The documentary record is clearly not as lively as the ethnographic record, but neither is it as distant, dead, or mute as the archaeological record. Like the ethnographic record, the documentary record often contains native taxonomies and sets of rules that can be used to construct descriptive grids. Moreover, other parts of the documentary record that discuss how things were used can shed light on organizational behavior. Given this analogy, four parts of middle-range theory are particularly useful for historical archaeology: (1) the independence of the archaeological and the documentary records, (2) the concept of ambiguity, (3) the use of descriptive grids, and (4) the idea of organizational behavior.

As noted earlier, most historical archaeological uses of the documentary record are limited and limiting searches for specific information, predicated on the hidden assumption that one line of evidence depends on the other. In fact, however, the archaeological and documentary records that we use were usually produced in different contexts, by people who usually had no direct connections with one another; those who created the documentary record were only infrequently the people who made, used, and discarded the material culture we recover archaeologically. Further, we would suggest that a creamware plate in the hands of a worker in Staffordshire is a fundamentally different thing from the same plate, three months later, in the hands of its ultimate owner in colonial Maryland. Someone making a patternbook in Staffordshire was describing the former but not the latter. Thus, in turning to 18th-century Staffordshire pottery records to obtain names for archaeological finds from colonial Massachusetts, Maryland, or Virginia—an archaeological convention that is useful but based on a false premise—we create a connection *that did not exist in the past.* As archaeologists, we attempt to describe plates excavated from colonial sites but those in Staffordshire creating the documentary record we often use to help us do so were performing an entirely different task, in a different context, and they could not possibly have anticipated us and our archaeological needs. Once we abandon the conceit that the documentary record was created for us, with our needs in mind—in other words, once we abandon the submerged premise of the dependence of the archaeological record on the documentary—we are left with two *independent* sources of evidence about the past and are able to work back and forth, from one to the other, using each to extend the meaning of the other.

The way to act on this independence between the two kinds of data and set up analytical byplay is to create descriptive grids, often based on insights from the documentary record, against which to array the archaeological record. One creates the framework, derives from it expectations of the archaeological record, and then uses the deviations from the expectations, the "ambiguity," in Binford's terms, as the basis for a new set of questions about the archaeological record *and* about the documentary record as well. In such an analysis, organizational behavior, which can also be learned from the documentary record, is the concept used to ascribe meaning to the ambiguities discovered through careful description and comparison.

An example may be helpful. Leone has conducted extensive work on 18th-century formal gardens, particularly the reconstructed William Paca Garden in Annapolis, Maryland, originally built circa 1765. He began that work by reading two bodies of literature: (1) the work of 20th-century garden scholars such as Lockwood (1934) and Mac-Cubbin and Martin (1984) and (2) 18th-century gardening books of the kind available to Paca and his contemporaries, such as Miller's *The Gardener's Dictionary* (Miller 1733) and the works of Langley (1726) and Switzer (1742). These writings served as the basis for constructing a descriptive grid. From the 20th-century scholarship Leone learned how to look at gardens as flat spaces with horticultural purposes, and from the 18th-century books he learned a set of names for parts of gardens and a set of rules for garden building. This body of knowledge became the basis for a descriptive vocabulary and a set of garden attributes on which to focus analytical attention. From this descriptive grid he formulated a set of expectations about the Paca garden itself, which was, in fact, recovered archaeologically so that the reconstruction became an archaeological context. As we explain below, the garden did not meet either set of expectations.

The clearest insights into the use of middle-range theory come from the expectations derived from 20th-century garden scholarship. Virtually all such scholarship treats 18th-century gardens as two-dimensional entities. Because gardens are graphically represented from a bird's-eye view, their topography is often overlooked or considered inconsequential. Leone's expectation was that the Paca garden was a two-dimensional entity, an expectation derived from one part of the descriptive grid. This expectation was violated by his experience in the garden. Standing at certain points, he noted that some distances appeared either greater or less than they actually were. These turned out to be optical illusions based on a conception of the garden as a volume, or as three-dimensional space. Three-dimensional space was the ambiguity. It was not supposed to be there, according to 20th-century garden scholars; and the 18th-century garden books, when read in the ways suggested by their 20th-century commentators, gave little indication of three-dimensionality, either. The typical historical archaeological move would be to dismiss the discovery of three-dimensionality as unintentional or idiosyncratic, as something other than data. Middle-range theory, however, would have us move back to the 18th-century garden books and read them from a new perspective, one based on experience in the archaeological garden. When read with a different set of questions in mind, these garden books indeed proved to contain a number of hitherto unnoticed rules for the manipulation of three-dimensional space, based on the placement of terraces, the use of converging and diverging lines, and other techniques. By giving something inexplicable in the archaeological record the status of data, Leone was able to reanalyze the documentary record and see something that was unnoticed when the documents were read using other assumptions. The next step was to use insights from a new understanding of the garden books to guide subsequent archaeology in other gardens (Hopkins 1986; Roulette, Williams, and Disimone 1986) to search for physical evidence of optical illusions such as nonparallel lines that otherwise would have been dismissed as the result of poor gardening, inattention to detail, or the lack of sophisticated gardening equipment.

The second expectation violated by the Paca garden comes directly from the 18th-century garden books. According to most of them, an up-to-date mid-18th-century garden was be a wilderness garden based on baroque principles of design and curvilinear geometry. By this standard, the Paca garden can be characterized as behind the times. About one-third of it is a wilderness garden, but the two-thirds nearest the house are terraced and formally planted in a style that harkens back to Renaissance gardens. But the argument that Paca was just slow to copy European fashion, like most diffusionist/time-lag arguments, relegates the differences between Paca's garden and the gardens in the books to the realm of nondata and makes the garden almost impossible to interpret. Middle-range theory, however, offers an alternative. If the deviation between Paca's garden and the up-to-date models is treated as ambiguity, then one may turn to the organizational behavior, the 18th-century context of garden use, to learn how the garden functioned and what the ambiguity means. The question was: Given what we know about how gardens were used, what would be the use of three-dimensionality? Leone has begun to answer this question in several pieces on the garden (Leone 1984, 1987), basing his interpretations of the messages communicated by optical illusions on the fact that 18th-century gardens were complex symbols, used for entertaining and for establishing and maintaining social position. In that context, Leone argues, the optical illusions represent a mastery of nature through geometry analogous to the mastery of society through law to which men like William Paca aspired about the time of the American Revolution.

In the first part of this example, the concept of ambiguity and the use of a descriptive grid directed a research strategy that moved from the documents to the archaeology back to the documents and back to the archaeology, a strategy that is expected to extend our knowledge of the past. The second part of the example demonstrates the value of the concept of organizational behavior for recovering meaning from ambiguity.

There is no denying that the Paca garden is a particularly rich archaeological context and is well-suited to middle-range research. But one need not have as ideal a setting as this to make use of middle-range theory. For example, Potter (1982) recently performed a study of ceramic acquisition in 19th-century Rockbridge County, Virginia, using general store sales and inventory records. The idea was to find out just which Staffordshire ceramics were available in Rockbridge County, to create a "universe of choice" against which to array the collections from various Rockbridge County archaeological sites.

The first step was to read a series of general store daybooks, from which Potter concluded that Rockbridge general store merchants did not use the same terms to describe ceramics that Noël Hume does and that the merchants offered considerably less detail. The traditional historical archaeological move would be to grant a superior status to those parts of the documentary record that were closer to the point of manufacture, which are the kinds of documents Noël Hume used, and then to call those documents created further away from the point of manufacture unusable because they were inept, inferior versions produced by the less well-informed. Middle-range theory, as we are adapting it for historical archaeology, would call both sets of documents independent and the differences between the two an ambiguity worthy of use.

Without using these particular terms, Potter proceeded along these lines. He recognized that the organizational behavior for general store daybooks was the daily context of sales and the purpose of descriptions of merchandise in the daybooks was to provide enough detail to show why a particular set of plates was sold for 50 cents rather than 25 cents. Using the independence of both sets of documents, the assumption of an internal logic to each, the idea of ambiguity, and the knowledge of the organizational behavior that produced the Rockbridge documentary record, Potter was able to create a grammar for the notation of ceramic items in 19th-century Rockbridge County general store daybooks.

Simply stated, plates described with no adjectives sold for the lowest prices, on the average, and plates described with the largest number of adjectives sold for the highest prices, on the average. Among plates described with a single adjective, those with an adjective describing size or shape sold for slightly more than plates with no adjective; plates with an adjective for decoration sold for slightly more still; and plates with an adjective for the kind of clay from which they were made were the most expensive single-adjective plates. If we accept the assumption that the basic unmarked category was the white earthenware dinner plate, the value of the grammar is that it allows us to know that in an archaeological assemblage the presence of china (versus earthenware) represents a larger "extra" expenditure than the presence of desert plates (versus dinner plates).

This grammar, which is derived from the ambiguity between two independent documentary records, can in turn be seen as the basis for a descriptive grid for 19th-century ceramics recovered from Rockbridge sites. Because it is based on locally assigned meanings, this grammar, rather than Noël Hume's typology, is the most appropriate way of classifying ceramic finds from 19th-century Rockbridge sites—if the goal in analyzing them is to gain local economic insights. Such insights could include the discovery of how various segments of Rockbridge society chose to spend their cash income, with ceramic purchases being a part of the overall pattern. A family that purchased expensive tableware and inexpensive building materials would have been living differently from one that did the reverse, buying inexpensive dishes and expensive building materials. The ability to make such discoveries is the archaeological payoff from using middle-range theory's idea of ambiguity.

The examples presented here are intended to demonstrate the value of middle-range theory. The documentary record used by historical archaeologists contains many types of documents that may be used to create descriptive grids. In addition to the garden books, dictionaries, and general store daybooks already mentioned, there are architectural pattern books, catalogues, and many other documents that describe material culture in a systematic way. Beyond these kinds of primary documents, there are syntheses derived from the documentary record, like Miller's Ceramic Price Index (Miller 1980), and syntheses derived from the archaeological record, like South's artifact patterns (South 1977), which may be used as descriptive grids to formulate expectations against which to array archaeological or documentary data. The critical move in using any of these frameworks is to follow through with the concept of ambiguity, to treat as data the differences between what the documents or models show and what the archaeology shows. This ambiguity can in turn be understood with the aid of organizational behaviors, also derived from the documentary record. The documents most helpful for this purpose are the ones that specify a set of relationships between people and things, the activities carried out using the material that we recover as the archaeological record. As the ambiguity is being analyzed, once it has been established, the researcher should assume that the result of understanding will be the illumination of both records, not just the archaeology. Once this is done, it will be clear that the archaeological record can even serve the historical record and can have as much integrity as the historical record. Precisely described, archaeological variation can be creatively challenging to further searches for data and meaning in the documents.

We recognize that some historical archaeological research is already following the pattern laid out here; Palkovich's Chapter 9 represents a tentative step in this direction, and as Leone and Crosby (1987) demonstrate, previously interpreted data may be used for reanalysis based on middle-range theory. Our point is that when more completely digested by historical archaeologists and more fully integrated into research strategies, middle-range theory, or our analogy of it, will serve to enrich the relationship between lines of evidence in historical archaeology. As a result, the meanings recovered by historical archaeologists may be extended as well.

ONE FINAL ISSUE

Historical archaeology needs to deal with one other issue, as we have already hinted. Whether or not historical archaeology is to be an archaeology of the emergence and development of capitalism has been settled in the affirmative. There never has been a choice even for those who were indifferent or hostile to the issue. Rather, the question is Are historical archaeologists going to bother to learn and use the concepts that will show them that they can either do the archaeology of capitalism under any name they choose, or continue to believe that the newly intensive search for Spanish remains in the United States just accidentally coincides with the rising Hispanic vote and the newly active political aspirations of the Roman Catholic church? In other words, we can either know our social context, which is the context of advanced industrial capitalism, or be prisoners of it.

The needed concepts are ideology and consciousness. Both come from several intellectual circles: Marxist theory, psychoanalysis, and the Frankfurt School of critical theory. Ideology usually means the set of ideas or notions used in everyday life (Althusser 1971), ideas like natural law and individual liberty in Leone's essay in this volume, ideas that misrepresent the actual conditions of everyday life. The exploration of current ideology that creates a past for modern political purposes is a concomitant issue. This is not explored in many of the essays in this book, but McGuire uses and amplifies the idea of ideology. Consciousness, meaning awareness of ideological constructions, implies the greater freedom to acknowledge and employ alternatives, once other factors like political or neurotic ones are visible. The whole point of this issue is epistemological. How does one discover the effect of modern capitalism's operation on history while doing historical archaeology? One school of thought says that the present constructs the past for its own purposes, but how is the constructing done? Further, once one knows or sees the construction of the past, what alternatives are there?

Or, to what should consciousness lead? These are critical questions for a few historical archaeologists, but no way has yet been found to link them to the practice of historical archaeology and in particular to the kind of research we proposed in the previous section on middle-range theory.

CONCLUSIONS

The preceding discussions of issues in historical archaeology corroborate, for historical archaeology, Warwick Bray's characterization of prehistoric archaeology cited earlier: Archaeologists borrow theory and pull out the useful parts to build an arsenal of ways to gain knowledge of the past; and with optimism we continue to do so. What Bray might have added is that archaeological data are an essential part of modern social fabrics, and its creators/discoverers are faced with theoretical options that invite them to see themselves as both political and active.

REFERENCES CITED

Althusser, Louis
  1971   Ideology and Ideological State Apparatuses. In *Lenin and Philosophy*, pp. 127–86. New York: Monthly Review Press.

Binford, Lewis R.
  1981   *Bones: Ancient Men and Modern Myths*. New York: Academic Press.
  1983   *Working at Archaeology*. New York: Academic Press.
  1987   Researching Ambiguity: Frames of Reference and Site Structure. In *Method and Theory for Activity Area Research*, ed. Susan Kent, pp. 449–512. New York: Columbia University Press.

Braudel, Fernand
  1981   *The Structures of Everyday Life*. New York: Harper and Row.
  1982   *The Wheels of Commerce*. New York: Harper and Row.
  1984   *The Perspective of the World*. New York: Harper and Row.

Bray, Warwick
  1986   Fifty Years On. *Nature* 322 (28 August): 784.

Deetz, James
  1977   *In Small Things Forgotten*. Garden City: Anchor Doubleday.
  1983   Scientific Humanism and Humanistic Science: A Plea for Paradigmatic Pluralism in Historical Archaeology. *Geoscience and Man* 23 (April 29): 27–34.

Hopkins, Joseph W., III
    1986   *A Map of the Ridout Garden, Annapolis, Maryland.* On file at Historic
            Annapolis, Inc., Annapolis, Maryland.

Jones, Steven L.
    1985   The African-American Tradition in Vernacular Architecture. In *The
            Archaeology of Slavery and Plantation Life*, ed. Theresa A. Singleton,
            pp. 195–211. New York: Academic Press.

Langley, Batty
    1726   *New Principles of Gardening.* London: Bettsworth and Batley.

Leone, Mark P.
    1984   Interpreting Ideology in Historical Archaeology: Using the Rules of
            Perspective in the William Paca Garden, Annapolis, Maryland. In
            Ideology, Power, and Prehistory, ed. Daniel Miller and Christopher
            Tilley, pp. 25–35. Cambridge: Cambridge University Press.
    1987   Rule by Ostentation: The Relationship between Space and Sight in
            Eighteenth Century Landscape Architecture in the Chesapeake Re-
            gion of Maryland. In *Method and Theory for Activity Area Research*,
            ed. Susan Kent, pp. 604–33. New York: Columbia University
            Press.

Leone, Mark P., and Constance A. Crosby
    1987   Epilogue: Middle-Range Theory in Historical Archaeology. *In Con-
            sumer Choice in Historical Archaeology*, ed. Suzanne M. Spencer-
            Wood, pp. 397–410. New York: Plenum Press.

Leone, Mark P., Parker B. Potter, Jr., and Paul A. Shackel
    1987   Toward a Critical Archaeology. *Current Anthropology* 28(3):
            283–302.

Lockwood, Alice G. B.
    1934   *Gardens of Colony and State.* New York: Charles Scribner's Sons.

MacCubbin, Robert P., and Peter Martin (eds.)
    1984   *British and American Gardens in the Eighteenth Century.* Williamsburg,
            Va.: Colonial Williamsburg Foundation.

Miller, George L.
    1980   Classification and Economic Scaling of 19th Century Ceramics.
            Historical Archaeology 14: 1–40.

Miller, Philip
    1733   *The Gardener's Dictionary.* London: Printed for the author.

Potter, Parker B., Jr.
    1982   *The Translation of Archaeological Evidence into Economic Understand-
            ings: A Study of Context, Naming, and Nineteenth Century Ceramics in*

Rockbridge County, Virginia. Unpublished master's thesis, Department of Anthropology, Brown University.

Roulette, Bill, Eileen Williams, and Laura Disimone
1986   *Map of the Carroll Garden.* On file at Historic Annapolis, Inc., Annapolis, Maryland.

South, Stanley
1977   *Method and Theory in Historical Archaeology.* New York: Academic Press.

Switzer, Stephen
1742   *Iconographia Rustica.* London: Printed for J. and J. Fox and B. and B. Barker et al.

Trigger, Bruce
1980   Archaeology and the Image of the American Indian. *American Antiquity* 45(4): 662–76.
1986   *Natives and Newcomers.* Montreal: McGill and Queen's University Press.

Wallace, Michael
1986a   Reflections on the History of Historic Preservation. In *Presenting the Past*, ed. Susan Porter Benson, Stephen Brier, and Roy Rosenzweig, pp. 165–199. Philadelphia: Temple University Press.
1986b   Visiting the Past: History Museums in the United States. In *Presenting the Past*, ed. Susan Porter Benson, Stephen Brier, and Roy Rosenzweig, pp. 137–61. Philadelphia: Temple University Press.

Wallerstein, Emmanuel
1974   *The Modern World-System I.* New York: Academic Press.
1980   *The Modern World-System II.* New York: Academic Press.

Wylie, Alison
1985   Between Philosophy and Archaeology. *American Antiquity* 50(2): 478–90.

PART I

Sixteenth-Century Spanish Settlement in the Southeast

There is no doubt about the importance of the history of 16th-century Spanish settlement on the East Coast of the United States—the history of places like St. Augustine, Santa Elena, and Santa Catalina. From the perspective of modern American culture, however, it is difficult to know how to handle this history, where to place it conceptually, and what to use it for. These questions arise because the Spanish colonization of the Southeast is popularly perceived as having gone nowhere if British colonization is used as a frame of reference, and American historiography from the 19th century onward suggests no alternatives. To rephrase the point, whose history is the history of places like Santa Elena and Santa Catalina? Today we have Sons and Daughters of the American Revolution, Daughters of the Confederacy, and families who proudly trace their origins on this continent to the Mayflower, but in schoolbook versions of American history direct links to the past end at 1620, or 1609 and Jamestown at the earliest, and the 130 years between Christopher Columbus's voyages and the landing at Plymouth Rock are usually dropped out. This does not necessarily mean that people like the various Spanish (and French) explorers in North America are not mentioned, only that they and their activities are seldom connected to today or made a part of any kind of cultural heritage. The subtextual message is that English people in North America after 1620 are a part of American history, whereas Spanish people in the part of North America that became the United States are not. In the face of this bit of contemporary ideology, archaeologists of 16th century Spanish sites have the double responsibility of doing good archaeology *and* of making it mean something to contemporary Americans who have been taught to feel no connection to the sites of such archaeology or to the people who lived on them.

As for the responsibility to do good archaeology, the work of both Stanley South and David Hurst Thomas may be seen as complementary to Deagan's (1983, 1987) work in St. Augustine. All three are making important contributions to the method and theory of a historical archaeology different in significant ways from the discipline founded in Virginia in the 1960s.

As for the second responsibility, to make the archaeology of Spanish America meaningful to contemporary Americans, South's approach to the historical archaeological record is particularly appropriate. He has clearly stated the ways in which he uses the theoretical position derived from Leslie White, which is that cultural systems are systems for the capture and use of energy, in its various forms. This energy-capture approach makes South's Santa Elena valuable in at least three ways. First, typical popular portrayals of 16th-century Spanish settlements that separate Spanish activity from mainstream American history make studies of Spanish America contextless; there is nothing to connect them to and no framework for seeing Spanish settlement as a part of anything else. South's frame of analysis restores context by making Santa Elena a part of a larger Spanish system of colonial settlement, a system with clearly defined goals and a full history. By referring to the goals of the system, South can suggest the purposes for which Santa Elena was created and can evaluate the mission's performance against these goals. Second, as hinted at by South, this approach makes it possible to compare various parts of the Spanish colonial system in terms of their different functions and the different local conditions to which they had to adapt.

Third, South's systems approach allows for the creation of context at the level of the site itself. Just as Santa Elena was a part of a world-wide colonial system, each individual, household, and social class in Santa Elena played a role in the functioning of the settlement. In all of these ways, South's systems approach and energy flow model provide the generalizing or universalizing ideas necessary to make the archaeological history of Santa Elena meaningful to American historical archaeology and to modern Americans. This is necessary because many modern Americans who will simply *assume* or take for granted that an English site from the 1670s is important will not make the same assumption for a Spanish settlement from the 1570s, for which they have no cultural frame of reference.

More explicitly than South, Thomas discusses the issue of the Anglo-American bias in American historiography and the parallel "black legend" that has come to stand for Spanish activity in the New World. Thomas's first step in redressing this bias has been to produce an essay similar to South's in its sophisticated use of historical background material, its well-articulated understanding of the purposes and techniques of Spanish colonization in North America, and the rich detail of its archaeological and artifactual data. Methodologically, whereas South's discussion focuses on arguments of relevance, Thomas's is concerned with remote sensing, a particularly valuable set of techniques given the almost total above-ground invisibility of Spanish colonial settlement in the American Southeast. In addition, while discussing various aspects of Santa Catalina, Thomas provides a comprehensive review of the archaeology of Spanish colonization in the Southeast.

Thomas relies more on the interpretation of historical documentation than on a theoretically derived model, as South does. Thomas makes data out of three grains of wheat, on the basis of a documented preference for a wheat bread host. Through a careful reading of Franciscan ideas about bells (the Franciscans name them and consider them living members of the religious community), he is able to interpret what would have been otherwise incomprehensible, a careful burial of fragments of several broken bells. Finally, using the same approach, Thomas is able to understand the apparent anomaly of Indians buried with fine *Spanish* grave goods of a religious nature in a church at the very edge of the Spanish borderlands—on the basis of the documented stages of conversion, one of which called for using the trinkets of Christianity as an inducement for conversion. The same doctrine calls for the eventual replacement of trinkets by true faith, at the point when the neophyte advances, and this knowledge serves to structure a set of archaeological signatures for the extent to which any given population of Indians, represented by their burials, had progressed down the path to complete conversion.

Both of the highly descriptive essays in this part of the book are rich with data and are based on the kind of functionalism described in the general introduction. In other circumstances any of these three characteristics might warrant criticism, but not in this case since each essay provides enough context for its data by way of parallel historical data and anthropological theory. Further, it bears repeating that South and Thomas, along with Deagan and a few others, are doing for Spanish colonial historical archaeology what was so ably done by Noël Hume (1969, 1970) for British colonial historical archaeology. The functionalism South and Thomas employ is a particularly productive approach for a research project at the stage where the archaeology of Spanish Colonial America currently finds itself.

REFERENCES CITED

Deagan, Kathleen
    1983   *Spanish St. Augustine: The Archaeology of a Colonial Creole Community*. Academic Press: New York.
    1987   *Artifacts of the Spanish Colonies of Florida and the Caribbean, 1500–1800. Vol. 1, Ceramics, Glassware, and Beads*. Washington: Smithsonian Institution Press.

Noël Hume, Ivor
    1969   *Historical Archaeology*. New York: Alfred A. Knopf.
    1970   *A Guide to Artifacts of Colonial America*. New York: Alfred A. Knopf.

CHAPTER 2

Santa Elena
Threshold of Conquest

STANLEY SOUTH

A major goal of historical archaeology should be to understand world cultural systems and the process of their operation, as they exploit the available energy resources through class distinctions (Marx 1906; White 1949, 1975; Finley 1954:397; Wallerstein 1974; Harris 1980; Odum and Odum 1981; Wolf 1982; Lewis 1984; Green 1986). All forms of life, as well as cultural systems, are based on the control of energy flowing from plant, animal, mineral, and human cultural resources (White 1949:364–65; Odum and Odum 1981; Green 1986). Models for expressing the energy flowing from processes represented by the artifacts that historical archaeologists recover, in relation to the cost of obtaining the energy, are badly needed if we are to express the archaeological record in terms of energy theory (Odum and Odum 1981). Halcott Green is already developing just such a model, which will be used to quantify artifact data from historic sites in energy terms (personal communication and Green 1986).

The control of energy resources from the environment leads to the concentration of economic power in the hands of individuals and families, and this power tends to become fixed as socioeconomic status within a society. Thus it behooves historical archaeologists to focus on such status in their studies of world cultural systems (White 1949, 1975; Finley 1954; Wallerstein 1974; 1980; Harris 1980:111, 228; Nash 1981;

Odum and Odum 1981:3; Lewis 1984; Green 1986a). By so doing they will be able to indirectly monitor the energy flow within the past cultural system under study. Fortunately, the archaeological record lends itself to such analysis since the processes related to socioeconomic status leave an indelible mark in the archaeological record. This chapter presents an illustration of how the archaeological record is connected— through the study of socioeconomic status differences and arguments of relevance—to energy flowing into and out of the past cultural system reflected by that record. The quantitative expression of socioeconomic status in terms of energy theory represents a major archaeological challenge for the future.

HISTORICAL BACKGROUND

In the process of colonizing the New World for the purpose of economic exploitation, Spain established the city of Santa Elena (1566–87) on what is now Parris Island, South Carolina, in Port Royal Sound (Lyon 1976; 1984a). It was founded by Pedro Menéndez de Avilés through a contractual agreement with the king (Lyon 1976:42, 118, 147, 185; 1984b). The Spanish colonial system was designed to efficiently control the energy flow to be found in the plant, mineral, animal, and human resources in Spanish Florida (Odum and Odum 1981:3). This could not be accomplished without a *military base to protect the settlement* and control the native population—the Indians— through *evangelization into the Catholic faith* (Lyon 1976:149; 1977; 1984a,b). In the initial period of their attempt at conquest, the Spanish adelantados officially agreed to treat the Indians fairly (although this policy often did not filter down to the local level), and religious conversion was undertaken (Lyon 1976:4, 50, 118, 149). During the second decade after Santa Elena was established, tribute was collected from the Indians (Quiros Papers, 1578–80).

Protecting the settlement population from Indian attack and from the incursions of the French and putting down mutiny became a major concern of Pedro Menéndez de Avilés. Both Santa Elena and the settlement at St. Augustine faced a constant threat from the English and French who hoped to avert the Spanish conquest of Florida by interfering with supply and trade routes (Lyon 1976; 7, 16, 42, 43, 119, 147, 153, 185). Effective settlement depended on a supply line to Spain and quieting the French corsair menace, a task that occupied the Spanish during the 20 years of Santa Elena's existence. The settlers also had to contend with hostility and attacks by the local Indians. Santa Elena's 21-year history came to an end in 1587, when it was abandoned, not because of the French or the Indians, but because of the English. Sir Francis Drake had already burned St. Augustine (Lyon 1984a:15), and when the military base in Santa Elena became threatened the authorities in Havana decided to abandon and burn it. This frontier foothold of Spain was thus withdrawn from the threshold of conquest and St. Augustine continued.

The population density needed to realize the agricultural potential of Florida eluded the Spaniards in the early years of the settlement (Lyon, 1976:155, 166, 205, 210). Thus, considerable energy was expended on constructing fortifications to protect the few hundred Spaniards residing in the Florida settlements. At Santa Elena, a succession of forts, from Ft. San Salvador to two Ft. San Felipes, together with a series of Ft. San Marcos additions, repairs, and alterations, attest to the emphasis on defense (Lyon 1984a; South 1984, 1985a; Hoffman 1978).

Santa Elena was composed of two basic social classes, the controlling Menéndez family on the one hand and settlers (consisting of the soldiers, artisans, craftsmen, merchants, and their wives and children) on the other (Lyon 1977; Manucy 1985:45). This latter group also included the 45 farmers who were in Santa Elena in 1573. In contrast, only 6 were in St. Augustine at that time (Connor 1925:83).

Menéndez's lieutenants were selected for leadership because of their Asturian background, or at least they were *norteno* noblemen related to Menéndez (Lyon 1976:76, 1977, 1984b). They constituted the highest social class in Santa Elena and in Florida and thus reproduced the hierarchical society of their native areas in Spain (Lyon 1976:117, 1977, 1984b). Santa Elena was therefore controlled by a family–oriented elite, which Hoffman has called the Menéndez Associated Families in America, or MAFIA (Lyon 1977). Some of the resources from trade, commerce, and tribute and the booty from French prizes and illegal trade went to benefit the Menéndez enterprise (Lyon 1977, 1984a:7); Manucy 1985:44).

At the other end of the socioeconomic scale were the slaves, settlers, and common soldiers. At times soldiers and other settlers did not have adequate food and were close to starving (Connor 1925:89). Of the 50 soldiers in the fort in 1570 only six had shirts, and all suffered "extreme need of everything" (Connor 1925:307,313). When they were not fishing or seeking food from the Indians or working on the Menéndez estate, the hungry soldiers passed the time by gambling, "which makes them stay quiet in the presidio" (Connor 1925:315; Lyon 1977).

Through trade, Menéndez became a minor power in the Indics and raided and took many French vessels involved in competitive trade there (Lyon 1976:7, 208). As a result, some French goods came into the hands of the Spaniards and found their way to Santa Elena and other Spanish settlements (Lyon 1976:9–16). Spanish goods included earthenware, swords, clothing, axes, nails, sugar, hides, gold, copper, wine, iron hardware, corn from Yucatan, oil, hogs, cattle, crossbows, padded cotton jackets (*escupiles*), cassava, honey, chickens, munitions, farm tools, wheat, and grapes. These goods were distributed by those in control (Lyon 1976:8, 48, 50, 150, 151, 174, 175, 203; 1984:6). In contrast to the seeming abundance among the members of the ruling class, rations were often meager for those lower on the socioeconomic scale. "In short supply were opportunities for entertainment and loot, the basic expectations of the sixteenth-century private soldier" (Lyon 1976:151, 1977). However, Menéndez's men were "fully armed with arquebuses, cross-bows, helmets, and shields" (Lyon 1976:48) since the fort was the center of authority and protection for the settlement.

Another source of subsistence for the Santa Elena citizens was the tribute collected from the Indians through the authority of the fort (Quiros papers 1578–80). This consisted of corn, furs, shells, pearls, money and other items, although such payments were seldom recorded officially (Lyon 1976:24, 25, 119; 1984a:9). The soldiers also took food and other items by force, and this practice eventually led to an Indian uprising in 1576.

Santa Elena was established "firmly upon . . . ancient urban customs," and the municipal institutions of Spain were used as a "significant instrument of conquest" (Lyon 1976:115–16; 1977). "There was thus created a microcosm of Castilian civilization to effect the conquest, as the Spanish ventured forth into new and uncertain territory" (Lyon 1976:116). Menéndez built Santa Elena alongside the Indian cultures to tap the resources of the land, in the hope that this activity would not disturb the Indians' rights in the land, but it did not work out as planned (Lyon 1976:118, 210). William Hunt has attributed the failure of Santa Elena, in contrast to the success in Peru, to differences in social organization (Hunt 1985).

The overall plan was for missionaries to gather the Indians into villages near the Spanish towns, where they could be encouraged to give up their old rites, ceremonies, and beliefs and thus change their way of life. As the Indians sensed, however, "it would, in fact, mean the total alteration of their culture" because their resources were being used to support the Spanish conquest system (Harris 1964:21–22; Lyon 1976:24, 205). Nonetheless, marriage and liaisons between Spanish men and Indian women occurred early in the contact, although hostility remained the rule (Deagan 1983:99). This flared into open warfare with the attack on Ft. San Felipe in July 1576 (Hoffman 1978:25; Lyon

1984:21?, which led the settlers to abandon Santa Elena for a year (Lyon 1976:12).

When Menéndez originally traveled from St. Augustine to Santa Elena in 1567, he carried with him some Tequesta and Timucuan Indians from the area of the St. Johns River (Lyon 1976:181). Such transport of native people, and their material goods, from one area to another was a common occurrence in the period.

The Indians grew hostile to Spanish attempts at colonization, not only because of the strict inculcation of Christian doctrine, a characteristic of Menéndez's enterprise, but also because the Spanish treated the natives harshly (Lyon 1976:205). Lyon points out that, according to a report on Spanish-Indian relations by the Jesuit priest, Juan Rogel, "it was the behavior of the Spanish soldiers which had outraged the natives in every area of occupation. They had demanded food from the Indians, beaten and killed natives, and abused their women. The Spaniards had been . . . overbearing, cruel, and harsh" (Lyon 1976:205). Rogel urged that the population be increased to allow the Gospel to be preached "in an atmosphere of community instead of one of lust and bloodshed" (Lyon 1976:205).

At the same time, there were strong counterinfluences to the ruling authority of the Menéndez family from within the Spanish colonial system (Eugene Lyon, personal communication September 16, 1986). One of these came from the soldiers under contract to Menéndez, whose semi-independent attitude at times brought them close to revolt. A second conflict developed between the ruling class and the clergy. When the Franciscans at Santa Elena attempting to excommunicate Governor Velasco, however, they were forced to flee the colony. Third, the settlers too rebelled against authority at times, through litigation, and asserted their rights under ancient Castilian municipal liberties. Lawsuits were a common occurrence in Santa Elena, so that the notary was fully occupied trying to keep up with the paper work involved (Eugene Lyon, personal communication, September 16, 1986).

THEORY

The archaeological study of a site such as Santa Elena serves to demonstrate the importance of studying nations as cultural systems (White 1975:158), and the effect of cultural systems on a world level (Wallerstein 1974; 1980). We have seen that the primary goal of the Spanish colonial system was to utilize energy flow through *economic control, fortification for protection* of the settlement and to control the native people through the mechanism of *conversion into the Catholic faith* (Lyon 1976,

1984: Odum and Odum 1981). To achieve this goal, the Spaniards relied on the technological, sociological, and ideological systems by
which man is articulated with his natural environment (White
1949:364).

A primary element in any cultural system is the technological system. According to White (1949:365):

> Man must have food. He must be protected from the elements.
> And he must defend himself from his enemies. These three things
> he must do if he is to continue to live, and these objectives are at-
> tained only by technological means.

The purpose of these activities, of course, is to utilize energy, since "all
life is a struggle for free energy" (White 1949:367; Odum and Odum
1981:3). Cultural systems evolve as energy utilization per capita per
year is increased (White 1975:19). As demonstrated by the Spaniards at
Santa Elena, who were endeavoring "to maximize their economic efficiency," *the primary function of culture is to harness energy for man's use*
(Green 1986a:13). Green (1986a:13, 27; 1986b:2) like White (1949,
1975), Odum and Odum (1981), and others (see Foster-Carter 1978;
Nash 1981:393) regard energy as a primary means of evaluating a cultural system:

> Differential control of things having energetic value led to com-
> plex status differentiations, which tended to become fixed as to
> persons and families. . . . The classes at the top exploited those at
> the bottom in the sense that they controlled important aspects of
> the behavior of individual members of the lower classes and ap-
> propriated a significant portion of their output, to be allocated at
> the discretion of those at the top. (Green 1986b:27)

The Menéndez family was certainly the elite at Santa Elena. However,
the private soldier also expected to share in booty taken from French
and English vessels and in the profits obtained by Menéndez through
his legal and illegal trade and hoped to obtain riches, particularly pre-
cious metals (Lyon 1976:151).

The archaeological study of the ruins of a city such as Santa Elena
can be organized around the concept of energy utilization, as described
here. Thus, status, ethnicity, fortification, social structure of the Indians, social structure of the Spanish colonial system, trade, settlement,
and evangelization can be seen to vary with the efficiency with which
the energy resources available to the controlling classes were utilized
beyond that necessary to maintain the system. In the pages that follow,

I examine the connection between the basic Spanish goal of economic production through *settlement, fortification,* and *evangelization* and the archaeological record.

An archaeologist who finds what appears to be a tooth fragment first tries to determine the source of the fragment. Once this is known to be a tooth, the archaeologist recognizes that other companion teeth in the set were at one time involved. When the animal from which the tooth came is identified, statements can be made about the biological system represented by the animal and the known subsistence system of that animal can be related to the site where the fragment was found.

This procedure is similar to what happens when a fragment of an artifact from a historic site is found and the archaeologist learns, through documentation, the place of that object in the past cultural system from a behavioral perspective and interpolates to the processual system of which it was a part. For example, a badly rusted hollow cone-shaped iron object 2 inches long may well be interpreted as a point for a crossbow bolt or quarrel. This information indicates that the item could not have functioned without the presence of a crossbow, which functioned in a hunting or military context (Payne-Gallwey 1958). The mechanical system of the crossbow, with goat's-foot lever, windlass, or other accouterments for cocking, is known from documentation, and thus a great deal can be said about it. However, when the artifact or the tooth fragment is associated with data on architecture, features, function, other artifacts, economic and social status, and other contextual information, the artifact's scientific value expands from the descriptive level to one that reflects cultural process.

The move from describing a rusty cone-shaped object to interpreting culture process requires a series of steps demonstrating (1) the relevance of the object to a quarrel and the relevance of a quarrel to a crossbow, (2) the relevance of a crossbow to hunting or defense, (3) the relevance of defense to the fortification where the fragment was found, (4) the relevance of the fortification to the settlement it was designed to protect, (5) the relevance of the settlement to the goals of the cultural system of which the settlement was a part, and (6) the relevance of that system to the exploitation of energy as a major function of all systems (White 1949, 1975; Odum and Odum 1981; Green 1986a,b).

In other words, the procedure by which the culture is interpreted consists of establishing arguments of relevance. First the artifact needs to be identified, and its technomic and other functional aspects determined. Next, one must establish the relevance of the functional behavioral aspects of the artifact to the site followed by the relevance of the functional-behavioral aspect to the social system of which the site was a part. Then the social system is related to the world cultural network involved. The final consideration is the relationship to the processes of energy use in the world system. At each step, an argument of relevance is presented linking that step to the one before. It is my view that a major goal of historical archaeology is to address the final step, the processes involved in the world system.

A common approach used in historical archaeology today is to proceed from artifact pattern recognition directly to an "explanation" of the meaning of the pattern without establishing the arguments of relevance to larger theoretical concepts. Some archaeologists move directly from the artifact pattern to a behavioral interpretation. The interpretation may focus on mentalistic structures and "different perceptions of the world" (Deetz 1977:151) rather than the processes of cultural systems (Harris 1980:59, 11). Cognitive explanations of archaeological patterning too often leap, or glide, over the chasm separating data and explanation on gossamer wings of mentalistic abandon, giving free reign to creative imagination rather than bridging the gulf with arguments of relevance. Harris (1980:60, 269) has compared this insistence of mind as a means of explanation in culture to the pre-enlightenment thinking prevalent before Darwin and Newton.

In this chapter I concentrate on bridging the historical and the archaeological material culture data sets. I begin by explaining the methodological strategy appropriate for establishing arguments of relevance between the historically derived hypotheses and the archaeological record.

METHOD

Many historical archaeology reports in recent years have implied that recognizing an artifact pattern is the goal of archaeology. Various patterns such as the Carolina Artifact Pattern, the Brunswick Pattern, the Slave Pattern, the Frontier Pattern, the Fur Trade Pattern, the Incarceration Pattern, the Public Interaction Pattern, and the like are being sought in artifacts from sites. Often, however, the reports do not go beyond the pattern recognition stage (South 1977; Foresman 1979; Wheaton, Friedlander, and Garrow 1983:277; Carnes 1984:1). As Leone (1982:6) has pointed out, "What is needed is a set of questions linking the archaeological record and the documentary record in complementary fashion." More disturbing to me, however, is the lack of any effort to link the archaeological patterns to past cultural *processes*. Frequently missing are arguments of relevance linking historical or processual concepts to the archaeological data patterns. The developers of the patterns mentioned above did not derive them simply as descriptive, inductivist,

34

ends in themselves, but as methodological tools that they hoped would be used to explore not only past behavior but also the *processes responsible for that behavior.*

Leone (1982:4), in reviewing the contribution made by my book *Method and Theory in Historical Archaeology* (1977), expresses a similar concern:

> South argued that historical archaeology was to employ scientific method including hypothesis testing, was to be concerned with universal patterns of human behavior, and draw its problems from the concept of culture defined as humanity's way of adapting to its environment. So that in investigating the colonial period in America and elsewhere the historical archaeologist was not solely concerned with whether or not the records were right or the folk tales accurate, he was concerned with the world cultural system associated with European expansion from the fifteenth century on. The expansion of European profit-making systems was not a matter of when some fort was built or how some house was constructed; those were what was now called historical problems, meaning that they were particular questions. Rather, historical archaeologists were concerned with *how different classes lived,* what they ate, how much imported ware they could afford; whether Africans retained any of their original culture after coming to the New World. *What were the class differences* between planters and overseers, and slaves; British officers and regular soldiers? *Class distinctions, clearly a product of economic conditions, were a chief consideration.* (italics mine)

Class differences are still a major interest, as I have moved from a concern with the British colonial system of the 18th century to the Spanish colonial system of the 16th century (South 1979, 1980, 1982, 1984, 1985a). *World cultural systems and the processes of their operation, as they exploit the available energy resources through class distinctions,* should in my opinion, be a major concern of historical archaeology (Marx 1906; Finley 1954:397; Wallerstein 1974; Harris 1980; Odum and Odum 1981; Wolf 1982).

In the next section I present the arguments of relevance that link energy theory via class structure to the patterned byproducts of the system to be found in the archaeological record. This linkage needs to be established if the patterns in the archaeological record, now being derived as a major activity in historical archaeology, are to have any relevance to past history and systemic processes of culture. As Binford (1972:98) has noted, "Any explanatory proposition must be reasoned in terms of relevance to the operation of the cultural system under study."

How are by-products of a system measured, and how does the variability thus found relate to class structure? What is the linkage between the settlement where they are found and the power center in Europe? Sixteenth-century settlements such as Santa Elena and St. Augustine (Deagan 1985) can be evaluated as to economic status by the degree of contact with the main supply line from the central power center in Spain, *as reflected by the presence of upper-class residents*. This presence can be measured by the *number of artifact types present*. The operative assumption here is that the ruling class can be expected to have available to them a wide range of artifact types, from "everyday" to the most expensive types, whereas the less economically advantaged people, the laboring people, would have fewer artifacts available for their use and these would reflect a utilitarian function, with few luxury items present. If a sufficiently large sample of artifacts, architecture, features, and their associations from these settlements is available through excavation of ruins of all social classes, a comparison *by settlement* can be made that will monitor the relative ability of each settlement to tap the economic resources of the Old World through trade and supply.

We know that Santa Elena was the capital of Spanish Florida, that St. Augustine was a defensive fortification in the 1560s, and that the ruling minority, Pedro Menéndez de Avilés and his family, made their home in Santa Elena (Lyon 1984a:4, 6). Given this access to a greater variety of material goods, we might therefore expect *Santa Elena to have a greater number of artifact types* (as opposed to fragments) *than St. Augustine* during the same period. Santa Elena was occupied largely by families rather than the unmarried soldiers that characterized St. Augustine (Deagan 1985:30), and, as mentioned above, some of these families were members of the ruling elite. Assuming that we have a representative sample of artifact types from St. Augustine and Santa Elena, we can compare artifact types from the two towns. We find a total of 104 artifact types from Santa Elena (South 1979–85a) and a total of 71 artifact types from St. Augustine (Deagan 1985:11–12). This is consistent with what we know of the history of the two sister settlements regarding the power structure (Deagan 1985:30).

Given this means of monitoring the status levels of communities such as Santa Elena through the presence of artifact types from the mother source of the world system involved in the colonization, it follows that the status of *individual family dwellings* can be similarly monitored, as well as the contrast between *domestic occupation* areas (as opposed to *military fort* occupations) and other sites reflecting functions related to socioeconomic status.

The presence of specific *high-status artifact types* is an important means of monitoring socioeconomic levels at occupation sites. Such artifacts include Chinese Ming dynasty porcelain and decorated majolica on 16th-century Spanish sites, and Chinese overglazed enameled porcelain on 18th-century sites of the British colonial system. In 16th-century contexts, porcelain is an indicator of the most elite group, whereas majolica reflects the class of merchants, craftsmen, and artisans (Kamer 1956; Cervantes 1977; South 1983:66–70).

Similar indicators of laboring-class occupation in 18th-century British contexts in South Carolina are the cheaply available lead-glazed earthenwares, colonoware made by black slaves (Ferguson 1978, 1980), and colono-Indian wares often utilized by people from the Old World in contact with Indian groups (Binford 1965). By comparing the relative quantities of these wares in relation to other status-sensitive data, one is able to interpret the status levels of the occupants of dwellings with which these artifacts are associated (Wheaton, Friedlander and Garrow 1983). This is done under the assumption that the elite of European origin would have had greater access to the flow of goods from the Old World than the slaves or Indians under their control, who had to produce their own alternatives. Other, nonceramic artifacts, such as the decorative *bordado* sewn onto the elite Spanish gentleman's costume, are also useful in monitoring the class structure reflected in various archaeological contexts (South 1982:55–57; 1984:23; 1983:57, 59). Thus, we have two basic means of monitoring social stratification using artifacts: quantitative and qualitative.

Architectural data, both the quality of the materials used and the size of the structures, also reveal socioeconomic status differences of the occupants. Larger structures, for example, probably reflect more affluence (South 1982:45, 99).

Variability in the *size of structures* and the artifacts associated with them (Architectural Pattern) *between artifact groups* (Carolina Pattern), *between artifact classes* (Kitchen Pattern), and *between artifact types* (Mean Ceramic Date Formula) are all analytical tools for determining socioeconomic status and temporal and functional differences reflected in the archaeological record (South 1977, 1978).

It should be noted that the contrast in socioeconomic status between a simple yeoman's cottage (where few European artifact types may be present) and a planter's house (where scores of artifact types are to be found) is a dramatic one. It should also be noted, however, that since slave quarters are such an integral part of the energy exploitation subsystem of the elite, a large number of European artifacts from the flow of goods to the controlling classes are found on such sites (Bullen and Bullen 1945; Wheaton, Friedlander, and Garrow 1983). In comparing the sites of slave quarters from such subsystems with a free black household or with a simple yeoman's cottage, one can use the number of artifact types as an indicator of the relative degree of dependence on imported European goods available to each household through the power structure. The slave quarters from the plantation subsystem would have had a far higher number of artifact types owing to the energy flow from the bond with the controlling class. The yeoman and the free slave would have had a more tenuous tie, if any, through their economically disadvantaged position, to the supply network, and, therefore, their artifact type inventory would have been less as a matter of energy efficiency (Finley 1954).

A comparison of the number of artifact types found at planter's house sites and plantation slave quarters sites may well reveal almost as many types in both contexts owing to the flow of goods between the two functional areas of the plantation system. The critical variable here for analysis is not the comparison at the *artifact type* level, but in the *relative frequency of European fragments* in the two contexts *in relation to the frequency of colonoware*. Colonoware is a primary indicator of slave occupation, since it is thought to have been manufactured and used by Afro-American slaves, for the most part (Ferguson 1978, 1980). A major consideration in such analyses, however, is the *architectural record*. Here a dramatic contrast is seen between the planter's subsystem composed of the main house and outbuildings, and the slave quarters area. The architectural quality and magnitude of the plantation owner's residence are in marked contrast to the slave's residence (Lewis 1985).

Otto (1977) has demonstrated that *specific ceramic types* such as annular wares and edged wares vs. transfer-printed wares may indicate socioeconomic status differences between overseer, slave, and planter. I have demonstrated elsewhere (South 1977:41, 42, 79, 230–31, 254–55), the extension of the tea ceremony to the far-flung corners of the British Empire as a status-enforcing ritual among the controlling classes. Because of their lack of economic resources and lack of concern for status-enforcing rituals such as the tea ceremony (which involved the acquisition of several expensive ceramic types and accompanying artifacts), the laboring farmers, trappers, cattle raisers, and frontier settlers were far less likely to possess artifacts that enforced or reinforced status than the wealthy controlling classes and consequently left behind a different archaeological record as they moved on.

In addition to using the methods mentioned here for determining socioeconomic status, function, ethnic difference, and other processes of culture at Santa Elena, I have also been concerned with testing archaeological methods in the process of recovering data from the site. I have examined the relationship between a 1 percent and a 3 percent sampling strategy when compared with the totally excavated archaeological universe. Because historical archaeology offers tremendous potential for controlling archaeological variables against the background of historical documentation, it is imperative that each excavation be designed with some aspect of method testing and refinement in mind so that methods and techniques can become increasingly predictive.

Without a predictive knowledge of the potential of archaeological data for interpreting past cultural behavior and the processes that caused it, historical archaeology may continue chasing its own pattern recognition tail instead of taking a bite out of past processes of culture. In the next section I present arguments of relevance linking the above sections on theory and method to the archaeological record at Santa Elena.

Arguments of Relevance
(Postulates concerning the Archaeological Record)

Once established, the cities of Santa Elena and St. Augustine became nodes for access to resources passing through the trade and supply network. They functioned in the production and exchange of goods, mercantilism, government, religion, recreation, and in the secular and ecclesiastic mechanism of coordination, integration, and regulation known as the state-church (White 1949:381). A major question facing the archaeologist dealing with a state-church system such as that represented at Santa Elena is, What is the relationship between the control of energy flow by the power structure and the quantification of the material by-products of that energy control in the archaeological record?

As we have seen, the first Santa Elena and its fortified outposts such as St. Augustine were controlled by Pedro Menéndez and his noblemen relations until his death in 1574. This constituted a class system with a minority at the top controlling a majority at the bottom that seldom had enough of anything (Green 1986a:13; White 1949:381). How is this control of human energy resources reflected in the archaeological record?

1. Through Menéndez's control of trade, commerce, and supply routes to Santa Elena, his power center was able to receive goods from the Spanish world trade network. Thus goods from Spain, Italy, China, France, the Caribbean, and Mexico would be imported to Santa Elena to become discarded in the refuse deposits. Therefore, the world trade system, through the flow of goods, would likely be reflected in the artifacts found at Spanish colonial settlements. Under Menéndez's control, the first Santa Elena (1566–76) was a power center, but the second Santa Elena (1577–87) functioned primarily to defend the settlers and collect tribute from the Indians. This should be reflected in the archaeological record from the two settlements.

2. Another important question is who would be likely to own these items from Spanish world trade? More such goods would most likely be found in the homes of the small, powerful, wealthy ruling class than in the settler's household. Therefore, *more artifact types would be expected to be discarded from elite class households than from laboring class homes.* The questions we are asking of Santa Elena pertain to the economic flow of energy in the form of goods and human labor through the mechanism of settlement, fortification, and evangelization of the Indians.

3. With this in mind we can compare the architecture expected in the town and the fort. We can expect *the house of Pedro Menéndez de Aviles to be larger and more elaborate and complex than that of the craftsman and merchant in the town.*

4. We can also expect *the dwellings of the laboring classes,* that is, the soldiers and servants, *to reflect the Indian model,* namely, a post-and-lintel, wattel-and-daub type thatched with palmetto fronds and having a central smokehole (Lyon 1976:154).

5. *We can expect the houses of the other residents* (the settlers, merchants, clerics, etc.) *to face along the street in the manner of those in St. Augustine* (Manucy 1985:36), *forming a rectangle around a courtyard or quadrangle,* laid out in a grid plan in the Spanish manner (Willis 1984:14).

6. We can also expect the *estates on land appropriated by the ruling class to be located away form the middle- and lower-class areas of the settlement* owing to the larger land areas involved.

7. In addition to the architectural data, we might look at the artifacts for possible contrast. *Colonoware,* pottery made by African slaves in a traditional manner *would be expected in a domestic context* where slaves are present (Ferguson 1977, 1980). More lead-glazed earthenware than expensive pottery might be expected in working-class households.

8. Detailed analysis of Santa Elena subsistence data alongside St. Augustine material indicates that subsistence strategies at both locations reflect the "adaptation and acculturation of the Spanish subsistence practices. The new strategies were energy efficient, emphasizing nearby adundant resources which could be attained with a minimum of effort. Variations within this overall theme were apparently correlated with socioeconomic status and ethnic affiliation" (Reitz and Scarry 1985:99). Because of the relatively high cost of chickens, as revealed by documentation, Reitz and Scarry have used their presence as an indicator of upper-class occupation within a site. The presence of porcelain, also expensive, supports this interpretation at Santa Elena (Reitz 1982:152; South 1982:152).

9. The soldiers and other laboring classes, however, seldom had enough to eat, suffering need for everything (Connor 1925:307, 313).

Therefore, we would expect their archaeological record to reveal fewer and less expensive artifacts.

One of the advantages of the data set from Santa Elena is that it can be pinpointed in time (1566 to 1587), with Ft. San Felipe dating from 1572 to 1576 (mean majolica date 1573.1), (Lyon 1976, 1977, 1984a, b; Hoffman 1978; South 1979, 1980, 1982, 1983, 1984, 1985a).

10. By definition, therefore, the Spanish features at the site can be seen as *a "time capsule" only slightly more generalized than a shipwreck site.* Another advantage of the site is that it has remained relatively undisturbed for the four hundred years since it was abandoned. Only an early 19th-century plantation period occupation, and an early 20th-century U.S. Marine Corps occupation (continuing to the present as a golf course) have been present since the Spanish period. The undisturbed Spanish features therefore represent at most 21 years, and those at Ft. San Felipe represent only a 4-year moment in time. The site lends itself, therefore, to addressing temporal questions of the data base not often possible when longer, more intense, and continuous occupations are involved, such as that at St. Augustine.

11. Because forts are necessarily built more solidly than domestic dwellings, and public energy in the form of labor control and resources is involved, we expect the following attributes to characterize fortification features seen archaeologically, as indicated by documentary research. *Wide ditches (moats) will be present, a feature not seen in association with domestic dwellings.* These and other military ditches will sometimes *be characterized by obtuse and acute angles* in plan view, a well-known characteristic of forts at bastions.

12. *Structures inside forts will be larger than domestic dwellings* because they housed large numbers of people upon occasion. This means *larger timbers* were used to construct such buildings and *larger postholes were dug to hold them.* Therefore, the *nails and spikes* at these sites are likely to be *larger* than those found on domestic house sites (South 1985b).

13. Artifacts at Santa Elena are likely to differ from those of the fort in terms of function and status. We would expect, because of the lower status of the soldiers, fewer *porcelain artifacts to be found in the forts than in the town of Santa Elena,* or in the homes of the ruling class leaders of the settlement, where the highest ration of porcelain would be expected. *Majolica,* although cheaper by far than porcelain, was still more expensive than the common lead-glazed earthenware and *is thought to reflect higher socioeconomic status than earthenware* (McEwan 1983:11). It was more commonly available to the more affluent socioeconomic class than to the laboring class. An important question to consider here is whether the fort was occupied primarily by lower-class soldiers or by members of the power structure who controlled the lives of the sol-

diers. Because the fort was both a literal and symbolic center of power, we projected that the refuse inside the fort would reflect occupation by the ruling class and the common soldiers garrisoned within, although we knew that some soldiers were quartered in the town (Eugene Lyon and Paul Hoffman, personal communication). We anticipated that *a higher ratio* of soldier's lead-glazed *earthenware* in relation to majolica *would be expected to be found in the fort than in the town*. In this, we were wrong, since large quantities of majolica were present.

14. Also *the ratio of locally produced Indian pottery*, which was part of the tribute required and collected by the controlling authority *would be expected to be higher in the fort than in the town* of Santa Elena.

15. The Indians imported by Menéndez and others to Santa Elena from the St. Johns area around St. Augustine may have brought their own pottery with them (St. Johns pottery), which is found on the site (Goggin 1947, 1949, 1952; Lyon 1976:181; Deagan 1978:30). If such imported Timucua Indians were allowed to live in Santa Elena, *their pottery would not likely be found inside the forts,* where their presence might well have been prohibited by the military authority.

16. Because of the controlling military function of the forts, we would expect to find *fewer nonmilitary artifact classes in the forts than in the domestic area of Santa Elena.* The *military-related artifacts,* however, such as arquebus balls, crossbow parts and bolts, cannonballs, and the like, *would be expected to occur in higher frequencies inside the forts.*

17. Because evangelization of the Indians was a major goal of the Spaniards, we would expect Santa Elena to contain *evidence of the strong interaction between local Indians and Spaniards.*

18. In the church, *we would expect Spanish burials to be clustered near the altar,* and *Christian Indian burials to be located away from the altar.* This was expected in accordance with the European model and from discoveries at the Mission of Santa Catalina (David H. Thomas, personal communication).

19. *Evidence for Indian-Spanish interaction* through servants, converts, mistresses, and wives *would likely occur through Spanish males and Indian females.* The main indication of this interaction would appear archaeologically through *the presence of locally made Indian pottery* in refuse deposits within the town.

20. *Crucifixes, rosary beads, and other religious symbols should reveal the Catholic nature of the town.*

21. Since Santa Elena functioned as the capital of Spanish Florida in the 1560s, whereas St. Augustine was an outpost fort, *we would expect from the higher-status individuals in Santa Elena a greater number of artifact types* reflecting the power-center role of Santa Elena *compared to that of St. Augustine.*

22. *This premise might also be true inside forts controlling such settlements, since fortifications were the actual and symbolic centers of power for such communities,* and ranking officials centered their activities there.

23. At the intersite level, we would expect that *after the abandonment of Santa Elena in 1587, tribute normally sent to Santa Elena by the Indians would be sent to St. Augustine,* because that settlement had taken over the role Santa Elena once played in the collection of tribute (Deagan 1980). This would produce *a higher percentage of Spanish contemporary Indian pottery from the area of Santa Elena in contexts in St. Augustine dating after 1587.* Such a question can be addressed with post-1587 data from St. Augustine, as Deagan has done (1980).

24. *Agricultural practices* at Santa Elena *might well be revealed through ditches* dug deep enough to plant crops, such as grape vines mentioned as being seen inside the town of Santa Elena by a visitor, Father Rogel, in 1568 (Lyon 1976:204). Such ditches dating from 1670 have been found at the settlement of Charles Towne, (South 1969:33), and some dating from the early years of the 19th-century have been found at William Moultrie's plantation (Powell 1986). Other crops such as sugarcane and corn were also grown in Santa Elena, and evidence of such crops may be found in the form of seeds or agricultural ditches for those species requiring deep planting.

25. We have seen that *one of the diversions of the soldiers* when not otherwise occupied *was gambling. Evidence for this recreational activity in the form of dice or other gaming devices* might well be expected from the archaeological record.

ARCHAEOLOGICAL PROJECT SUMMARY

The postulates outlined here, which are based on historical research and reflected in the archaeological record, are designed to monitor energy flow through socioeconomic status differences. This has been the main approach of my research at Santa Elena since 1979 (South 1979, 1980, 1982, 1983, 1984, 1985a).

A sampling strategy designed to discover the distribution of the material remains of Santa Elena and its forts San Marcos (1577–87) and San Felipe (1572–76) made it possible to find the remains of the ruins of the city between the two forts (Figure 2.1) (South 1979; Lyon 1984a:9–15). Subsequent archaeology in the city of Santa Elena (beneath the Parris Island Golf Course) (Figure 2.2) revealed five houses, one of which was a hut made in the Indian manner with a central hearth, probably once occupied by a foot soldier or a servant. The other four structures were rectangular and were 20, 26, 32, and 42 feet long and about

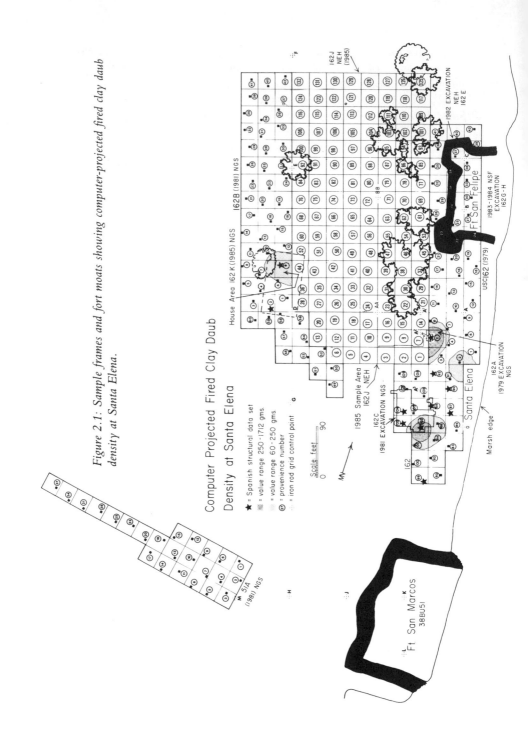

Figure 2.1: Sample frames and fort moats showing computer-projected fired clay daub density at Santa Elena.

44

Figure 2.2: Spanish features beneath the Parris Island golf course.

10 feet wider (Figure 2.3). They are thought to represent settler's dwellings. These excavations exposed 6,775 square feet in the town of Santa Elena (South 1980:12, 46; 1982:14; 1983:7).

The entire area inside Ft. San Felipe and the northwest bastion and moat were revealed in excavations exposing 11,560 square feet, almost twice the area excavated in the city (Figures 2.4, 2.5). The excavation of the interior of Ft. San Felipe, half of which has been lost through erosion, revealed a fortified house or *casa fuerte*, measuring 50 by 70 feet (Figure 2.6) (South 1983:52; 1985a:13).

These excavations yielded artifacts from a *domestic occupation* in the town of Santa Elena (Figure 2.7) and a *military occupation* inside Ft. San Felipe (Figure 2.8), as well as the remains of a hut once occupied by *a laboring-class individual*. Table 2.1 summarizes the analytical tools and

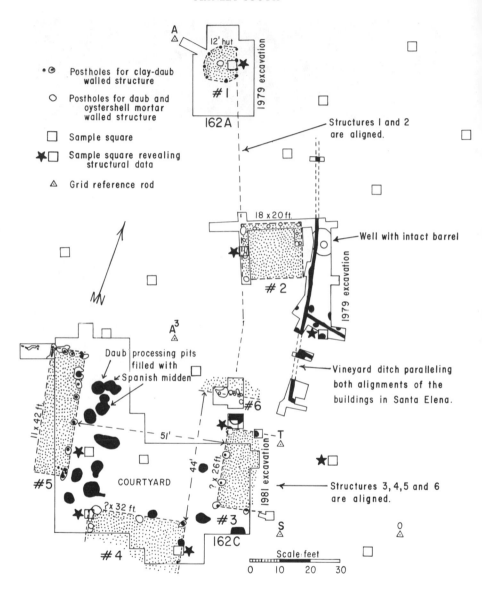

Figure 2.3: Structures in the Spanish city of Santa Elena.

assumptions used in our Santa Elena research. The arguments of
relevance link the theoretical ideas to the archaeological data by means
of these analytical tools and assumptions.

Figure 2.4: Excavation at the northwest bastion of Ft. San Felipe.

ARCHAEOLOGICAL DATA SUMMARY

Settlement and Socioeconomic Status Data

The predominant class of Spanish colonial artifacts recovered at Santa
Elena consists of ceramics imported from the various countries involved in the Spanish trade network. These include Ming dynasty porcelain from China (Cervantes 1977; South 1982:50), majolica from
Spain and Italy (Lister and Lister 1974, 1976, 1982:73; South 1982:6,
46), burnished red-painted ware from Mexico (Thomas Charlton 1968,

Figure 2.5: Excavation in progress inside the area of Ft. San Felipe.

and personal communication), and many types from Spain (Deagan 1978; Goggin 1960, 1968; Lister and Lister 1974, 1976, 1982; H. Smith 1949; R. Smith 1971; South 1982:5, 45–46). These ceramic types clearly reflect the world trade network of which Santa Elena was a part.

It is interesting to note that, although there was a great deal of interaction between Spain and France during the 16th-century struggle for control of the New World, we have yet to positively identify French ceramics at Santa Elena or on other 16th-century Spanish occupation sites. This is, in my opinion, not because such ceramics are not present, but because we have as yet not learned how to distinguish attributes di-

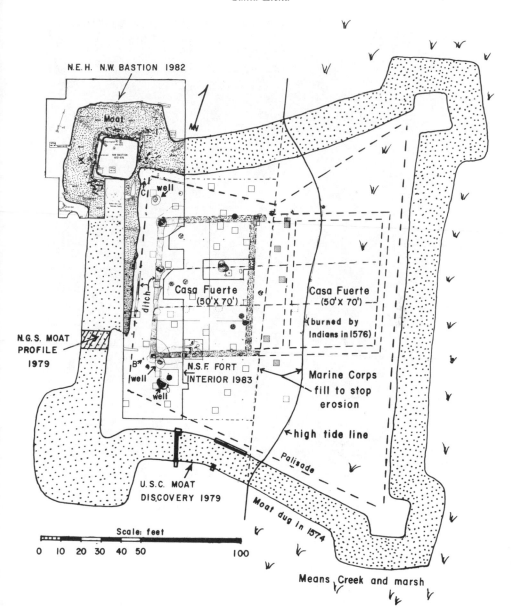

Figure 2.6: Interpretive plan of Ft. San Felipe at Santa Elena showing the position of the two casas fuertes *known to have been inside the fort.*

Figure 2.7: Spanish majolica from a feature in Santa Elena.

agnostic of French ceramics of the period. We are likely dealing with a French-Spanish-Iberian ceramic tradition with little differentiation among some attributes.

The power over the exploitation of Spanish Florida was centered in Santa Elena during the 1560s and was in the hands of the controlling elite-status individuals residing there. In contrast, St. Augustine was a frontier garrison fort at the time. Therefore, we can expect more artifact classes and types reflecting control of energy and resources by the

Figure 2.8: Spanish armor being revealed at the northwest bastion of Ft. San Felipe.

elite class to be found in Santa Elena than in the outpost settlement at St. Augustine. In keeping with our expectations, 104 artifact types have been found at Santa Elena (South 1979, 1980, 1982, 1983, 1984, 1985a) and 71 at St. Augustine (Deagan 1985:11–12). Socioeconomic status within settlements such as Santa Elena can be determined through architectural data. Our expectations are that the dominant class of dwellings will consist of larger buildings that settler's structures will be smaller and grouped around the courtyards, and that the laborers probably lived in the smallest huts set back from the town plaza. We have not found the estate of Pedro Menéndez de Avilés, known to have been located on the edge of Santa Elena, but we have found four rectangular structures measuring 18 × 20, ? × 26, ? × 32, and 11 × 42 feet in length, in contrast to a small (12-foot-wide) Indian style, D-shaped hut with a central hearth and a central roof smokehole (Figure 2.3) (South 1980). Three of the larger buildings were positioned around a courtyard (Figure 2.3). In contrast, the public-funded *casa fuerte* located inside Ft. San Felipe measures 50 by 70 feet.

The data used to compare architectural size or artifact quantities and dispersion for functional interpretations must come from a similar

TABLE 2.1

*Tools and Assumptions Used in Archaeological Analysis
at Santa Elena*

World system	1.	Artifact type variability as a measure of the link of colonial sites to the European power center
World system	2.	Artifact types as indicator of world trade network (ceramics from Spain, Italy, Caribbean, Mexico, China, etc.)
Status	3.	Artifact type variability as a measure of elite- vs. laboring-class occupancy
Status	4.	Frequency and quality of artifact types and fragments as a measure of status in domestic dwellings
Status	5.	The presence of elite status-related artifact types (bordado, porcelain, etc.)
Status	6.	The presence of laboring-class artifact types (colonoware, earthenware, etc.)
Status	7.	The presence of ceramics typical of Santa Elena settlers (majolica)
Status	8.	Architectural artifact quality as indicator of elite-status structure
Status	9.	Size of architectural feature as indicator of elite-status dwelling (larger)
Architecture	10.	Density of artifact fragments as an indication of entryways (Brunswick pattern; South 1977)
Architecture	11.	Architectural artifacts as indicator of structures (architectural artifact pattern; South 1978)
Function (domestic)	12.	Artifact type frequency relationships as a measure of domestic household activity (Carolina pattern; South 1977)
Function (nondomestic)	13.	Artifact type ratios as a measure of nondomestic function (military, craft, industrial, etc.)
Function	14.	Architectural size as indicator of public structure vs. private

TABLE 2.1—*continued*

Function	15. Larger nail size as indicator of public vs. private structure
Function	16. Archaeological features as indicators of military vs. civilian function (broad ditches, moats, obtuse and acute bastion angles, larger timber = larger posthole, etc., vs. small drainage and agricultural ditches, small postholes, etc.)
Function	17. The ratio of food preparation and consumption artifacts as an indicator of domestic activities (kitchen pattern; South 1977)
Chronology	18. Artifact types and fragment frequency as a measure of occupation period (mean ceramic date formula and mean majolica date formula; South 1977)
Ethnicity	19. Artifact type ratios as an indicator of ethnicity (slaves, Indians, Spaniards) or socioeconomic status
Religion	20. Specific artifact types as indicators of religious belief system (crucifixes, figas, etc.)
Religion	21. Burial features as a measure of religious belief system
Sex roles	22. Artifact type ratios as an indicator of male-female role differentiation
Agriculture	23. Artifact types (pruning shears, hoes, etc.) and features (vineyard ditches) as indicator of agricultural practices
Formation processes	24. Spatial distribution of cross-mended vessels as an indicator of site formation processes (mended sherds from wells, pits, and levels, etc.)
Association	25. Association of artifacts, architectural features, and pits as functional, status, ethnic, religious, etc. indicators

Note: I use "artifact" to refer to a sherd, for instance. I use "artifact type" to refer to a taxonomic type, such as majolica. I use "artifact class" to refer to several artifact types, such as ceramics. I use "artifact group" to refer to a group of artifact classes, such as kitchen group (see South 1977).

time period. At Santa Elena, all materials connected with the Spanish occupation date from 1566 to 1587, (Lyon 1976), the median occupation date being 1576.5. This gives the data sets a tight time frame. Within this frame, I have used the mean majolica date formula to compare dates using majolica with the known occupation of the town (South 1977:238; 1983:40), with a date of 1572.5 being derived using this method.

Another temporal method being used at Santa Elena to date features prior to 1577 is based on the fact that lime from Havana was ordered at that date, and no lime was used in the fort built before then (Connor 1930:13). Also, oyster shell mortar was used after 1580 and not before (Connor 1930:283; South 1984:22). These diagnostic lime and oyster shell mortar attributes are used to separate the features of the first Santa Elena occupation from those of the second decade of occupation. The mortar was used to make a thin lime coating over clay walls and flat roofs (in the Southwest manner) to protect against damage by rain (Quiros Papers, 1578–80; South 1984).

The mention of a thriving vineyard in Santa Elena in 1568 (Lyon 1976:204) reminds us that evidence of vineyard ditches and other agricultural activity by the Spaniards might well be found archaeologically. Indeed, vineyard ditches are found in almost all excavation contexts, some clearly intruded on by subsequent Spanish features (South 1980:13; 1982:2–8, 22, 25; 1983:1, 11–21, 49, 53, 60; 1984:16–17).

The possibility of the presence of slave-made colonoware in Spanish archaeological contexts exists (Lyon 1976:49; Ferguson 1978, 1980). However, such ware has been found in only limited quantity among the pottery from Spanish features at Santa Elena (Chester DePratter in preparation). It may well be that slaves were not numerous in Santa Elena. However, there is a possibility that slaves used Indian pottery, in which case their presence would not be noticed through pottery in the archaeology record. In any case the excavated ceramics, the number of artifact classes, the size of the architectural structures, specific status-related artifacts such as bordado and Chinese Ming porcelain, agricultural practices such as those represented by vineyard ditches, and the chronology from ceramics all reflect the socioeconomic status differences, agricultural practices, and time differences, as expected from our arguments of relevance.

Fortification and Socioeconomic Status Data

We have argued that, because of the need for protection, public buildings inside fortifications would be expected to be larger, to be built of heavier timbers, and to have larger postholes, and we can expect the timbers to be joined by larger spikes and nails (South 1985b). The average width (or diameter) of the postholes at Santa Elena is 1.2 feet, and the average size of the postholes for the *casa fuerte* inside Ft. San Felipe is 3.5 × 4.3 feet, which is more than three times the size of the postholes in the domestic dwellings (South 1980:9–13, 44–49; 1982:39–43; 1984:14, 21–56; 1985a:13). We have also suggested that military fortification construction would be marked by wider ditches than would domestic construction, and this is indeed the case. At Ft. San Felipe, the moat is 16 feet wide with obtuse and right angles at the bastion instead of the expected acute angles seen on later forts. The fortified *casa fuerte* ditch measures 2.5–3 feet in width. No such ditches have been found in the domestic area of Santa Elena (South 1983:52; 1984:14, 21–56; 1985a:13) or on other domestic nonfortified sites.

Table 2.2 compares the nail types between the town of Santa Elena and Ft. San Felipe. Large nails (sizes 7 through 10) make up 36.6 percent of the nails from Santa Elena domestic contexts, but 52.0 percent of the nails from the fort. These data support our argument that larger timbers and thus larger nails would be involved in fortification construction on historic sites (South 1985b). As we have seen, the postholes for such construction were three times the size of those in the domestic dwellings.

An interesting contrast emerged from the comparison of nails involving the quantity of nails from the domestic town versus the military fort context. The ratio of excavated area in Santa Elena compared to the fort is 1 to 1.7. The 437 nails from Santa Elena multiplied by 1.7 is 743, the projected number of nails for the fort if the quantity of nails used in Santa Elena and the fort were the same. However, the fort nail count is only 383, less in fact, than for Santa Elena, being a ratio of 1 to minus 1.1 for the fort. This tells us that far fewer nails were used in the *casa fuerte* than in Santa Elena structures. Perhaps this has to do with the use of larger timbers in the fort, where nails may have been less common than mortise-and-tenon construction. In wooden forts, therefore, the nails and spikes may be larger in size but fewer in number than in domestic post-and-lintel, wattle-and-daub construction.

Elsewhere, I have demonstrated that fortification use areas can be distinguished from domestic use areas through the greater number of artifact types in the military class (South 1977:175–76). The comparison at Santa Elena is summarized in Table 2.3 (see South 1980:70; 1982:64–65; 1983:24–28, 54–65; 1984:58, 68, 146; 1985a:55–60, 67).

This simple comparison of military artifact types hints at the presence of a military function versus a domestic function without the ben-

TABLE 2.2

Nail Types from Santa Elena and Ft. San Felipe

Nail Type No.	Nail Size (mm)	Santa Elena		Ft. San Felipe	
		Count	%	Count	%
1[a]	—	—	—	—	—
2	20–30	12	2.74	6	1.57
3	30+–40	19	4.35	16	4.18
4	40+–50	37	8.47	17	4.44
5	50+–63	47	10.75	36	9.40
6	63+–90	162	37.07	109	28.46
7	90+–135	124	28.38	140	36.55
8	135+–185	26	5.95	43	11.23
9	185+–230	9	2.06	10	2.61
10	230+–280	1	.23	6	1.56
		437	100.00	383	100.00
Large nails, types 7–10		160	36.61	199	52.00

[a]Large-headed tacks, *estoperoles*, not included here.

efit of the architectural features from the two areas; that is, there are three times more military artifact types inside Fort San Felipe than in the town of Santa Elena.

We have suggested through our arguments of relevance that majolica might well be a typical settler's indicator in contrast to the humble artifacts available to the laborers. To test this idea, we compare the majolica from the hut site with that from the total excavation in Santa Elena in relation to that from Ft. San Felipe (Table 2.4).

We find that the residents of the rectangular, Spanish-style houses in Santa Elena did indeed have far more majolica (24.9 percent) than the residents of the hut (8.9 percent). The occupants of the fort, however, had the most majolica in relation to other Spanish imported ceramic types. They also had the most majolica types (14). The surprise, however, is the large quantity of majolica recovered inside the fort compared with Santa Elena (77.8 percent of all majolica). Also, the number of sherds of all types of Spanish imported ceramics, which total 20,763, is far higher than one would expect even when considering the larger area excavated inside the fort. We can project the number expected in-

TABLE 2.3

Military Artifact Types from Santa Elena and Ft. San Felipe

From Santa Elena	From Ft. San Felipe
1. Lead shot	1. Lead shot
2. Lead sprue	2. Lead sprue
3. Bullet mold	3. Bullet mold
4. Arquebus or crossbow trigger	4. Arquebus or crossbow
	5. Goatsfoot lever for crossbow
	6. Chain mail link
	7. Crossbow bolt point (quarrels)
	8. Serpentine with thumbscrew
	9. Bandolier bag for holding shot
	10. Cannonball
	11. Armor (iron)
	12. Copper disc from quilted armor

side the fort (to obtain comparable data from the excavated areas involved) by multiplying the quantity in Santa Elena (7,352) by the 1.7 greater ratio of excavated area in the fort. This gives a projected figure of 12,498, still far short of the actual quantity of Spanish imported ceramics present. This finding suggests that a far higher use of Spanish imported ceramics, and thus energy, was available to those occupying the fort than those in the town and is consistent with the fort's being the center of the administrative power structure of the settlement, both symbolic and actual. Access to the flow of goods, both Spanish and Indian, in and out of the fort was greater than in the town of Santa Elena.

In contrast to the high percentage of majolica and other Spanish imported ceramics in Ft. San Felipe, which indicate the fort's role as a center for the exploitation of economic resources moving in and out of Santa Elena, Chinese Ming dynasty porcelain is all but absent. The settlement of Santa Elena yielded one sherd of Ming porcelain to five sherds of earthenware, whereas Ft. San Felipe yielded 1 porcelain sherd to 176 sherds of earthenware (South 1982:108; 1983; 1984:79;

TABLE 2.4

Majolica Found at Study Sites

	Count	Percent	Percentage of majolica to total Spanish introduced wares	Total Spanish ceramic wares	Total majolica types present
Hut	85	1.0	8.9	955	5
Santa Elena	1,834	21.2	24.9	7,352	13
Ft. San Felipe	6,710	77.8	32.3	20,763	14
	8,629	100.0			

Sources: South (1980:22; 1982:70–71; 1983:34–36, 67–69; 1984:105, 116; 1985a:123, 125).

1985a:123– 25, 127–34). Clearly, porcelain was relatively rare inside Ft. San Felipe compared with Santa Elena. Porcelain in any quantity probably would have been in the possession of only the most affluent among the ruling class at conquest settlements such as Santa Elena (Kamer 1956; Cervantes 1977). Its virtual absence within the fort and its greater availability within the town of Santa Elena suggests that porcelain did not function within the military context of the fort. Majolica, too, might be found to be an elite as well as a settler status indicator if split into Italian majolica and decorated types vs. cheaper undecorated types.

A specific socioeconomic status indicator as diagnostic as porcelain is seen in the braid sewn onto clothing of the Spanish elite, known as bordado. Bordado has been found in Santa Elena as well as in the fort of San Felipe (South 1982:55–57; 1984:57–59). Its presence is an indicator of activities related to individuals of upper socioeconomic status.

To our knowledge, we have not discovered the residence estate of Pedro Menéndez de Avilés on the edge of Santa Elena, but I suspect that if we do there will be a higher ratio of porcelain and decorated and Italian majolicas than we have seen in Santa Elena itself. Porcelain is a good indicator of the highest ruling class in the settlement and is hardly present in the fort, whereas majolica is present in the fort in larger quantity than in the town. This suggests that majolica may well be a reflector of soldier and craftsman status, just as porcelain was an upperclass indicator, and earthenware and Indian pottery (and perhaps plain majolica) were the types of ware most used by the laboring class in Spanish colonial settlements.

One other point of interest is the fact that bone dice and gaming discs made of sherds of Indian pottery and Spanish olive jars have been found at Santa Elena. This is archaeological evidence for the gambling said to have been taking place among the soldiers there (Lyon 1977).

Evangelization and Indian Data

The historical background and the arguments of relevance indicate that a major goal of the Spaniards in the conquest of Florida was to evangelize and convert the Indians. We know that considerable interaction with Indians took place in St. Augustine and Santa Elena through tribute and trade and that "intermarriage and intermating between Spaniard and Indian were extremely widespread" (Deagan 1973:56; 1980:4), with the result that mestizos were born in both settlements. The mestizaje process came about primarily "by Indian women in Spanish or mestizo household units within a predominantly male-oriented cultural milieu" (Deagan 1973:63). By this means, Indian pottery (made by women) came to be a functional item within Spanish colonial households.

The strength of this connection at Santa Elena can be seen in the fact that, of all the artifacts recovered in the town, 42.4 percent were fragments of Indian pottery, while at Ft. San Felipe the figure was 47.9 percent. Does this mean that more Indians were in the fort, as suggested by the higher percentage of Indian pottery inside the fort? A more likely interpretation might relate to Indian tribute. Access to the flow of goods by those in control from within the power center of the fort might be seen, in this case, through Indian pottery. It may be that goods such as corn, beans, squash and other tribute being paid by the Indians to the Spaniards were delivered to the fort in Indian pottery, which was subsequently used there, and broken. This would account for the higher percentage of Indian pottery there.

The relative percentage of Indian pottery in features is thought to be a means of determining the presence of Indian women in Santa Elena households. By using 55 percent of Indian pottery as a criterion for separating features associated with Structures 3, 4, and 5 in Santa Elena, we found that all such features were located near Structures 3 and 4, whereas all those pit features associated with Structure 5 had 55 percent or more Spanish pottery (Figure 2.9). This suggests that Structure 5

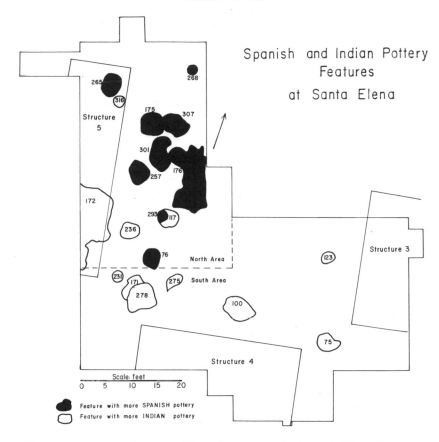

Spanish and Indian Pottery
Features

at Santa Elena

265
268
316
Structure
5
175
307
301
176
257
172
293
117
236
76
North Area
123
Structure 3
231
171
275
South Area
278
100
75
Structure 4

Scale: feet
0   5   10   15   20

Feature with more SPANISH pottery
Feature with more INDIAN pottery

Figure 2.9: Note the clustering of Spanish pottery at the largest building, Structure 5. Indian pottery reflects the presence of Indian women at the smaller buildings, Structures 3 and 4.

was likely an elite-status structure. Other items such as chicken bones also suggest that Structure 5 was a more elite household, as does its larger size (42 feet long) in comparison with other structures (South 1982:69–85).

The degree of contact between Santa Elena and nonlocal Indians—for example, the Timucua along the St. Johns River near St. Augustine—can be monitored through the presence of St. Johns Pottery and other nonlocal Indian pottery (Goggin 1947, 1949, 1952; Deagan 1978:30; DePratter, in preparation). As we have seen from the documentary summary, Pedro Menéndez de Avilés brought some of these Indians with him to Santa Elena, along with some Tequesta Indians (Lyon 1976:181). I believe that such Indian ware would not have come into the fort by means of tribute as did the local Indian pottery, but would have come by way of Indian women into the households of Santa Elena. We can archaeologically monitor the Florida Indian presence through the presence of St. Johns pottery.

A comparison of the ratios of locally made Irene and other contemporary Indian pottery from the Santa Elena area (Caldwell and McCann 1941; DePratter, in preparation) with imported St. Johns pottery from the area near St. Augustine has yielded the following results: For every sherd of St. Johns pottery in Santa Elena there are 14 sherds of locally made ware, clearly a majority of local Indian pottery. In Ft. San Felipe, however, the ratio is one St. Johns sherd to every 318 sherds of locally made ware. This indicates the scarcity of St. Johns pottery in the fort and supports the argument that this St. Johns ware is associated with the dwellings in Santa Elena rather than the fort, where cohabitation by Indian mates in soldier's beds may well have been discouraged (South 1982:64–65, 109; 1983:35–36; 1984:81). In any case, the evidence is far greater for local Indians in Ft. San Felipe than for Timucua Indians.

After Santa Elena was abandoned and burned in 1587, tribute to the ruling authorities was then paid at St. Augustine (Deagan 1980). From this information, Deagan hypothesized that there should be a higher percentage of Irene (Pine Harbor) Indian pottery from around Santa Elena (DePratter personal communication) in St. Augustine features dating after that time. Using the mean majolica dating formula (South 1977:238) to date each feature and arranging them into five-year increments, she examined the associated Indian pottery and found that a marked increase in Irene and associated types of pottery from the Santa Elena area occurred in features dating after 1585. "This corresponds to the prediction of a notable increase in non-local [Irene-Pine Harbor] wares after 1585 based on the shift in tribute from the northern regions to St. Augustine" (Deagan 1980:10). As more data are recovered from both cities, additional analyses designed to address intersite questions will be undertaken. As Deagan's study shows, the archaeological record reflects the cultural process of tribute and the flow of energy it represents from the Indian to the Spanish cultural system.

Because Santa Elena was a Catholic settlement, a goal of which was to evangelize and convert the Indians, one would expect to recover artifacts, architecture, or features relating to this process. The church would be the center for the recovery of data on religion, with burials being located according to status in the system. The controlling-class individuals would be buried nearest the altar in the tradition of the

Christian church in Europe. The church has not been found at Santa Elena, and was probably destroyed by erosion along with about half of the town site. Some scattered objects have been recovered, however, and reflect through archaeology, the religious orientation of the occupants. The direct influence of evangelization would most likely be found among converted Indians who may have been interred with Catholic symbols revealing their new-found god.

A brass Maltese cross with a relief figure of Christ, recovered from Santa Elena, is the emblem of the Order of the Hospital of St. John of Jerusalem (Post 1974:48). The Spanish elite were members of the Maltese order and had to show noble birth to become a member. Donate members could, upon making a generous donation to the order, be admitted at somewhat less than full status (Hume 1940; South 1982:59). Obviously, this Christian religious object reflects ownership by a member of the ruling or elite class at Santa Elena.

A series of small (1/2-inch) delicately carved objects made of jet may also have religious significance, perhaps as symbols of saints, for example. They all have a small hole drilled on a tab for fastening onto garments. One of these is a version of the Millrine Cross, whereas two are trefoil in shape, which is symbolic of the Holy Trinity (Post 1974:22, 65). One of the miniature objects is a triple figa or clinched fist motif representing the clinched hand of God holding the souls of the righteous, an amulet designed to turn away the evil eye (*Catalogo de la collection de amuletos* n.d.:16–18; Cooper 1978:78–79; South 1984:57–59). Such amulets were also believed to have the power to turn away bullets (Held 1957:34), and often were sewn onto children's clothing as protection (Lopez-Rey 1968:143, Plate VI). A scallop shell represents St. James the greater, the patron saint of Spain and of pilgrims (Post 1974:18; Hulme 1976:201), the first of the disciples to go on a missionary journey. Such objects reflect the belief system of the people who once wore them. Indians converted to Christianity may well have been attracted to these delicately carved symbols and the power they supposedly contained, but no direct connection between these symbols from the evangelization and conversion process of the Indians has been found at Santa Elena.

Another artifact class, also diminutive (1/2 inch) and probably tied to a religious symbolism, is copper or silver stars (South 1983:23–24; Radisch 1986). The function of these objects was unknown until research into 16th-century paintings revealed that the symbol is commonly found on doorways, tiles in floors and on walls, on coats of arms and shields and is sewn onto clothing, diadems, and so on as a religious motif (Angulo 1954:67, figs. 53, 55, 68, 94, 96, 100, 110, 114, 120, 125, 220, 232, 325, 338; Anderson 1979:131, figs. 7, 308).

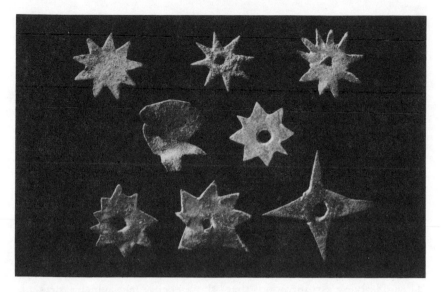

Figure 2.10: Copper stars with various points probably having religious symbolism.

From a strictly technomic point of view, these stars (with 4, 7, 8, 9, and 10 points, with central holes) could have functioned as backing plates for dispersing the needle holes in leather when the round ball-shaped buttons found on the site were being sewn on. They were made at Santa Elena and the by-product of their manufacture has been recovered from Spanish features along with the stars (Figure 2.10). These stars probably acted in the ideological system much as the carved ebony amulets did—to ward off evil, bring good luck, and so on, when sewn onto clothing— because such stars with various points have religious symbolism. The well known five-pointed star of the Epiphany and the six-pointed star have not been found thus far. The seven-pointed star symbolizes the seven gifts of the spirit, the eight-pointed star is the symbol of regeneration, the nine-pointed star represents the nine fruits of the spirit, and the twelve-pointed star represents the twelve tribes of Israel (Post 1974:67). These copper and silver stars are very likely symbols of the belief system held by those residents of Santa Elena devoted to Christianity. I suggest that these stars relate to the religious belief among the Spaniards and thus support the argument of relevance between archaeology and the religious system.

CONCLUSION

The research described in this chapter has been concerned with the Spanish strategy of energy control used at the colonial settlement of

Santa Elena through economic control, fortification, and conversion of the Indians into the Catholic faith, as revealed in the archaeological record. The discussion has focused on arguments of relevance connecting these energy controlling mechanisms to the subsistence, technological, social, symbolic, and world trade subsystems (Renfrew 1977:109) Through status differentiation as revealed in the artifacts and architecture, we have learned "how different classes lived, what they ate, and how much imported ware they could afford."

The basic assumption here is that "important traits will be important in energy terms and therefore should be expressed materially" (Price 1979:278). We have examined through architecture the energy output needed to construct a simple round hut using an Indian model and a large rectangular Spanish house using a Spanish model, contrasted with the energy in labor, size of materials, and scale of public defensive architecture. We have also examined site stratification by comparing the frontier outpost at St. Augustine and the colonial capital city of Santa Elena as reflected in the number of artifact classes present. The underlying assumption is that "those phenomena which represent, or encapsulate, or remove from circulation, the greatest quantities of energy should provide the best foundation for explanation" (Price 1979:275).

This chapter has also examined the contrast in ethnicity through Spanish local, and Florida Indian material remains in order to determine who produced the remains, when and where they lived, and the significance of the contrasts in historical, cultural, and processual terms (Renfrew 1977:92). The quantitative expression of socioeconomic status levels in terms of energy theory represents, in my opinion, a major archaeological challenge for the future. The processual strategies being used by elites in exploiting environmental and human energy resources are clearly encoded in the archaeological record and are therefore a major means of monitoring sociocultural processes.

This study has illustrated the importance of arguments of relevance as links bonding evolutionary energy theory to the appropriate artifact types, classes, and groups as seen in the archaeological record. This approach should be used more widely in historical archaeology if we hope to move from the site or regionally specific level to the level of world cultural systems and the processes of their operation as they exploit the available energy resources. The power of evolutionary theory in addressing the energy exploitative processes of cultural systems lies in the compatability between theoretical concepts and material remains within the archaeological record. No other theoretical tool set enables the historical archaeologist to study the cultural processes at the scale of world cultural systems.

ACKNOWLEDGMENTS

The data used in this chapter are from projects carried out between 1979 and 1985 that were funded through the South Carolina Institute of Archaeology and Anthropology at the University of South Carolina by the National Geographic Society, the *National Geographic* magazine, the U.S. Marine Corps, the Explorers Club of New York, the National Endowment for the Humanities, the National Science Foundation, and the Government of Spain through the Cultural Office of the Spanish Embassy. Without this support the research summarized here would not have been possible. I also want to thank the following colleagues for taking the time to read and comment on the chapter: Chester DePratter, Roy Dickens, Leland Ferguson, Halcott Green, William Hunt, Mark Leone, Eugene Lyon, James L. Michie, William Radisch and Carl Steen. Thanks also go to Kenn Pinson and Diane Moses for editing and producing the manuscript.

REFERENCES CITED

Anderson, Ruth Matilda
1979   *Hispanic Costume, 1480–1530*. New York: Hispanic Society of America.

Angulo, Diego Iniguez
1954   *Ars Hispaniae Universial del Arte Hispanico*. Volumen Decimosegundo, Pintura del Siglo XVI. Madrid: Editorial Plus-Ultra.

Binford, Lewis R.
1965   Colonial Period Ceramics of the Nottoway and Weanock Indians of Southeastern Virginia. *Quarterly Bulletin of the Archaeology Society of Virginia* 19 (4): 78–87.
1972   *An Archaeological Perspective*. New York: Seminar Press.

Bullen, Adelaide K., and Ripley P. Bullen
1945   Black Lucy's Garden. *Bulletin of the Massachusetts Archaeological Society* 6 (2). Massachusetts Archaeological Society, Boston.

Caldwell, Joseph R., and Catherine McCann
1941   *Irene Mound Site, Chatham County, Georgia*. Athens: University of Georgia Press.

Carnes, Linda F.
1984   *Archaeological Investigations at the Third Halifax Jail, Historic Halifax State Historic Site*. Raleigh: North Carolina Department of Cultural Resources, Division of Archives and History, Historic Sites Section.

Catalogo de la Collección de Amuletos
En trabajos y Materiales del Museo del Pueblo Espanol. Madrid: Talleres
Tipograficos "AF," n.d. 16–18. (Reference courtesy of Kathleen A.
Deagan, 11/7/83)

Cervantes, Gonzalo Lopez
1977   Porcelena Oriental en la Nueva Espana. Anales de Antropologia e
Historia, Epoca 8a. Tomo I. Instituto Nacional de Anthropologia e
Historia. Mexico, pp. 65– 82.

Charlton, Thomas H.
1968   Post-conquest Aztec Ceramics: Implications for Archaeological Interpretation. The Florida Anthropologist 21(4): 96–101.

Connor, Jeannette T.
1925   Colonial Records of Spanish Florida: Letters and Reports of Governors
and Secular Persons, Trans. and ed. J.T.C. Vol. 1. Florida State Historical Society, Publication 5. Deland.
1930   Colonial Records of Spanish Florida: Letters and Reports of Governors
and Secular Persons. Trans. and ed. J.T.C. Vol. 2. Florida State Historical Society, Publication 5. Deland.

Cooper, J. C.
1978   An Illustrated Encyclopedia of Traditional Symbols. London: Thames
and Hudson.

Deagan, Kathleen A.
1973   Mestizaje in Colonial St. Augustine. Ethnohistory 20(1): 55–65.
1978   The Material Assemblage of 16th Century Spanish Florida. Historical Archaeology 12:25–50.
1980   Spaniard and Indian in Sixteenth Century La Florida. Paper presented at the Southeastern Archaeological Conference Meeting,
New Orleans.
1983   Spanish St. Augustine. New York: Academic Press.
1985   The Archaeology of Sixteenth Century St. Augustine. The Florida
Anthropologist 38(1–2), pt. 1. The Florida Anthropological Society,
Inc.

Deetz, James
1977   In Small Things Forgotten. Garden City, N.Y.: Anchor Press/
Doubleday.

DePratter, Chester
In preparation.
Spanish Contemporary Indian Pottery. In Spanish Artifacts at Santa
Elena by Stanley South, Chester DePratter, Richard Johnson and
Russell Skowronek. University of South Carolina Institute of Ar-
chaeology and Anthropology Anthropological Studies Series. Co-
lumbia.

Ferguson, Leland
    1978   Looking for the "Afro" in Colono-Indian Pottery. The Conference
            on Historic Site Archaeology Papers 1977, 12. The Institute of Ar-
            chaeology and Anthropology, The University of South Carolina,
            Columbia.
    1980   Looking for the "Afro" in Colono-Indian Pottery. In *Archaeological*
            perspectives on Ethnicity in America, ed. Robert L. Schuyler, pp.
            14–28. Farmingdale, N.Y.: Baywood Press.

Finley, M. I.
    1954   *The World of Odysseus*. New York: Viking Press.

Foresman, Michael
    1979   Artifact Pattern Recognition and Comparison. *Pattern and Meaning*.
            The Conference on Historic Site Archaeology. The Institute of Ar-
            chaeology and Anthropology, The University of South Carolina,
            Columbia.

Foster-Carter, Aiden
    1978   Can We Articulate 'Articulation'? In *The New Economic Anthropol-*
            ogy, ed. John Clammer. New York: St. Martin's Press.

Goggin, John M.
    1947   A Preliminary Definition of Archaeological Areas and Periods in
            Florida. *American Antiquity*. 13(2): 114–27.
    1949   Cultural Traditions in Florida Prehistory. In *The Florida Indian and*
            His Neighbors, ed. John W. Griffin, pp. 13–44. Winter Park, Fla.:
            Inter-American Center, Rollins College.
    1952   Space and Time Perspective in Northern St. Johns Archaeology,
            Florida. Yale University Publications in Anthropology. No. 47.
            New Haven.
    1960   *The Spanish Olive Jar: An Introductory Study*. Yale University Publi-
            cations in Anthropology no. 62. New Haven, Conn.
    1968   *Spanish Majolica in the New World*. Yale University Publications in
            Anthropology no. 72. New Haven, Conn.

Green, Halcott P.
    1986a   *Power and Evolution: the Disequilibrium Hypothesis*. Occasional Pa-
            pers no. 1. Institute of International Studies, University of South
            Carolina. Columbia.
    1986b   Original Sin and the Social Order: The Social Prediction of the
            Disequilibrium Hypothesis. Manuscript on file at the University of
            South Carolina Institute of International Studies. Columbia.

Harris, Marvin
    1964   *Patterns of Race in the Americas*. New York: Walker and Co.
    1980   *Cultural Materialism: The Struggle for a Science of Culture*. New York:
            Vintage Books.

Held, Robert
1957   *The Age of Firearms*. New York: Harper and Brothers.

Hoffman, Paul
1978   Sixteenth-century Fortifications on Parris Island, South Carolina. Ms. on file at the National Geographic Magazine, Washington.

Hulme, Edward
1976   *Symbolism in Christian Art*. Poole, Great Britain: Blandford Press.

Hume, E. E.
1940   *Medical Work of the Knights Hospitallers of Saint John of Jerusalem*. Baltimore, Md.: Johns Hopkins Press.

Hunt, William
1985   A Comparison of Sixteenth Century Spanish Colonization at Santa Elena in Florida with the Andean Region of Peru. Manuscript on file. South Carolina Institute of Archaeology and Anthropology. University of South Carolina, Columbia.

Kamer, Aga Oglu
1956   Late Ming and Early Ching Porcelain Fragments from Archaeological Sites in Florida. *Florida Anthropologist* 8(4): 1–51.

Leone, Mark
1982   Historical Archaeology and Reshaping the Myths of American Origins. Prepared for a conference on protection of cultural and natural resources. Washington, D.C.

Lewis, Kenneth E.
1984   *The American Frontier: An Archaeological Study of Settlement Pattern and Process*. New York: Academic Press.

1985   Plantation Layout and Function in the South Carolina Lowcountry. In *The Archaeology of Slavery and Plantation Life*, ed. Theresa A. Singleton, pp. 35–66. New York: Academic Press.

Lister, Florence C., and Robert H. Lister:
1974   Majolica in Colonial Spanish America. *Historical Archaeology* 10: 28–41.
1976   Italian Presence in Tin Glazed Ceramics of Spanish America. *Historical Archaeology* 10: 28–41.
1982   *Sixteenth Century Maiolica Pottery in the Valley of Mexico*. Tucson: University of Arizona Press.

Lopez-Rey, Jose
1968   *Velazquez' Work and World*. London: Faber and Faber.

Lyon, Eugene
1976   *The Enterprise of Florida.* Gainesville: University Presses of Florida.
1977   St. Augustine 1580: The Living Community. *El Escribano* 16. St. Augustine Historical Society. St Augustine.
1984a   Santa Elena: a Brief History of the Colony, 1566–1587. South Carolina Institute of Archaeology and Anthropology, Research Manuscript Series 193. University of South Carolina, Columbia.
1984b   The Florida Mutineers, 1566–67. *Tequesta* 44: 44–61.

Manucy, Albert
1985   The Physical Setting of Sixteenth Century St. Augustine. *The Florida Anthropologist* (1-2), pt.1. Florida Anthropological Society, Inc.

Marx, Karl
1906   *Capital.* New York: Modern Library.

McEwan, Bonnie Gair
1983   Spanish Colonial Adaptation on Hispaniola: The Archaeology of Area 35, Puerto Real, Haiti. Masters Thesis. University of Florida, Gainesville.

Nash, June
1981   *Ethnographic Aspects of the World Capitalist System.* Annual Review of Anthropology. Annual Reviews Inc.

Odum, Howard T., and Elizabeth C. Odum
1981   *Energy Basis for Man and Nature.* New York: McGraw-Hill. New York.

Otto, John Solomon
1977   Artifacts and Status Differences: a Comparison of Ceramics from Planter, Overseer, and Slave Sites on an Antebellum Plantation. In *Research Strategies in Historical Archaelogy*, ed. Stanley South, pp.91-118. New York: Academic Press.

Payne-Gallwey, Ralph
1958   *The Crossbow.* New York: Bramhall House.

Post, W. Ellwood
1974   *Saints, Signs, and Symbols.* Wilton, Conn.: Morehouse-Barlow.

Powell, Nena
1986   Emergency Evaluation of Impending Impact on General William Moultrie's Plantation site. University of South Carolina Institute of Archaeology and Anthropology, Research Manuscript Series. Columbia.

Price, Barbara J.
1979   Turning State's Evidence: Problems in the Theory of State Formation. In *New Directions in Political Economy*, ed. M. B. Leóns and F. Rothstein. Westport, Conn.: Greenwood Press.

1982   Cultural Materialism: A Theoretical Review. *American Antiquity* 47(4): 709–741.

Quiros Papers
1578–80 Archivo General de Indias. Santo Domingo 125, no. 150D.

Radisch, William
    1986   Classification and Interpretation of Stars from Santa Elena: Some Problems and Potential Solutions. Manuscript on file at the University of South Carolina, South Carolina Institute of Archaeology and Anthropology. Columbia.

Reitz, Elizabeth J.
    1982   Vertebrate Remains from Santa Elena 1981 Excavations. University of South Carolina, Institute of Archaeology and Anthropology, Research Manuscript Series 184. Columbia.

Reitz, Elizabeth, and C. Margaret Scarry
    1985   *Reconstructing Historic Subsistence with an Example from Sixteenth-Century Spanish Florida.* Special Publication Series, (3). The Society for Historical Archaeology.

Renfrew, Colin
    1977   Space, Time and Polity. In *The Evolution of Social Systems*, ed. J. Friedman and M. J. Rowlands. London: Gerald Duckworth.

Smith, Hale G.
    1949   *Two Historical Archaeological Sites in Brevard County, Florida.* Florida Anthropological Society Special Publication, no. 1.

South, Stanley
    1969   Exploratory Archaeology at the Site of 1670–1680 Charles Town on Albemarle Point in South Carolina. University of South Carolina, Institute of Archaeology and Anthropology, Research Manuscript Series 1. Columbia.
    1977   *Method and Theory in Historical Archaeology.* New York: Academic Press.
    1978   Pattern Recognition in Historical Archaeology. *American Antiquity* 43(2): 223–30.
    1977   *Method and Theory in Historical Archaeology.* New York: Academic Press.
    1978   Pattern Recognition in Historical Archaeology. *American Antiquity* 43(2): 223–30.
    1979   The Search for Santa Elena on Parris Island, South Carolina. University of South Carolina, Institute of Archaeology and Anthropology, Research Manuscript Series 150. Columbia.
    1980   The Discovery of Santa Elena. University of South Carolina, Institute of Archaeology and Anthropology, Research Manuscript Series 165. Columbia.

1982   Exploring Santa Elena 1981. University of South Carolina, Institute of Archaeology and Anthropology, Research Manuscript Series 188. Columbia.

1983   Revealing Santa Elena 1982. University of South Carolina. Institute of Archaeology and Anthropology, Research Manuscript Series 188. Columbia.

1984   Testing Archaeological Sampling Methods At Fort San Felipe 1983. South Carolina Institute of Archaeology and Anthropology, Research Manuscript Series 190. University of South Carolina, Columbia.

1985a   Excavation of the Casa Fuerte and Wells at Ft. San Felipe 1984. South Carolina Institute of Archaeology and Anthropology, Research Manuscript Series 196. University of South Carolina, Columbia.

1985b   Building a Model for Use in a Typological Analysis of Nails from Santa Elena. Manuscript dated 10/10/1985, on file at the University of South Carolina Institute of Archaeology and Anthropology. Columbia.

Wallerstein, Immanuel

1974   *The Modern World-System.* New York: Academic Press.

1980   *The Modern World-System II: Mercantilism and the Consolidation of the European World-economy, 1600–1750.* New York: Academic Press.

Wheaton, Thomas R., Amy Friedlander, and Patrick H. Garrow

1983   *Yaughan and Curriboo Plantations: Studies in Afro-American Archaeology.* Marietta, Ga.: Soil Systems.

White, Leslie

1949   *The Science of Culture.* New York: Grove Press.

1975   *The Concept of Cultural Systems.* New York: Columbia University Press.

Willis, Raymond F.

1984   Empire and Architecture at 16th Century Puerto Real, Hispaniola: An Archaeological Perspective. Ph.D. diss. University of Florida.

Wolf, Eric R.

1982   *Europe and the People without History.* Los Angeles: University of California Press.

CHAPTER 3

Saints and Soldiers
at Santa Catalina
Hispanic Designs for Colonial America

DAVID HURST THOMAS

I try to achieve two goals with this chapter. My first wish is to emphasize the burgeoning field of mission archaeology currently being pursued in the American Southeast. Over the past decade, our knowledge
regarding this important arena of European–Native American interaction has increased at an exponential pace. I illustrate the thrust of such
research with some preliminary findings coming to light from my
ongoing excavations at Mission Santa Catalina (Georgia).

At a more general level, I also stress the wide variability in colonial
strategies that conditioned the early European conquest of Native
North America. Almost by default, mainstream American history has
been constructed from a marked Anglo perspective, and rarely does an
awareness of Hispanic colonialization transcend the heavily documented, but unrepresentative, conquests of 16th-century Mexico and
Peru. The recent flurry of interest in the historical archaeology of
Spanish towns and missions in *La Florida* serves to highlight the
diversity in early European colonial attitudes toward Native Americans
and their homeland.

DAVID HURST THOMAS

SOME SMALL THINGS SEEM MORE READILY
FORGOTTEN THAN OTHERS

Three generations of Spanish borderland historians have attempted to demonstrate that American history consists of more than the establishment and expansion of English settlements along the eastern seaboard of North America. Bolton argued that U.S. history had been written almost solely from the standpoint of the East and of the English colonies with the importance of the Spanish period in American History not fully recognized. This general perception seems not to have changed significantly over the past six decades (see Sturtevant 1962; Scardaville 1985:185; Washburn 1985:146–47).

This systematic historical bias has fostered a persistent *leyenda negra*, a "black legend," that, for nearly four centuries, has systematically overlooked and belittled Spanish achievements in general (Gibson 1971; Maltby 1971; Scardaville 1985:188). One particularly succinct sketch unwittingly characterizing the "black legend" is provided in a 1892 history text:

> The Spaniards were brave, and they could rule with severity. But they thirsted for adventure, conquest, and wealth, for which their appetite was early encouraged; their progress in Mexico, Peru, and the West Indies had been too rapid and brilliant for them to be satisfied with the dull life and patient development of an agricultural colony. . . . Their aims were sordid, their State was loosely knit, their commercial policy was rigidly exclusive, their morals were lax, and their treatment of the savages was cruel, despite the tendency of the colonists to amalgamate with the latter, and thus to descend in the scale of civilization. (Thwaites 1892:47)

In more general terms, the black legend seems to embrace four related beliefs:

1. Spaniards were never true colonizers in the New World; only the English set out to establish permanent colonies. Rather than being settlers, the Spanish were perceived as being interested solely in "glory, God, and gold" (Jones 1979:4).

2. Spaniards contributed little, if anything, of lasting value to New World civilization.

3. The Spanish were not only exceptionally cruel in the conquest of the Americas, but they refused to engage in manual labor— especially agriculture.

4. Something "peculiar" in the national Spanish character fostered bigotry, pride, and hypocrisy.

This conventional textbook wisdom portrays St. Augustine as a second-rate foil to the more noble British colonies, with Spanish language, law, religion, and worldview contrasted, always unfavorably, with those of the English (Patrick 1964:xi; see also Sturtevant 1962: 42–43; McAlister 1964; Hoffman 1980:1–2; Fitzhugh 1985).

Decades of Spanish borderlands research has done little to redress the balance. The United States still seems to view its own history through decidedly Anglo-colored glasses.

Contrasting Strategies in Colonial North America

The Hispanophobic bias obscures significant variability within the early colonial strategies. From Greenland to Virginia, the earliest European contacts with the New World were largely mercantile ventures initiated by privateers operating with crown permits or charters, which granted rights to trade and exploit resources within a given territory (Fitzhugh 1985:272). In this area of the New World, European governments exercised little control over the day-to-day conduct of activities. Although influenced strongly by European politics, interactions between European colonists and Native Americans in the northern and central regions of the East Coast were largely entrepreneurial and highly individualistic (Fitzhugh 1985). Anglo-American colonists felt only a vague, and largely after-the-fact sense of mission to civilize the Native American (Spicer 1962:343).

The institutional character of European settlement south of British-held Virginia differed radically from this pattern. Spanish contact with Native Americans south of Virginia was governed by formal policies "designed both to apply Christian principles to the governance of a new state and to help realize the economic potentials of the colonies and meet the needs of the colonists and the crown" (Deagan 1985a:282). From the start, Spanish policy was based on a sense of duty to change the Indians from heathen barbarians into good Christians. The southlands were not settled by private individuals acting in their own interest (or on behalf of commercial corporate concerns); throughout Spanish Florida, Native Americans were confronted by the priest, the soldier, and the bureaucrat, each of whom answered to a much higher authority (Fitzhugh 1985:272).

DAVID HURST THOMAS

THE MISSION AS AGENT OF SPANISH
FOREIGN POLICY

The 15th- and early 16th-century Spanish conquests in the New World relied on an *encomienda* strategy, evolved during the reconquest of Islamic Spain. The *encomienda* assigned Native American inhabitants of a region basically as vassals to individual Spaniards, the Indians "exchanging" goods and services for military protection and instruction in Christianity. But their experiences in Hispaniola and the Caribbean convinced mid-16th-century Spaniards that the *encomienda* system was—and always had been—"a serious mistake" (Fairbanks 1985:138; see also Bolton 1917; Lyon 1976:24–26; McAlister 1984:157–67; Deagan 1985a:292–94).

Encomienda was considered patently inappropriate for the relatively late colonization of Spanish Florida, which lacked economic activities requiring intensive, large-scale labor, such as mines or plantations; a different strategy was implemented at St. Augustine:

> In the rest of the Indies, debate had been going on for years about Indian rationality, just wars and slavery, forced conversions, *encomiendas* (allotments of tribute or service), and the alienation of native lands. . . . By the time the Florida conquest began, these questions were more or less settled. Although not advanced enough to be subject to the Inquisition, the Indian had been determined a rational being. He could not be held in servitude or have his lands taken. It was forbidden to enter his territory with arms and banners or to resettle him anywhere against his will. Florida was to be conquered through the Gospel. (Bushnell 1981:7–8; see also Hanke 1964:19–25)

As Spaniards moved into the borderlands, *encomienda* was replaced by the mission outpost, which, almost by default, became the most important way of deliberately modifying Native American culture to suit Spanish ethnocentric values (Bolton 1917:43, 55–61; Montgomery, Smith and Brew 1949:9; Fairbanks 1985:138).

A *mission* comprised an entire settlement—not just the religious edifices—in which the tribal economy was reorganized (even new crops and European methods of cultivation were introduced). Because scattered Native American groups were commonly nucleated into new settlements where diverse instruction was provided (Kubler 1940:6–7), missions also had an explicit enculturative function. Whereas the primary task of the Franciscan was to effect religious conversion,

it was his aim also to raise the aborigines from their primitive
state, often characterized by a very low degree of culture, to that
of civilized and responsible citizens of the Spanish empire. Lacking
a sufficient number of colonists, the Spanish crown made use of
the missions, together with the presidios which were established at
strategic points, as frontier agencies to occupy and hold and settle
its vast domains. (Habig 1976:18)

To Bolton (1917), the mission was a pioneering, "frontier" institution
that, theoretically, was to vanish with the advance of civilization; like
the presidial garrison, missions were to become secular parish churches
once sufficient political, social, and economic change had eliminated
the need for them.

Years of New World experience had permitted Spanish friars to
perfect techniques for the wholesale conversion of Indians to the Catholic faith (Lyon 1985:157; see also Hann 1986). Pedro Menéndez de
Avilés, founder of St. Augustine, wished the newly founded Jesuit
order to continue such evangelical work in *La Florida*. Although the Jesuits did not succeed in proselytising the natives of Spanish Florida, their
energetic Franciscan successors built some of the first churches in what
is now the United States, mastered numerous native languages, and
wrote the first dictionaries based on the Indian dialects. Friars provided
instruction not only in the catechism, but also in music, reading, and
writing, "so developing their program as to become in truth important
political as well as spiritual leaders in the Spanish provinces governed
from St. Augustine" (Chatelain 1941:26).

Father Pareja, stationed for years in *La Florida*, boasted that "we are
the ones who are conquering and subduing the land" (quoted in
Sturtevant 1962:63). With some effect, 16th- and 17th-century church-
men at St. Augustine argued that their success in controlling the Indians
"made them not only an indispensable but also a superior instrument of
frontier defense, as compared with the military personnel" (Chatelain
1941:25), influencing not only religious and social conduct within the
colony, but also acting as primary agents in placing new settlements,
determining the nature of defensive installations, and deciding the primary emphasis of agrarian policy throughout Spanish Florida.

With unabashed hyperbole, Bolton argued that the Spanish mission was a force

which made for the preservation of the Indians, as opposed to
their destruction, so characteristic of the Anglo-American frontier.
In the English colonies the only good Indians were dead Indians.
In the Spanish colonies it was thought worth while to improve the

natives for this life as well as for the next. (Bolton 1917:61; see also Fitzhugh 1985:273)

Throughout 16th-century Spanish Florida, the Catholic church unquestionably served to counterbalance the exploitive tendencies in Spanish-Indian relations (Deagan 1985a:297).

Florida's Invisible Spanish Missions

The Franciscan mission remains a highly visible feature on America's landscape—but only in California and the Southwest, where the mission heritage forms an integral part of one's childhood. In fact, the first archaeological site I ever visited was Mission Santa Clara, near San Jose, California. But when I began doing archaeology on St. Catherines Island in 1974, I was astonished to learn that a Franciscan mission had once flourished there. Not only had I never heard of Santa Catalina de Guale, but I was also unaware of the extensive mission system that once operated throughout 16th- and 17th-century Spanish Florida.

Why so? In reviewing the literature, I found that the southeastern mission system was fully comparable to its better-known western counterparts. By the mid-17th century, *La Florida* had perhaps 70 Franciscans serving approximately 25,000 Indians in 38 missions (Bolton 1917:50; Chatelain 1941:26; Gannon 1965:57; cf. Matter 1972:vii). At the same time, 50 or so missions were operated in the Southwest under the direction of 26 friars (Kubler 1940:7). The 650-mile-long chain of Franciscan outposts in Alta California was home to 60 friars who, just before secularization in 1830, were preaching to 18,000 Indians (Cook 1976:261).

Despite their former numeric and strategic importance, the missions of Spanish Florida barely exist in America's perception of its own past. Part of this relative invisibility is due to the so-called black legend mentioned earlier—that systematic bias that has overlooked and belittled Spanish achievements for centuries. Although some degree of anti-Spanish sentiment lingers throughout the English-speaking world, the black legend drapes a particularly dark cloud over Spanish Florida—an apparently permanent stigma attached to Menéndez de Avilés, for actions against Jean Ribault and the other shipwrecked Frenchmen at Matanzas Inlet (Solís de Merás 1922:115–22; Lyon 1976: 121-24).

Spanish Florida also lacks the historical continuity of the American West, which is still home to substantial populations of Spanish-speaking Native Americans (many of whom remain at least nominally Catholic). Hispanicized Native Americans disappeared long ago from *La Florida*. By the 1750s, only two small villages of Christianized Indians remained outside St. Augustine. When the Spaniards turned over rule to the British in 1763, the 83 surviving Native American converts fled from Florida as well (Siebert 1940; Deagan 1983:32).

The physical elements surely conspired against *La Florida*. Viewing St. Augustine in the 1620s, one eyewitness remarked that the walls of the fort were so dry that firing one of the guns would have set them aflame (Bushnell 1983:47). St Augustine was indeed fired several times, most notably by Sir Francis Drake in 1586 and Carolinian Governor James Moore in 1702. Not a single mission structure in Guale survived the Juanillo Rebellion of 1597, and Moore's 1702–1704 attacks totally leveled mission churches across Apalachee and Timucua (Boyd, Smith, and Griffin 1951:11–13).

In 1599, while some Spaniards were setting the torch to Native American towns in Guale as retribution for the rebellion two years earlier, a fire swept through St. Augustine, burning the Franciscan friary and surrounding buildings; hurricane-tossed seas then rose to carry away several houses (Bushnell 1983:39). Hurricanes also leveled parts of "The Oldest City" in 1638, 1655, 1674, 1685, 1822, 1894, and during the 1940s (Waterbury 1983:255).

The combination of "flimsy" construction methods, periodic fires and hurricanes, and British military superiority effectively erased 16th- and 17th-century *La Florida* from the landscape (Manucy 1983:51). Except for the sturdy coquina walls of Castillo de San Marcos, not a single building—mission or secular—survives. The absence of structural reminders is responsible, in part, for allowing *La Florida* to slip from the historical consciousness.

By contrast, Spanish mission sites—and their conspicuous ruins— litter the landscape of the American West. Each year, thousands tour mission ruins at national monuments such as Pecos, Quarai, Abo, Gran Quivira, and Tumacacori. Still operating mission churches are highly visible at Taos, Zuni, Laguna, and Acoma pueblos. The "Mission Trail" connects the Alamo (itself a former Spanish mission) to three other 18th-century missions within the city limits of San Antonio and another just over the city line.

Each one of the 21 Alta California missions can today be visited: 14 are now parish churches, 3 have become museums, 1 houses a seminary, another is a university chapel, and 2 are state historical parks. Religious services are regularly held in all but two.

The physical mission presence throughout the West has inspired significant architectural "revivals" that further enhance the visibility of western missionization. In contrast, the architectural legacy of the eastern United States is decidedly non-Spanish, and for good reason.

In the late 19th century, when an expanding middle class drifted away from Victorian excess to embrace more properly "American" forms, many turned to the homes of early American colonists for inspiration. Countless 17th- and 18th-century (British- and Dutch-derived) houses survived along the eastern seaboard, providing architectural roots that ultimately fostered the widespread Dutch and Colonial Revival styles.

Post-Victorian architecture evolved along a very different pathway in Alta California, where colonial precedents were largely Spanish (Gowans 1986). Although 18th-century mission structures were falling into disrepair, public-spirited citizens had begun to clamor for their restoration by 1880. Hundreds of tourists were already undertaking California mission pilgrimages by the turn of the century.

A distinctive *Mission Revival* architectural style was legitimized by architect A. Page Brown's design for the California State Pavilion at the World Columbian Exposition in Chicago in 1893: "At the fair that brought America the triumphs of French classical architecture . . . California told the story of its founding by reassembling the missions and their forms in an eclectic pile of porous architecture "which reminded visitors of the climate and open-ended possibilities of the new state" (Betsky 1985:66). Virtually overnight, house facades in America's West began to look like church fronts, with prominent scalloped ornamentation, reddish-brown tiled roofs, round-headed window openings, and clearly recognizable parapets. Ceilings were built to resemble the open timberwork still visible in some California missions. Arcades defined entryways and side porches, and bell towers sprouted from public buildings—not only schools, libraries, and courthouses, but also Santa Fe railroad stations, city halls, movie theaters, and the newly constructed campus of Stanford University. The evolution of Mission Revival architecture and the restoration of Franciscan prototypes proceeded hand in hand, defining the romantic mission style that has become a lasting cultural tradition in California.

In the Southwest, where earlier forms were more Native American than strictly Spanish, post-Victorian architecture followed parallel lines. Since Native Americans supplied most of the material and labor in New Mexico, Spaniards adopted the distinctive *Pueblo Revival* style more from necessity than choice. Although surely Spanish to some degree, the characteristic low silhouette, massive pillars, and overall proportions of Southwestern buildings derived largely from limitations in aboriginal adobe technology. As in California, this overwhelmingly popular architectural style—deeply rooted in Native American and Spanish tradition—ensured the survival of the mission as institution in the American Southwest.

Florida architects, in the meantime, searched in vain for suitable historical prototypes: Not only was traditional English-style housing rare, but legitimate Spanish mission architecture had vanished. The distinctive 18th-century "St. Augustine Look" was rejected as merely "quaint" (Manucy 1978:7), with little appeal beyond the outskirts of "The Oldest City."

Floridians ultimately borrowed domestic architectural elements directly from the Mediterranean, at times also incorporating details from Islamic North Africa. Florida eventually spawned a so-called *Venetian Revival* style, a term derived primarily to publicize Miami and Coral Gables, where developers simulated the canals and lagoons of Venice, providing bridges, islands, and other exotics.

Understanding the past has always been heavily conditioned by attitudes of the present. The early missions of Alta California, Texas, New Mexico, and Arizona remain highly visible. It is no coincidence that hundreds of volumes have been written on America's western missions, and that dozens of these archaeological sites have been excavated. One simply does not overlook the "mission heritage" in the West—if the historical mission buildings are not enough, the countless revival replicas keep that tradition in the forefront.

Such reminders disappeared from *La Florida*. Both visibility and historical continuity are lacking; only the barest outline exists today of how the extensive Spanish mission system operated in the American Southeast. Few mission sites have been excavated, and even fewer books have been written. Although archival research has great promise, much of this history can be retrieved only from evidence preserved in a relatively intractable archaeological record.

Mission Archaeology in La Florida

Spanish Florida was divided into four major provinces: Apalachee, Apalachicola, Timucua, and Guale (Figure 3.1). Less than half of the four dozen or so Spanish missions in these provinces can today be identified with archaeological sites—and several of these correlations remain tenuous.

Our most complete picture comes from Apalachee, where archaeologists have been actively researching mission sites for three decades (Boyd, Smith, and Griffin 1951; Morrell and Jones 1970; Jones 1980; Marrinan 1985; Shapiro 1987; Thomas 1987). More than half the Apalachee mission sites have been securely located and, to one degree or another, investigated archaeologically (see Figure 3.1: *San Lorenzo de Ivitachuco* (Jones 1970a:3, 1972:2), *La Concepción de Ayubali* (Boyd, Smith, and Griffin 1951:112–20; Smith 1956:56–59; Morrell and Jones 1970:26; Loucks 1979:130) *San Juan de Aspalaga* (Boyd, Smith, and

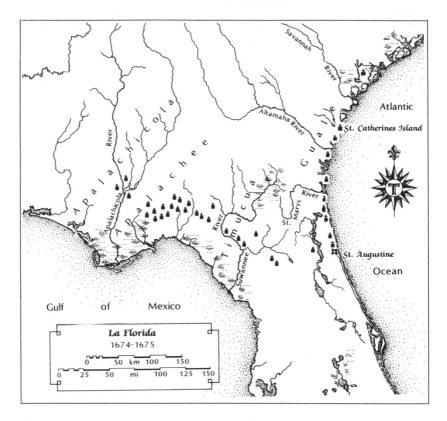

Figure 3.1: The provinces and missions of La Florida *at the time of Bishop Calderón's visitation, 1674–75 (after Gannon 1965:64, facing). Each mission is indicated by a cruciform symbol.*

Griffin 1951:62–63; Morrell and Jones 1970), *San Joseph de Ocuya* (Jones 1970a:3, 1972, 1973:6), *San Pedro y San Pablo de Patale* (Jones 1970a, 1971, 1972:2; Byrne and Marrinan 1984; Shapiro and Marrinan 1986), *San Damian de Escambi* (Jones 1970a:1–2), and *San Luis de Talimali* (Boyd, Smith, and Griffin 1951; Smith 1956; Shapiro and Poe 1984; Shapiro 1985, 1987; Shapiro and Marrinan 1986). Six missions have not been located.

Three 17th-century Spanish missions were founded in the Apalachicola Province, west of Apalachee (Calderón in Wenhold 1936:9). These sites have been identified archaeologically in the vicinity of

Chattahoochee—*Santa Cruz de Sabacola* (Boyd 1958:215, map 8 and fig. 10), *San Carlos* (Bullen 1950; Boyd 1958:258), and *San Nicolás* (Boyd 1958:260)—but virtually nothing is known about them.

Missions of Timucuan Province were more scattered than settlements to the west, so that their archaeological identification is more difficult. The following 17th-century Timucuan mission sites have been identified with some security: *San Diego de Salamototo* (Goggin 1953:5; Smith 1956:46; Deagan 1978:106), *San Francisco de Potano* (Goggin 1960; Symes and Stephens 1965:65; Loucks 1979), *Santa Catalina de Afuerica* (Smith 1956:49–50, Deagan 1972:23; Loucks 1979), *San Augustin de Urica* (Loucks 1979), *San Pedro de Potohiriba* (Loucks 1979; see also Jones 1972), *San Miguel de Asile* (Jones 1970a:3, 1972). In addition, Milanich (1972a:36) has excavated the Richardson site, possibly the secondary mission (*visita*) of Apalo. The Zetrouer site was apparently a late 17th-century Spanish–Indian cattle ranch, established in Potano territory to supply beef to St. Augustine (Boyd, Smith, and Griffin 1951:68; Smith 1956:47–48; Milanich 1972a:36, 1978:63, 79). Locations of six other Timucuan mission sites are unknown.

Archaeological investigations have also taken place at *Nombre de Dios*—the first Christian mission to the North American Indian (Gannon 1965:27)—on the outskirts of St. Augustine (Seaberg 1951; Goggin 1952:54, 1968; Merritt 1977). The Florida State Museum is currently conducting further research there (Kathleen Deagan and Michael Gannon, personal communication).

Additional sites along the northern frontier have been located for post-1658 *Nuestra Señora de Guadalupe de Tolomato* (Goggin 1953:6, 1960; Deagan 1978:106; Larson 1978:136), *San Juan del Puerto* (Milanich and Sturtevant 1972:11–12; Milanich 1972b; McMurray 1973:15; Dickinson and Wayne 1985), *Santa María* (Hemmings and Deagan 1973), *Santa Catalina de Guale de Santa María* (Hardin 1986; Clark Spencer Larsen and Jerald Milanich, personal communication), *San Pedro de Mocamo* (Larsen 1958:16; Milanich 1972b:289–90), and *San Pedro y San Pablo de Puturibato* (Adams 1985:67).

Considerably less is known about the archaeological record in the province of Guale. The exact locations of *Santo Domingo de Asao* (J. R. Caldwell 1943; S. K. Caldwell 1953, 1954; Goggin 1960; Kelso 1968; Larson 1980), the pre-1658 *Nuestra Señora de Guadalupe de Tolomato* and *Tupique* (Larson 1953, 1958, 1978; Fryman, Griffin, and Miller 1979; Braley, O'Steen, and Quitmyer 1986), and *San José de Zápala* (Larson 1952:2, 1980; Crook 1980) all remain problematical. With the exception of *Santa Catalina de Guale*—the subject of this chapter—not a single mission has been accurately identified within Guale proper.

THE SEARCH FOR SANTA CATALINA

For nearly a decade, our primary research objective on St. Catherines Island (Georgia) has been to seek and excavate the 16th- and 17th-century Mission Santa Catalina de Guale. The American Museum of Natural History has been exploring the archaeology of St. Catherines Island since 1974, and our research objectives have evolved markedly since then. Some years ago, we published an overview of the natural and cultural history of St. Catherines Island, and that monograph serves as a backdrop for this discussion as well (Thomas, Jones, Durham, and Larsen 1978).

Early objectives on St. Catherines Island were decidedly bio-cultural in emphasis, initially focusing on the Refuge and Deptford phase complex (Thomas and Larsen 1979). Larsen (1982) subsequently conducted a detailed examination of prehistoric biocultural adaptations on St. Catherines Island. Drawing upon a skeletal sample of more than 600 individuals, he found that the shift to agriculture-based subsistence coincided with a general rise in infectious disease, a modification attributed primarily to increasing population density and a diet high in carbohydrates (see also Larsen 1981, 1984). This program in mortuary archaeology continued in 1977 and 1978, when two St. Catherines period burial mounds—Marys Mound and Johns Mound—were excavated and analyzed (Larsen and Thomas 1982). More recently, we reported on excavations at two additional prehistoric burial mounds (Larsen and Thomas 1986). South End Mound I, an Irene period mortuary site, had been initially excavated by C. B. Moore during the winter of 1896–97. South End Mound II, a previously unrecorded St. Catherines/Savannah period burial mound, was discovered not far from Moore's excavations. Other related mortuary excavations are reported elsewhere (Thomas, South, and Larsen 1977).

Since 1978, we have focused our attention on the archaeology of Mission Santa Catalina de Guale (Thomas 1987; Garrison, Baker, and Thomas 1985). Although five years of intensive excavations are now complete, we are still digging. In this chapter I discuss how the archaeological site of Santa Catalina de Guale was located and I provide a few preliminary findings and implications of our research.

Ethnohistory of the Guale

The Guale were among the first indigenous peoples met by Europeans exploring north of Mexico (Swanton 1922:81, 1946:603; Sturtevant 1962; Larson 1978; Jones 1978). After brief contact with the Spanish in 1526, this Muskhogean-speaking group encountered the French in

1562–63. Then, beginning in 1566, the Guale were exposed to a long, intensive period of Spanish colonization. By 1684, the gradual withdrawal of the Spanish to the south, and the correlative expansion of the Carolina colony southward prompted relocation and reorganization of the vastly reduced Guale population.

St. Catherines Island may (or may not) have been an important settlement during the earliest phase of European contact; but there is no doubt that an important Guale town existed there by at least 1576 (Jones 1978:203). Spanish mission efforts were minimal at this point; the year 1584 found only four Franciscan friars stationed throughout all of *La Florida*, and they spent their time attending to Spanish needs at St. Augustine and Santa Elena and had little time for missionizing the Guale and Timucua (Sturtevant 1962:58).

The Spanish named the Guale Indians for the chiefdom centered at the principal town on this island; the associated Franciscan mission eventually became known as *Santa Catalina de Guale*. By 1597, a decade after the fall of Santa Elena, (see Chapter 2), 14 friars were stationed in *La Florida*, and several of these served in Guale (Geiger 1940). That year, the Indians of Guale staged a major revolt, partly played out on St. Catherines Island (see also Larson 1978:133; Deagan 1978:113; Wallace 1975:200)—an uprising with distinctly nativistic overtones (Sturtevant 1962:58).

After resettlement of the missions in the early 17th century (Ross 1926), Spanish hegemony remained unchallenged until 1670, when the English settled at Charles Town, South Carolina. The territory from there south to St. Augustine became a region of contention between England and Spain. This area, the so-called debatable land, remained the scene of conflict between the two countries until 1763 (Bolton and Ross 1925).

Spanish missions on the barrier islands of coastal Georgia became the first victims of this basically European conflict. In 1670 the English and Spanish agreed, through the Treaty of Madrid, that Britain might forever hold the areas in America and the West Indies that were already regarded to be in her possession. Conflicting interpretations resulted, and the Spanish intended to settle the problem by sending an expedition to attack and destroy Charles Town, the southernmost British settlement. Although the expedition destroyed Port Royal, it was disrupted by storms and forced to retreat before even threatening Charles Town. The only tangible consequence of this episode was the establishment of a Spanish garrison on St. Catherines Island in 1673 and the beginning of a stone fort at St. Augustine.

The year 1680 was a turning point as the English began a steady push down the coast and across the interior toward the Mississippi.

"For a decade the English cloud hovered over Santa Catalina, guardian of the Guale border. . . . The Guale missions were a menace, and their neophytes would make good slaves on Carolina plantations" (Bolton and Ross 1925:35).

That year, a force of 300 British-led Yamassee Indians appeared at Santa Catalina, apparently killing a few Christian Guale guards. The surviving sentries spread the alarm through the small fortified mission settlement. The hastily organized defense force—five Spaniards and less than four dozen Guale—took refuge in the fortified mission church, where they withstood siege for more than a day (Bolton and Ross 1925:36). When Governor Salazar heard of this attack, he dispatched reinforcements from St. Augustine. Although the Guale had held off the invaders, they were horrified by the attack and abandoned Santa Catalina immediately and completely. Retreating toward the relative safety of St. Augustine, they stopped first at Sapelo Island, then, in 1686, withdrew to the mouth of the St. Mary's River. Although no formal war had been declared between England and Spain, the English had cleared the Georgia coast of Spanish missions, fortifications, and influence.

The earlier fall of Santa Elena in 1586 had been critical because it exposed Spain's inability to stake out by colonization the middle North American coast against the incursions of other nations (Lyon 1984:16). A century later, the failure of Santa Catalina likewise underscored the inability of Spain to retain this same coast through missionization.

St. Catherines Island was all but abandoned in the early 1680s. Although British travelers in 1687 and 1738 described the ruins of Santa Catalina (Dunlop 1929:131, Hvidt 1980:39), the mission site was "lost" soon thereafter.

Previous Attempts to Find Santa Catalina

Historians and ethnographers have debated the whereabouts of Santa Catalina de Guale for decades. Swanton (1922:50–55) thought that the principal town of Guale and its associated mission were initially established on St. Catherines Island in the spring of 1566. In his recent assessment of the same evidence, Jones (1978:203) argued that prior to 1575, the town of Guale was *not* on St. Catherines Island, but rather to the north, either near Skidaway Island or on Ossabaw. There is no question, however, that by 1587, both the Guale chiefdom and the associated Franciscan mission existed somewhere on St. Catherines Island (e.g., Bolton and Ross 1925; Ross 1926; Gannon 1965:39; Lyon 1976:154; Jones 1978:204).

This geographic and historic conjecture was then supplemented to some degree by hands-on archaeological investigation. As part of the Georgia Historical Commission search for 16th- and 17th-century Spanish mission sites along the Georgia coast, Lewis Larson visited St. Catherines Island in 1952. Among the "good candidates for the location of a mission," Larson (1952:2) listed "Wamassee Head on St. Catherines as the location of Santa Catherina de Guale," but he cautioned that "no final and conclusive identification of a mission site can be made until adequate excavation . . . has been undertaken."

Larson returned to excavate at Wamassee Creek six years later. The sherd sample recovered consisted primarily of aboriginal wares dating to the Spanish period, but included majolica comparable to that from Spanish mission sites in Florida. No structural evidence of Santa Catalina emerged in these limited tests.

In April 1965, John W. Griffin (then staff archaeologist, National Park Service) visited St. Catherines Island to gather information regarding the eligibility of the site of Santa Catalina mission as a registered national historic landmark. He subsequently reported that "further work on the site of Santa Catalina mission is in some respects of the highest priority" (Griffin 1965a:10–11), but he warned that given "the perishable nature of the structures themselves—they were of poles and thatch, not masonry—it can readily be seen that extensive archaeological work would be needed to pinpoint individual buildings of the settlement" (Griffin 1965b:5–7).

Joseph R. Caldwell and students from the University of Georgia then conducted three seasons of archaeological fieldwork on St. Catherines Island (1969–71). Although they excavated mostly in mounds elsewhere on the island (see Larsen and Thomas 1982), they sank several test pits in the Wamassee Creek area. In unpublished field notes, Caldwell concluded, "There is no reason to believe, at present, that this is not the site of the mission of Santa Catalina. So far, however, our excavations have yielded little structural detail" (Caldwell n.d.).

Such was the state of knowledge regarding the location of Mission Santa Catalina when the American Museum of Natural History began long-term fieldwork on St. Catherines Island in 1974 (see also Thomas 1987). The combined French, English, and Spanish historic documentation available in the late 1970s supplied little more than general geographic clues. The limited archaeological evidence suggested only that—*if* mission structures remained intact—they were likely to be buried somewhere near the southwestern marsh on St. Catherines Island.

Discovering Mission Santa Catalina: 1977–1981

We began our own search for Santa Catalina with an extensive program of reconnaissance and site evaluation for all of St. Catherines Island, employing a research design deliberately patterned after our earlier work at Pleistocene Lake Tonopah, Nevada (Thomas 1979:292–99). This survey generated a 20 percent sample of the island, obtained in a series of 31 east-west transects, each 100 meters wide. We found 135 archaeological sites, ranging from massive shell heaps to small, isolated shell scatters; each "site" was explored with two or more 1-meter square test units. More than 400 such test pits were dug in this phase of excavation (Thomas 1987).

In addition to providing data on the overall regional patterning, the survey sampling showed that 16th- and 17th-century Spanish period ceramics occurred at only 5 of the 135 archaeological sites. Relevant Hispanic materials clearly clustered around the Wamassee Creek drainage.

This regional approach confirmed and complemented earlier archaeological investigations: Mission Santa Catalina almost certainly was in a 10-hectare area adjacent to Wamassee Creek. But the nature of that archaeological deposit was almost totally unknown. Did Santa Catalina survive merely as 16th- and 17th-century garbage middens, or was structural evidence buried somewhere nearby?

In 1980 the research focus shifted from systematic regional to intrasite sampling. Where in these 10 hectares should we begin digging? Although we tried randomized test pitting, we found such blind testing to be slow, tedious, and rather unproductive. Ample cultural materials were recovered—most from the Spanish period—but feature recognition was hampered by the relatively small "window" provided by 1-meter test pits. At Santa Catalina, randomized test pitting told us little more than where not to dig.

Looking around for better ways to find that needle hidden somewhere in this haystack, we heard about Kathleen Deagan's successful search for 16-century St. Augustine. Following her example, we initiated a systematic auger test survey throughout the high probability area at Wamassee Creek (Deagan 1981; see also Percy 1976; South and Widmer 1977; McManamon 1984); similar techniques have been used recently with great success at other Spanish mission sites in Florida (Shapiro and Poe 1984; Shapiro and Marrinan 1986; Shapiro 1987; Dickinson and Wayne 1985).

Auger testing generated useful data at three levels. Once field testing was complete (by mid-1981), we plotted the distribution of Spanish period materials in a series of simple dot density maps. Sherd density varied considerably across the 10 hectares sampled, but the central and western zones contained extremely high densities of Spanish-period aboriginal sherds and Hispanic ceramics. If one applied the conventional wisdom that Hispanic/aboriginal sherd ratios reflect "social status" (e.g., South 1977:172–75; Deagan 1983:114–16) in the mission context, a single tract measuring 100 by 100 meters seemed to emerge as the most probable location for the central mission complex.

This area, termed Quad IV, was a totally undistinguished piece of real estate, covered by the same scrub palmetto and live oak forest typical of the western margin of St. Catherines. The only evidence of any human occupation was a little-used field road for island research vehicles. Although shell-midden scatters were evident here and there, there was absolutely no surface evidence to distinguish Quad IV from its surroundings. In effect, the simple and expedient auger testing had narrowed the focus from 10 hectares to 1 hectare.

Moreover, Quad IV contains relatively little shell midden. This was, after all, a "sacred" precinct, kept fairly clear of everyday (secular) garbage. Had we followed the conventional search strategy (find-the-largest-shell-midden-and-center-punch-it), we would have absolutely precluded our ultimate discovery of the mission church, cemetery, and associated *convento* complex.

At this point, we shifted methods from relatively destructive subsurface testing toward noninvasive, nondestructive remote sensing. In its strictest usage, *remote sensing* applies only to various applications of photogrammetry (e.g., Avery and Lyons 1981; Ebert 1984), but in current archaeological circles, remote sensing has come to embrace the variety of technology employed in geophysical observation (e.g., Dunnell 1982:516, 1984:495; Parrington 1983; Lyons and Avery 1984): not only visual and infrared aerial sensing, but also a broad range of chemical and geophysical techniques, most notably magnetometry, resistivity, ground-penetrating radar, and, most recently, differential heat analysis (Benner and Brodkey 1984).

Specific remote sensing efforts at Santa Catalina pursued three objectives: to locate and define the mission complex, to determine the size and configuration of buried features and structures *before they are excavated*, and to build a baseline library of geophysical signatures projected against ground-truthed archaeological evidence.

Our first goal was to narrow the zone of potential excavation, to derive progressively higher levels of probability for locating mission structures *prior to excavation*. The initial instrument prospection at Santa Catalina was a proton magnetometer survey, conducted in May 1981 by Ervan G. Garrison and James Tribble (both then associated with Texas A&M University); subsequent surveys took place over the

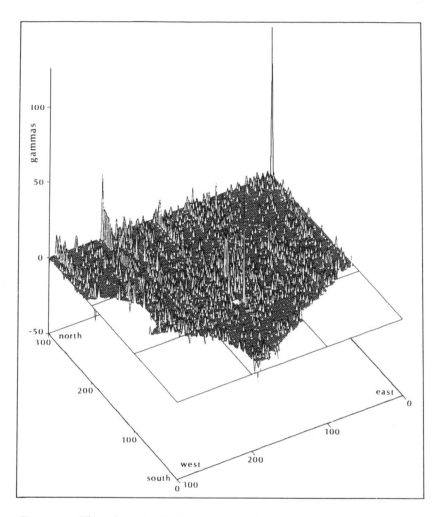

Figure 3.2: Three-dimensional ("birds-eye" view) magnetic map covering 10 hectares at Santa Catalina. Grid interval equal to 2 meters; values within ± 4 gammas plotted as equal to zero (after Garrison, Baker, and Thomas 1985: fig. 8).

next two years. Although several computer graphic techniques helped filter and refine the magnetic survey data (as discussed in Garrison, Baker, and Thomas 1985; Thomas 1987), such remote sensing paid off significantly even before the computer plots were available (see Figure 3.2).

As the Texas A&M team left to work up the data, they pointed out three major subsurface anomalies, suggesting we begin test excavations even without computer filtering of the magnetometer data. Exploring these three anomalies in the few remaining days of the May 1981 field season, we found that

1. The first anomaly, near an auger hole that had previously produced daub, turned out to be the remarkably well-preserved Franciscan church (*iglesia*), Structure 1, now known to have contained 400–450 Christian Guale Indian burials.

2. The second anomaly was the mission kitchen (*cocina*), now denoted as Structure 2.

3. The third magnetic anomaly was a Hispanic period barrel well, comprising seven decomposing iron rings above the well-preserved remains of an oak casing. Olive jar, majolica sherds, and a metal plate were found within the construction pit of the well.

Even without the benefit of computer enhancement and graphics, the magnetometer data were sufficiently powerful to pinpoint three significant Hispanic-period structural features at Santa Catalina. These important subsurface landmarks could doubtless have been located by extensive test trenching, but remote sensing proved considerably more cost-effective and less destructive.

Although magnetometer survey yielded accurate indications of daub wall segments, soil resistivity provided a better way to define the configuration and extent of the unexcavated buildings. Soil resistivity, an "active" method of site prospection (see Weymouth 1986:314), monitors the electrical resistivity of soils in a restricted volume near the surface. Perhaps because of its relatively low cost, soil resistivity has been a popular technique of geophysical prospection over the past three decades (esp. Carr 1982:5–8; see also Carr 1977; Parrington 1983:113–15; Bevan 1983; Weymouth 1986:331–40).

In the spring of 1982, Gary Shapiro and Mark Williams conducted a pilot study to determine the potential and feasibility of larger-scale resistivity prospection at Santa Catalina (Thomas 1987; see also Shapiro 1984). Not only did soil resistivity provide a general projection of site structure across the central mission precinct, but it also gave us structure-by-structure detail, defining the shape, orientation, and extent of unexcavated buildings at Santa Catalina.

These projections were then tested against independent data generated from ground-penetrating radar studies, which in some ways proved to be the most promising method of geophysical exploration tried at Santa Catalina. Ground-penetrating radar, another "active" method of geophysical prospection, is one of the more expensive techniques. Although the cost is offset to some degree by the speed with which it can proceed under ideal circumstances, neither radar equipment nor interpretation is simple (Bevan and Kenyon 1975; Weymouth 1986:315).

The ground-penetrating radar study at Santa Catalina was conducted in 1984. By this time, we had completed the magnetometer and soil resistivity prospection, and intensive excavations were being conducted at the church (Structure 1), kitchen (Structure 2), and friary (Structure 4). We were also employing large-scale testing to determine the nature of the associated Guale Indian village.

Quad IV had been defined as a 1-hectare control area, to be saturated by diverse methods of remote sensing, then extensively excavated to compare the efficacy and results of each method against in-the-ground archaeological evidence. Moreover, we had become such great believers in remote sensing technology that we worried about extending our excavations into areas not first surveyed geophysically. Remote sensing is not very effective in partly excavated areas, and we knew that important information can be lost when subsurface features are excavated "cold," without benefit of geophysical survey. It may be that remote sensing will one day be required as baseline documentation prior to the destruction of sites through excavation.

Extant documentation suggested that Santa Catalina had been fortified as a precaution against British attack (e.g., Bolton and Ross 1925:36; Lanning 1935:215), and we thought that palisades and bastions must have protected mission structures immediately adjacent to the central plaza. Despite three years of prospection and excavation, we had failed to locate any trace of defenseworks at Santa Catalina.

Test excavations, guided by radar profiles, led directly to the discovery, in 1984, of the palisade and bastion complex encircling the central buildings and plaza at Santa Catalina. Excavations proceed on these features.

Several other radar transects, run across the northern end of the church, produced a series of pulses corresponding to the post pits encountered in our excavations. A series of point echoes also apparently correspond to the dozens of extended, supine Christian Guale burials, subsequently excavated. Similar pre-excavation radar data are likewise available for the other Spanish-period structures currently being excavated at Santa Catalina.

Beyond the building-specific results, remote prospection was designed to establish a baseline library of radar signatures for Quad IV. Such prior information not only guided excavation strategy, but also provided data about those structures and features deliberately left unexcavated. These ensure that significant parts of the archaeological record at Santa Catalina remain intact for investigation by future archaeologists (who presumably will employ superior techniques not now available).

Remote sensing technology potentially provides all archaeologists with cost-effective means of generating noninvasive, nondestructive assessments of the archaeological record (Weymouth 1986:311). In the developmental stage, emphasis has necessarily been on technology. But if the technological improvements are to realize their full potential in archaeology, remote sensing studies must now be integrated into the theoretical fabric of working archaeology. Newer developments in technology and field technique are not merely refined ways of generating traditional data.

It is critical not only to compare results between geophysical survey and actual excavation, but also to examine the efficacy of geophysical media per se. If successful, this exercise could ensure that in future excavation at Santa Catalina (and similar sites), destructive exploratory efforts—such as randomized test pitting—could be avoided. The subsurface research design could be guided instead by a sequence of unambiguous, nondestructive geophysical signatures.

Constructing a comprehensive and cross-cutting library of remote sensing signatures is an exercise in midrange theory building in archaeology—a way of assigning meaning to our empirical observations (Schiffer 1976; Binford 1977:2–10; Thomas, Winterhalder, and McRae 1979; Hayden and Cannon 1984; Thomas 1986:238, 1987). Midrange theory determines how we perceive the past, and our construction of such theory differs from our attempt to explain that past (Binford 1981:29; Thomas 1983a:17).

In the past, "empirical observation" in archaeology was conducted by "tactile sensing"—you know what something *is* after you've dug it up and can hold it. To many, these objects comprise the "hard data" of archaeology. But this confuses just what *data* really are: "Data are not people, objects, or things; data are counts, measurements, and observations *made on* people, objects, and things. . . . There are no data until an anthropologist observes them. Data do not passively exist. Data must be generated" (Thomas 1976:7). Remote sensing is simply another way to generate archaeological data—in this case, data from unexcavated objects and features. That these phenomena still lie beneath the ground is irrelevant in an epistemological sense.

Remote sensing will ultimately provide new ways of defining traditional concepts—*provided* that we work out unambiguous relationships between things still buried and how we know they are there. We need to define the "if and only if" statements (Grayson 1982) linking more traditional archaeological concepts (walls, structures, and features) to the way they are perceived ("remotely") by the sensors of geophysical machinery. Defining these linkages became the ultimate methodological objective of the archaeological research at Santa Catalina.

EXCAVATING AT SANTA CATALINA: 1981–1988

We have been digging at Santa Catalina for the past seven years and, although our field investigations continue there, a few observations seem warranted even at this relatively preliminary stage. Future excavations will doubtless refine these interpretations, but we think the basics of mission structure are now apparent.

Site Structure at Santa Catalina

Before we found Santa Catalina, what little we knew about mission structure in Spanish Florida came mostly from excavations in the Apalachee Province. Another important clue came from a rare map surviving from the period (see also Boyd, Smith, and Griffin 1951: plate I; Manucy 1985: fig. 1). Although not a map of the mission on St. Catherines Island, this plan view, dated 1691, depicts the fortified mission compound built on Amelia Island (then called Santa María) by refugees who had fled St. Catherines in the 1680s (Figure 3.3).

The inscription on the Santa María map reads as follows:

> Stockade made on the Island of Santa María and place of Santa
> María in the Province of Guale; it is 3 *varas* in height with loop-
> holes for the firing of arms cut into its little bulwarks terraplained
> to half the height with its moat; inside is the church (*iglesia*), the
> *convento* of the priest, the barracks of the infantry, and a little
> house for cooking (*cocina*) as it appears in the plan with its scale in
> *varas*.

This map is scaled in Spanish yards (*varas*), thought to be about 84 centimeters (32.9 inches) in St. Augustine (Boyd, Smith, and Griffin 1951: plate II; Manucy 1978:165). If we assume that mission outliers of St. Augustine used the same units of measurement, the Santa María map may be used to generate some expectations for the archaeological record on St. Catherines Island and elsewhere in Spanish Florida.

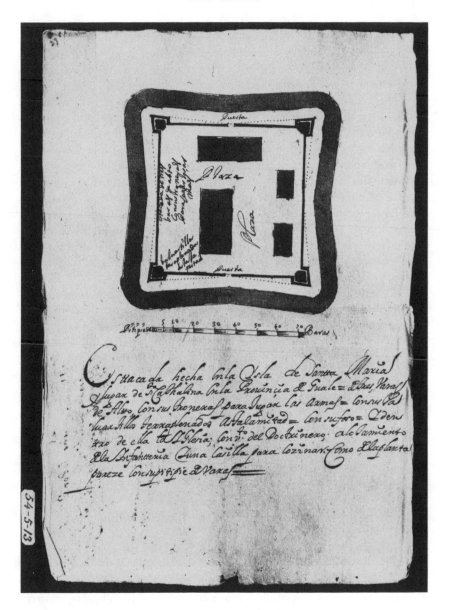

Figure 3.3: Plan view (1691) of Mission Santa Catalina de Guale, located on the Island of Santa María (courtesy of P. K. Yonge Library of Florida History, University of Florida).

The mission on Amelia Island may have been, to some degree, planned as a replica of the mission on St. Catherines Island. Although we do not know whether the projected mission compound at Santa María was ever executed, the map does provide a model of what such a settlement *should have* looked like.

The actual settlement pattern at Santa Catalina, as reconstructed archaeologically, rather closely corresponds to the idealized expectations from the Santa María map. We now know that the entire mission complex and surrounding Guale village at Santa Catalina followed a rigid grid, the long axis of the church being oriented 45 degrees west of magnetic north. The church building (Structure 1) defines the western margin of the *central plaza*; the presumed *cocina* and *convento* structures defined the eastern margin. The central plaza at Santa Catalina is more nearly square, measuring 23 meters wide by approximately 40 meters (the northwest-southeast dimension is less well-defined at present) and is considerably larger than that depicted on the Santa María map (measuring 15 meters × 17 meters).

We have found at Santa Catalina no analog to the "garrison" structure shown at the top of the Santa María map. Perhaps the remains of this structure are still to be discovered. But I think it more likely that a specific facility for housing infantry was absent at Santa Catalina, having been added only to later missions in response to British attacks after 1680.

The Mission Church

The church (*iglesia*) at Santa Catalina has been completely exposed, but the subfloor deposits have been only partly excavated (and excavations continue). We know that the 16th-century *iglesia* was burned to the ground in September 1597; these ruins were personally inspected by Governor Canzo, who had traveled north from St. Augustine to observe for himself the aftermath of the Guale Rebellion (discussed in Geiger 1937:103–104). After a period of abandonment, Santa Catalina was resettled by the Spanish in 1604, and the mission church was reconstructed (apparently on the 16th-century site). Although detailed stratigraphic relationships are still being worked out, Structure 1 at Santa Catalina is, without question, the 17th-century church, abandoned shortly after the British siege in 1680.

The church at Santa Catalina was constructed on a single nave plan, lacking both transept and chancel (e.g., Kubler 1940:30). This rectangular structure is 20 meters long and 11 meters wide. The church depicted on the Santa María map is somewhat larger (measuring 26 × 13.5 meters), but the structures are proportioned almost identically.

The church facade, facing southeast, was made entirely of wattle and daub. This wall, the only one built strictly of wattlework, was anchored to four round uprights, set in shell-lined postholes spaced on 3.7 meter centers. Although the facade wall is only about half the length of the lateral walls, these supportive uprights are more than twice the size of corresponding members employed elsewhere in the 17th-century church. Either a pointed gable was elevated to support a steep thatch roof (as in Manucy 1985: fig. 5), or the facade had a false front projecting above the single-story construction of the nave. The public entryway was centered in the facade wall, which, when fired, fell toward the southeast (outward across the churchyard).

The lateral church walls were constructed both of wattlework and pine planking. The nave portion, 16 meters long, was built entirely of wattle and daub, which, when encountered archaeologically, consisted of a densely packed linear rubble scatter consisting of roughly 50 percent sterile sand fill, the remainder being fired and unfired daub, sherds, and occasional shell lenses. The appearance of oyster shell in places between concentrations of fired and unfired daub, suggests that the nave walls toppled over after a long period of formal abandonment (during which a "squatter midden" apparently accumulated). The relatively straight margin of the northeastern edge of the wall suggests that the wall had decomposed down to a height of only about 1 meter when it toppled inward.

The symbolic separation between nave and sanctuary was emphasized by a composite construction technique. The *sanctuary* (northwestern) end of the church, constructed entirely of wooden planking, was apparently elevated above the lateral wattle-and-daub walls of the nave. Hundreds of shot-sized metal balls were recovered in the charcoal scatter of the sanctuary; although most of the slag has not yet been identified, several pieces appear to be copper and silver. If so, the interior of the sanctuary may have been decorated with a permanently affixed *reredo*, decorative metal panels that were not removed before the church was abandoned.

A clearly demarcated *sacristy*, measuring 5 meters wide by 3 meters deep, was built on the Gospel side of the church (the left-hand side of the sanctuary as one faces the altar). This room was presumably used for storage of vestments, linens, candles, processional materials and other ritual paraphernalia essential to performance of the Mass. Both the placement and configuration conform to 16th- and 17th-century structures in New Mexico, where "the sacristy is invariably a modest room of which the function is indicated only by location and furniture" (Kubler 1940:71–72).

Inside the sacristy we found a cache of charred kernels, and all grains so far examined have been provisionally identified as wheat, *Triticum* spp. (Donna L. Ruhl, personal communication), an unusual find in Spanish Florida.

To early Europeans colonizing the New World, wheat bread was an indispensable item of diet (Crosby 1972:65). Wheat was among the foodstuffs listed as imports into 16-century Spanish Florida (Lyon 1976:133–57). Despite inhospitable climate and soils, the Spanish colonists tried to grow wheat and other familiar grains at Santa Elena (Lyon 1981:288; Reitz and Scarry 1985:47, 55), apparently without much success (see also Sauer 1966:206). By 1580, imported wheat had been largely replaced by maize grown locally or acquired from Indians (Lyon 1977:23).

The historic records are corroborated by the archaeological evidence: Wheat is entirely absent from 16th-century St. Augustine (Scarry 1985: Table 1), and only two wheat grains (*Triticum* sp.) are known from Santa Elena (Reitz and Scarry 1985:55).

From the Spanish viewpoint, the situation improved somewhat during the 17th century, when ranchers reported some success at raising wheat at the interior Apalachee and Timucuan missions. Bishop Calderón, for example, reported "excellent" and "abundant" wheat grown at the inland missions "as alms for the missionaries and the needy widows" (Wenhold 1936:13).) Wheat grains have also been recovered archaeologically from two Apalachee mission sites (Reitz and Scarry 1985:55).

We suspect that the wheat recovered from the sacristy at Santa Catalina was destined to be baked into the "host," flatbread used in the Eucharist. Contemporary Catholic custom clearly specifies that only wheat bread be used for the Eucharist because "bread is the staple food in the diet of most people" (Kilgallon, Weber, and Ziegmann 1976:180). Although wheat probably never had assumed great dietary importance to Spaniards living in *La Florida*, the wheat kernels cached in the *sacristy* underscore the effectiveness of the Franciscan Order in obtaining the supplies necessary for the proper conduct of church ritual—even on the most remote northern frontier of Guale Province.

Roman Catholic liturgical regulations—and a sense of architectural balance—further dictate that a second room must have been built on the opposite side of the altar, to balance the sacristy. But at present we lack evidence for such a room.

Fronting the church at Santa Catalina is a square shell-covered subplaza, measuring about 15 meters on a side. This churchyard (or *atrio*) was probably a low-walled enclosure demarcating the public entrance to the church. Ubiquitous features of New World religious architecture, churchyards served not only as a decorous entryway into the church, but also as outdoor chapels, areas to contain overflow congregations, and sometimes as cemeteries (Kubler 1940:73–75; Montgomery, Smith, and Brew 1949:54).

The churchyard at Santa Catalina was constructed of water-rolled marine shell, available from naturally occurring deposits scattered along the intracoastal waterway; these massive shell bars, accessible only by watercraft, today continue to provide building aggregate. Low-level aerial photography has disclosed a faint pathway leading across the *atrio* into the church doorway. This narrow line of crushed, compacted shell was created by hundreds of 17th-century processions, neophytes moving single-file to attend services at Santa Catalina.

The Campo Santo *(Cemetery)*

The only known cemetery at Santa Catalina occurs inside the church, where we encountered approximately 400–450 burials beneath the floor of the nave and the sanctuary (none were encountered beneath the sacristy). Project physical anthropologist, Clark Spencer Larsen, has supervised the complete excavation of the cemetery; the last burial was removed in May 1986.[1]

Roughly one-third of the burials occurred in primary context, buried in a supine position with feet toward the altar and hands across the chest or (less commonly) across the abdomen. The remaining individuals were found as scattered, disarticulated bone in the upper grave fill—a secondary zone of disturbance created when previous interments were disturbed by later interments.

The cemetery at Santa Catalina contained a truly astounding array of associated grave goods (several of these are illustrated in Figures 3.4–3.6). These materials are still being analyzed but a partial listing includes 4 complete majolica vessels, several projectile points, a chunky stone, a rattlesnake shell gorget in the "Citico" style, 2 complete glass cruets, 12 crosses of metal and wood, 10 small glass and gold leaf cruciform ornaments, 10 bronze religious medals, 1 gold medallion, 1 silver medallion, 2 mirrors, 15 finger rings, 2 hawks bells, 1 rosary, 8 shroud pins, 2 copper plaque fragments, 1 clay tablet (with depictions of saints on both sides), a large piece of shroud cloth, and glass trade beads numbering (at least) in the tens of thousands. Some implications of this unusual assemblage are explored later in this paper.

The Friary (Convento) *Complex*

Eastward across the plaza stood the *convento* and *cocina* complex. The *convento* (usually translated as monastery, convent, or friary) comprised

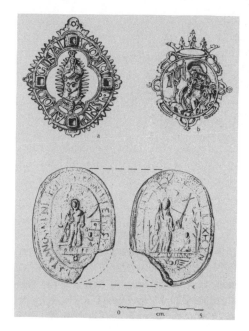

*Figure 3.4: Some religious arti-
facts recovered from the cemetery at
Santa Catalina. a. copper,
enamel, and possibly gold* venera
*(28.0/6509) depicting Our Lady
of Guadalupe; inscription reads*
CONCEBIDA SIN PECADO
ORIGINAL *("conceived without
original sin"); b. gold-plated silver
medallion (28.0/6503) depicting
Pietá with shroud-draped cross in
background; c. clay tablet with seal
impressions (28.1/1624), probably
depicting St. Francis (on the left)
and St. Helen (obverse side).*

one or more subsidiary buildings in which friars and lay brothers lived
their cloistered lives, according to the rules of their order (Kubler
1940:72).

At least two superimposed *conventos* exist at Santa Catalina. The
earlier structure was probably built in the late 1580s shortly after the
Franciscans arrived. Second only in size to the church itself, it measured
16 meters long, and roughly 7 meters wide, the long axis running
roughly northwest-southeast (at an angle of 310 degrees). Construction
was entirely of rough wattle and daub (considerably coarser than that
employed in building the church).

I suspect that the kitchen and *refectory* were housed inside the 16th-
century *convento* structure, the other rooms probably used for living
quarters and storage. Kitchen debris and table scraps were tossed out
the backdoor, where a fringe of shell midden accumulated against the
rear wall—well out of sight from the church.

Although perhaps a minor nuisance to the barefoot friars living
there, this backyard midden served a useful function. When torrential
Georgia rains hit the *convento*—driving gallons of rainwater off the
thatched roof—the midden dispersed and drained the runoff. A clearly

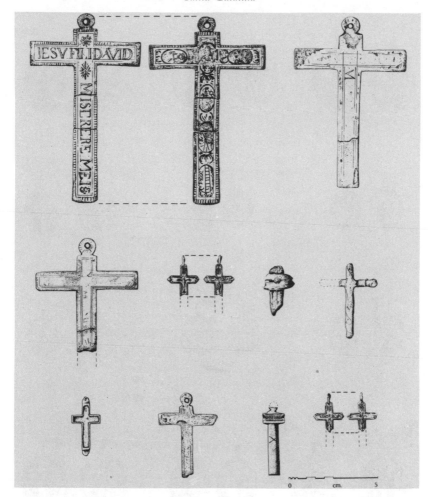

Figure 3.5: Some of the crosses found in the graves of Santa Catalina. Inscription on the large cross at the upper left reads IESU FILI DAVID. MISERERE MEI *("Jesus, Son of David. Have mercy on me").*

incised dripline demonstrates that the 16th-century *convento* had eaves extending about 100 centimeters beyond the rear wall.

This early *convento* was destroyed by burning, probably by rebellious Guale in 1597. Temporarily abandoned, Mission Santa Catalina was resettled in 1604. When Fray Ruiz supervised the reconstruction, he apparently separated sacred from secular, because a distinctive *cocina* was erected 20 meters to the north of the new *convento*. The detached

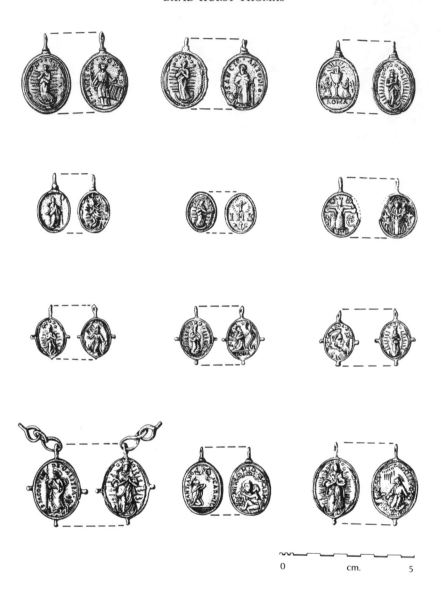

Figure 3.6: Various religious medals from Santa Catalina.

kitchen was also a common feature within urban St. Augustine (Deagan 1983:247). A barrel well was excavated between the two buildings, and a well-beaten path connected the well with a north-facing doorway of the friary.

The southeastern wall of both 16th- and 17th-century *conventos* was built on the same location. But the later structure was somewhat smaller, measuring only 12 meters long, and 8 meters wide. Moreover, the long axis of the 17th-century *convento* is 325 degrees; the 10-degree difference in orientation greatly facilitates separating the two buildings during excavation.

The later friary consists of three well-defined daub walls and one that is less well preserved, accompanied in all cases by in situ wall posts. Because excavation continues in the subsurface daub pits and wall trenches, it is difficult to assign specific functions to individual rooms in the friary. But at this point, it appears that the 17th-century *convento* was subdivided into several small rooms arranged around a central enclosure. A slightly larger room defined the southern end of the friary. Either the refectory or a library, this evidently communal room was apparently heated by a circular charcoal *brazier* (see Manucy 1978:33). A doorway passed directly from this room to the outside.

Set into the clay floor of the central room was a curious floor feature: a rectangular clay foundation, standing 25 centimeters above the floor, scooped out to receive an oval, metallic receptacle. Although this floor font might have held holy water, this feature was more likely employed for personal hygiene. The Franciscans serving at Santa Catalina de Guale (and elsewhere throughout *La Florida*) wore no footgear. Writing to the King of Spain in 1635, Fr. Francisco Alonzo de Jesus wrote "The friars suffered greatly in this mission field. They must walk barefooted in this cold land when going about from mission to mission" (cited in Gannon 1965:54). Moreover, Friar Antonio de Badajoz, who was martyred at Santa Catalina, was a lay brother of the Friars *Descalcados*—the Order of the Barefoot Friars. Great concern with footcare survived among Franciscans into the early 20th century.

The western wall was enclosed by a well-defined arcade, probably a colonnaded porch marking the eastern margin of the central plaza. At least three doorways faced the church to the west. This porch was exactly aligned with the western wall of the *cocina*.

The new friary was about 15 percent smaller than its predecessor, but this size differential was more than counterbalanced by the new *cocina* (kitchen) built 20 meters to the northwest. The 17th-century kitchen, measuring 4.5 × 6 meters, was constructed of wattle and daub on three sides. These walls were supported by squared-off pine posts, placed in pits with a center-center distance of 230 centimeters. The southern end of the kitchen was apparently left open, presumably to facilitate both access and ventilation.

The cooking for the friars and important visitors was probably shifted to this new structure early in the 17th century. Although most kitchen debris was discarded some distance away (probably outside the walled mission compound), some midden accumulated in pits within and near the *cocina*. Garbage was also tramped underfoot, being thus incorporated in the kitchen floor.

Although the 17th-century *convento* was apparently kept considerably cleaner than its predecessor, a thin scatter of shell midden occurs near the doorways. This trash appears to be squatter debris, discarded after the building had been abandoned, but was still standing.

Immediately outside the back of the *convento*, we found nearly four dozen bronze bell fragments (other fragments have been found haphazardly scattered about Santa Catalina). Several pieces show punch and axe marks, indicating that the bells were deliberately destroyed; at least four different bells are represented. Somewhat similar bell fragments, apparently also deliberately broken, have been recovered from Mission San Damian de Escambi (Jones 1970a:2, 3) and the Franciscan mission at Awatovi, Arizona (Montgomery, Smith, and Brew 1949:56).

The mission bell always held a special significance, at times symbolizing the entire mission enterprise. Like all sacred vessels of the church, bells were consecrated or blessed. This ceremony is similar to baptism: use of exorcisms, application of water, salt, and holy oils, bestowing of a Christian name (usually chosen after a specific saint), and the naming of godparents (see Walsh 1934:234 for an account of one such blessing conducted at Mission Santa Clara, California). The church bell was viewed literally as a member of the Hispanic Christian community (Foster 1960:159). This status continued even after the breaking of a bell; bell fragments were collected at missions San Miguel and San Luis Rey, in Alta California, and sent to Mexico, ultimately to be recast into new bells (Walsh 1934:32).

The finds at Santa Catalina suggest an interesting and, at this point, speculative scenario: I suspect that the fragments found behind the 17th-century *convento* were from bells broken by rebellious Guale, probably during the uprising of 1597. Eyewitness accounts describe how the artifacts of the church and belongings of the friars were torn apart, to be worn as heirlooms or simply broadcast about the mission ruins (e.g., Quinn 1979:72–73, 77). Friars who returned to Santa Catalina some years later undoubtedly encountered some of these fragments, and I believe that the broken bells found behind the *convento* were a deliberate cache of still-consecrated fragments, perhaps to be later recycled into new bells.

SPANISH COLONIAL STRATEGIES

Zéndegui (1977) has argued that after the fall of the Roman Empire no world power was faced with so great a need to conquer, populate, and hold a vast new territory under its dominion until the discovery of America (see also Crouch, Garr, and Mundigo 1982:xvi):

> To conquer and to found—that was the twofold task of captains-general and their lieutenants. The first is an act of force. . . . [But] to found occurs only when the plans for a new town are drawn up, a new church is built, a new town council is installed. . . . This is true even though the church might be a shack, the council a symbol, and the entire city nothing more than a hamlet. (Zéndegui 1977:S-1)

European intrusion into Spanish Florida was a heavily regimented endeavor, conditioned by social and economic policy ingrained in the fabric of Spanish consciousness. Deagan (1985b:31) contrasts the "conservative" bent of Spanish colonial life in Florida with the rather different course followed by evolving Anglo-American culture in New England (e.g., Deetz 1977). "In theory and law, little was left to chance" (Crouch, Garr, and Mundigo 1982:xviii); Spain attempted to regiment everything from economy to religion, from art to architecture.

The Preferred Hispanic Design for New World Living

Between the 16th and 18th centuries, Spain issued thousands of regulations promoting, regularizing, and controlling the American colonies. But one document in particular—"The Royal Ordinances Concerning the Laying Out of Towns" issued in 1573 by Philip II—stands out because it prescribed an idealized system for promoting colonization and laying out civil settlements throughout 16th-century Spanish America (Zéndegui 1977; Jones 1979:6–7; Crouch, Garr, and Mundigo 1982: 13–16).

These royal ordinances were a comprehensive compilation of 148 regulations dictating the practical aspects of New World site selection, city planning, and political organization, effectively removing these tasks from the Spanish military. New Hispanic towns were to be established only where vacant lands existed, or where Indians had consented freely to their establishment. Urban centers were supposed to be located on an elevated site, surrounded by abundant arable land for farming and pasturage. The ideal town site was also within easy reach of fresh water, fuel, timber, and native peoples (presumably for labor purposes). Sufficient space was to be left in the original townsite to allow for growth. The ordinances stipulated that, before any construction began, a detailed town plan was to be drafted, showing exact locations of major buildings, lots, streets, and plazas.

The plazas were to be laid out first, then the rest of the town oriented accordingly. The principal plaza was to be located near the landing place in coastal towns, in the center of the community for inland settlements. Always rectangular in form, the length of the plaza was to be one and one-half times its width, a design thought both to provide most efficient traffic movement and also ample room for holding fiestas (Jones 1979:7).

Spanish borderlands archaeology has great potential for assessing the degree of compliance between this idealized blueprint and on-the-ground reality. In St. Augustine, for instance, the 16th-century town plan was clearly laid out according to a standardized grid, with the size of town lots corresponding almost precisely to those stipulated by the ordinances (Deagan 1982:189–90).

But this preferred Hispanic plan, a direct attempt to transplant a "civilized" lifeway upon a Florida wilderness, remained highly "frontier" in character (Deagan 1982:191). The founders of St. Augustine chose not to construct a central plaza—the hallmark of Spanish urban planning and a mainstay of the ordinances (Deagan 1982:185–91). Phillip II's rigid urban plan would have usurped the highest, most desirable residential land for a centralized plaza. The public buildings of St. Augustine, including the earliest church, were grouped at the northern end of town—rather than in the center as dictated by the ordinances. Recognizing the ecological realities in low-lying St. Augustine, the early urban planners positioned the grid in response to local patterns of drainage and microtopography.

Designed for an entire continent, the royal ordinances defined ideal spatial arrangements that, in reality, were often modified to suit local environmental conditions. Frontier variability frequently fostered compromise, and no single settlement anywhere in the New World followed all these regulations (Jones 1979).

The Spatial Structure of La Florida Missions

Ordinance 36 stipulated "that they [new settlements] should be populated by Indians and natives to whom we can preach the gospels since this is the principal objective for which we mandate that these discoveries and settlements be made" (Crouch, Garr, and Mundigo 1982:8). Whereas the ordinances theoretically applied only to permanent civic settlements—not temporary missions or military encampments—in practice there was little distinction between types of settlement in North America. The familiar ordinances seem to have been applied equally to urban centers and mission outposts (Crouch, Garr, and Mundigo 1982:28; see also Bolton, 1917:44).

Mission archaeology in Spanish Florida is only now coming of age. But enough is known to allow a preliminary examination of the degree to which the Laws of the Indies were played out in a mission context. To begin with, it is clear that—whenever we have sufficient archaeological data to tell—the missions of *La Florida* contained the same basic architectural components: the now-familiar church, *convento*, *cocina*, and cemetery complex (Jones 1980; Marrinan 1985: Thomas 1987).

In addition to the church at Santa Catalina, church structures are known from several sites in the Apalachee Province: La Concepción de Ayubale (Boyd, Smith, and Griffin 1951; Morrell and Jones 1970), San Juan de Aspalaga (Boyd, Smith, and Griffin 1951; Morrell and Jones 1970) and possibly two church structures at San Pedro y San Pablo de Patale (Jones 1970a, 1971, 1972).

Some regularity is evident in the churches of *La Florida*. Assuming the identifications to be correct, the typical 17th-century church in Apalachee was almost precisely the same size as that excavated at Santa Catalina, about 10 meters in width to slightly over 20 meters in length (Boyd, Smith, and Griffin 1951:119; Jones 1970a, 1971, 1972; Morrell and Jones 1970; see also Thomas 1987). The churches at Santa Catalina and Aspalaga exhibit multiple construction techniques, employing both board planking and wattlework; at Santa Catalina, this architectural variability served to reify the symbolic distinction between sanctuary and nave. In all cases, the church is the largest of the buildings identified in the compound.

Several *conventos* have also been located archaeologically at Santa Catalina de Guale (described above), San Lorenzo de Ivitachuco (Jones 1970a:3, 1972:2), La Concepción de Ayubale (Boyd, Smith, and Griffin 1951:119; Morrell and Jones 1970:26), San Juan de Aspalaga (Boyd, Smith, and Griffin 1951:62–63; Morrell and Jones 1970), San José de Ocuya (Jones 1970a:3, 1972:2). Possible *conventos* have also been identified at both San Pedro y San Pablo Patale (Jones 1970a, 1971, 1972; Marrinan 1985) and San Luis de Talimali (Boyd, Smith, and Griffin 1951; Smith 1956; Shapiro 1985; Shapiro and Marrinan 1986).

The mission structures seem to have been laid out along a rigid grid pattern, as stipulated by Ordinance 110. At Santa Catalina, a rectangular plaza defined the center of the complex (Ordinance 112), flanked on one side by the mission church (Ordinance 124: "separated from any nearby building . . . and ought to be seen from all sides"), on the other by the friary (Ordinances 118, 119, 121). The plaza was surrounded by (and separated from) the Guale *pueblo*: "In the plaza, no lots shall be assigned to private individuals; instead, they shall be used [only] for the buildings of the church and royal houses" (Ordinance 126). Housing in the *pueblo* consisted of rectangular buildings, perhaps separated by "streets." Native American structures were apparently built as an extension of this initial gridwork. A similar pattern may hold at Santa Catalina de Guale de Santa María (Jerald Milanich, personal communication), and perhaps at some of the Apalachee missions as well.

Church orientation was a matter of both secular and sacred concern (Kubler 1940:23). Although some variability has been observed throughout the New World (Montgomery, Smith, and Brew 1949:132–33), orientation seems to have been highly standardized throughout Spanish Florida. The structures at Santa Catalina are oriented along an axis of 45 degrees west of north (we attribute the variability of about 10 degrees to errors in surveying and measurement); this same 45-degree orientation is also evident at San Juan de Aspalaga, San Luis, and San Pedro y San Pablo de Patale, and probably also at San Juan del Puerto (Dickinson and Wayne 1985). To my knowledge, the only exception in Spanish Florida is La Concepción de Ayabali (Boyd, Smith, and Griffin 1951:118–21), which is oriented in a north-south direction.

At Santa Catalina, the orientation may be explained by local topography. The long axis of this church parallels the intracoastal waterway, the major route of transport along the Georgia coast. We know that, in the late 17th century, the mission compound was surrounded by "much clear ground in our view for 7 or 8 miles together" (Dunlop 1929:131). So situated, even a one-story wattle-and-daub church would have been easily visible for miles up and down the nearby intracoastal waterway. The brilliant whitewash and shell-covered churchyard would further enhance its visibility.

This placement precisely follows Ordinance 120, which urged that "the temple of the cathedral [principal church] where the town is situated on the coast shall be built in part so that it may be seen on going out to sea and in a place where its buildings may serve as a means of defense for the port itself (Crouch, Garr, and Mundigo 1982:14).

Both religious and secular regulations dictated the configuration of Franciscan *conventos* (Kubler 1940:72–74; Montgomery, Smith, and Brew 1949:202–205). The friary was, above all, "cloistered," a monastic enclosure separate and apart; women were not permitted inside. Poverty, the hallmark of the Friars Minor, dictated that the friary consist of very small, sparsely furnished rooms ("cells"). Such complexes usually followed a simple plan, often a single row of rooms, sometimes defining the sides of a quadrangle that contained the sacred garden (or garth). Inside the *convento* were the refectory, the cells or suites of the friars, and perhaps some specialized rooms, such as a kitchen, offices, workshops, or granary (Bolton 1917:59; Montgomery, Smith, and Brew 1949:14, 48). Meals were to be taken in silence inside a refectory. Water assumed great significance in Franciscan rite, and a source of fresh water was always a matter of concern when positioning a friary. Because of the importance of *visitation*—by superiors and other friars— friaries were sometimes built to serve needs far beyond those of one or two lonely friars.

We are still excavating the *convento* at Santa Catalina, but preliminary evidence strongly suggests that such rules were closely followed. Rooms are indeed very small, and they appear to surround two central enclosures (one of which is probably the refectory). A barrel well was excavated nearby and a pathway connects it to the 17th-century *convento*; an apparent floor font was constructed inside the central room. A covered, colonnaded walkway parallels the southwestern wall (Ordinance 115), defining porticoes along the northeastern margin of the plaza.

Although comparative data from other Franciscan *conventos* in Spanish Florida are scarce, those of which we know seem to have contained several small rooms. The *convento* at San Juan de Aspalaga even has a floor feature reminiscent of the "floor font" at Santa Catalina (Morrell and Jones 1970: Figure 2). But the size of these structures varies considerably: The *convento* at San Lorenzo de Ivitachuco measured 6.2 × 4.3 meters (Jones 1970a:3; 1972:2); that at Mission La Concepción de Ayubale (Morrell and Jones 1970:26) was 6.0 × 5.0 meters (Boyd, Smith, and Griffin 1951:119); the *convento* at San José de Ocuya, one of the three distinct artifact concentrations, was 10.4 by 9.4 meters (Jones 1970a:3; 1972:2). In other words, although friaries were highly stylized, their overall appearance was considerably less uniform than that of the churches of *La Florida*.

The Franciscan missions of Spanish Florida, as elsewhere in the New World, clearly followed long-established rules and time-honored sequences of construction. These matters were not subject to priestly whim. Considerable paperwork was involved to ensure compliance, and high-level visitations were sufficiently frequent to ensure a high degree of conformity (e.g., Wenhold 1936; Pearson 1974). Native Americans at these missions lived a regimented life, and the Hispanic architecture of these settlements reflects the "rigid organization of space by a formal sixteenth century Iberian template" (Deagan 1985b:29).

Paradoxically, the plaza and grid arrangement is virtually nonexistent in homeland Spain, where town planning was "rather formless" (Foster 1960:43). This ideal plan was deliberately abstracted from a few selected cases, which were then projected into mainstream urban planning in the New World.

> City planning in Spanish America represents, therefore, not the diffusion of a material trait, but the utilization of an idea in a new context, with specific goals in mind. The process of the founding and growth of cities, towns, and villages in America illustrates particularly well the "formal" side of conquest culture in which careful planning and direction rather than the customs and forms familiar to conquistadors and administrators were instrumental in developing new patterns. (Foster 1960:49)

The spatial organization of mission life in Spanish Florida exemplifies what Foster (1960:15–16) termed a deliberate simplification or "stripping down" of Spanish culture.

That the grid plan characterizes only a half-dozen pre-Conquest Spanish towns is irrelevant. The ordinances reflect an idealized Spanish template, upon which New World forms were modeled. The great variety of plans in Spanish towns and cities was deliberately replaced throughout Spanish America by variations upon a single theme.

VARIABILITY WITHIN THE MISSION SYSTEM

There exists without question an overriding air of uniformity and conformity in Spanish colonial strategies for *La Florida*; this is not to imply that Spanish Florida was either homogeneous or monotonous. Considerable chronological, ethnographic, and ecological variability clearly exists within the archaeological record of *La Florida*, and the perceived degree of diversity will escalate in direct proportion to the amount of field archaeology conducted: The more we choose to dig, the more diversity we will find in our data.

Even at this relatively early stage of inquiry, one is particularly struck by the variable mortuary behavior evident throughout *La Florida* (see also Marrinan 1985:246). An urban burial sample is available from Nuestra Señora de la Soledad, located in downtown St. Augustine (Koch 1980, 1983). Soledad was initially the site of a Spanish hospital, dating back at least to 1597. It was subsequently converted to a convent, and finally employed as a parish church serving both Spanish and later British congregations. Through all these periods, Soledad apparently also functioned as a cemetery. In addition, half a dozen mission cemeteries have been investigated archaeologically, excavations ranging from brief preliminary testing (as at San Joseph de Ocuya and San Miguel de Asile) to full-blown biocultural explorations at Santa Catalina and Santa María.

Not surprisingly, the Catholic cemeteries of 16th- and 17th-century Spanish Florida share certain basic similarities. Soledad was located near one of the primary parish churches of St. Augustine, some graves excavated directly into the church floor, and others concentrated in a *campo santo* immediately adjacent to the church (Koch 1983:203). Mission cemeteries were also juxtaposed to churches, but the pattern varies from mission to mission. The only known graves at Santa Catalina have been found beneath the church floor, where 400–450 people had been buried. After the church at San Pedro y San Pablo de Patale was burned in 1647, the ground was leveled, and graves were apparently dug through the floor of the burnt church (Jones 1970b, 1971, 1972:2). But most cemeteries at the Apalachee missions were located along one side of the church (Jones 1980:164). The cemetery at San Damian de Escambi was about 30 meters from the suspected church (Jones 1970b:1), and that at San José de Ocuya was southeast of the apparent *convento* (Jones 1972:2; 1973:6). The *campo santo* at San Miguel de Asile was positioned about 15 meters north of the church (Jones 1972:2). The recently discovered cemetery at Mission Santa María may have been similarly positioned (Clark Spencer Larson and Jerald Milanich, personal communication); this could also be the pattern at Mission Nombre de Dios, where the church must surely be somewhere nearby, but its exact location has yet to be identified.

Orientation and burial posture is also quite similar between urban St. Augustine and its mission outposts. Citizens of St. Augustine usually buried their dead with the head oriented toward the east and arms crossed on the chest (Koch 1983:203), a characteristic "Christian" burial posture recognized at all the known mission cemeteries through Spanish Florida. The exact orientation varies somewhat, but most such graves were positioned parallel to the primary mission axis; the observed variability in grave orientation thus probably reflects only differing site orientations rather than deviations in mortuary practices per se.

St. Augustinians were buried in a highly standardized fashion, usually wrapped in a simple shroud and without grave goods. Occasionally an unembellished coffin was used. Only one of the 21 first Spanish period (pre-1763) graves at Soledad contained any grave goods at all. Burial 16 was accompanied by a silver crucifix, and a rosary. Koch (1983:224) quite properly speculates that this individual was a parish priest. These simple pauperlike burials reflect the prevalent Hispanic Catholic customs of the 16th and 17th centuries (Foster 1960:144).

The same is true for some of the mission cemeteries. No grave goods accompanied Indian burials at missions San Joseph de Ocuya (Jones 1972:2) and San Miguel de Asile (Jones 1972:2). The more than 100 burials excavated at Nombre de Dios were also accompanied by very little: a few hundred beads of glass, amber, shell, and seeds, plus five metal cone-shaped tinklers and an amber pendant (Seaberg 1951; see also Geiger 1940:23; Goggin 1952:54, 1968; Merritt 1977; Larson 1978:120). Although investigators working at Santa María have found 80–90 mission-period burial pits and a large ossuary containing another 56–60 individuals, very little was found in association with the remains: a bone pin (or projectile point), a small crucifix, an oval glass pendant (or mirror), and about a dozen trade beads (Hardin 1986:77; Clark Spencer Larsen and Jerald Milanich, personal communication).

But some mission cemeteries in *La Florida* contained large grave assemblages. The surprisingly rich inventory from the Santa Catalina graves was described earlier in this chapter. Thirteen of the 64 graves excavated at San Pedro y San Pablo de Patale were accompanied by numerous artifacts of personal adornment: multifaceted glass trade beads, cigarette-sized rolled brass beads, brass finger rings, dumbbell-shaped shell pendants, a shell gorget, shell beads, a brass crucifix, and a broken hawk bell (Jones 1971, 1972:2). Grave goods at San Damian de Escambi were also mostly of personal adornment, associated primarily with children: multicolored glass trade beads, rolled sheet brass beads, and grooved dumbbell-shaped shell pendants (Jones 1970a:1, 2, 3; 1970b:2); one well-preserved piece of heavy woven cloth was recovered. Two adults and one child had been placed in wooden coffins fastened with wrought iron nails.

Although the Catholic continuities are readily understood, we are at present unable to account for the extreme variability in some specific aspects of burial practice between St. Augustine and its mission outposts (and among the missions themselves). But we can isolate some factors that are doubtless involved. As suggested above, the mortuary diversity evident in Spanish Florida is at least partly procedural, itself an artifact of archaeological technique. It is well established that such diversity in many (if not most) archaeological assemblages is a direct, linear function of sample size (Thomas 1983b:425–31; Jones, Grayson, and Beck 1983): The more bones one excavates, the more species will be represented; the more artifacts one surface-collects, the more types will be represented. Although I am unaware of any analysis of the precise relationship of size to diversity within mortuary samples, I strongly suspect that the same effect operates here: The more graves one digs, the more diverse will the assemblage of grave goods appear.

Implications for the cemeteries of Spanish Florida are clear. The obvious diversity in the mortuary assemblage from Santa Catalina must be due (in part) to the fact that we excavated the remains of 400–450 individuals. Conversely, the apparent paucity of grave goods that accompanied Indian burials at missions San José de Ocuya and San Miguel must be due (in part) to the small sample of graves actually excavated.

Whereas the sample size–sample diversity relationship is undoubtedly a factor, it alone will not satisfactorily account for all known mortuary variability in Spanish Florida. Plenty of graves were excavated at Nombre de Dios and Santa María, but little beside bones was recovered; on the other hand, the five dozen grave pits at Patale produced a rather large, diverse sample of grave goods.

The process of archaeological sampling can introduce a second skewing factor into such interpretation. In South's (1977:48) Brunswick pattern of refuse disposal, debris commonly accumulates at structural points of entrance and exit. But Deagan (1983:258) has recently demonstrated how excavation strategy can influence such pattern recognition. Had the St. Augustine excavations been limited to a few test squares around the structure entrances, a Brunswick pattern would have been incorrectly suggested. Fortunately, Deagan and her associates likewise excavated in areas further back in the lot, finding considerably heavier concentrations of refuse in pits and wells.

Similar bias can easily occur in mortuary excavations, and in no case—either in urban St. Augustine or any of its satellite missions— have archaeologists recovered a mortuary sample adequate for reliable pattern recognition studies. Had we restricted our excavated sample at Santa Catalina to the outer nave portion of the church, we would have recovered few grave goods; conversely, had we excavated only near the altar, we would have radically overestimated the projected nature of the grave assemblages. Moreover, potential sampling bias plagues even such large-scale excavations. We cannot rule out the possibility that our samples do not adequately represent the entire site. Perhaps burials laden with grave goods remain to be discovered within St. Augustine, Nombre de Dios, or Santa María. Or perhaps an artifact-free cemetery is yet to be discovered somewhere in the mission compound at Santa Catalina. Not until bias-controlled sampling has been successfully instituted at such sites can we hope to obtain a fully adequate explanation of mortuary variability in Spanish Florida.

One further potential bias must be considered. Over the past decade, historical archaeologists have become increasingly fond of ascribing such variability to status differentiation, commonly perceived in relative economic, social, military, or racial terms (e.g., Miller and Stone 1970): the officer-enlisted man dichotomy (South 1974; Ferguson 1975), the planter-overseer-slave continuum (Otto 1984), plus such generic categories as "adaptive success" (Honerkamp 1982) and "ethnicity" (Schuyler 1980).

Similar mechanisms of interpersonal differentiation operated within Spanish Florida, but with a few added twists. The rigid Spanish class hierarchy, emphasizing both wealth and social position, was transferred wholesale to *La Florida*, where "people differentiate themselves wherever there are disparities of background or belongings to be envied or flaunted" (Bushnell 1981:15). In St. Augustine, relative social status was also conditioned by birthplace: "*Criollos* [people of Hispanic descent born in the New World] were generally believed to be inferior both mentally and physically to *peninsulares* [those born in Spain] due to the enervating effects of the New World climate" (Deagan 1983:30). Native Americans and free blacks also lived in St. Augustine, and the socioeconomic hierarchy was complicated by an assortment of racial admixtures.

Approaching mortuary variability within Spanish Florida requires an appreciation of the multiplicity of potential factors involved. In particular, the manifest inseparability of church and state within *La Florida* requires that we consider "status" within a religious framework.

One's perceived "status" relative to God unquestionably influenced where (and how) one encountered the afterlife. Some cemeteries were divided into districts for the holy and the unholy (Koch 1983:220), and burial placement inside a church was conditioned at times by dichotomies such as clergy-lay person, blessed-unblessed, single-married, child-adult, poor-affluent.

> Even after death there were class distinctions. The hidalgo was
> buried in a private crypt, either in the sixteen-ducat section or the
> ten-ducat section. Other plots of consecrated earth were priced at
> three or four ducats. A slave's final resting place cost one ducat,
> and a pauper was laid away free. (Bushnell 1981:26; see also Foster
> 1960:144)

Such distinctions were variously reified in space. At times, the Gospel and Epistle sides of the church were differentially employed. Whereas parishoners were usually buried with feet facing the altar, members of the priesthood were buried in reverse posture, "facing" their congregation.

Considerable research will be required to forge a sufficiently multifaceted explanation of mortuary variability within 16th- and 17th-century Spanish Florida. But even at this relatively primitive stage of research it is clear that simplistic categorizations such as "high status" and "low status" serve to obscure considerably more than they clarify.

THE METHODOLOGY OF MISSIONIZATION

St. Augustine was a hardship post—"a struggling, military outpost on the fringe of empire with few of the amenities of civilization" (TePaske 1965:104)—and residents complained bitterly about the frontier conditions encountered there (Bushnell 1981:139). In 1606, the visiting Bishop of Santiago described a modest wooden church so poor it lacked even a single candle; in 1623, the same edifice is described as old and crumbling: "The parish was so poverty-stricken by 1673 that during a portion of that year the sacristan-priest complained that Mass could not be celebrated for lack of hosts and wine" (Gannon 1965:60).

But if St. Augustine was perched on the frontier, the mission outliers surely defined the frontier of the frontier. Father Pareja described what he considered the utter privation of the friars working along the Guale coast; they lacked not only food and clothing, but sometimes even vestments for conducting Mass. At one point, Fathers Pareja and Ruiz were reduced to fashioning a chalice from lead, complaining that funds designated for the missions had been siphoned off by officials in St. Augustine "since it seems to them that the soldiers are the necessary ones [here], and that we are of no use" (cited in Gannon 1965: 53–54).

It seems curious, in the light of such apparent poverty, that the archaeological record of Santa Catalina, presumably one of these destitute outposts, should contain such a rich inventory, in some cases, the very best examples of European "art" in Spanish Florida. Why and how did such a profusion of religious paraphernalia find its way into the hands of heathen converts, a people whose primary contact with the Spanish Empire was filtered through a handful of friars (who themselves had taken vows of abject poverty)? This apparent paradox in the archaeological record can be resolved only by placing the Franciscan missionary enterprise in Spanish Florida into its larger global context.

Religion as an Extension of Spanish Hegemony

The Age of Discovery could not have been more timely for a badly battered Catholic church. By the 16th century, the Inquisition finally had diverted its energies from punishing Jews and Moors to marshaling doctrine and ideology against the threat of Protestantism. Spaniards planted the cross at St. Augustine less than 20 years after the death of Martin Luther, thereby opening potential new fields to spiritual conquest at the very time Catholicism had sustained grave setbacks in Europe (Ellis 1965:22–23).

Religion so thoroughly permeated everyday life in 16th- and 17th-century Spain that all aspects of individual and collective life were, one way or another, touched by it. Catholicism became such a dominant force at home that virtually 25 of every thousand Spaniards were religious figures of one sort or another: monks living in monasteries, nuns residing in convents, lay clerics drawn from the population at large (Defourneaux 1971:107).

Unlike their European competitors along the Atlantic seaboard, Spaniards colonizing *La Florida* made no pretense of separating church from state. At the time of New World colonization, Catholicism had become a uniquely secular enterprise. Previous rights of lay patronage conceded by the Vatican were so broadly interpreted that "ultimately the Church in the Spanish colonies came to be almost as completely subordinate to the crown as the army itself" (Ellis 1965:16). As a result, the cult of the Virgin Mary was deliberately spread throughout the Americas, a legacy that remains today. "From the Rio Grande to Patagonia . . . the same saints are honored on the same days and in essentially the same fashion, and the same Mass draws the faithful each Sunday" (Foster 1960:3– 4).

Spreading Religion to the Native American Masses

Although the Catholic church was ultimately responsible for the well-being of Spanish Florida, specific ecclesiastical policy varied significantly between the town and the mission (and at times even among missions themselves). Urban religious life was overseen by one or more "secular" or "diocesan" priests working within geographically fixed parishes (at St. Augustine, under the direct supervision of the Bishop of Santiago; Gannon 1965:xiv, 45). Although secular priests occasionally chose to spend time among the Indians, their primary responsibility was to care for the Spanish settlers.

Missionary activities per se were conducted by "regular" or "religious" priests, each a member of a mendicant order, primarily Franciscan, Jesuit, or Dominican. Rather than being assigned to a parish, the friars were committed to special duties such as charity, education, or missionization. Each primary mission (termed a *doctrina*) was served by a resident priest, who also visited one or more subsidiary mission stations (a *visita*), preferably on Sundays and holy days.

Whereas the ultimate objective of all such missionization was to convince the Indians to lead good Christian lives, it was clearly recognized that this goal would hardly be achieved overnight.

THE ENTRADA (PRE-MISSION) PHASE.   Missionization throughout the Spanish borderlands proceeded according to an explicit sequence of evolutionary steps (Spicer 1962:288–97; Polzer 1976:39–58). The process began with a "pre-mission" (or *entrada*) phase, during which the missionary introduced himself and attempted to establish certain sacramental links to the Indians. Likely locations were scouted out for projected mission sites, and the friars assessed the linguistic/cultural areas involved.

The priests deliberately emphasized the symbolic trappings of Catholicism during these initial encounters, ever conscious of the lasting impression they were making: their distinctive garb, the sacred images, the ubiquitous crosses, the paintings, the statuary. When Pedro de Ybarra, governor of St. Augustine, visited Santa Catalina in 1604 to oversee reconstruction of the church burnt in the rebellion seven years before, he urged the Guale leaders to place crosses throughout the mission and along the roads "because it is the true indication of a Christian." When possible, the more portable iconographic items were selectively passed into Native American hands, as part of the overall strategy of emphasizing conversion of *caciques*, who then could be called upon to help convert their followers (Deagan 1985a:299).

The archaeological visibility of such pre-mission contact is low, and patterning difficult to discern. I suspect that several of the artifacts listed by DePratter and Smith (1980) as "trade materials" from the Juan Pardo expedition of 1567–68 actually resulted from *entrada*-level missionization conducted by the Jesuit Father Juan Rogel, known to have distributed not only religious artifacts, but also utilitarian items such as bolts of cloth, mattocks, and seed-corn (Lyon 1984:4).

THE MISSION (OR PRE-PAROCHIAL) PHASE.   A successful pre-mission *entrada* soon led to the establishment of the actual mission outposts. Friars assigned to specific missions quickly attempted to master the native language and commence instruction in the catechism. The objective of these catechetical lessons was to ensure that the neophytes understood the rudiments of Christian belief and devotional practice, emphasizing the common prayers used by the church and also the frequent confession of sins (e.g., Milanich and Sturtevant 1972).

At this stage of development, the mission became basically an educational institution. Always a hands-on enterprise, Catholicism was symbolized by processions of believers fingering rosaries and wearing medallions, bearing canopies, crosses, and statues. As during the *entrada* phase, religious instruction was greatly facilitated by concrete expressions of faith. The bulk of the material assemblage at Santa Catalina was generated during this stage of missionization.

But even granting an awareness of such standardized procedures, one is unprepared for the quantity and quality of religious art recovered at Santa Catalina: the crucifixes, rosaries, religious seals, potsherds inscribed with crosses, and especially the religious medals and medallions. This distinctive mission assemblage reflects a preoccupation with, and direct access to, the artifactual expressions of faith—artifacts that functioned as concrete reminders of religious truths or teachings, as incitements to prayer and acts of virtue (Ewing 1949).

The religious assemblage at Mission Santa Catalina likewise reflects a worldview generated half a world away. Nowhere is the rigidity and formality of the 16th- and 17th-century Spanish worldview better portrayed than in the Spanish attitude toward art. By this time, art had become a form of zealous propaganda for reinforcing unification at home and colonizing the world at large through religion. In a move that would parallel the later royal ordinances of 1573, the Council of Trent (1563) had established protocols that governed Spanish art throughout the 17th century, thus fostering the singular homogeneity characteristic of Spanish baroque art and repressing the liberalism of the Renaissance.

Rather than seeking new modes of expression, conservative Spanish scholars and artists looked to the church for guidance. Once accepted—especially by members of the Society of Jesus— specific iconographic styles were rapidly incorporated and repeated by wary artists fearing criticism and punishment. Arbiters of art, employed by the Inquisition, ensured that artists focused on the correct depictions of religious subjects. In cities throughout Spain, painters' guilds required formal examinations to certify that potential masters possessed not only skill, but also a knowledge of approved religious themes. Formal contracts were even drawn up to spell out matters of exact content, appropriate style, and precise accoutrements (Brown 1978:64).

Rigid artistic and religious superstructure is manifest in the suite of stylized medals recovered at Santa Catalina, several of which commemorate special events in the history of the church (Figure 3.6). Scenes range from St. Francis receiving the stigmata (symbolizing the five wounds on Jesus' crucified body) to angels kneeling around a chalice, from St. Anthony of Padua to an IHS medal (an abbreviation of *Iesus*

Hominum Salvator: "Jesus Savior of Mankind"), from Our Lady of Mt. Carmel to several renderings of the Blessed Virgin (characteristically standing above the half moon and surrounded by a *gloria* of light, a halo crown, and seven stars symbolic of her "joys"). Several medallions are ringed with the characteristic Franciscan cord, an important component of the habit worn, then as now, by Franciscan friars.

Such items of religious art were almost certainly presented to important neophytes at occasions such as christenings, baptisms, and confirmations. These medallions are emblematic of an important adage that permeated the mission philosophy:*Abusus non tollat usum* ("the abuse of a thing should be corrected, but it is not a reason for abolishing the proper use of that thing," Ewing 1949:103).

Native Americans of the Southeast had, for instance, long worn shell gorgets to symbolize a wealth of sacred and secular beliefs. The display of a Christian medallion became a logical extension of that practice. In fact, an adolescent was buried near the altar at Santa Catalina wearing a traditional style rattlesnake gorget. The Franciscans had "baptized" a pagan custom in order to effect conversion.

Guale wearing religious medals not only possessed reminders of their faith, but also proclaimed that faith publicly. These objects comprised concrete demonstrations of basic Christian ideas and provided a visual means for reinforcing repetitious acts of prayer, singing, and church-centered ritual (Spicer 1962:295–96).

The same is true of the rings worn by Guale buried at Santa Catalina. Whereas rings recovered in colonial Anglo-America often symbolize personal sentiments such as betrothal or mourning, those at Santa Catalina are manifestly religious in content and function. Unlike colleagues digging in colonial Virginia or Massachusetts, archaeologists working in a borderlands mission should not expect to find personalized artifacts like "posy rings" with such amorous inscriptions as "I LOVE ERVE, I LOVE V EUER, or LOVE THY TRV FRIND" (Noël Hume 1976:265). Instead, the artifacts of Santa Catalina reflect more institutionalized messages; two of the medals are inscribed with "ROMA," which strongly suggests that they were manufactured in the Vatican (and perhaps obtained by a friar on pilgrimage).

The finger rings from Santa Catalina likewise differ from the "Jesuit rings" that occur by the hundreds in 18th-century French-Indian sites. Once strictly "religious" in nature, these cheaply mass-produced brass rings came to assume a secular function as currency along the frontiers of New France (e.g., Cleland 1972; Hauser 1982). The individualized, hand-crafted silver rings of Santa Catalina retained their original, more strictly religious function. Such Hispanic religious art belongs to a category of material culture wholly distinct from the "trade goods" that characterized Anglo- and French-American colonies to the north.

These object lessons reflect the differing strategies employed throughout the northern New World. Native American cemeteries in colonial Anglo-America likewise contain a wealth of grave inclusions (e.g., Robinson, Kelley, and Rubertone 1985; Chapter 5), but most of these objects are utilitarian items of both European and aboriginal manufacture: spoons, scissors, bottles, kettles, buttons, knives, rings, and so forth. By sharp contrast, Spanish policy strictly prohibited trading with or arming Native Americans. Although the occasional utilitarian artifact made its way into the Guale graves of Santa Catalina, items of religious significance overwhelmingly dominated the mortuary assemblage. Quite clearly, the Franciscan friars diverted a significant portion of their limited resources toward the trappings of religion, making available the symbolic paraphernalia proven to be effective in the conversion effort.

> The Fathers realized this practice bordered on idolatry, but they were wise enough to understand that an intermediate level was necessary in the transfer of religious veneration from demonolatrical objects to monotheistic faith. Pictures and statues also identified a sacred area for the Indians who needed to understand Spanish insistence on the holiness of a church and its attendant buildings . . . it was an enticement . . . a kind of social seduction. (Polzer 1976:48–49)

Such apparent contradictions are commonplace during an intermediate, pre-parochial stage of missionization. As long as the Indians accepted the most fundamental sacraments of the church—especially baptism, monogamy, participation in the Mass, and Christian burial—allowances were made for the sake of conversion. Church belief viewed neophytes as people who had accepted the faith, but were not "fully formed" in it (Polzer 1976:5).

To the schooled Franciscan mind, this juxtaposition of Christian and pagan could be justified as a necessary step in the overall evolutionary process of conversion.[2] The Guale were encouraged to bury their dead in Christian fashion—in unmarked graves beneath the floor of the church, hands crossed on the chest with feet toward the altar, in accordance with prevalent church teaching.

But the archaeology of St. Catherines Island and elsewhere demonstrates that the Indians of coastal Georgia were accustomed to placing valued objects in the graves of their departed; for millennia, they had believed that "you really can take it with you."

Thus, to achieve an important outward symbol of conversion—
and to stamp out offensive pagan burial mounds and charnel houses—
friars apparently "allowed" the Guale to continue their tradition of
grave goods, even though the practice directly violated church practice.
Not "fully formed" in Christianity, the Guale enjoyed the luxury of
seeking salvation through conversion while simultaneously retaining
selected traditional customs.

These two important transitional methodologies of missionization—the perception of neophytes as not fully formed in Christianity
coupled with an emphasis on religious artifacts as symbols of
conversion—account for much of the archaeological patterning at Santa
Catalina.

SECULARIZATION: THE MISSIONARY'S ULTIMATE GOAL.   The mission, as a frontier institution, was theoretically designed to be only a
temporary installation. Previous experience in Central and South
America led Spanish missionaries to expect to effect complete conversion within a decade, turn the neophytes over to secular clergy, and
then move on to new frontiers (Bolton 1917:46). At this point, the
faithful would have been elevated to the status of "fully formed Christians and full fledged members of the Church" (Polzer 1976:5). Neophyte communities were to graduate from simplified doctrinal instruction into mainstream Hispanic society.

Mission methodology, accordingly, should eventually merge im-
perceptibly with traditional pastoral practice and technique. Whereas
church furnishings and items of personal devotion remained important
under secular guidance, the clergy no longer felt the need to distribute
the quantity (or quality) of church-related artifacts so critical during a
pre-parochial, mission phase of outreach.

Furthermore, in strictly mission times, the Franciscan effort was
heavily subsidized from public coffers (Sluiter 1985:6)— rationalized by
the crown as a means of pacifying natives without the use of force. But
support for the secular churches of *La Florida* relied upon crown-
controlled personal tithes. This agriculturally based tribute fluctuated
dramatically in St. Augustine. During the famine year of 1697, for instance, the bishop commented that "in times of hunger all men quar-
reled and all had reason" (Bushnell 1981:79). Whereas the earlier Franciscan missions enjoyed an inflated symbolic status and economic base
compared with the rest of the Florida enterprise, parish churches of St.
Augustine were always reflective of the relative status of that community within the Spanish Empire at large (see also TePaske 1965).

This ontological perspective takes into account both the apparent
abundance of religious objets d'art at mission sites and their paucity at

the contemporaneous urban archaeological sites of *La Florida*. This impression is reinforced by the manifests of supplies assembled by Menéndez de Avilés for his conquest of Spanish Florida (Lyon 1976:91). Although the *adelantado* contributed eight church bells and the altar furnishings necessary to conduct Mass in the new settlement, this inventory pales in comparison with the massive supplies of artillery, ammunition, marine supplies, foodstuffs, bulk iron, and agricultural tools.

Accordingly, although the occasional crucifix or rosary bead turns up at St. Augustine (Koch 1983:224) and Santa Elena (South 1982:59, fig. 19c, d), these artifacts of religion are swamped by the assemblages generated from the military, domestic, and bureaucratic sectors. Although an absolutely indispensable component of the Hispanic lifestyle, religious items constituted but a tiny fraction of the baggage necessary to transfer Castilian civilization to the shores of *La Florida*.

With the rights of full citizenship in the Spanish Empire and the Catholic church came restrictions and responsibilities. Not only would the "fully Christian" Indian be subject to taxation, but, at least in theory, he or she would also be required to live up to the full measure of church membership. Unlike the previous mission phase, when accommodating friars made exceptions to the neophyte status, the secular clergy would expect full compliance with the regulations of the church—and in 17th-century Spain, these expectations could be considerable.

Indians achieving this ultimate "parochial" stage of conversion were, at least in the eyes of the church, to be elevated to the level of Spaniards and Creoles living in towns such as St. Augustine. The operative assumption in both cases was that the faithful were "fully formed Christians and full fledged members of the Church (Polzer 1976:5). The citizenry was expected to participate fully in the belief system and ritual prescribed by the church and administered by the diocesan priest. It is hardly surprising that the graves at Soledad, a cemetery intended exclusively for the use of parishioners in St. Augustine, contained almost exclusively simple shroud burials.

Was any mission in *La Florida* elevated to the fully parochial status anticipated in the "methodology of missionization"? We do not know. But *should this have happened*, one can anticipate two important trends in the material inventory of such a site:

1. The overall frequency of religious-specific artifacts (beyond church adornment and items of personal devotion) in any such secularized mission should decline precipitously. The iconographic professions of faith so critical during the mission stage are not needed to sustain faith among full-fledged Christians.

2. Moreover, in such contexts, we expect that grave goods—an apparent "exception" permitted in pre-parochial times—would be strictly prohibited (except in the case of the vestments and adornment worn by members of the clergy).

This dichotomy may help explain some of the mortuary variability discussed earlier: Perhaps such sites with rich grave-associated assemblages—such as Santa Catalina and Patale—reflect mostly pre-parochial missionization; whereas missions with only minimal grave goods (particularly Santa María and some of the Apalachee missions) might reflect the transition to secularized outposts, with ritual more rigorously conditioned by church doctrine.

Specifics aside, Spanish Florida clearly has much to offer the discipline of historic archaeology. Our rapidly increasing knowledge of this area already requires that archaeologists immersed in the early colonial history of the United States come to grips with diversity: not only the escalating variability within the empirical base, but also an increasingly diverse perception of early European motivations in approaching Native North America.

ACKNOWLEDGMENTS

I express my sincere thanks to the Trustees of the St. Catherines Island and Edward John Noble Foundations, particularly Mr. and Mrs. Frank Y. Larkin, for providing both the opportunity and the support to conduct the archaeological research described here. Additional funding has been provided by the Richard K. Lounsbery Foundation, the National Science Foundation, the Georgia Endowment for the Humanities, Mr. Donald McClane, the James Ruel Smith Fund, the Ogden Mills Fund, and Earthwatch.

Several friends and colleagues helped out by reviewing earlier drafts of this paper and providing insights, manuscripts, unpublished data, obscure references, and helpful advice: Richard Ahlborn, Chad Braley, Amy Turner Bushnell, Morgan Crook, Kathleen Deagan, Chester DePratter, John Hann, Grant Jones, Clark Spencer Larsen, Lewis Larson, Jerald Milanich, Gary Shapiro, and Mark Williams. I also thank the staff of the St. Catherines Island Archaeological Project for their assistance in preparing this paper: Margot Dembo, Karen Ilyse Katz, Melanie LeMaistre, Lorann S. A. Pendleton, and Debra Peter. Dennis O'Brien prepared Figure 3.1 and Nicholas Amorosi illustrated the artifacts from Santa Catalina. I gratefully acknowledge the P. K.

Yonge Library, University of Florida, for permission to reproduce Figure 3.2.

NOTES

1. The Guale cemetery at Santa Catalina has potential to provide unique biocultural information, but before proceeding we wished to ensure that our investigations would be carried out with appropriate dignity and respect. We also felt it was necessary to determine from the outset the ultimate disposition of the remains. We therefore temporarily suspended our mortuary excavations in the cemetery pending resolution of both matters.

The appropriate first step required that we contact individuals of demonstrable biological affinity to the people buried there. Tracking down the biological descendants of the Santa Catalina Guale was fruitless. After St. Catherines Island fell to the British in the 1680s, many Guale apparently remained in the area, aligning with the British and being absorbed by the Yamassee. Missionized Guale were removed closer to St. Augustine (Swanton 1922:136; Lanning 1935:218; Barcia 1951:312), and by the early 18th century, the Guale had become the dominant Indian element in St. Augustine (Deagan, 1973). But the latest reference we can find to the Guale occurred in 1735, at Mission Nombre De Dios, on the outskirts of St. Augustine (Geiger 1940:23; Larson 1978:120). After that, the Guale disappeared as an ethnic and biological entity.

Since there was no possibility of contacting demonstrable *biological* descendants, we focused on establishing those with the closest *cultural and/or religious affinity* to the Guale at Santa Catalina. Our initial test excavations indicated a mortuary pattern clearly mandated by 16th- and 17th-century Catholic liturgical custom. Those Guale buried at Mission Santa Catalina—or at least their immediate families—had without question opted for Christian burial. We view this decision—made three to four centuries ago—as unequivocal evidence of religious preference, and on this basis, the contemporary Catholic church became the appropriate organization with which to discuss the disposition of the human remains.

Accordingly, in September 1982, I contacted Father Raymond Lessard, bishop of Savannah, asking if the church objected to scientific investigation of this 16th- and 17th-century Franciscan cemetery. Bishop Lessard assured me that the Catholic church supported our excavations; in his view, Santa Catalina ceased to be consecrated when the missionaries and neophytes abandoned the site in the 1680s.

Bishop Lessard and I also discussed the ultimate disposition of remains. We agreed that (1) the most appropriate action was reburial after suitable analysis, and (2) the most appropriate venue for reinterment would be the original cemetery itself.

The St. Catherines Island Foundation agreed to this plan and on May 25, 1984, Bishop Lessard returned to Santa Catalina to conduct a service dedicated to "Reblessing the Ground and Re-burial of Remains." He also supervised reinterment of three Guale Indians in an excavated portion of the nave. We feel that this solution represents the most satisfactory course of action for all concerned. Additional remains will be reinterred as biocultural analysis is completed.

2. How the conflict between traditional values and Christianity was resolved in the Guale mind is an entirely different, and unresolved, issue. Quite clearly, the Guale employed some form of syncretic integration, probably through some form of contextual relativism (see Geertz 1960), but the specifics at present elude our grasp.

REFERENCES CITED

Adams, William Hampton (ed.)
   1985   *Aboriginal Subsistence and Settlement Archaeology of the Kings Bay Locality*. Vol. 1. *The Kings Bay and Devils Walkingstick Sites*. University of Florida Department of Anthropology Reports of Investigations, no. 1. Gainesville.

Avery, T. E., and T. R. Lyons
   1981   *Remote Sensing: Aerial and Terrestrial Photography for Archaeologists*. National Park Service, Supplement 7.

Barcia, Andres Gonzales
   1951   Barcia's Chronological History of the Continent of Florida. Trans. with an introduction by Anthony Kerrigan. Gainesville: University of Florida Press.

Benner, S. M., and R. S. Brodkey
   1984   Underground Detection Using Differential Heat Analysis. *Archaeometry* 26: 21–36.

Betsky, Aaron
   1985   The Spanish Influence: Architecture in America. *Horizon* 28 (10): 53–68.

Bevan, Bruce W.
   1983   Electromagnetics for Mapping Buried Earth Features. *Journal of Field Archaeology* 10 (1): 47–54.

Bevan, Bruce W., and J. Kenyon
   1975   Ground-penetrating Radar for Historical Archaeology. *MASCA Newsletter* 11 (2): 2–7.

Binford, Lewis R.
   1981   *Bones: Ancient Men and Modern Myths*. New York: Academic Press.

Binford, Lewis R. (ed.)
   1977   *For Theory Building in Archaeology*. New York: Academic Press.

Bolton, Herbert E.
1917   The Mission as a Frontier Institution in the Spanish-American Colonies. *American Historical Review* 23:42–61.
1921   *The Spanish Borderlands: A Chronicle of Old Florida and the Southwest.* New Haven, Conn.: Yale University Press.

Bolton, Herbert E., and Mary Ross
1925   *The Debatable Land.* Berkeley: University of California Press.

Boyd, Mark F.
1958   Historic Sites in and around the Jim Woodruff Reservoir Area, Florida-Georgia. *Bureau of American Ethnology, Bulletin* 169(9–14): 195–314.

Boyd, Mark F., Hale G. Smith, and John W. Griffin
1951   *Here They Once Stood: The Tragic End of the Apalachee Missions.* Gainesville: University of Florida Press.

Braley, Chad O., Lisa D. O'Steen, and Irvy R. Quitmyer
1986   *Archaeological Investigations at 9 McI 41, Harris Neck National Wildlife Refuge, McIntosh, Georgia.* Report to the U.S. Department of the Interior, Fish and Wildlife Service. Atlanta, Ga.

Brown, Jonathan
1978   *Images and Ideas in Seventeenth Century Spanish Painting.* Princeton, N.J.: Princeton University Press.

Bullen, Ripley P.
1950   An Archaeological Survey of the Chattahoochee River Valley in Florida. *Journal of the Washington Academy of Science* 40: 101–25.

Bushnell, Amy
1981   *The King's Coffer: Proprietors of the Spanish Florida Treasury 1565–1702.* Gainesville: University Presses of Florida.
1983   The Noble and Loyal City 1565–1688. In *The Oldest City: St. Augustine, Saga of Survival,* ed. Jean Parker Waterbury, pp. 27–56. St. Augustine, Fla.: St. Augustine Historical Society.

Byrne, Stephen C., and Rochelle A. Marrinan
1984   1984 Excavations at the Mission of San Pedro y San Pablo de Patale. Paper presented at the 1984 Southeastern Archaeological Conference, Pensacola.

Caldwell, Joseph R.
1943   Cultural Relations of Four Indian Sites of the Georgia Coast. Master's thesis, Anthropology Department, University of Chicago.
n.d.   Unpublished field notes on file, laboratory of anthropology, St. Catherines Island, Georgia.

Caldwell, Sheila K.
    1953   Excavations at a Spanish Mission Site in Georgia. *Southeastern Ar-chaeological Conference Newsletter* 3(3): 31–32.
    1954   A Spanish Mission House near Darien. *Early Georgia* 1(3): 13–17.

Carr, C.
    1977   A New Role and Analytical Design for the Use of Resistivity Survey-ing in Archaeology. *Mid-Continental Journal of Archaeology* 2(2): 161–93.
    1982   *Handbook on Soil Resistivity Surveying: Interpretation of Data from Earthen Archeological Sites.* Evanston, Illinois: Center for American Archeology Press.

Chatelain, Verne E.
    1941   *The Defenses of Spanish Florida: 1565– 1763.* Washington, D.C.: Carnegie Institution of Washington.

Cleland, Charles E.
    1972   From Sacred to Profane: Style Drift in the Decoration of Jesuit Fin-ger Rings. *American Antiquity* 37(2): 202–10.

Cook, Fred C.
    1976   The Kent Mound Burials: A Protohistoric Indian Population on the Georgia Coast. Anthropology Department, University of Georgia.

Crook, Morgan R., Jr.
    1980   Spatial Associations and Distribution of Aggregate Village Sites in a Southeastern Atlantic Coastal Area. In Sapelo Papers, ed. Juengst, D. P., pp. 77–87. *West Georgia College Studies in the Social Sciences*, Carrollton, Ga.

Crosby, Alfred W., Jr.
    1972   *The Columbian Exchange: Biological and Cultural Consequences of 1492.* Westport, Conn.: Greenwood Press.

Crouch, Dora P., Daniel J. Garr, and Axel I. Mundigo
    1982   *Spanish City Planning in North America.* Cambridge, Mass.: MIT Press.

Deagan, Kathleen
    1972   Fig Springs: The Mid-Seventeenth Century in North-Central Flor-ida. *Historical Archaeology* 6:23– 46.
    1973   *Mestizaje* in Colonial St. Augustine. *Ethnohistory*, 20:55–65.
    1978   Cultures in Transition: Fusion and Assimilation among the Eastern Timucua. In *Tacachale: Essays on the Indians of Florida and Southeast-ern Georgia during the Historic Period*, ed. Jerald Milanich and Samuel Proctor, pp. 89–119. Gainesville: University Presses of Florida.
    1981   Downtown Survey: The Discovery of Sixteenth-Century St. Augustine in an Urban Area. *American Antiquity* 46(3):626–34.

1982 St. Augustine: First Urban Enclave in the United States. *North American Archaeology* 3(3): 183– 205.

1983 *Spanish St. Augustine: The Archaeology of a Colonial Creole Community.* New York: Academic Press.

1985a Spanish-Indian Interaction in Sixteenth-Century Florida and Hispaniola. In *Cultures in Contact: The European Impact on Native Cultural Institutions in Eastern North America,* A.D. 1000–1800, ed. William W. Fitzhugh, pp. 281–318. Washington, D.C.: Smithsonian Institution Press.

1985b The Archaeology of Sixteenth Century St. Augustine. *The Florida Anthropologist* 38(1–2)Part 1: 6–33.

Deetz, James
1977 *In Small Things Forgotten: The Archaeology of Early American Life.* New York: Anchor Press/Doubleday.

Defourneaux, Marcelin
1971 *Daily Life in Spain in the Golden Age.* Trans. Mewton Branch. Palo Alto, Calif.: Stanford University Press.

DePratter, Chester B., and Marvin T. Smith
1980 Sixteenth Century European Trade in the Southeastern United States: Evidence from the Juan Pardo Expeditions (1566–1568). In *Spanish Colonial Frontier Research,* ed. Henry F. Dobyns, pp. 67–78. Albuquerque: Center for Anthropological Studies.

Dickinson, Martin F., and Lucy B. Wayne
1985 *Archaeological Testing of the San Juan del Puerto Mission Site (8Du53), Fort George Island, Florida.* Report prepared for Fairfield Communities. Jacksonville, Fl.; Gainesville, Fl.: Water & Air Research.

Dunlop, Captain
1929 Journall Capt. Dunlop's Voyage to the Southward, 1687. *South Carolina Historical and Genealogical Magazine* 30(3): 127–33.

Dunnell, Robert C.
1982 Americanist Archaeological Literature: 1981. *American Journal of Archaeology* 86:509–29.

1984 The Americanist Literature for 1983: A Year of Contrasts and Challenges. *American Journal of Archaeology* 88:489–513.

Ebert, James I.
1984 Remote Sensing Applications in Archaeology. In *Advances in Archaeological Method and Theory,* Vol. 7, ed. Michael B. Schiffer, pp. 293–362. New York: Academic Press.

Ellis, John Tracy
1965 *Catholics in Colonial America.* Baltimore, Md.: Helicon Press.

Ewing, J. Franklin
1949   Appendix. The Religious Medals. In Franciscan Awatovi, ed. Ross
        Gordon Montgomery, Watson, Smith, and John Otis Brew, pp.
        100–106. *Papers of the Peabody Museum of American Archaeology and
        Ethnology* 36.

Fairbanks, Charles H.
1985   From Exploration to Settlement: Spanish Strategies for Coloniza-
        tion. In *Alabama and the Borderlands: From Prehistory to Statehood*, ed.
        R. Reid Badger and Lawrence A. Clayton, pp. 128–39. University:
        University of Alabama Press.

Ferguson, Leland B.
1975   Analysis of Ceramic Materials from Fort Watson: December
        1780–April 1781. *The Conference on Historic Site Archaeology Papers
        1973* 8: 2–28.

Fitzhugh, William W.
1985   Commentary on Part IV. In *Cultures in Contact: The European Im-
        pact on Native Cultural Institutions in Eastern North America, A.D.
        1000–1800*, ed. William W. Fitzhugh, pp. 271–79. Washington,
        D.C.: Smithsonian Institution Press.

Foster, George M.
1960   Culture and Conquest: America's Spanish Heritage. *Viking Fund
        Publications in Anthropology*, no. 27. New York: Warner Green Foun-
        dation for Anthropological Research, Inc.

Fryman, Mildred L., John. W. Griffin, and James J. Miller
1979   *Archeology and History of the Harris Neck National Wildlife Refuge,
        McIntosh County, Georgia*. Report to the U.S. Fish and Wildlife Ser-
        vices, Atlanta.

Gannon, Michael V.
1965   *The Cross in the Sand: The Early Catholic Church in Florida,
        1513–1870*. Gainesville: University of Florida Press. [Reprinted
        1967]

Garrison, Ervan G., James G. Baker, and David Hurst Thomas
1985   Magnetic Prospection and the Discovery of Mission Santa Catalina
        de Guale, Georgia. *Journal of Field Archaeology* 12: 299–313.

Geertz, Clifford
1960   *The Religion of Java*. London: The Free Press of Glencoe.

Geiger, Maynard J.
1937   *The Franciscan Conquest of Florida (1573– 1618). Studies in Hispanic-
        American History*. Vol. 1. Washington, D.C.: The Catholic Univer-
        sity of America.

1940   Biographical Dictionary of the Franciscans in Spanish Florida and Cuba (1528–1841). Paterson, N.J.: *Franciscan Studies, Vol. 21.*

Gibson, Charles (ed.)
    1971   *The Black Legend: Anti-Spanish Attitudes in the Old World and the New.* New York: Alfred A. Knopf.

Goggin, John
    1952   Space and Time Perspective in Northern St. Johns Archeology, Florida. *Yale University Publications in Anthropology, no. 47.* New Haven, Conn.
    1953   An Introductory Outline of Timucua Archaeology. *Southeastern Archaeological Conference Newsletter* 3(3): 4–17.
    1960   The Spanish Olive Jar: An Introductory Study. *Yale University Publications in Anthropology,* no. 62. New Haven, Conn.
    1968   Spanish Majolica in the New World. *Yale University Publications in Anthropology,* no. 72. New Haven, Conn.

Gowans, Alan
    1986   *The Comfortable House: American Suburban Architecture 1890–1930.* Cambridge, Mass.: MIT Press.

Grayson, Donald K.
    1982   Review of *Bones: Ancient Men and Modern Myths,* by Lewis R. Binford. *American Anthropologist* 84: 439–40.

Griffin, John W.
    1965a   Notes on the archaeology of St. Catherines Island, Georgia. Prepared for and submitted to Edward John Noble Foundation. Copy on file, Department of Anthropology, American Museum of Natural History (unpublished). New York.
    1965b   Santa Catalina Mission, Liberty County, Georgia. Documentation for Consideration as a Registered National Historic Landmark. Copy on file, Anthropology Department, American Museum of Natural History (unpublished). New York.

Habig, Marion A.
    1976   *The Alamo Chain of Missions, a History of San Antonio's Five Old Missions.* Chicago: Franciscan Herald Press. (First published 1968)

Hanke, Lewis
    1964   *The First Social Experiments in America.* Gloucester, Mass.: Peter Smith. (First published 1935)

Hann, John H.
    1986   Demographic Patterns and Changes in Mid-Seventeenth Century Timucua and Apalachee. *The Florida Historical Quarterly* 64: 371–92.

Hardin, Kenneth
    1986   The Santa Maria Mission Project. *Florida Anthropologist* 39(1–2): 75–83.

Hauser, Judith Ann
    1982   Jesuit Rings from Fort Michilimackinac and Other European Contact Sites. *Mackinac Island State Park Commission, Mackinac Island, Mi. Archaeological Completion Report Series*, no. 5.

Hayden, Brian, and Aubrey Cannon
    1984   The Structure of Material Systems: Ethnoarchaeology in the Maya Highlands. *Society for American Archaeology Papers*, no.3. Washington, D.C.: Society for American Archaeology.

Hemmings, E. Thomas, and Kathleen A. Deagan
    1973   Excavations on Amelia Island in Northeast Florida. *Contributions to the Florida State Museum of Anthropology and History*, no. 18. Gainesville, Fl.

Hoffman, Paul E.
    1980   *The Spanish Crown and the Defense of the Caribbean, 1535–1585: Precedent, Patrimonialism and Royal Parsimony*. Baton Rouge: Louisiana State University Press.

Honerkamp, Nick
    1982   Social Status as Reflected in Faunal Remains from an Eighteenth Century British Colonial Site. *The Conference on Historic Site Archaeology Papers* 1979 14: 87–115. Columbia, S.C.: Institute for Archaeology and Anthropology.

Hvidt, Kristian
    1980   *Von Reck's Voyage: Drawings and Journal of Philip Georg Friedrich von Reck*. Savannah, Ga.: Beehive Press.

Jones, B. Calvin
    1970a   Missions Reveal State's Spanish-Indian Heritage. Florida Division of Archives, History and Records Management. *Archives and History News* 1(2): 1, 2, 3.
    1970b   17th Century Spanish Mission Cemetery Is Discovered near Tallahassee. Florida Division of Archives, History and Records Management. *Archives and History News* 1(4):1,2.
    1971   State Archaeologists Unearth Spanish Mission Ruins. Florida Division of Archives, History and Records Management. *Archives and History News* 2(4): 2.
    1972   Spanish Mission Sites Located and Test Excavated. Florida Division of Archives, History and Records Management. *Archives and History News* 3(6): 1–2.
    1973   A Semi-Subterranean Structure at Mission San Joseph de Ocuya,

Jefferson County, Florida. *Florida Bureau of Historical Sites and Properties Bulletin*, n. 3, pp. 1– 50.

1980   Interview with Calvin Jones. *Florida Anthropologist* 33(4): 161–71.

Jones, George T., Donald K. Grayson, and Charlotte Beck

1983   Artifact Class Richness and Sample Size in Archaeological Surface Assemblages. In *Lulu Linear Punctated: Essays in Honor of George Irving Quimby*, ed. Robert C. Dunnell and Donald K. Grayson, pp. 55–74. *Museum of Anthropology, University of Michigan*, no. 72. Ann Arbor.

Jones, Grant D.

1978   The Ethnohistory of the Guale Coast through 1684. In The Anthropology of St. Catherines Island: 1. Natural and Cultural History, David Hurst Thomas, Grant D. Jones, Roger S. Durham, and Clark Spencer Larsen, pp. 178–210. *American Museum of Natural History Anthropological Papers* 55(2).

Jones, Oakah L., Jr.

1979   *Los Paisanos: Spanish Settlers on the Northern Frontier of New Spain.* Norman: University of Oklahoma Press.

Kelso, William M.

1968   *Excavations at the Fort King George Historical Site: Darien, Georgia— the 1967 Survey.* Atlanta: Georgia Historical Commission.

Killgallon, James, Gerard Weber, and Leonard Ziegmann

1976   *Life in Christ.* Rev. ed. Chicago: Foundation for Adult Catechetical Teaching Aids.

Koch, Joan K.

1980   Nuestra Senora de la Soledad: A Study of a Church and Hospital Site in Colonial St. Augustine. Master's thesis, Florida State University.

1983   Mortuary Behavior Patterning and Physical Anthropology in Colonial St. Augustine. In *Spanish St. Augustine: The Archaeology of a Colonial Creole Community*, ed. Kathleen Deagan, pp. 187–227. New York: Academic Press.

Kubler, George

1940   *The Religious Architecture of New Mexico.* Colorado Springs: The Taylor Museum.

Lanning, J. T.

1935   *The Spanish Missions of Georgia.* Chapel Hill: University of North Carolina Press.

Larsen, Clark Spencer

1981   Functional Implications of Postcranial Size Reduction on the Prehistoric Georgia Coast. *U.S.A. Journal of Human Evolution* 10: 489–502.

1982   The Anthropology of St. Catherines Island: 3. Prehistoric Human Biological Adaptation. *American Museum of Natural History Anthropological Papers* 57(3): 157–276.

1984   Health and Disease in Prehistoric Georgia: The Transition to Agriculture. In *Paleopathology at the Origins of Agriculture*, ed. Mark N. Cohen and George J. Armelagos, pp. 367–92. New York: Academic Press.

Larsen, Clark Spencer, and David Hurst Thomas

1982   The Anthropology of St. Catherines Island: 4. The St. Catherines Period Mortuary Complex. *American Museum of Natural History Anthropology Papers* 57(4):271–341.

1986   The Archaeology of St. Catherines Island: 5. The South End Mound Complex. *American Museum of Natural History Anthropological Papers* 63(1):1–46.

Larson, Lewis H., Jr.

1952   1952 Season, Georgia Historical Commission, Archaeological Survey of the Georgia Coast. Report on file, University of Georgia, Athens.

1953   Coastal Georgia Survey. Unpublished manuscript. Copy on file Archaeology Laboratory, American Museum of Natural History.

1958   Cultural Relationships between the Northern St. Johns Area and the Georgia Coast. *Florida Anthropologist* 11(1): 11–21.

1978   Historic Guale Indians of the Georgia Coast and the Impact of the Spanish Mission Effort. In *Tacachale: Essays on the Indians of Florida and Southeastern Georgia during the Historic Period*, ed. Jerald Milanich and S. Proctor, pp. 120–140. Gainesville: University Presses of Florida.

1980   The Spanish on Sapelo. In Sapelo Papers, ed. D. P. Juengst, pp. 35–45. *West Georgia College Studies in the Social Sciences* 19. Carrollton, Ga.

Loucks, Lana Jill

1979   Political and Economic Interactions between Spaniards and Indians: Archeological and Ethnohistorical Perspectives of the Mission System in Florida. Ph.D. diss., University of Florida.

Lyon, Eugene

1976   *The Enterprise of Florida: Pedro Menéndez de Avilés and the Spanish Conquest of 1565–1568.* Gainesville: University Presses of Florida.

1977   St. Augustine 1580: The Living Community. *El Escribano* 14: 20–33.

1981   Spain's Sixteenth-Century North American Settlement Attempts: A Neglected Aspect. *Florida Historical Quarterly* 59(3): 275–91.

1984   Santa Elena: A Brief History of the Colony, 1566–1587. *University of South Carolina, Institute for Archaeology and Anthropology, Research Manuscript Series*, 193.

1985   Continuity in the Age of Conquest: The Establishment of Spanish
        Sovereignty in the Sixteenth Century. In *Alabama and the Border-*
        lands: From Prehistory to Statehood, ed. R. Reid Badger and Lawrence
        A. Clayton, pp. 154–61. University: University of Alabama Press.

Lyons, T. R., and T. E. Avery
1984   *Remote Sensing: A Handbook for Archeologists and Cultural Resource*
        Managers. Washington, D.C.: National Park Service, U.S. Depart-
        ment of the Interior.

McAlister, Lyle N.
1964   Introduction. In *Pedro Menéndez de Avilés: Memorial*. ed. Gonzalo
        Solis de Merás, pp. xiii– xxxiv. Gainesville: University of Florida
        Press.
1984   *Spain and Portugal in the New World: 1492– 1700*. Minneapolis: Uni-
        versity of Minnesota Press.

McManamon, Francis P.
1984   Discovering Sites Unseen. In *Advances in Archaeological Method and*
        Theory, ed. Michael B. Schiffer, vol. 7, pp. 223–92. New York:
        Academic Press.

McMurray, Judith Angley
1973   The Definition of the Ceramic Complex at San Juan del Puerto.
        Master's thesis, University of Florida.

Maltby, William S.
1971   *The Black Legend in England: The Development of Anti-Spanish Senti-*
        ment, 1558–1660. Durham, N.C.: Duke University Press.

Manucy, Albert
1978   *The Houses of St. Augustine*. Tallahassee: St. Augustine Historical
        Society.
1983   Building Materials in 16th-Century St. Augustine (part I). *El*
        Escribano 20: 51–71.
1985   The Physical Setting of Sixteenth Century St. Augustine. *Florida*
        Anthropologist 38(1):34–53.

Marrinan, Rochelle
1985   The Archaeology of the Spanish Missions of Florida: 1565–1704. In
        Indians, Colonists, and Slaves, K. W. Johnson, J. M. Leader, and
        R. C. Wilson, ed. *Florida Journal of Anthropology Special Publication*
        no. 4: 241–252. Gainesville, Fl.: Florida Anthropology Student As-
        sociation.

Matter, Robert Allen
1972   The Spanish Missions of Florida: The Friars versus the Governors
        in the "Golden Age," 1606–1690. Ph.D. diss., University of Wash-
        ington, Seattle.

Merritt, J. D.
1977   Excavations of a Coastal Eastern Timucua Village in Northeast
        Florida. Master's thesis, Florida State University, Tallahassee.

Milanich, J. T.
1972a   Excavations at the Richardson Site, Alachua County, Florida: An
        Early 17th Century Potano Indian Village. *Florida Bureau of Histori-
        cal Sites and Properties Bulletin* 2: 35–61.
1972b   Tacatacuru and the San Pedro de Mocamo Mission. *Florida Histori-
        cal Quarterly* 50(3): 283– 91.
1978   The Western Timucua: Patterns of Acculturation and Change. In
        *Tacachale: Essays on the Indians of Florida and Southeastern Georgia dur-
        ing the Historic Period*, ed. Jerald Milanich and Samuel Proctor, pp.
        59–88. Gainesville: University Presses of Florida.

Milanich, Jerald T., and William C. Sturtevant
1972   *Francisco Pareja's 1613 Confessionario: A Documentary Source for
        Timucuan Ethnography*. Tallahassee: Florida Division of Archives,
        History, and Records Management.

Miller, J. Jefferson, and Lyle M. Stone
1970   Eighteenth-century ceramics from Fort Michilimackinac. *Smithson-
        ian Studies in History and Technology, no. 4*. Washington, D.C.

Montgomery, Ross Gordon, Watson Smith, and John Otis Brew
1949   Franciscan Awatovi: The Excavation and Conjectural Reconstruc-
        tion of a Seventeenth Century Spanish Mission Establishment at a
        Hopi Indian Town in Northeastern Arizona. *Papers of the Peabody
        Museum in American Archaeology and Ethnology* 1:36.

Morrell, L. Ross, and B. Calvin Jones
1970   San Juan de Aspalaga: A Preliminary Architectural Study. *Florida
        Bureau of Historical Sites and Properties Bulletin* 1:25–43.

Noël Hume, Ivor
1976   *A Guide to Artifacts of Colonial America*. New York: Alfred A.
        Knopf.

Otto, John Solomon
1984   *Cannon's Point Plantation, 1794–1860*. New York: Academic Press.

Parrington, Michael
1983   Remote Sensing. *Annual Review of Anthropology* 12:105–24.

Patrick, Rembert W.
1964   Editorial Preface. In *Pedro Menéndez de Avilés: Memorial*, ed.
        Gonzalo Solís de Merás, p. xi–xii. Gainesville: University of Florida
        Press.

Pearson, Fred Lamar, Jr.
  1974   Spanish Indian Relations in Florida, 1602–1675: Some Aspects of
          Selected Visitas. *Florida Historical Quarterly* 52(3): 261–273.

Percy, George
  1976   The Use of a Mechanical Earth Auger at the Torreya Site, Liberty
          County, Florida. *Florida Anthropologist* 29(1): 24–32.

Polzer, Charles W.
  1976   *Rules and Precepts of the Jesuit Missions of Northwestern New Spain.*
          Tucson: University of Arizona Press.

Quinn, David B. (ed.)
  1979   *New American World.* Vol. 5. New York: Arno Press and Hector
          Bye.

Reitz, Elizabeth J., and C. Margaret Scarry
  1985   Reconstructing Historic Subsistence with an Example from
          Sixteenth-Century Spanish Florida. *Society for Historical Archaeology
          Special Publication Series* No. 3. Glassboro, N.J.: Society for His-
          torical Archaeology.

Robinson, Paul A., Marc A. Kelley, and Patricia E. Rubertone
  1985   Preliminary Biocultural Interpretations from a Seventeenth-Century
          Narragansett Indian Cemetery in Rhode Island. In *Cultures in Con-
          tact: The European Impact on Native Cultural Institutions in Eastern
          North America, A.D. 1000– 1800*, ed. William W. Fitzhugh, pp.
          107–30. Washington D.C.: Smithsonian Institution Press.

Ross, Mary
  1926   The Restoration of the Spanish Missions of Georgia, 1598–1606.
          Georgia Historical Quarterly 10(3):171–199.

Sauer, Carl Ortwin
  1966   *The Early Spanish Main.* Berkeley: University of California Press.

Scardaville, Michael C.
  1985   Approaches to the Study of the Southeastern Borderlands. In *Ala-
          bama and the Borderlands: From Prehistory to Statehood*, ed. R. Reid
          Badger and Lawrence A. Clayton, pp. 184–96. University: Univer-
          sity of Alabama Press.

Scarry, C. Margaret
  1985   The Use of Plant Foods in Sixteenth Century St. Augustine. *Florida
          Anthropologist* 38(1):70–80.

Schiffer, Michael B.
  1976   *Behavioral Archeology.* New York: Academic Press.

Schuyler, Robert L. (ed.)
   1980   *Archaeological Perspectives on Ethnicity in America: Afro-American and Asian American Culture History.* Farmingdale, N.Y.: Baywood.

Seaberg, Lillian M.
   1951   Report on the Indian Site at the "Fountain of Youth," St. Augustine. Unpublished manuscript.

Shapiro, Gary
   1984   A Soil Resistivity Survey of 16th-Century Puerto Real, Haiti. *Journal of Field Archaeology* 11(1): 101– 10.
   1985   The Apalachee Council House at Seventeenth Century San Luis. Paper presented at the 1985 Southeastern Archaeological Conference, Birmingham, Ala.
   1987   Archaeology at San Luis: 1984–1985 Broad-scale Testing. *Florida Archaeology*, no. 3. Tallahassee: Florida Bureau of Archaeological Research.

Shapiro, Gary, and Rochelle A. Marrinan
   1986   Two Seventeenth Century Spanish Missions in Florida's Apalachee Province. Paper presented at the Society for Historical Archaeology, Sacramento, Calif.

Shapiro, Gary, and Charles Poe
   1984   Broad-scale Archaeological Testing at a Seventeenth Century Spanish Mission in North Florida. Paper presented at the Southeastern Archaeological Conference, Pensacola, Florida.

Siebert, Wilbur H.
   1940   The Departure of the Spaniards and Other Groups from East Florida, 1763–1764. *The Florida Historical Quarterly* 19(2): 145–54.

Sluiter, Engel
   1985   The Florida Situado: Quantifying the First Eighty Years 1571–1651. *Research Publications of the P. K. Yonge Library of Florida History.* No. 1. University of Florida, Gainesville.

Smith, Hale G.
   1956   *The European and the Indian: European-Indian Contacts in Georgia and Florida.* Florida Anthropological Society Publication no. 4.

Solís de Merás, Gonzalo
   1922   *Pedro Menéndez de Avilés.* Trans. Jeannette Thurber Connor. DeLand, Florida State Historical Society. Facsimile ed. Gainesville: University of Florida Press [1964].

South, Stanley

1974   *Palmetto Parapets: Exploratory Archaeology at Fort Moultrie, South Carolina 38CH50.* Institute of Archaeology and Anthropology, University of South Carolina, Anthropological Studies, no. 1. Columbia.

1977   *Method and Theory in Historical Archeology.* New York: Academic Press.

1982   Exploring Santa Elena 1981. Institute for Archaeology and Anthropology, University of South Carolina, Research Manuscript Series, No. 184. Columbia.

South, Stanley, and Randolph Widmer

1977   A Subsurface Sampling Strategy for Archeological Reconnaissance. In *Research Strategies in Historical Archeology*, ed. Stanley South, pp. 119–50. New York: Academic Press.

Spicer, Edward H.

1962   Cycles of Conquest: The Impact of Spain, Mexico, and the United States on the Indians of the Southwest, 1533– 1960. Tucson: University of Arizona Press.

Sturtevant, William C.

1962   Spanish-Indian Relations in Southeastern North America. *Ethnohistory* 9(1): 41–94.

Swanton, John R.

1922   Early History of the Creek Indians and Their Neighbors. *Smithsonian Institution, Bureau of America Ethnology Bulletin* no. 73. Washington, D.C.

1946   The Indians of the Southeastern United States. *Smithsonian Institution, Bureau of American Ethnology Bulletin* no. 137. Washington, D.C.

Symes, M. I., and M. E. Stephens

1965   A 272: the Fox Pond Site. *Florida Anthropologist* 18: 65–76.

TePaske, John J.

1965   Funerals and Fiestas in Early Eighteenth Century St. Augustine. *Florida Historical Quarterly* 44(1 & 2): 97–104.

Thomas, David Hurst

1976   *Figuring Anthropology: First Principles of Probability and Statistics.* New York: Holt, Rinehart and Winston.

1979   *Archaeology.* New York: Holt, Rinehart and Winston.

1983a   The Archaeology of Monitor Valley: 1. Epistemology. *American Museum of Natural History Anthropological Papers* 58(1): 1–194.

1983b   The Archaeology of Monitor Valley: 2. Gatecliff Shelter. *American Museum of Natural History Anthropological Papers* 59(1): 1-552.

1986   Contemporary Hunter-Gatherer Archaeology in America. In *American Archaeology Past and Future: A Celebration of the Society for Ameri-*

can Archaeology 1935– 1985, ed. David J. Meltzer, Don D. Fowler, and Jeremy A. Sabloff, pp. 237–76. Washington D.C.: Smithsonian Institution Press.

1987   The Archaeology of Santa Catalina de Guale: 1. Search and Discovery. *American Museum of Natural History Anthropological Papers* 63(2):47–161.

Thomas, David Hurst, Grant D. Jones, Roger S. Durham, and Clark Spencer Larsen
1978   The Anthropology of St. Catherines Island: 1. Natural and Cultural History. *American Museum of Natural History Anthropological Papers* 55(2): 155–248.

Thomas, David Hurst, and Clark Spencer Larsen
1979   The Anthropology of St. Catherines Island: 2. The Refuge-Deptford Mortuary Complex. *American Museum of Natural History Anthropological Papers* 56(1): 1–179.

Thomas, David Hurst, Stanley South, and Clark Spencer Larsen
1977   Rich Man, Poor Men: Observations on Three Antebellum Burials from the Georgia Coast. *American Museum of Natural History Anthropological Papers* 54(3): 393– 420.

Thomas, R. B., Bruce Winterhalder, and S. McRae
1979   An Anthropological Approach to Human Ecology and Adaptive Dynamics. *Yearbook of Physical Anthropology* 22: 1–46.

Thwaites, Ruben Gold
1892   *The Colonies: 1492–1750.* 3d ed. New York: Longmans, Green.

Wallace, Ronald
1975   An Archeological, Ethnohistoric, and Biochemical Investigation of the Guale Aborigines of the Georgia Coastal Strand. Ph.D. diss., University of Florida, Gainesville.

Walsh, Marie T.
1934   *The Mission Bells of California.* San Francisco: Hart Wagner.

Washburn, Wilcomb E.
1985   The Southeast in the Age of Conflict and Revolution. In *Alabama and the Borderlands: From Prehistory to Statehood,* ed. R. Reid Badger and Lawrence A. Clayton, pp. 143–53. University: University of Alabama Press.

Waterbury, Jean Parker (ed.)
1983   *The Oldest City: St. Augustine, Saga of Survival.* St. Augustine, Fla.: St. Augustine Historical Society.

Wenhold, Lucy L. (trans.)
    1936   A 17th Century Letter of Gabriel Diaz Vara Calderón, Bishop of
            Cuba, Describing the Indians and Indian Missions of Florida. *Smith-*
            sonian Miscellaneous Collection 95(16).

Weymouth, John W.
    1986   Geophysical Methods of Archaeological Site Surveying. In *Advances*
            in Archaeological Method and Theory, ed. Michael B. Schiffer, vol. 9,
            pp. 311–95. New York: Academic Press.

Zéndegui, Guillermo de
    1977   City Planning in the Spanish Colonies. *Américas*, Special Supple-
            ment 29(2): s1–s12.

PART II

Native Americans and Europeans in 17th-Century Southern New England

The 17th century history of the eastern United States is almost inevitably difficult to comprehend, especially on its own terms. The lives led and the problems faced by Europeans, principally the English, in New England and the Chesapeake region are foreign to modern Americans. The lives and problems of the Native Americans displaced by Europeans in the 17th century can only be more alien, when they are recognized at all. The gap to be crossed to gain understanding is both temporal and cultural. The work of Deetz (1977) goes a long way toward at least painting a picture of the communality, the naturalness, and all the other traits that characterized Anglo-American life during this time period. But for all our understanding, Anglo-American life in the 17th century was not just a simpler version of our contemporary way of life; it was different. The dishes were different, the houses were different, time was calculated differently, food was eaten differently, and so on.

As foreign as the 17th century is to us, it is also important. Anglo-American settlement, from the first decade of the 1600s on, was, from a strictly adaptive viewpoint, a success. Old World building techniques were adapted for a new climate (Carson et al. 1981). Some settlers became acclimated, or "seasoned," survived, and reproduced. Anglo-Americans began to learn how to govern themselves and how to take land away from the Native Americans they found living in it, inventing a set of land-exchanging techniques that were to be used by European Americans for close to three centuries of westward expansion.

The essays in Part II take up the issue of European contact with Native Americans in 17th-century southern New England. Both authors approach things from the Native American side of the issue, trying to understand the mental world of people who are both temporally and culturally distant. Attempting to understand the native point of view is the key move in each essay. By making this move and exploring Native American culture and society on terms approaching its own, Elise Brenner and Constance Crosby are able to avoid arguing that European domination of Native American populations was *solely* a matter of European technological superiority. This is important for two reasons.

First, when European domination is understood only in terms of things—such as the superiority of iron over shell hoes and metal over clay pots—people drop out and so, too, does European responsibility. But when 17th-century European domination is not technologically inevitable, as in Crosby and Brenner's essays, then it is possible to ask why it happened and also to examine in a new way the 20th-century consequences of this 17th-century social phenomenon. Second, and even more important from the perspective of the connections between past and present, if we believe that technology is what decimated Native American society, then it becomes very easy to propose technological solutions to contemporary Native American problems that ignore Native American culture just as completely as it was ignored by those who nearly destroyed it in the past. The approach taken by both Brenner and Crosby is an antidote to portrayals of 17th-century Native Americans that deny them the integrity and the complexity of their culture.

Specifically, Brenner presents an argument for the social function of European grave goods from 17th-century southern New England Native American cemeteries. She begins with the rapid and profound social consequences of European contact, principally European diseases to which Native Americans had little resistance. Then she observes that in the most completely furnished graves from this time period, those presumably of individuals of the highest social standing, the principal kind of European grave goods are those that would have had a social function. Those include items that required considerable social and political skills to acquire as well as items like red European coats that would signal the social status of their owners at great distances. Brenner hypothesizes that such items were most highly valued because they demonstrated the shape of a social order in rapid flux and that such items came to be grave goods because they were earned individually, demonstrating achieved rather than ascribed status, which was, as such, nontransferable. Correct or not— and it is likely on the mark —Brenner's most provocative argument gives 17th-century Native Americans the same status as creators and assigners of meaning that we insist on for ourselves.

Whereas Brenner understands grave goods in social terms, Crosby turns to the ideational realm to interpret a similar body of data. She first describes the categories in Native American cosmologies before contact that were capable of encompassing Europeans, the impact of European expansion across southern New England, and the restrictions this expansion imposed on Native American life. More important, Crosby recognizes that Native American ideology played a major role in the acceptance of the European goods that found their way into Native American graves. She discusses *manit*, the concept that Native Americans used to evaluate European goods and to accept, on their own terms, items of European material culture. *Manit* allows us to go beyond etic arguments of efficiency to understand the acceptance, adaptation, and rejection of European goods by Native Americans. Crosby's 17th-century Native Americans, like Brenner's, are seen as persons who assigned meanings to items of material culture, not as passive consumers of European technology and European meanings. Using copper kettles did not make *these* Native Americans European; rather, these Native Americans made European goods distinctly Native American by using them and thinking about them in Native American ways.

The cultural relativism that lies behind the work of both Bren-

ner and Crosby does not deny the ultimate effects of European expansion on Native Americans, but it does keep archaeology from
being just another tool in the continuing domination of Native
Americans by white Americans, an issue discussed at length by Trigger (1980, 1986). Trigger urges historians and archaeologists to pay
attention to the categories through which the past is created, particularly the often submerged idea that history is for Europeans while
anthropology (or science) is for Native Americans. The classic product of this idea is the frequent separation of Euro-American and Native American history, with Europeans in history museums and Native Americans in natural history museums along with the woolly
mammoths and other stuffed animals. What is more, this perspective
presents Native Americans as unreliable producers of and commentators on their own past and as dependent on and dominated by white
scholars and scholarship. Brenner and Crosby, understanding the
problem Trigger discusses, have found an alternative that allows their
own scholarship to continue without so severely compromising the
position of the objects of their research.

A subsidiary value of both essays arising from their careful consideration of the social and ideational aspects of Native American
views of European goods is the set of questions generated by turning
the same kind of sophisticated attention to the European side of
things. If we assume that the shape of European expansion was not
inevitable and choose to go beyond the technomic, then we have to
ask What did Europeans think about Native Americans? More specifically, What place did the emergent ideology of European capitalism
have for Native Americans? Were they producers, consumers, or
both? Were Native Americans as producers treated differently from
Native Americans viewed as consumers? Or, were Native Americans
considered capital? Answers to these questions are important. Further, what was the perceived relationship between Native Americans
and the natural resources such as furs that they were used to exploit?
Were Native Americans treated the same way as beavers, or differently? Were there shifts in the European treatment of Native Americans that were *actually* shifts in the European conservation ethic?
Were European efforts to control Native American populations ana-
logs of their attempts to control nature? Most pointedly, perhaps,

what of European conversion efforts? Were Native Americans converted, put in churches on Sundays, and moved into praying towns to bring them closer to God, or were they converted because the discipline necessary to be a good Christian was like the discipline necessary to be a predictable and reliable, producing and consuming member of society? These lines of questioning all grow out of the sophisticated analytical frameworks brought to their data by Brenner and Crosby here and by Trigger elsewhere. Some of the answers lie in their essays, and much could be gained by asking these questions of other contact studies and other contact period sites.

REFERENCES CITED

Carson, Cary, Norman F. Barka, William M. Kelso, Garry Wheeler Stone, and Dell Upton
> 1981   Impermanent Architecture in the Southern American Colonies. *Winterthur Portfolio* 16(2/3): 135–196.

Deetz, James F.
> 1977   *In Small Things Forgotten*. Garden City, N.Y.: Anchor Books.

Trigger, Bruce
> 1980   Archaeology and the Image of the American Indian. *American Antiquity* 45(4):662–76.
> 1986   *Natives and Newcomers*. Kingston and Montreal: McGill and Queen's University Press.

CHAPTER 4

Sociopolitical Implications of Mortuary Ritual Remains in 17th-Century Native Southern New England

ELISE M. BRENNER

An important research domain in protohistoric northeastern United States is the nature of social and political changes experienced by native communities as they interacted increasingly with various colonial interest groups. In the absence of many systematically excavated contact-period habitation sites in southern New England, I have turned to cemetery data to evaluate hypotheses concerning changing native sociopolitical relations during the 17th century. This chapter describes my initial investigation into the sociopolitical implications of native American mortuary ritual remains in 17th-century southern New England using both archaeological and ethnohistorical records.

The chapter is organized around four topics: (1) the theoretical approaches to the interpretation of mortuary ritual remains; (2) the perspective I employed to interpret 17th-century southern New England native mortuary remains; (3) 17th-century southern New England native political organization as manifested in burial data; and (4) 17th-century southern New England aboriginal mortuary remains.

PERSPECTIVES ON THE INTERPRETATION OF MORTUARY RITUAL REMAINS

One approach to the interpretation of burial evidence is that employed by Winters (1968), Saxe (1970), Brown (1971), Binford (1972), Buikstra

(1976), Peebles and Kus (1977), Tainter (1977), and Braun (1979). These researchers believe that mortuary remains reflect the social organization of the living population. They argue that qualitative and quantitative differences in burial treatment of deceased individuals reflect status asymmetries operating in the living society. Furthermore, they see a positive and direct correlation between the status of the deceased and the quantity/quality of associated grave goods, amount of labor expended in mortuary rites, and energy expended in mortuary treatment (Peebles and Kus 1977:431–33).

A second group holds that burial ceremonialism is a specific example of a broader concept—that of the "ideological legitimation of the sociopolitical order" (Shanks and Tilley 1982:129). In their view, it is necessary to account for the ideological system that determines in what manner political and social differentiation is expressed in mortuary ritual. Ritual practices and their material correlates are interpreted as means of symbolically (and not necessarily directly) expressing social and political roles. That is, such symbolic expression of the sociopolitical order may *not* be a *direct* reflection of actual social relations in the living society, as the first group would argue.

In asking how social relations should be translated into material symbols, Hodder (1982a:10) underscores the fundamental difference between his and Binford's approaches. Hodder argues that "burial pattern is not a direct reflection of social pattern. Instead, it is structured through symbolically meaningful strategies. . . . The concern must be to examine the role of material culture in the ideological representation of social relations" (1982a:10).

Hodder (1982a:10, 1982b) has identified three general strategies that may be played out in mortuary ritualism: (1) a naturalizing strategy wherein political inequalities are symbolically expressed as an integral and inherently necessary part of the hierarchical order attributed to the natural world; (2) a masking strategy wherein political inequalities are denied or hidden behind a facade of equality and egalitarianism; (3) a marking strategy wherein political relations of inequality are clearly and overtly expressed. The specific strategy in any given context and its material patterning are "generated by symbolic structures within a cultural matrix" (Hodder 1982a:10).

Proponents of the second approach have criticized the first one for its inability to explain the specific context of mortuary ritualism (Shanks and Tilley 1982:152). It fails to explain, the critics claim, why certain items are selected as grave furniture, what the spatial arrangement of grave goods in the burials signifies, and why other forms and spatial arrangements are *not* selected (Hodder 1982a:9–10; Shanks and Tilley 1982:152).

The fact that there are two interpretations of mortuary ritual raises three important questions: (1) To what extent does material culture patterning reflect sociopolitical arrangements in the living society? (2) To what extent is material culture patterning that results from specific strategies of ideological legitimation a constructed reality that does not passively reflect actual sociopolitical arrangements? and (3) To what extent can we *determine* the symbolic structures that will generate a particular patterning of material remains? Note, however, that material culture and its patterning contain several possibilities for messages that can be manipulated in various ways in relation to specific historical conditions (Silverman 1981:163). Certain possibilities for symbolic communication are elaborated upon under given conditions. The unstable political climate of 17th-century southern New England leads me to expect that a *marking* strategy would have been used in mortuary ritual as a way of clarifying political relations. With this last point in mind, I now turn to the theoretical perspective employed in my analysis of 17th-century mortuary remains in southern New England.

THEORETICAL APPROACH

Ritual is an important resource of power available to leaders, especially during times of sociopolitical upheaval (Firth 1955:23; Laughlin and Brady 1978:13–14; Royce 1982:225– 227). Such sociopolitical upheaval occurred in native 17th-century southern New England when colonial policies were directed at political domination and cultural suppression of native peoples at the same time that new economic demands and opportunities were confronting native individuals and communities. Binford has noted that "when a cultural system is altered in its internal organization, new units of organizational relevance are generated for the human participants. The recognition of such referential units by participants in the system may prompt the act of symboling and thereby result in a proliferation of symbols within the sociocultural system" (1972:225). The symbolic acts and symbolic objects do not simply proliferate in times of change, but may be actively manipulated as part of a political actor's strategy of legitimizing power and authority. Emergent leaders are likely to institutionalize and objectify their authority in the form of ritual (Shanks and Tilley 1982:133).

Hodder (1982:10), as already mentioned, has argued that three strategies may be played out in mortuary ritualism concerning the relationship between sociopolitical realities and their representations: (1) a naturalizing strategy, (2) a masking strategy, and (3) a marking strategy. I believe that 17th-century aboriginal cemeteries in southern New England are contexts in which political roles and relations were clearly and overtly marked. To cope with the instability in the 17th century, native communities had to be capable of mobilizing collective action vis-à-vis the various colonial interest groups as well as neighboring aboriginal communities. Following Pearson (1982:112), I suggest that in the context of this period of political instability, competition, and reorganization in native New England communities, "social advertisement in death ritual" was "expressly overt" owing to "changing relations of domination" that resulted in "status re-ordering and consolidation of new social positions" (Pearson 1982:112).

The role of material culture in the overt expression of sociopolitical relations in 17th-century native southern New England is best discussed in terms of imported goods. One reason for this approach is that, in the context of the contact period, when native political actors were taking advantage of new opportunities for economic and political leverage and new roles, European commodities served as important material resources. Many writers concerned with change in native sociopolitical organization during the contact period confirm that trade goods were given symbolic and social meanings by the native system, frequently as prestige items (Martin 1975; Trigger 1976; Bishop 1979, to name a few). However, little attention has been paid to the question of who actually assigns value to trade goods, who benefits from this signification, and what the consequences of such signifiers really are.

Braithwaite notes (1984:93) that in looking at the relationship between signs and social structure one must distinguish analytically between (a) "signs that are primary in relation to position in the social structure," that is, a system of prestige "in which rights to signs are derivative from social position" and (b) "signs which are secondary or derivative in relation to social position," that is, a system of prestige "in which social position is derived from the possessions of signs" (1984:93, 94). It appears that, during the contact period, the second form noted by Braithwaite began to operate: Political actors and entrepreneurs could achieve a new position in the social structure through the possession and strategic manipulation of European commodities. Once in the new position, however, the individual most likely had to constantly validate his or her status through continual manipulation and strategic redistribution of trade goods and skillful decisionmaking in order to maintain a following (see Thomas 1979, 1985:139, 148).

Second, imported goods in cemeteries serve most effectively as signifiers of sociopolitical differentiation because (a) trade goods occur with great frequency in the mortuary context once they are introduced into the native system through exchange (European commodities are associated with nearly every grave lot in the 17th-century cemeteries sampled); (b) trade goods, especially particular classes, are differentially distributed among the grave lots and thus perhaps indicate something of their use in the ritual communication of sociopolitical differentiation; (c) imported goods were assigned different meanings and values by the native system from those given by the English and were put to symbolic and sociopolitical uses. The notion that material culture has different meanings in different contexts is the significant characteristic of what a symbol *is* (Hodder 1982a:9). An important point that derives from the one above is that the quantity of trade goods at a contact-period site does not directly and necessarily reflect the degree of "acculturation" that the community had undergone. Rather, the presence and patterning of trade goods may be more suggestive of the social and political processes that were played out by the native community (see, for example, Ray's 1974 analysis of native middlemen).

Hodder (1982a:9) has asked why certain items are repeatedly selected as grave furniture, and why other forms of material culture are not chosen. Although I discuss this question in detail later in the chapter, it is important at this point to briefly comment on the imported material culture classes used as markers of political status in mid-17th-century native cemeteries in southern New England. These trade goods found in the most lavishly furnished graves could be acquired only with a high degree of personal effort, political resourcefulness, and diplomacy. It was not goods that were more generally available or everyday domestic articles that distinguished richly furnished graves from plainer ones. Rather, native actors were apparently selecting particular material classes of goods to signify political differentiation.

ANALYSIS OF POLITICAL ORGANIZATION

In order to evaluate the patterns that emerged in the cemeteries sampled, it is necessary to review the political processes of the contact period. In the initial decades of the contact period, European goods were scarce, and individuals competed for access to, and control over, trade contacts, trade routes, and the pelts needed to acquire the scarce imports. At the same time that imported goods entered the native regional system, European diseases were introduced. Epidemics caused severe social and demographic dislocations among native communities. Entrepreneurial individuals, seeking to fill power gaps in the now unstable political system, found that they could achieve and strengthen their prestige and authority and consolidate a following by attaining control over the imported valuables via the expanding trade. Such a leader would have to redistribute a share of the wealth he acquired in order to maintain and add to his following, as does a big man (Sahlins 1963; Thomas 1979, 1985). However, he could also retain a portion of the imported wealth and use it for display purposes.

When a community disposed of trade goods in graves as a strategy to mark political differentiation, it prevented the oversupply of particular imports. This meant that material signifiers of political power and authority would not become diluted. The same material signifiers and contexts for display of political claims could be used for a long period of time, lending an element of stability to an unstable situation (Brenner 1984). Theoretically, if this were not the case, it would be necessary to continually adopt new symbols of political differentiation as soon as an increasing number of individuals gained access to the current symbols of rank.

This raises an important question that concerns the interpretation of burial data in general: Why are the goods used to mark and reaffirm political inequalities put out of circulation when they could serve the next generation as signifiers of claims to status? Simmons (1970) suggests that lavishly furnished graves served to reaffirm an individual's status in the afterworld. Thus, signifiers of status were put out of circulation because it was necessary to arrive in the afterlife materially and socially prepared. An alternative explanation cites changing relations of power in contact-period native communities.

The classes of goods that differentiate graves of dominant individuals from other burials appear to be those acquired through personal skill, resourcefulness, political entrepreneurship, and diplomatic connections. Furthermore, such goods were apparently put to personal, political use and were displayed to validate claims to authority and to positions of leadership. Once trade goods became signifiers of authority and prestige, individuals seeking political authority in the competitive situation were forced to manipulate the goods as part of their strategy for attaining and legitimating their own authority. The result could be intensified competition for control over trade goods and exchange networks with both European interest groups and aboriginal communities. However, the symbols of political differentiation were put out of circulation by being buried with their owners, so that succeeding leaders had to compete to acquire such goods anew. What would be the advantage of such a situation, and who would benefit from it?

If ascribed status was being reinforced via mortuary ritualism, then material goods that mark political differentiation would be expected to be passed down to individuals with ascribed rights to positions of authority. The mortuary evidence seems to indicate, however, that deceased dominant individuals took their material markers of office with them to the grave, and did *not* pass them down to their heirs. At present we have no definite archaeological evidence indicating ascribed status in 17th-century southern New England, but I suggest that future archaeological and ethnohistorical research be undertaken to evaluate the problem.

If achieved status was being reinforced via mortuary ritualism, then the removal from circulation of material markers of political status would appear to be consistent with a cultural emphasis on individual achievement and demonstrated ability. The successful leaders would have to acquire the symbols of office anew through their own personal political skills and acumen. Once an individual successfully mobilized a community of followers under his or her direction, this authority would be expensively expressed in the mortuary ritual context.

Still another problem to consider is that we do not know precisely the manner in which grave goods were deposited with the deceased during the contact period. Items in burial lots within the cemeteries investigated may represent: (1) gifts bestowed by followers upon their leaders; (2) gifts presented by kin to another deceased member; (3) the personal possessions of the deceased; or (4) some combination of all of these alternatives.

If the grave goods were given by followers to their leaders, those in the richest interments represent the domestic and personal goods acquired and contributed by common people; and those in the commoner graves may simply represent the personal goods of the deceased, or a few items donated by close kin, perhaps. However, the richest graves in the mid-17th-century cemeteries sampled contain many goods that could only have been acquired through great personal effort and political skill. Moreover, such goods are *not* among the general domestic items that are ubiquitous in the plainer graves. Therefore, it is doubtful whether such items were owned and donated by common folk to their deceased leaders only.

If grave goods represent gifts from kin to deceased relatives, the only explanation for richly furnished graves would be that these deceased individuals had wealthier relatives than did those individuals buried with few and more common grave goods. This second possibility, like the first, does not satisfactorily explain the special nature of the goods that accompany the most lavish interments—nondomestic, highly visible items that take special effort to acquire.

If grave goods were the personal possessions of the deceased, and if, as argued above, entrepreneurial individuals manipulated imported material culture as part of a strategy to consolidate a following, then lavishly furnished graves would be marking those political actors' achieved status. The common household goods included in these high–

status burials may represent either gifts by followers or kin, or they may simply be the common domestic goods of the dominant individual.

In an analysis of burial goods from a 17th-century cemetery in North Kingstown, Rhode Island (site RI-1000), Turnbaugh (1984:7, 10) takes an important step toward elucidating the nature of goods deposited with the dead by performing use-wear analysis on selected grave good classes. He was able to determine which items saw heavy use prior to burial. For example, iron hoes and European clay smoking pipes showed heavy use prior to deposition, whereas bottles and latten spoons saw little use.

SEVENTEENTH-CENTURY BURIAL RITUALISM

It is not by chance that contact-period burials like those of seventeenth-century southern New England are the context for the symbolic expression of the sociopolitical order. Death is a phenomenon that marks the boundary between one world and another. The point at which an individual passed from the unstable, competitive world of Europeans and native Americans into the domain of Cautantowwit, the creator, was chosen as the time to emphasize status. Unresolved problems, contradictions, and ambiguities in the material world of 17th-century southern New England could be resolved in ritual space.

Before discussing the mortuary remains in southern New England I review the evidence for late prehistoric burial patterns in this area in order to demonstrate the changes in mortuary ritual behavior that followed contact with Europeans.

Late Woodland Burial Patterns in Southern New England

The evidence for late prehistoric burial patterns in aboriginal southern New England is quite sparse because most sites are undated. In those burials dated with reasonable certainty to the Late Woodland period, individuals were usually buried in a flexed position, lying on their right or left side, with the head oriented toward the south or southwest (toward Cautantowwit's House), and the face toward the east (Simmons 1970; Axtell 1981:113). The deceased were buried with few, if any, grave goods (Rogers 1935; Robbins and Bullen 1945; Torrey and Bullen 1946; Bullen and Brooks 1947; Russell 1947; Robbins 1956; Coffin 1963; Stockley 1969; Schambach and Bailet 1974; Bradley et al. 1982; Taylor 1982; Turchon 1982).

Most interments are isolated features (Robbins and Bullen 1945;

Robbins 1956; Stockley 1969; Turchon 1982) or occur in small groups of one to six individuals (Torrey and Bullen 1946; Bullen and Brooks 1947; Taylor 1982). The fact that some interments have been found covered with mixed soil and refuse matter consisting of fragments of animal bone, broken shell, and other debris indicates that Late Woodland period burial pits were commonly dug through middens and even through refuse pits in soft ground (Robbins and Bullen 1945; Bullen and Brooks 1947; Russell 1947; Schambach and Bailet 1974; Turchon 1982). Later pits were dug into human interments (Stockley 1969). Thus, artifacts associated with Late Woodland interments are more often than not fill rather than deliberate grave offerings (Robbins and Bullen 1945; Bullen and Brooks 1947; Russell 1947; Robbins 1956; Coffin 1963; Schambach and Bailet 1974; Turchon 1982). In sum, Late Woodland burials appear to be predominantly isolated features in midden fill with few, if any, associated grave goods.

An exception to the above pattern is seen in the early Late Woodland ossuary at Indian Neck, Wellfleet, Massachusetts (Bradley et al. 1982:54). At least 56 individuals were represented in the excavated portion of the ossuary (Bradley et al. 1982:57), so this feature is clearly *not* an isolated interment, but a cemetery—the only Late Woodland feature of this kind reported east of New York.

With the exception of the Wellfleet ossuary, collective cemeteries are unknown in southern New England in the late prehistoric period until the protohistoric period (which I date from the end of the Late Woodland period, ca. A.D. 1550, through approximately 1630). Further, the known Late Woodland burials are accompanied by few, if any grave goods. An explanation of the lack of such goods in the Late Woodland interments may be found in Root's discussion of egalitarian relations (1983:210–12). Root argues that, in order "to perpetuate the conditions for egalitarianism, namely to keep information in circulation," artifacts that are highly visible will be curated, conserved, and exchanged, not put into burials or caches, "because both take information out of circulation and imply hoarding," which would suggest the breakdown of egalitarian conditions (Root 1983:210). "Caches or concentrations of surplus labor are not expected if hoarding of information is avoided" (Root 1983:212). Thus, if Late Woodland bands were characterized by relatively egalitarian relations, we would expect little, if any, grave furniture.

The practice of isolated interments, as opposed to burial in cemeteries, may indicate that the living group had little need for outward objectification of its collective identity. It is likely that Late Woodland bands in southern New England were characterized by varying degrees of mobility, fluid group membership, largely egalitarian social relations, and achieved, ephemeral group leadership. In such a situation there may be no stable or permanent group whose corporate, collective identity has to be reaffirmed during such crises as the death of one of its members.

Protohistoric Period Burial Patterns

Several well-documented burial sites from the late 16th century and the first decades of the 17th century shed some light on the years between the late prehistoric and the period of sustained interaction between Native Americans and Euro-American colonists (see Table 4.1 a–c).

Two changes in mortuary practices emerge during the protohistoric period: the appearance of cemeteries, as opposed to individual inhumations, and the appearance of grave goods.

In the protohistoric period, cemeteries may imply that, even prior to sustained interaction with Euro-Americans, the pressures generated by direct and indirect contacts precipitated the consolidation of a collective identity that was expressed, perhaps among other ways, by burial in collective cemeteries. In any case, the collective cemeteries that appeared during the protohistoric period persisted throughout the 17th century.

The presence of grave goods is another feature that persists and intensifies throughout the 17th century (see Turnbaugh 1984:15). Again, Root's arguments regarding the maintenance and breakdown of egalitarian conditions may account for the presence of grave goods.

> As the costs of maintaining equal access to information [egalitarianism] increase, it is expected that there should be evidence for constraints on information flow, increasing the directionality of information flows. Constraints on the movement of information may be expressed by concentrations of portable information, thereby creating competition for participation in the information pool. These processes may be manifested by burials that contain elaborate and/or large quantities of burial goods. (Root 1983:211)

Therefore, in the first decades of the contact period we may be witnessing evidence of a breakdown in egalitarian conditions as new opportunities opened for attaining political and economic leverage, instability increased with the spread of disease, and the initial interaction with colonial interest groups produced political competition and reorganization.

Two protohistoric cemeteries are of particular interest. One is a cemetery in Winthrop, Massachusetts, that dates from as early as 1580

–1634 (Willoughby 1924). Nine graves at the Winthrop cemetery contain the remains of three adult males, one female, and three children under the age of three years, as well as a group burial of an adult male, an adult female, and two children (Willoughby 1924). The ratio of preserved aboriginal grave goods to imported grave goods at Winthrop is approximately 3:2, and the children's graves are particularly well furnished with goods. The burial position of the skeletons is flexed (Willoughby 1924). The preserved imported grave goods are predominantly glass beads and sheet copper beads—decorative items; the preserved aboriginal goods include a high proportion of shell beads and utilitarian items such as bone tools and pottery (see Table 4.1a). The Titicut cemetery in Bridgewater, Massachusetts, dates from 1500–1620 (Robbins 1959). The majority of grave goods at this site, especially the imported trade goods, are associated with one adult male (see Table 4.1b).

The quantity of grave goods at the Winthrop and Titicut cemeteries increases substantially per burial over the Late Woodland period. Differential distribution of grave goods is evident throughout the burial lots; some contain many grave goods, others contain only a few. Children in the Winthrop cemetery may receive special treatment in the way of grave furniture, whereas at the Titicut cemetery one adult male is associated with the most lavishly furnished lot.

Many of the preserved imported goods in the protohistoric cemeteries are metal cutouts. These are made of imported materials (e.g., sheet brass and copper, brass and copper kettles) and are formed into aboriginal utilitarian and ornamental forms, such as projectile points and pendants (Fowler 1973:24).

Furthermore, the majority of preserved grave goods from the protohistoric cemeteries are nonutilitarian. Such items include unworked shell, perforated seeds, sharks' teeth, and polished pebbles (in the sphere of aboriginal goods), and European bells, copper discs, brass pendants, copper and brass pieces, sheet copper beads, and sheet copper tubes (in the sphere of imported goods). These nonutilitarian goods function in the realm of information exchange, broadcasting messages of social and political differentiation and affiliation (Wobst 1977).

Patterns in Mid-17th-Century Cemeteries

The following burial sites have been investigated in the light of the theoretical perspective outlined above: four small cemeteries from southeastern Massachusetts and Rhode Island (Chapin 1927); Burr's Hill, a 1655–80 cemetery in Warren, Rhode Island (Gibson 1980); and

TABLE 4.1

Seventeenth-Century Burial Sites in Southern New England

a. Proto-Historic Burials at Winthrop, Massachusetts, ca. 1580–1634 (Willoughby 1924)

#	Sex	Age	Good types	# of Abor:Imp goods	Aboriginal goods		Imported goods		
					Domestic or utilitarian	Decorative	Domestic or utilitarian	Decorative	High value
1	M	AD	3	2:1	10 bone points, 1 bone awl				iron bar
2	M	AD	2	1:1		tubular white shell beads		5 tubular glass beads	
3	M	AD	1	1:0	bone awl				
4	F	AD	2	1:1		unworked shell		20 sheet copper beads	
5	F	AD	5	3:2	potsherds	48 shell beads discoidal, mussel shell beads		30 blue and white glass beads, copper beads	
6		CH	10	5:5	potsherds, terra-cotta pipe, skin bag, coiled net bag	perforated seeds	iron adze blade, sheet copper spoon, sheet brass spoon	blue and white glass beads, 5 brass pendants	

7	CH	4	4:0	pottery vessel, pestle with animal-head shape, antler spoon	water-worn stone, with animal-head shape		

b. Proto-Historic Burials at Bridgewater, Massachusetts (Titicut Cemetery), ca. 1500–1620 (Robbins 1959)

1	M	AD	11	5:6	12 birch bark bags (one containing infant bones), quartz point	quartz crystals, hundreds of shell beads, bone beads	2 brass triangular projectile points	8 copper discs, brass pendant, copper beads, copper/brass items in birch bark bag, 4 brass/copper rectangular items
2	M	AD	0		(individual was killed by projectile point, no associated goods)		
3	M	AD	0		(individual was killed by projectile point, no associated goods)		
4	M	AD	3	3:0	large triangular projectile point, large flat stone	red ochre	
5	M	AD	6	6:0	fire-making set projectile points, clay pipe stem polished steatite fragments, bone points	shark's tooth	

TABLE 4.1—*continued*

#	Sex	Age	Good types	# of Abor:Imp goods	Aboriginal goods		Imported goods		
					Domestic or utilitarian	Decorative	Domestic or utilitarian	Decorative	High value
6	M	AD	1	1:0	steatite pipe stem	(individual was killed by projectile point)			
7	?	AD	1	0:1				2 brass discs	
8		CH	1	1:0	atlatl weight (?)				

c. Proto-Historic Burials at Ipswich and Marblehead, Massachusetts, ca. 1600s (Hadlock 1949)

Marblehead

#	Sex	Age	Good types	# of Abor:Imp goods	Aboriginal goods		Imported goods		
					Domestic or utilitarian	Decorative	Domestic or utilitarian	Decorative	High value
1	M	AD	3	2:1	bear skin pouch	whelk skin		8 rolled copper tubes	
2	F	AD	8	5:3	steatite pipe, 3 pestles, (one with animal-head shape), pottery vessel	2 shells, box-turtle shell	copper pot, ears of second copper pot	string of glass beads	
3		CH	2	0:2				bell, 2 glass beads	

Ipswich

| 1 | M | AD | 3 | 1:2 | grit-tempered potsherds | | | string of rolled copper beads, sheet copper pendant | |
| | buried with child | | | | | | | | |

d. 17-Century Burials from Rhode Island (Tiverton, Westerly, Apponaug, Charlestown) and Fall River, Massachusetts (Chapin 1927)

Tiverton, Rhode Island

1	M	AD	8	4:4	whetstone, stone axe, stone chisel	wampum	glass bottle, 6 copper spoons, Dutch clay pipes	glass beads
2	M	AD	1	0:1				7 gun barrels

Westerly, Rhode Island

1	M	AD	6	2:4	stone pipe	wampum	square glass bottle, 2 round glass bottles, copper kettle	bell

Apponaug, Rhode Island

1	M	AD	12	4:8	stone mallet, pottery projectile points, stone pipes	wampum	glass bottle, metal spoon, iron kettle fragments, spoon handle, large metal pots, iron axe head, English clay pipes	ring marked I.H.S.

TABLE 4.1—continued

#	Sex	Age	Good types	# of Abor:Imp goods	Aboriginal goods		Imported goods		
					Domestic or utilitarian	Decorative	Domestic or utilitarian	Decorative	High value
Charlestown, Rhode Island									
1	M	AD	1	0:1					sword
2	M	AD	6	2:4	pottery	wampum	spoon bowl, 3 copper kettles	blue glass tube	blue cloth
Fall River, Massachusetts									
1	M	AD	6	1:5		wampum	perforated triangular projectile point, brass plate, kettles		musket, brass cylinder belt

e. Burr's Hill, Warren, Rhode Island, ca. 1655–1680 (Gibson 1980)

#	Sex	Age	Good types	# of Abor:Imp goods	Domestic or utilitarian
1	M	AD	1	0:1	stippled cup
2	M	AD	3	0:3	copper kettle, iron kettle, glass bottle

3	M	AD	11	1:10		white shell beads	2 kettles, 9 glass bottles, scissors, 4 metal spoons	3 horseshoes	bullet mold, blanket fragments, pistol barrel, iron key, flintlock
4	M	AD	14	4:10	pestle	120 sharks' teeth, shell beads, 2 pottery beads	2 plates, glass bottle, 4 small brass kettles, brass spoon bowl, nails, bowl, iron axe	2860 glass beads iron bar	blanket
5	M	AD	10	0:10			kettle, glass bottle, 2 brass kettles, spoon	3 glass rosette buttons, medallion, 2 metal breast ornaments, glass bead belt, 6,117 glass beads	blanket fragments
6	M	AD	7	1:6		shell beads	brass kettle, brass spoon, knife, copper fishhook	glass beads, copper segment	

TABLE 4.1—continued

#	Sex	Age	Good types	# of Abor:Imp goods	Aboriginal goods		Imported goods		
					Domestic or utilitarian	Decorative	Domestic or utilitarian	Decorative	High value
7	M	AD	17	3:14		wampum, shell beads, shell tubes	10 glass bottles, Bellarmine jug, spoon bowl, spoon handle, 2 hoes, brass kettle fragments	mirror fragments, metal comb with bird ornament, copper beads, glass beads, brass wire	ring, brass key, blanket fragments
8	M	AD	4	4:0	hammer cleaver, clay pipe	claw			
9	M	AD	2	0:2			iron knife	spur	
10	M	AD	4	0:4			broken glass bottle, broken spoon handle, iron cup, fragments		blanket fragments
11	M	AD	1	0:1			clay pipe		

12	M	AD	7	0:7			3 brass kettles (damaged) bell-mouthed glass bottles, crockery cup, spoon handle	copper beads, 6 glass beads	2 metal rings
13	M	AD	6	2:4		wooden comb, periwinkle shell	brass spoon fragment, iron knife, 2 pipes		blanket fragments
14	M	AD	2	2:0		quahog shell fragment, periwinkle shell, columnella			
15	M	AD	7	3:4	2 tomahawks	periwinkle shells, 5 sharks' teeth	brass spoon, pipe stem, iron kettles, 2 iron knives		
16	M	AD	5	2:3		2 periwinkle shells, quahog shell	3 pipes		lead bullets, gun
17	M	AD	8	3:5	lithic projectile point	white shell beads, periwinkle shell, fragments	nails	brass tube, copper fragments	flints, bullet mold

TABLE 4.I—continued

#	Sex	Age	Good types	# of Abor:Imp goods	Aboriginal goods		Imported goods		
					Domestic or utilitarian	Decorative	Domestic or utilitarian	Decorative	High value
18	M	AD 2 bodies in grave	17	2:15		2 sharks' teeth white shell beads	2 copper mess kits, 2 brass kettles, iron pintle, iron-handle spike	iron rod, iron chain	sword fragments, rapier fragments, gun-lock fragments, small key, locked chest, blanket with colored stripes, 2 iron keys, powder
19	M	AD	2	1:1	stone pipe				gun
20	M	AD buried with child	17	5:12	wooden spoon fragments	wampum belt squash seeds, shell beads, periwinkle shell fragments	copper spoon fragments, pewter tankard fragments	glass beads, copper beads	fine cloth fragments, woolen cloth, ring fragments, box with metal parts, brass rings,

No.	Sex		Age	Ratio					
21	M	AD	18	4:14	bone tool, wooden spoon fragments	shell beads, shell tube	4 scissors, brass spoon, bird bottle, 9 glass bottles, brass kettle, 3 brass kettle ears, 2 iron knives	glass beads, chain, wooden shield, covered with brass/copper	sword in scabbard, flint, blanket, iron key, match lock gun, brass pistol, barrel, lock-guard, 3 ball locks
22	F	AD	2	0:2			iron hoes, iron kettle		
23	F	AD	3	0:3			glass bottle, iron hoe		iron box
24	F	AD	7	2:5	skin bag	shell beads	copper kettle, 2 iron kettles, 3 iron hoes	hair ornament, glass beads	
25	F	AD	2	1:1	2 stone pestles		3 iron hoes		
26	?	SA	1	0:1			iron knife		
27	?	SA	1	0:1			iron knife		
28	?	AD	5	1:4		78 shell beads		2 bells, metal band, 130 glass beads	3 rings
29	?	AD	3	0:3			large kettle small kettle		blanket

TABLE 4.1—*continued*

#	Sex	Age	Good types	# of Abor:Imp goods	Aboriginal goods		Imported goods		
					Domestic or utilitarian	Decorative	Domestic or utilitarian	Decorative	High value
30	?	AD	6	1:5	animal-headed pestle		broken glass bottle, iron axe, 2 iron hoes	horseshoes, iron fragments	
31	?	AD	7	2:5	pottery	shell beads	iron spoon, broken glass bottle, kettle	glass beads	blanket
32	?	AD	4	1:3		shell beads	brass kettle, nails, spoon		
33	?	AD	2	1:1		shell beads	glass bottle		
34	?	AD	1	0:1			mug		
35	?	AD	8	2:6		red ochre, periwinkle shell	spoon, brass kettle	glass beads, 2 brass bells, leather book cover fragments	iron key

f. *West Ferry Site, Conanicut Island, Jamestown, Rhode Island, ca. 1610–1660 (Simmons 1970)*

1	M	AD	6	2:4		shell discs, unfinished wampum	4 whetstones, kaolin pipe	4 glass beads, iron piece	
2	M	AD	13	3:10	wooden spoon	unfinished wampum, wampum	2 kettles, 2 knives	glass beads	key, musket, iron lock, European cloth, wooden truck, 2 lead balls, 8 powder flasks
3	M	AD	3	0:3				copper tube, copper shred, glass beads	
4	M	AD	8	1:7		polished pebble	iron projectile point, brass fishhook, iron axe heads, iron hooks, 2 iron knives, kaolin pipe	copper tube	
5	M	AD	6	1:5	quartzite point		brass projectile point, iron chisel	brass bell, brass belt hook, iron piece	
6	M	AD	7	3:4	wampum drill, whetstone	shell beads	iron nail	glass bead, iron piece	gun flint

TABLE 4.1—*continued*

#	Sex	Age	Good types	# of Abor:Imp goods	Aboriginal goods		Imported goods		
					Domestic or utilitarian	Decorative	Domestic or utilitarian	Decorative	High value
7	F	AD	2	0:2			brass kettle, iron hoe		
8	F	AD	2	0:2			2 brass kettles, 3 iron hoes		
9	F	AD	1	0:1				copper sherd	
10	F	AD	6	1:5		shell beads	brass kettle, latten spoon	iron bar, glass beads, pewter measure	
11	F	AD	1	0:1			2 iron hoes		
12	F	AD	4	2:2	3 graphite pebbles	shell beads		ear pendants, glass beads	
13	F	AD	no grave goods						
14	?	CH	4	1:3		3 shell pendants	5 latten spoons	iron buckle	brass ring
15	?	CH	2	0:2				brass hawk bell, glass beads	
16	?	CH	2	1:1	clay pot		brass spoon		
17	?	CH	4	1:3		shell beads	latten spoon	brass thimbles, brass hawk, bells	

	Sex	Age						
18	?	CH	1	1:0		shell beads		
19	?	CH	3	2:1	clay pot	clay balls	brass spoon	
20	?	CH	1	1:0	clay pot			
21	?	CH	2	1:1		shell beads	iron hatchet	
22	?	CH	4	0:4			iron axe, iron knife, iron scissors	iron box
23	?	CH	1	1:0	potsherd			

g. North Middleboro, Massachusetts (Fowler 1974)

	Sex	Age						
1	F	AD	9	3:6	2 Shantok-type pots, stone pestle	bone beads	copper kettle, 2 iron hoes, 2 knives	broken hand mirror with metal handle, glass beads, 3 buttons
2	?	CH	2	1:1	Shantok-type pot			glass beads

Note: Sex: M = male, F = female. Age: AD = adult, CH = child, SA = sub-adult. Grave goods: Abor = aboriginal, Imp = imported.

171

West Ferry, a 1620–60 cemetery on Conanicut Island in Jamestown, Rhode Island (Simmons 1970 see Table 4.1d-g).

The period of sustained interaction with colonial interest groups saw an intensification of those burial ritual trends that began in the protohistoric period. The quantity of preserved grave goods increases significantly through time; the earliest cemeteries have the fewest artifact classes, whereas the latest cemetery has the greatest number of classes (Turnbaugh 1984:15). Moreover, imports greatly exceed aboriginal goods by a ratio of roughly 3:1. The ratio of imported grave good classes to aboriginal good classes includes only preserved and reported counts and associations. Any bias in the artifact counts and associations that result from differential preservation in the archaeological record or differential recovery and reporting by investigators remains a persistent problem in this and similar analyses.

As in cemeteries of the protohistoric period, grave furniture in the mid-17th-century cemeteries sampled is differentially distributed among burial lots. This refers not only to the quantity of grave goods but, perhaps more significantly, to the quality of the imports.

Evidence from the burial data (see Table 4.1) points to repetition and redundancy in grave good associations. Thus, certain classes of imports may indeed be interpreted as signifiers that marked political differentiation. Several items recur together in only the most lavishly furnished interments, but never occur together and rarely appear alone in the plainer grave lots. These items are European clothing, imported weaponry, locks and keys (often associated with the remains of wooden boxes or chests), rings (unusual ornamental pieces), and extraordinarily large quantities of glass and shell beads. In contrast, such grave goods as kettles, spoons, glass bottles, smaller quantities of glass beads, iron hoes, knives, and iron axes occur with greater frequency and are more evenly distributed throughout the burial lots in the cemeteries sampled.

The more ubiquitous class of items includes the less perishable of the imports, but the absence of the "prestige" grouping of imports (equally as nonperishable) from the majority of grave lots, indicates a qualitative difference in the classes of goods associated with each burial lot. The more ubiquitous grouping may represent the domestic goods of a typical household, except for the glass and shell beads, which may represent items that were personally acquired and accumulated.

I will briefly describe the grave good classes that are associated with the most lavishly furnished burial lots, and that are set apart qualitatively from the household/domestic class of imported grave goods.

During the 17th century, English coats, especially those of bright colors, were presented to, or earned by, individuals who cooperated in one way or another with the colonists, colonial administrators, and missionaries. For example, a coat was given to the sagamore of Ag-awam in 1655 in order to "encourage him to know God and excite other Indians to do the like" (Pulsifer 1859:14; cf. Dillon 1980:104). In 1660 coats were bestowed upon six native leaders "to encourage them in their service to the English in governing the Pequot" (Pulsifer 1859:250; cf. Dillon 1980:104).

Roger Williams (1936:124) attests to the symbolic, as opposed to strictly utilitarian, use of imported clothing:

> Our English clothes are so strange unto them, and their bodies in-ured so to indure the weather, that when (upon gift &c.) some of them have had English cloathes, yet in a showre of raine, I have seen them rather expose their skins to the wet than their cloaths, and therefore pull them off, and keep them drie. . . . While they are amongst the English they keep on the English apparell, but pull of all, as soone as they come againe into their owne Houses and Company.

Moreover, Williams reports that if the native people he encountered could not have the color of cloth they preferred— "sad" colors of cloth, mostly deep blues and reds—"they would take their furs elsewhere to trade" (Williams 1936:160).

Peter Thomas (1979:184–85) has discussed the use of European cloth as a symbol of social prestige—of "status signaling": "What bet-ter symbol to attest to one's social prestige than a large red or blue coat which could be seen from a considerable distance?" (Thomas 1979:184). Thus, fine European clothing, a personal and highly visible article and an item that was preferentially available to leaders or to those vying for positions of leadership, may well have served to affirm the prestige of its owner, aid in the creation of that prestige, and broadcast its owner's social position.

Items of imported weaponry, such as muskets and pistols, were powerful, visible, and dangerous articles. It would be to the clear ad-vantage of leaders or entrepreneurs to monopolize access to ownership of firearms and ammunition, given the capacity for control inherent in arms. As Axtell notes, "A gun, powder, and shot could be obtained only from an English trader at considerable expense" (1981:259).

Locks and keys, often found in association with the remains of wooden or metal chests or boxes, may imply that the individuals buried with these possessed valuables to secure under lock and key. Burton (1976:93) notes that "sachems and other prominent Indians began keep-ing English chests filled with European eating utensils, clothing, and other amenities." According to Roger Williams (1936:121, quoted in

Burton 1976:93), such utensils were used only "while they are amongst the English." Lechford (1833:105), writing in 1642, notes, "He is a Sachem, whose wife hath her cleane spoons in a chest for some chiefe Englishmen, when they come on guest wise to the wigwam."

Rings are found most frequently in the most lavishly furnished interments and come in several types in the cemeteries sampled: decorative cast brass rings, possibly signet rings; Jesuit rings, originally distributed by French Jesuit missionaries; and plain brass rings, possibly made locally from brass materials (Groce 1980:109, 112). Unlike European clothing, rings are visible only from a short distance; yet rings are items of personal adornment of the sort that frequently surround individuals of high status.

The large quantities of glass and shell beads deposited with the most richly furnished grave lots indicate increasing ornamentation and marking of key individuals. Indeed, the association of rings and other highly ornamental pieces (such as medallions and pendants) with only the most lavishly furnished burials is undoubtedly part of this increasing ornamentation and marking of dominant individuals. A number of English observers have commented on the use of shell beads in the personal adornment of leaders. Roger Williams (1936:157), for example, has observed that "the princes make rich Caps and Aprons (or small breeches) of these Beads." Lechford (1833:103), too, comments on the wearing of shell beads: "Some of theire chief men goe so, with pendants of wampom, and such toyes in their ears. And some of the chiefe women, have faire bracelets, and chaines of wampom." Josselyn (1833:306), writing about his observations from 1638–73 notes: "They dril them and string them, and make many curious works with them to adorn the persons of their sagamores and principal men and young women." In short, wampum was used for ornamentation and to symbolize rank (Ceci 1977:12–14).

The repetition of European clothing, imported weaponry, locks and keys, rings, and unusually large quantities of beads in association with only the most lavishly furnished interments may indicate the use of such imports as markers of political roles in a time of instability and competition. These specific classes of artifacts are personal items, not common household articles; they are powerful items or highly visible goods, and they are items of imported material culture that took great political effort, diplomatic skills, and entrepreneurial abilities to acquire.

CONCLUSION

In nonstate, lineage-based societies, relations of inequality or differentiation can be established and maintained through repeated social acts
that involve redundant elements (Cohen 1981; Shanks and Tilley 1982;
H. Martin Wobst, personal communication). In the absence of state coercion, form tends to become redundant in order to make a message
clear to all members of a society (Cohen 1981). The context for such
clear expression of sociopolitical relations through the use of material
symbols is often ritual.

Ritual is frequently the setting for the mobilization of material
symbols; it provides a context for the repetition of symbolic forms and
acts (Donley 1982:70). Furthermore, ritual can be used by leaders (or
emergent leaders) as a power source, especially in times of sociopolitical upheaval (Laughlin and Brady 1978). Emergent leaders may institutionalize their acquired power through the use of symbolic forms in the
ritual context (Shanks and Tilley 1982:133).

To reiterate Pearson's argument, "Social advertisement in death
ritual may be expressly overt where changing relations of domination
result in status re-ordering and consolidation of new social positions"
(1982:112). Pearson refers to situations characterized by political instability and competition. The new political roles that emerge are in need
of explicit definition. Such overt expression of sociopolitical relations
occurs in contact-period cemeteries. The display of personally acquired
wealth in specific grave lots suggests that, in this particular historical
and cultural context, ritual served to clarify sociopolitical roles and to
orient social relations in a time of rapid sociopolitical change. At a time
when the political situation was in flux and in need of definition and
resolution, there was an increase in the degree of objectification of sociopolitical roles and relations (Kus 1982:51).

Although contact with colonial agents has had a differential impact
on native societies around the world, it is safe to assert that one result
of colonial penetration usually entails political restructuring of some
sort on the part of both the aboriginal and colonial communities.
Under the impact of newly introduced epidemic diseases, intensified
warfare, new trade relations, imported material culture, new opportunities for individual economic activity, missionization, and ever-
expanding settlement, social and political relations in native communities undergo rapid change. In southern New England, the pressures,
demands, and opportunities presented by the above variables created
conditions that intensified competition for positions of political-economic power, status, and authority. New avenues for attaining such positions were opened via interaction with Europeans. Display of sym-

bols of authority, most notably of certain classes of imported goods that required great political effort to acquire, was part of a political entrepreneur's strategy for validating his claims to prestige and authority.

I have argued that in the context of 17th-century native southern New England, a strategy of clearly marking political roles was expressed and objectified in mortuary ritual. The differences among burial lots in the cemeteries sampled are part of a strategy of clarifying and resolving the conflicts and contradictions surrounding political relations in a time of rapid sociopolitical change, cultural stress, and competition. It appears that, in 17th-century southern New England native mortuary ritualism, the role of material culture in the ideological representation of social relations (Hodder 1982a:10) was to clarify redundantly and expensively, political roles and relations in a time of instability.

REFERENCES CITED

Axtell, James
  1981   The European and the Indian: Essays in the Ethnohistory of Colonial North America. New York: Oxford University Press.

Binford, Lewis
  1972   Mortuary Practices: Their Study and Their Potential. In An Archaeological Perspective, ed. L. Binford, pp. 208–43. New York: Seminar Press.

Bishop, Charles
  1979   Northeastern Indian Concepts of Conservation and the Fur Trade: A Critique of Calvin Martin's Thesis. Paper presented at the 1979 annual meeting of the American Society for Ethnohistory, Albany, New York.

Bradley, James, Francis McManamom, Thomas Mahlstedt, and Ann Magennis
  1982   The Indian Neck Ossuary: A Preliminary Report. Massachusetts Archaeological Society Bulletin 43(2): 47–58.

Braithwaite, Mary
  1984   Ritual and Prestige in the Prehistory of Wessex c. 2.200–1,400 B.C: A New Dimension to the Archaeological Evidence. In Ideology, Power, and Prehistory, ed. Daniel Milles and Christopher Tilley, pp. 93–110. Cambridge: Cambridge University Press.

Braun, David
  1979   Illinois Hopewell Burial Practices and Social Organization: A Re-

examination of the Klunk-Gibson Mound Group. In *Hopewell Archaeology, The Chillicothe Conference*, ed. D. Braun and N. Greber, pp. 66–79. Kent, Ohio: Kent State University Press.

Brenner, Elise M.
1984   Strategies for Autonomy: An Analysis of Ethnic Mobilization in Seventeenth Century Southern New England. Ph.D. diss., University of Massachusetts, Amherst.

Brown, Joseph
1971   The Dimension of Status in the Burials at Spiro. In *Social Dimensions of Mortuary Practices*, ed. J. Brown, pp. 92–112. American Antiquity Memoir no. 25. Washington, D.C.

Buikstra, Jane
1976   Hopewell in the Lower Illinois Valley. *Northwestern Archaeology Program Scientific Paper* 2. Washington, D.C.

Bullen, Ripley, and Edward Brooks
1947   Three Burials at the Hughes Site, Nantucket, Massachusetts. *Massachusetts Archaeological Society Bulletin* 10(1): 14.

Burton, William
1976   Hellish Fiends and Brutish Men: Amerindian-Euroamerican Interactions in Southern New England, An Interdisciplinary Analysis, 1600–1750. Ph.D. diss., Kent State University.

Ceci, Lynn
1977   The Effect of European Contact and Trade on the Settlement Pattern of Indians in Coastal New York, 1524–1665: The Archaeological and Documentary Evidence. Ph.D. diss., City University of New York.

Chapin, Howard
1927   Indian Graves. *Rhode Island Historical Society Collections* 20: 14–32.

Coffin, Claude
1963   Connecticut Burials. *Bulletin of the Connecticut Archaeological Society* 32:61–64.

Cohen, Abner
1979   Political Symbolism. *Annual Review of Anthropology* 8: 87–114.
1981   Variables in Ethnicity. In *Ethnic Change*, ed. Charles Keyes, pp. 307–31. Seattle: University of Washington Press.

Dillon, Phyllis
1980   Trade Fabrics. In *Burr's Hill: A 17th Century Wampanoag Burial Ground in Warren, Rhode Island*, ed. S. Gibson, pp. 100–107. Haffenreffer: Brown University.

Donley, Linda
    1982   House Power: Swahili Space and Symbolic Markers. In *Symbolic and Structural Archaeology*, ed. Ian Hodder, pp. 63–73. Cambridge: Cambridge University Press.

Firth, Raymond
    1955   *The Fate of the Soul: An Interpretation of Some Primitive Concepts.* Cambridge: Cambridge University Press.

Fowler, William
    1973   Metal Cutouts of the Northeast. *Massachusetts Archaeological Society Bulletin* 34(3–4): 24–29.
    1974   Two Indian burials in North Middleboro. *Massachusetts Archaeological Society Bulletin* 35(3–4): 14–18.

Gibson, Susan (ed.)
    1980   *Burr's Hill: A 17th-Century Wampanoag Burial Ground in Warren, Rhode Island.* Providence, R.I.: Brown University.

Groce, Nora
    1980   Ornaments of Metal: Rings, Medallions, Combs, Beads, and Pendants. In *Burr's Hill: A 17th Century Wampanoag Burial Ground in Warren, Rhode Island*, ed. S. Gibson, pp. 108–17. Providence, R.I.: Brown University.

Hadlock, Wendell
    1949   Three Contact Burials from Eastern Massachusetts. *Massachusetts Archaeological Society Bulletin* 10: 63–71.

Hodder, Ian
    1982a   Theoretical Archaeology: A Reactionary View. In *Symbolic and Structural Archaeology*, ed. I. Hodder, pp. 1–16. Cambridge: Cambridge University Press.
    1982b   The Identification and Interpretation of Ranking in Prehistory: A Contextual Perspective. In *Ranking, Resource and Exchange: Aspects of the Archaeology of Early European Society*, ed. C. Renfrew and S. Shennan, pp. 150–54. Cambridge: Cambridge University Press.

Josselyn, John
    1833   An Account of Two Voyages to New England. *Massachusetts Historical Society Collections*, 3d. ser., 3: 311–54.

Kus, Susan
    1982   Matters Material and Ideal. In *Symbolic and Structural Archaeology*, ed. Ian Hodder, pp. 47–62. Cambridge: Cambridge University Press.

Laughlin, Charles, and Ivan Brady
    1978   Introduction: Diaphasis and Change in Human Populations. In *Extinction and Survival in Human Populations*, ed. Charles Laughlin and Ivan Brady, p. 1048. New York: Columbia University Press.

Lechford, Thomas
    1833   Plain Dealing: Or Newes From New England. *Massachusetts Historical Society Collections*, 3d. ser., 3: 55–128.

Martin, Clavin
    1975   Four Lives of a Micmac Pot. *Ethnohistory* 22(2): 111–33.

Pearson, Michael
    1982   Mortuary Practices, Society, and Ideology: An Ethnoarchaeological Study. In *Symbolic and Structural Archaeology*, ed. I. Hodder, pp. 99–114. Cambridge: Cambridge University Press.

Peebles, Christopher, and Susan Kus
    1977   Some Archaeological Correlates of Ranked Societies. *American Antiquity* 42: 421–28.

Pulsifer, David (ed.)
    1859   *Acts of the Commissioners of the United Colonies of New England.* 2 vols. Boston.

Ray, Arthur
    1974   *Indians in the Fur Trade: Their Role as Hunters, Trappers, and Middlemen in the Lands Southwest of Hudson Bay, 1660–1870.* Toronto: University of Toronto Press.

Robbins, Maurice
    1956   An Indian Burial at Gardner's Neck. *Massachusetts Archaeological Society Bulletin* 17(2): 22–25.
    1959   Some Indian Burials from Southwestern Massachusetts—Part 1. *Massachusetts Archaeological Society Bulletin* 20:17–32.

Robbins, Maurice, and Ripley Bullen
    1945   An Indian Burial at South Dartmouth, Massachusetts. *Massachusetts Archaeological Society Bulletin* 6(3): 44–45.

Rogers, Edward
    1935   A Double Burial from Niantic. *Bulletin of the Archaeological Society of Connecticut* 1: 2–3.

Root, Dolores
    1983   Information Exchange and the Spatial Configurations of Egalitarian Societies. In *Archaeological Hammers and Theories*, ed. J. Moore and A. Keene, pp. 193– 220. New York: Academic Press.

Royce, Anya Peterson
    1982   *Ethnic Identity: Strategies of Diversity.* Bloomington: Indiana University Press.

Russell, Lyent
    1947   Indian Burials at Niantic, Connecticut. *Bulletin of the Archaeological Society of Connecticut* 21: 39–43.

Sahlins, Marshall
    1963   Poor Man, Rich Man, Big Man, Chief: Political Types in Melanesia and Polynesia. *Comparative Studies in Sociology and History* 5: 285–303. The Hague: Mouton.

Saxe, Arthur
    1970   Social Dimensions of Mortuary Practices. Ph.D. diss., University of Michigan, Ann Arbor.

Schambach, Frank, and Howard Bailet
    1974   The Purcell Site: Evidence of a Massacre on Cape Cod. *Massachusetts Archaeological Society Bulletin* 35(3–4): 18–22.

Shanks, Michael, and C. Tilley
    1982   Ideology, Symbolic Power and Ritual Communication: A Reinterpretation of Neolithic Mortuary Practices. In *Symbolic and Structural Archaeology*, ed. I. Hodder, pp. 129–54. Cambridge: Cambridge University Press.

Silverman, Sydel
    1981   Rituals of Inequality: Stratification and Symbol in Central Italy. In *Social Inequality: Comparative and Developmental Approaches,* ed. G. D. Berreman, pp. 163–82. New York: Academic Press.

Simmons, William
    1970   *Cautantowwit's House: An Indian Burial Ground on the Island of Conanicut in Narrangansett Bay.* Providence: Brown University Press.

Stockley, Bernard
    1969   A Late Woodland Burial on Martha's Vineyard. *Massachusetts Archaeological Society Bulletin.* 31(1–2): 30–31.

Tainter, Joseph
    1977   Modeling Change in Prehistoric Social Systems. In *For Theory Building in Archaeology*, ed. L. Binford, pp. 327–51. New York: Academic Press.

Taylor, William
    1982   The Taylor Farm Site. *Massachusetts Archaeological Society Bulletin* 43(2): 40–46.

Thomas, Peter
    1979   In the Maelstrom of Change: The Indian Trade and Cultural Pro-
            cesses in the Middle Connecticut River Valley, 1635– 1665. Ph.D.
            diss., University of Massachusetts, Amherst.
    1985   Cultural Change on the Southern New England Frontier,
            1630–1665. In *Cultures in Contact: The European Impact on Native
            Cultural Institutions in Eastern North America, AD 1000–1800*, ed.
            William M. Fitzhugh, pp. 131–62. Anthropological Society of
            Washington Series. Washington, D.C.: Smithsonian Institution
            Press.

Torrey, Howard, and Ripley Bullen
    1946   A Burial Pit at Taylor Hill, Wellfleet, Massachusetts. *Massachusetts
            Archaeological Society Bulletin* 7(4): 65–67.

Trigger, Bruce
    1976   *The Children of Aataentsic I and II: A History of the Huron People to
            1660*. Montreal: McGill-Queen's University Press.

Turchon, Frederic
    1982   A Woodland Burial from Nantucket. *Massachusetts Archaeological So-
            ciety Bulletin* 43(2): 34–37.

Turnbaugh, William A.
    1984   The Material Culture of RI-1000, A Mid-17th-Century Narragan-
            sett Indian Burial Site in North Kingstown, Rhode Island. Depart-
            ment of Sociology and Anthropology, University of Rhode Island,
            Kingston, R.I.

Williams, Roger
    1936   *A Key into the Language of America*. 5th ed. Providence: Rhode Is-
            land and Providence Tercentary Commission.

Willoughby, Charles
    1924   Indian Burial Place at Winthrop, Massachusetts. *Papers of the Pea-
            body Museum of American Archaeology and Ethnology* 11: 2.

Winters, Howard
    1968   Value Systems and Trade Cycles of the Late Archaic in the Mid-
            west. In *New Perspective in Archaeology*, ed. S. Binford and L.
            Binford, pp. 175–222. New York: Aldine.

Wobst, H. Martin
    1977   Stylistic Behavior and Information Exchange. *Michigan Anthropolog-
            ical Papers* 61: 317–42.

CHAPTER 5

From Myth to History, or Why King Philip's Ghost Walks Abroad

CONSTANCE A. CROSBY

The rapid incorporation of European materials and goods into the lives of southern New England Indians presents an interesting problem. Bruce Trigger has observed that among the Huron and other Iroquoian-speaking peoples, the presence of European goods in graves was all out of proportion to their economic and technological significance (1985:161–63).[1] The same observation can be made for groups such as the Wampanoag, Massachusett, Narragansett, and Montauk in southern New England. The excavation of several cemetery sites in southern New England dating from the 1500s to the mid 1700s has revealed that both the amount and variety of grave goods increased over time. Included in the graves were European goods such as copper and brass cooking pots, iron tools, glass beads, bottles, kaolin pipes, and ceramic vessels.

The presence of European goods in graves can be interpreted in a variety of ways:[2] as part of a cultural revitalization movement fueled by the disruption of disease (Axtell 1981), as an index of increasing status differentiation (Johannsen 1980), as an index of increasing participation in capitalism (as reflected in the differential penetration of certain items of European material culture over time), or all of the above.

Yet none of these explanations alone or in combination addresses the question of how it was that European material culture could be so readily incorporated into the daily and ritual life of these Indians. What has been overlooked is the crucial role that native cosmology and ideology played in their acceptance of European ideas and material culture.

From the point of view of the southern New England Indians, certain items such as copper kettles and iron tools were placed in graves because of their spiritual power or *manit*.[3] This spiritual power could take almost any form and in the seventeenth century was observed in the following ways:

1. In its efficacy, as in the ability of an iron plough to quickly till a field for planting

2. In its strangeness or unfamiliarity, as in a ship under sail or in a windmill grinding corn

3. In its manifestation of great spiritual power, as in the power of the Englishman's god, the Bible, and reading and writing in general

4. In Hobbamock as the personification of *manit* in the many forms in which he was said to appear.

Hodder (1982a, 1982b) has called upon archaeologists to give more consideration to cosmology and cognitive systems in their effort to explain cultural change. In this chapter I explore the difficult question of *why* these southern New England groups accepted European goods and later adopted Christianity in the ways that they did. To answer this question, one must recover the meaning that these new objects and ideas had in the context of Native American life. I combine archaeological, ethnohistorical, and linguistic sources to examine the mortuary practices and the cosmology of the southern New England Indians and to document their reaction to the new concepts and goods.

These sources reveal the transformation of the southern New England Indians from a people whose sense of group identity was grounded in myth, to a people whose folklore interpreted their history for and to themselves. This transformation of their ideological base from myth to history occurred during the seventeenth century as a result of their interaction with and eventual subjugation by the English. The transformation was crucial to their continued survival in a world that was moving beyond their political, economic, and social control. The concept of *manit*, as spiritual power manifested in any form, was extended to things English. This extension enabled the Indians to value the incorporation of new things, new ideas, and even a new language, not in the Western sense of change as progress, but in their own cultural terms of change as a means to acquiring spiritual power.

Mortuary rituals and the treatment of the dead exhibit a marked degree of continuity and similarity through time and space. From the Late Archaic period into the historic period (ca. 2000 B.C. to A.D. 1700), red ocher was used in primary burials, secondary bundle, and cremation burials throughout the northeast. Cremation became the dominant form of interment in the Late Archaic and Early Woodland periods. By the Late Woodland period (ca. A.D. 1000), burial in the flexed posture had replaced cremation throughout southern New England, but most of these graves did not contain much in the way of grave goods.[4]

In this section I examine the archaeological evidence from four cemetery sites scattered across southern New England and covering the period 1500–1750. During this time, Indian groups in southern New England had intermittent and then continuous interaction with Europeans. First they encountered European diseases, then traders, fishermen and explorers, and finally settlers. The impact on Native American societies and cultures was often swift and dramatic. European material culture was increasingly incorporated into the everyday life of these societies: Copper pots replaced bark cooking vessels, iron tools replaced stone, and cloth replaced furs and leather. English missionaries worked to convert the Indians to Christianity, set up schools, and encouraged them to live as the English did, in permanent settlements.

By 1700 the effects of disease and conflict had so decimated these groups that they no longer posed any real military or political threat to the English settlements in southeastern New England. The surviving groups were placed on small reservations. Usually they were not removed from their former lands but restricted to ever smaller and smaller tracts; their cultural expressions became confined, restricted, and prescribed by circumstances and sometimes by law.

The period from 1500 to 1750 can be divided into three parts: 1500–1620, 1620–76, and 1676–1750. The years up to 1620 saw intermittent contact between Native Americans in southern New England and European explorers, traders, and fishermen. Goods and materials of European manufacture were placed in graves almost as soon as they became available, yet their presence in graves is sparse during this pre-settlement period. At the Titicut site (ca. 1500–1620) in southeastern Massachusetts, about half the graves contained grave goods, but the amount was small.[5] A kaolin pipe stem and some projectile points, beads, and spoons fashioned from copper were the only items of European origin (Robbins 1959).

During the years 1620–76 more trade items came into Indian hands through direct trade for furs and land, alliances with other sachems and the English, and the spoils of conflict. European ideas and concepts of time, history, religion, work, dress, and behavior were also introduced. At the West Ferry site, used by the Narragansett from ca. 1620 to 1660, half the undisturbed graves contained goods, which consisted of European items such as kettles, knives, hoes, axes, drills, spoons, glass beads, thimbles, bells, buckles, muskets, and cloth.[6] Overall, the graves were much more richly furnished than those at Titicut (Simmons 1970).

In the 17th century, hunting, fishing, tobacco use and production, and wampum manufacture were all considered proper labor for men, whereas women engaged in agriculture and food preparation. Simmons noted that the sexual division of labor was reflected in the types of goods associated with skeletons identified as male or female (1970:44–47). Iron hoes and most of the brass kettles were found with women. Projectile points, fishing gear, a musket, kaolin pipes, unfinished wampum and iron drills, and many of the chopping, cutting, and honing tools such as axes, knives, and whetstones were found with men. Children's graves also contained specific items, such as clay pots of native manufacture, bells, thimbles, rattles, and beads.

Simmons made good use of the available ethnographic descriptions to link the archaeological remains with the beliefs and rituals recorded for the Narragansett. These early reports made clear the significance of the body's orientation toward the southwest and the flexed position of the body: "There they say (at the South-west) is the Court of their great God Cautantowwit: At the Southwest are their Forefathers soules: to the South-west they goe themselves when they dye" (Williams [1643] 1973:86).

The link between birth and death is also seen in the archaeological evidence and historical descriptions. For example, this group believed that, just as a child enters the world head first, so at death a person should enter the afterworld head first. Furthermore, a baby was often covered with soot and grease at birth, and after a death mourners blackened their faces and bodies. The red ocher used in burials may be analogous to blood and the placenta at birth. Another link is evident in the practice of not naming a child immediately at birth and of avoiding a person's name at death. After a birth, the mother followed certain restrictions, including a period of ritual separation from the group. Similarly a period of separation was mandatory for the close relatives of the deceased, especially the surviving spouse (Simmons (1970:60–61). Generally the fit between the archaeological record and the recorded ethnographic details appears to be excellent.

The third period begins in 1676, after the King Philip's War, when the groups in southern New England were confined to reservations and lost their political, military, and economic power. Some had converted to Christianity before the war, but others—like the Narragansett and the Montauk—did not convert until the Great Awakening in the 1740s.[7] Between 1676 and 1750 they all became subject to the authority of the English colonial government.

The cemeteries at the Burr's Hill site and the Pantigo site cover the periods ca. 1650–1720 and ca. 1660–1730/50, respectively. The Burr's Hill site was used by the Wampanoag both before and after the war.[8] Two of the individuals buried at this location were extended in the English manner and the rest were flexed. All individuals were oriented with the head toward the southwest, south, or southeast (Gibson 1980:13).

What distinguishes Burr's Hill from the other three sites is the sheer volume of grave goods. Thirty-six of the 42 burials, or 86 percent, contained grave goods, in comparison with about 50 percent at the other three sites. Altogether, Burr's Hill contained three to four times the amount of goods found at West Ferry and Pantigo, respectively (Gibson 1980:14).

At the Pantigo site, 21 of the burials were flexed, whereas 17 were extended in the English manner.[9] The extended burials probably reflect the direct influence of the Christian missionaries sent among the Montauk group in the 18th century. The extended burials tended to date later than the flexed ones, but both methods may have occurred simultaneously. A higher percentage of the flexed burials (57 percent, or 12 of 20) were accompanied by grave goods than the extended burials (47 percent, or 8 out of 17).

All the graves with such items also contained evidence of personal adornment or clothing in the form of glass or pewter buttons and many varieties of glass and shell beads. As a group, the extended burials seemed slightly richer than the flexed burials. Other goods accompanying the burials included spoons, iron kettles, a clay pipe, English combed and dotted slipware, basins and dishes (of pewter, brass and iron), iron knives mounted in wood or antler handles, a thimble, and brass buckles. This site also yielded three projectile points and two native pottery vessels showing European influence in their form.

In contrast to Burr's Hill and West Ferry, the Pantigo graves did not contain any hoes (iron or otherwise), grinding equipment, fishing and hunting gear, or axes. Many of the items found in these graves appear to be associated with personal adornment, food preparation, and food consumption. Three of the graves each had a kaolin pipe, and several others had the remains of a small cloth or mat bag containing small items such as bells, rings, beads, and thimbles.

Some information on these items comes from the Reverend Sampson Occum, a Mohegan Indian and an ordained Anglican minister, who spent a number of years teaching and preaching among the Montauks in the 1750s (Kellaway 1961:190–91): "They use to bury great many things with the dead, especially things that belonged to the dead, and what they did not bury they would give away" (Occum [1761] 1809:110). This may explain why certain items of personal adornment and food consumption were included in the Pantigo graves whereas others, such as tools, were not. During the Great Awakening, many of the Montauks "renounced all their heathenish idolatry and superstition, and many of them became true christians" (Occum [1761] 1809:110). Occum may have been premature in his pronouncement since the number of extended burials with grave goods suggests that the Montauk were yielding to missionary pressure, but that they had not yet abandoned all their pre-Christian practices.

With the arrival of Europeans and their material culture, the Indians may have increased the practice of placing grave goods with the deceased. Yet the orientation of the grave southwest to northeast, the placement of the body (with the head toward the southwest), and the flexed position of the body (with the knees drawn up to the chest) were all part of a well-established pattern in the late prehistoric period. That pattern continued throughout the 17th century and well into the 18th. The new practice of including European materials in the grave and of extending the body did not conflict with the old rituals surrounding the burial of the dead.

Patterns of artifact use reflected native practices as a rule. When items such as copper kettles and iron axe heads were introduced, they were used without any regard for how these items functioned in the European context. For example, in the 1500s axe heads were first worn as pendants, until the English explained how to fix the head on a wooden handle. The first brass and copper kettles served as raw material for tubular beads, spoons, projectile points, breastplates, and so on.

By the second quarter of the 17th century, European items, although they continued to be valued as manifestations of spiritual power and as symbols of prestige, were becoming part of everyday life. Here the pattern becomes more one of replacement, with one material replacing another, one form replacing another, or both. Copper kettles continued to be valued for their metal, but they also began to replace ceramic, bark, and basket cooking vessels; wool blankets or duffils replaced skins and furs; and iron knives, axes, and hoes replaced stone forms of the same tools.

Toward the end of the 17th century, European ceramic vessels and glass bottles began to replace wooden bowls and bark containers. Commenting on the number and type of European items used in their households at the time, Daniel Gookin wrote: "Since the English came among them, some of them get tin cups and little pails, chests of wood, glass bottles, and such things they affect" (Gookin [1674] 1970:16). Such things as iron tools, muskets, and metal cooking pots were improvements over the indigenous technologies. But there was no advantage in other cases. For example, the cloth that replaced leather wore out more quickly and soiled more easily.

COSMOLOGY

Cautantowwit, the great god of the southwest among the Narragansett, was variously known among the Massachusett and Wampanoag as Kiehtan, Kytan, or Ketan, and among the Montauk as Cauhlantoowut. (Winslow [1624] 1832:91; Morton [1632] 1838:35; Wood [1638] 1967:92; Occum [1761] 1809:109).[10] Although Cautantowwit was one god among the many (upward of 37) honored by the southern New England groups, he was the one accorded the greatest power and authority and he was considered the Creator. He was the source of agriculture in the form of corn, beans, and squash and the source of the warm winds and gentle rains that made all things grow. He had power over life and death; mortal wounds and disease resulted from his anger and whim. The souls of the dead traveled to the southwest, where they were allowed to enter the house of Cautantowwit to dwell with the ancestors. There, life continued, free from want and with all one's friends and relatives together once again (Winslow [1624] 1832:91–92; Morton [1632] 1838:34–35; Williams [1643] 1973:161, 164, 190, 194, 197; Van der Donck [1656] 1841:215, 251; Occum [1761] 1809:108–10). Roger Williams provides the best contemporary description.

> Lastly, it is famous that the Southwest *(Sowaniu)* is the great Subject of their discourse. From thence their *Traditions*. There they say (at the *South-west*) is the Court of their *great God Cautantowwit*: At *the South-west* are their *Forefathers* soules: *to the South-west* they goe themselves when they dye; From the *South-west* came their *Corne*, and Beans out of their Great *God Cautantowwits* field: And indeed the further *Northward* and *Westward* from us their Corne will not grow, but to the *Southward* better and better. (Williams [1643] 1973:86)

Hobbamock (also known as Hobbamoqui, Abamocho, and Cheepi), the other principal deity, was very much involved in people's daily lives. He was identified in 17th-century accounts as the source of personal spiritual power and knowledge and he was the spiritual force behind the power of the powwows (shamans). Hobbamock was not always a benevolent deity, and the power of the powwows to heal was also a power to hurt or injure. Hobbamock was blamed for sickness and misfortune, and powwows would seek Hobbamock's aid in curing the sick and healing the wounded. Hobbamock could appear to people in dreams and waking visions, taking a variety of forms, both human and animal. In contrast, Cautantowwit did not appear to people in dreams or visions and he remained remote and distant from everyday life. Yet he could be placated with prayers and he was honored with feasts and celebrations. The English quickly drew parallels between the Christian god and Cautantowwit on the one hand, and Satan or the Devil and Hobbamock on the other.[11]

The souls or spirits of the wicked were turned away from Cautantowwit and bid *quachet*, "walk abroad." They belonged to Hobbamock, who resided to the east or northeast and who often directed them to plague the living (Winslow [1624] 1832:91–2; Wood [1638] 1967:105; Van der Donck [1656] 1841:215; Williams [1643] 1973:194). Perhaps the strong taboo against uttering the name of the deceased came from the fear that using the deceased's personal name would call him or her back to the world of the living. The spirits of the dead were feared and respected because of the belief in their power to cause sickness or bring misfortune.

The themes of separation, transition, and incorporation—which are typically found in most life-crisis rituals, according to van Gennep (1960)—run through many of the symbolic schemes expressed in the mortuary rituals. The dead were physically and spiritually separated from the living by burial and mourning rituals.[12] The soul of the deceased traveled to Cautantowwit's house, joining family and friends and making the web of social relationships whole once again. At the same time, the individual's identity and personality were lost to the living, and the dead person was never spoken of by name again. The idea of separation was also expressed in the words used to refer to the dead (*chepeck, chippeu, chepassotam,* and *chepasquaw*), the east and northeast winds (*wutchepwash* and *chepewssin*) and the name Cheepi. All derived from the same root, *chepe,* denoting separation.[13]

The corpse existed in a transitional or liminal state between the world of the living and the world of the gods and spirits. The two words for corpse, *ahchunk* and *napuk*, expressed this sense of a thing between two worlds. A corpse had not been buried nor had the soul begun its journey to the southwest, yet the breath of life was gone (Trumbull 1903:238). Other words (*mauchautom* and *kitonckquei*) that referred to the dead person emphasized the departure of the life force, the second form of the soul that resided in the chest or heart.[14] All these terms convey either a sense of something leaving, going, departing, or something separate and apart.

To summarize, there was a continuous flow between the world of the living and the land of Cautantowwit. Souls went to the southwest and dwelt there together as forefathers or ancestors. Cautantowwit was the source of traditional authority voiced by the old men who taught the younger ones. The physical and the spiritual were joined in a dynamic relationship through the mediation of corn and earth-mother.[15] According to their traditions, the body was planted in the ground from whence corn and other plants sprang, and the soul traveled to the southwest from whence corn originated. The body entered the womb of earth-mother via the grave and enriched her, bringing forth more corn, while the soul returned to the southwest and joined Cautantowwit and the ancestors, thus enriching the group's tradition. Thus the relationship between birth and death was a cycle of continuous renewal for both the community of the living and the community of the ancestors in Cautantowwit's house.

The relationship between the sociopolitical structure and cosmology of southern New England Indians appears to fit the structural-functionalist model in which the traditional political leaders (sachems) and the traditional religious leaders (powwows) had their counterparts in the cosmological systems. Thus cosmology appears to maintain the status quo by legitimating the power and authority of the sachems. Cautantowwit was to the sachems as Hobbamock was to the powwows, and just as Cautantowwit was more powerful than Hobbamock, so the sachems had control over the powwows.

Yet the status quo was not maintained, and as the power and authority of the sachems diminished in the face of superior English military force and economic position, so did the faith in Cautantowwit as the principal god. The English god was increasingly acknowledged in the second half of the 17th century as the more powerful. Regard for the powwows also diminished as their efforts to combat the European disease epidemics and conduct spiritual warfare against the English failed. In addition, *powwowing*—the performance of curing, conjuring, or divining rituals by powwows—was eventually outlawed by the English.

Durkheim's observation that what people worshiped as a deity or deities was "only the figurative expression of the society," and the power attributed to divine beings and things sacred was "the moral power" of society itself, can be used to explore the interdependence between the cosmology and the social structure in these Indian groups (1965:257–258).

In other words, people invent their Gods and their cosmology in society's own image; each different type of social organization has its corresponding form of religious ideology. It follows that if the underlying structure of society changes, then the religious ideology should also change. This is exactly the case among the Indian groups in southern New England at the end of the 17th century.

Robinson et al. (1985) state in their discussion of a 17th-century Narragansett cemetery (RI-1000) that the inclusion of European goods in graves, along with the increased attention devoted to the burial of the dead (especially the arrangement of the graves in close rows), "was an expression of group solidarity and cohesiveness" directed against European encroachment (p. 109). At the same time the recent intensification of mortuary practices was the means by which "new social values were incorporated and rationalized" (p. 124).

We have seen how 17th-century mortuary practices appeared to celebrate group solidarity and the renewal of the social order. Yet we also see a growing emphasis on the individual, evidenced by both the amount and the increasingly personal nature (especially among the Montauk) of the goods buried with the dead. Thus even as religion appeared to uphold the existing structures, it also served as a vehicle for incorporating change and transforming the ideology of the group.

Whereas the power and authority of the traditional leaders waned throughout the 17th and 18th centuries, the important role and function of the ancestors as bearers of tradition did not disappear, but were transformed, reflecting the enhanced importance of the individual relative to the group. Throughout the 17th century, people acquired and used European goods and knowledge, namely Christianity and literacy, to negotiate their social position within their own groups. The increased emphasis on the individual in mortuary practices directly parallels the growing opportunities for wealth and autonomy for certain individuals in 17th-century Indian societies. The ancestors no longer dwell far off to the southwest, but take up residence in the nearby landscape of each group. Personal encounters with these spirits of the dead take on additional significance. This transformation and the roles played by *Manit* and folklore are developed in the remainder of the chapter.

MANIT AND MATERIAL CULTURE

In this section I discuss how the southern New England Indians extended the concept of *manit*—namely, spiritual power that could be manifested in any form—to cover everything from iron hoes to Puritan Christianity. The concept of *manit* was crucial to the successful transformation of the ideology of southern New England Indians in the 17th century. The placing of European materials in graves, the adoption of Christianity, the learning of a new language, and other changes in everyday life take on new meaning when viewed as a means to acquiring greater spiritual power. The different ways in which the Indians used European material culture in ritual contexts represented attempts to control or capture the *manit* or spiritual power inherent in them, and thereby control both the Europeans and their diseases. To the Indians, the more powerful technology of the English and their resistance to disease meant that the English and their god possessed greater *manit* than the Indians and their gods. This paralleled the changing political situation in the 17th century, as the balance of power (political, economic, and spiritual) shifted from the southern New England Indians to the English colonists.

The names of all persons, places, and things conveyed meaning, and it was through the naming of a thing that its spiritual power, its *manit* quality, could be invoked. Personal names were given and changed at pivotal points in one's life, such as coming of age or after experiencing some significant event or performing a certain deed (Winslow [1624] 1832:97; Occum [1761] 1809:108). Experience Mayhew wrote in a letter in 1722 that the traditional names of Christian Indians on Martha's Vineyard were "generally very significant, by far more so than those of the English. . . . For with them the way was to call every place person and thing by a name taken from something remarkable in it or attending of it" (quoted in Bragdon 1981:73). Many of the Christian converts were known by both English or biblical names and their traditional names.

Manit as spiritual power was observed as a quality or an ability expressed in the appearance, behavior, or strangeness of animals, plants, people, and things, both Indian and European. However, many 17th-century observers such as Roger Williams or John Eliot simply interpreted *manit* or *manitou* to be equivalent to "God" or "god":[16]

> Besides there is a generall Custome amongst them [the Narragansett], at the apprehension of any Excellency in Men, Women, Birds, Beasts, Fish, &c. to cry out, *Manittoo,* that is, it is a God, as thus if they see one man excell others in Wisdome, Valour, strength, Activity &c. they cry out *Manitoo;* a God: and therefore when they talke amongst themselves of the *English* ships, and great buildings, of the plowing of their Fields, and especially of Bookes

and Letters, they will end thus: *Mannittowock* They are
Gods: *Cummanittoo,* you are a God, (Williams [1643] 1973:191)

In discussing religion with the Narragansett, Williams found that they
believed "1. That God is. 2. That hee is a rewarder of all them that diligently seek him" ([1643] 1973:189). Like many of his contemporaries,
Williams took *manit* to refer to "God," whereas it actually denoted a
power beyond and higher than that of humans—spiritual power. Thus
we can rephrase the second statement as follows: If one diligently seeks
out and acquires *manit,* one will be rewarded by its benefits.

Trumbull (1870) attempted to shed light on the etymology of
manit but was careful not to go beyond literal meanings and associations. Nor did he speculate much on its metaphoric extensions and applications. To better understand how these southern New England
groups applied *manit* to define their world and give meaning to European material culture and Puritan Christianity, we return to the ethnohistorical record for evidence.

Several 17th-century observers noted the attitude of the Indians to
European goods. Their accounts clearly show how the Indians perceived these objects in their own terms, and how they readily extended
the concept of *manit* to items that were previously unknown to them.
The Indians remarked, for example, on the power manifested in a
plow, which could turn over much more ground than their shell hoes.
They acknowledged the greater spiritual power of the English god as
manifested in certain signs and small miracles, usually pertaining to disease and the weather. Furthermore, they held books and other written
texts in some esteem since the power of the English, particularly with
regard to religion, seemed to come from such items. According to William Wood,

> These *Indians* being strangers to Arts and Sciences, and being un-
> acquainted with the inventions that are common to a civilized peo-
> ple, are ravisht with admiration at the first view of any such
> sight:They tooke the first Ship they saw for a walking Iland, the
> Mast to be a Tree, the Saile white Clouds, and the discharging of
> Ordinance for Lightning and Thunder, which did much trouble
> them, . . . They doe much extoll and wonder at the *English* for
> their strange Inventions, especially for a Wind-mill, which in their
> esteeme was little lesse than the worlds wonder, for the
> strangenesse of his whisking motion, and the sharpe teeth biting
> the corne (as they terme it) into such small peeces; . . . the *Indians*
> seeing the plow teare up more ground in a day, that their Clamme
> shels could scrape up in a month, desired to see the workmanship

of it, and viewing well the coulter and share, perceiving it to be
iron, told the plow-man, hee was almost *Abamocho* [Hobbamock],
almost as cunning as the Devill; but the fresh supplies of new and
strange objects hath lessen'd their admiration, and quickened their
inventions, and desire of practicing such things as they see. ([1638]
1967:87–88)

Wood remarked on the quick-wittedness and dexterity of the Indian
men and noted that they rapidly learned to use English versions of such
tools as the ax and hatchet. He speculated that "they would soon learne
any mechanicall trades" and therefore benefit the English as well as
themselves "if they were not strongly fettered in the chaines of idle-
nesse" ([1638] 1967:88).

Roger Williams noted that the Narragansett, too, were quick to
adopt English tools such as iron drills to make wampum and iron axes
to fell trees, yet "some old & poore women (fearfull to leave the old tradition)" continued to use wooden or shell hoes (Williams[1643]
1973:213). Similarly, Daniel Gookin observed, "They delight much in
having and using knives, combs, scissors, hatchets, hoes, guns, needles,
awls, looking glasses, and such like necessaries, which they purchase of
the English and Dutch with their peague, and then sell them their
peltry for their wompeague" ([1674] 1970:18). In general, the Indians
raised few objections to items that afforded some savings in labor or effort or that simply replaced indigenous materials or forms with European ones.

European goods were also readily incorporated into religious and
curing rituals with seemingly little or no anxiety over their presence
and place in the spiritual as well as the material realm. The Narragansett sacrifices, which comprised long and elaborate ceremonies to Cautantowwit, included items such as "kettles, skins, hatchets, beads,
knives, etc all which are cast by the priests into a great fire. To this of-
fering every man bringeth freely and the more he is known to bring,
hath the better esteem of all men" (Winslow [1624] 1832:93–94). The
Wampanoag told Winslow that they approved of this behavior and
hoped that their sachems would do likewise "because the plague hath
not reigned at Nanohigganset [Narragansett] as at other places about
them, they attribute to this custom there used" (p.94).

A powwow on Martha's Vineyard described his *pawwawnomas* or
"guardian spirits" as possessing him "from the crowne of the head to
the soal of the foot . . . not onely in the shape of living creatures, as
Fowls, Fishes, and creeping things, but Brasse, Iron, and Stone" (Whitfield [1652] 1834:187). The association of brass, iron, and stone with
spiritual power that could be employed by a powwow shows that the

concept of *manit* was extended to include items of European origin. Also powwows clearly had the ability to call upon and control such *manit* for their own purposes.

However, this control over the *manit* of English things did not extend to the *manit* of the English themselves or their spirits. Hobbamock in his various forms did not appear when English persons were present, and the English testified that they never saw any of these spirits either (Winslow [1624] 1832:93). The powwows complained of their inability to harm or control the English by their witchcraft and conjuring, although they tried. A powwow who cured an Indian woman warned her that the spirit of a drowned Englishman, who was the cause of her illness, might return since he (the powwow) was not able to contain the "English Spirit" long (Mayhew 1694:15). These accounts reflect the growing doubts of the Indians regarding the efficacy and power of their rituals and beliefs to control their world in the face of mounting evidence that there existed a more powerful form of *manit,* the "Englishman's god."

> They acknowledge the power of the *Englishmans* God, as they call, him, because they could never yet have power by their conjurations to damnifie the *English* either in body or goods; and besides, they say hee is a good God that sends them so many good things, so much good corne, so many cattell, temperate raines, faire seasons, which they likewise are the better for since the arrivall of the *English.* (Wood [1638] 1967:94)

When the Narragansett compared the power of their own Cautantowwit to create things with the power of the English god, they conceded, after a little persuasion by Williams, "that the *God* that made *English* men is a greater *God,* because Hee hath so richly endowed the *English* above *themselves*" with things like "Clothes, Books, [and] Letters" which "their fathers never had" (Williams [1643] 1973:85).

Recently some groups of Massachusett and Wampanoag had been decimated by disease with one result being the loss of considerable cultural knowledge. This experience had a profound impact on the native cosmology. For example, the Indians told stories about once knowing God some time in the past, forgetting him, and now finding him again. Such stories may represent an attempt to reconcile the conversion to Christianity with their own past (Simmons 1986:67), or they may be seen as the last attempt to employ myth as precedent for change before the whole mythic structure collapsed. Consider the response of the Cape Cod Wampanoag to John Eliot's preaching in the late 1640s about the Ten Commandments and the creation of the world by God: "They had heard some old men who were now dead, to say the same things, since whose death there hath been no remembrance or knowledge of them among the *Indians* untill now they heare of them againe." (Shepard [1648] 1834:43). The emphasis Puritan missionaries placed on the contents of the Bible as preserved cultural knowledge impressed most Indian groups, whether they were sympathetic to Christianity or not.

Even powwows, who owed their allegiance to Hobbamock and drew strength and power from the various spirits under his control, acknowledged that their spiritual power was no match for the English *manit*. The conversion of Hiacooms, a man of low status living on Martha's Vineyard, illustrates this point. He was the first successful convert, and the sachems and powwows were so angered by his act that at a public confrontation they threatened to kill Hiacooms with their "Witchcraft." Hiacooms responded before the assembly that "the god they Worrshipped had *great Power,* but *Limited,* and was Subservient to the God he now had chosen" (Mayhew 1694:18). Some time later, however, one of the powwows whose spirit helper appeared to him in the form of a snake, and who had tried to conjure Hiacooms, confessed that he and the others had failed to harm Hiacooms and therefore "he resolved to worship the *true God,* from which time during *Seven years,* the said Snake gave him great disturbance, but that he never after his Praying to God in Christ ever imployed that said *Snake* in any thing, which about that time ceased to appear to him" (Mayhew 1694:44).

The growing doubts also extended to the authority of the "forefathers," the voice of tradition, as Williams attests. The sachem Miantunnomu of the Narragansett had heard Roger Williams preach that after death souls went either to heaven or hell and not to the southwest. The sachem debated this notion with another Indian:

> The *Sachim* answered, But how doe you know your selfe, that your soules goe to the *Southwest;* did you ever see a soule goe thither?

> The *Native* replyed; When did he (naming [Williams]) see a soule goe to Heaven or Hell?

> The *Sachim* againe replied: He hath books and writings, and one which God himselfe made, concerning mens souls, and therefore may well know more than wee that have none, but take all upon trust from our forefathers. (Williams [1643] 1973:198–199)

The reluctance and ambivalence felt by these people when they saw their traditional beliefs and old way of life challenged can be illustrated by two instances of group hysteria recorded by the English. In 1638 the

Massachusett who resided with the English in their towns "were much frightened with Hobbamock (as they call the devil) appearing to them in divers shapes, and persuading them to forsake the English and not to come at the assemblies nor to learn to read" (Winthrop, quoted in Bragdon 1981:42).

In 1643 a similar phenomenon was observed among the inhabitants of Martha's Vineyard who had just recently been exposed to systematic missionizing efforts:

> They ran up and down as if delerious, till they could run no longer; they would make their faces as black as a Coal and snatch up any weapon, as tho they would do Mischief with it, and speak great swelling words, but yet they did no Harm. Many of these *Indians* were by the *English* seen in this Condition. Now this and all other Calamities which the *Indians* were under, they generally then attributed to the departure of some of them from their own heathenish Ways and Customs. (Mayhew 1727:3)

However, not all powwows were hostile or antagonistic toward the inroads Christianity was making. The conversion to Christianity and acceptance of the Englishman's god did not conflict with their own belief system, which already included many gods and spirits of varying abilities and strengths. For example, although the wife of a former powwow on Martha's Vineyard was counted a true Christian convert her husband "declared that he could not blame her, for that she Served a God that was above *his;* but that as to himself, his gods continued kindness, obliged him not to forsake his Service" (Mayhew 1694: 12–13). Thus, from the Indian point of view, belief in the Englishman's god, the practice of Christian prayer, keeping the Sabbath, and so on did not conflict with the Indian categories for religious behavior.

Although the Indians failed to control the English through ritual and spiritual means (or any other means), they were more successful in resisting the English on an ideological level. By extending *manit* to English material culture and ideas, these southern New England groups were able to incorporate the new with the old and transform their ideological base from one centered around myth to one grounded in the landscape and historical time.

FROM MYTH TO HISTORY

By the close of the 17th century, the larger cultural continuum embracing all of these southern New England groups and beyond had been broken, and their political power and autonomy, even over their own people, were in decline. Although sachems continued to rule in hereditary fashion among the Narragansett and Gay Head Wampanoag well into the 1700s, their power and authority were severely restricted and even questioned by their own people at times. The powwows, whose power derived from a personal relationship with Hobbamock, also disappeared under the direct attack of Christian missionaries and colonial authorities. Their cultures became increasingly confined and defined in English terms.

At the same time the seat of their cultural power and authority was transformed and transferred from a remote, distant and far-off place and personage—Cautantowwit's House—to the local landscape, where real people—one's ancestors—were born, lived, and died. The voice of tradition became embodied in the visitation of ghosts of ancestors admonishing the living who had strayed in some way from the proper path.

The practice of burying a person's possessions with the dead, which continued at least into the first half of the 18th century, was probably the key to the transformation of the role played by the spirits of the dead. In the long run, the practice of including items belonging to the individual, and items representative of a person's wealth or status, helped to create a more personalized and personified link between the living and the dead. This ran counter to the attempts of the Indians to celebrate social solidarity through mortuary ritual and maintain a clear boundary between the world of the living and the world of the dead.

Tradition, its spiritual and cultural power, became localized and embedded in a particular landscape as each group was confined to separate reservations and no longer resided contiguously. The groups of Narragansett, Mohegan-Pequot, Montauk, Massachusett, and Wampanoag became bounded geographically as well as socially; they were isolated and separate from English society, yet lived under colonial control. The surviving enclaves became more and more enmeshed in the political, social, and economic structures of the larger society over time. (Much more could be said regarding the social and political implications of this process, but that goes beyond the bounds of the present chapter.) Yet in each locale, the land becomes saturated with meaning and spiritual power, *manit*. Each group develops its own folklore which strengthens and deepens the relationship between the local landscape and *manit*. The land itself becomes the most potent and enduring symbol of and metaphor for both group and personal identities.

William Simmons (1986) recently published an extensive collection of southern New England Indian folklore, oral and written, from the period 1620–1984. This material gave him a unique opportunity to study how folklore responds to changing conditions over time. He concludes that "folklore, as we have seen in the New England texts, is the major vehicle for expressing and perpetuating a persistent Indian identity, and the Indians' claim to being a people is more strongly proclaimed in folklore than in any other aspect of their culture" (1986:267).

Most of the folklore consists of memorates and legends. Legends serve to link people with their past and their environment, grounding them in the present context but providing a bridge to the past. In addition, legends remain loosely structured and improvisational and thus are sensitive and responsive to historical and social change (Simmons 1986:7). Memorate, "a concrete account of a personal encounter with the supernatural," often served to sanction someone who had violated traditional norms and values (Simmons 1986:6).

In contrast to legends and memorates, myths function as "the authority for existing social institutions, religious beliefs and rituals" (Simmons 1986:7). Simmons notes, however, that myth is almost totally absent from the texts he collected "for although early Europeans recorded bits of indigenous mythology, Christianity swept this genre away, or rather, replaced it with Christianity's own biblical equivalents" (Simmons 1986:7). However, he fails to explain why myth did not continue to proliferate in the way that legends and memorates did. Some groups, notably the Narragansett, did not adopt Christianity until the 1740s, more than a hundred years after they first heard Roger Williams's discourse on the Gospel. The answer is that these people experienced a transition from myth time to historical time in the 17th century.

The folklore collected by Simmons contains numerous accounts of individual encounters with spirits, ghosts, and supernatural beings. King Philip's ghost walks abroad in the vicinity of where his head is traditionally said to be buried.[17] The spirits of the ancestors grow *very* restless: They continue to function as the keepers and bearers of tradition, but they now appear to anyone and everyone. They no longer live far off in a remote place in myth time, unseen and unheard except through the authority offered by the traditional political and religious leaders such as sachems, powwows, and pnieses. The ancestors now dwell nearby in the local landscape, in the land itself, which becomes a metaphor for group identity even after the land is sold off, as reflected in the abundant place names and rich folklore that incorporate them. The living and the dead now share the same restricted space and time —historical time. Simmons writes:

Former generations speak in folklore through anonymous spirits of
the dead, through ghosts of remembered persons, and even
through purely legendary figures. . . . Legends about ghostly pres-
ences in spruce trees, rhododendrons, rock formations, corn
fields, and streams all speak of historical injustices to earlier generations. The ghosts that lived around taverns or memorials urged
the living to respect custom as their predecessors had or else lose
their luck. Persons whose last wishes are ignored return to chide
relatives for neglecting their obligations. The dead appear every-
where to tell the living who they were and how their descendants
should behave toward one another in the present. Even domestic
dogs, cats, horses, and cattle, which also participate in human social life, were believed to be attuned to the ancestral presence. To
acknowledge the ghosts and other legendary figures known to
one's parents and grandparents connects the living and the dead
and affirms one's commitment . . . to the collective, symbolic life
of the group. (1986:267)

Although Simmons is writing about the present-day Narragansett,
Mohegan-Pequot, Wampanoag at Mashpee and Gay Head and several
other smaller groups, his words apply to the late 17th and early 18th
century as well. Many of these stories express ambivalence, conflict,
and uncertainty and reflect the tenuous and marginal social position of
these groups. Many of the legends and stories were first recorded in the
1600s and early 1700s, and since then legend and memorate have grown
increasingly important as they have come to supplant the ideological
functions of myth and to embody the Indian's ability to change.

Rather than being an iron hand that grips their identity regardless
of historical circumstances, the ancestral voice in folklore imparts a
group spirit, an awareness on the part of the living that they belong to a particular people who have survived dramatic obstacles
and will continue to do so, even though specific areas of indigenous custom are lost and replaced with alien practice and belief.
(Simmons 1986:268)

There is a long and strong tradition among these southern New England groups of a willingness and ability to adapt and change (see, for
example, Bragdon 1981; Salisbury 1982; and Simmons 1986). Bragdon
writes that changes in political organization, religious belief and practice, land tenure, inheritance, and the adoption of literacy, among other
things, "included many instances of reinterpretation of elements

adopted from English culture, as well as examples of the syncretic use of old and new traits and ideas." (1981:161).

These groups were able to reformulate their ideologies of identity and adjust to their changed and changing circumstances. They incorporated new systems of belief, new forms of social organization, new economic modes of production, new forms of communication, and new material culture, but on their own terms. Conversion and acceptance of Christianity sooner or later formed a keystone of their cultural transformation and transition into the European world.

CONCLUSION

The incorporation of European material culture into mortuary ritual, exchange networks, and daily life during the 17th century contributed to the growing importance and autonomy of individuals, often at the expense of group interests. Although the concept of *manit* was a cultural value shared by the whole group, in practice it enabled and encouraged people to make their own choices and decisions regarding the acceptance or rejection of change. In most instances people opted for the new or novel, as acquisition of European material culture, literacy, and religious knowledge came to represent access to the greater spiritual power the Indians saw as inherent in these things.

According to Roy Wagner (1981), anthropologists use their concept of culture as their way of coping with the experience of culture shock suffered while doing fieldwork. In the process of coming to grips with his or her situation, through interviewing people, taking notes, making kinship charts, and so on, the anthropologist "invents" the native's culture. The Melanesian cargo cults are an analogous phenomenon; they are the Melanesian means of comprehending the sudden and unexplained appearances and disappearances of Europeans and their incredible material wealth (1981:31–34).

Following Wagner's line of reasoning, I would like to suggest that the southern New England Indians extended their concept of *manit* to accomplish the same end—to give meaning to the European presence and make sensible their material culture and ideas. *Manit* acted as a metaphor providing the southern New England Indians with a logic they could use to create bridges of understanding and to link two disparate cultures and worldviews, and in the process, transform themselves and their ideology. They did not simply become Puritans or Yankees of a different color.

ACKNOWLEDGMENTS

I wish to thank the following people for their comments, suggestions, encouragement, and support: Mark Leone, William Simmons, Parker Potter, Robert and Gundel Bowen, and Dirk Bavendamm. I owe a special debt of gratitude to William Simmons for both his excellent teaching and for the use of materials from his book *The Spirit of the New England Tribes,* without which this paper would not have been possible.

NOTES

1. I wish to thank Mark Leone for drawing my attention to Trigger's recent work and his observation regarding the rapid acceptance of European material culture among the Huron.

2. Salisbury appears to misinterpret the absence of grave goods from some early 17th-century burials in the vicinity of Boston and a description of the unburied dead after the severe epidemic that struck the Wampanoag and Massachusett ca. 1617–19 as evidence that the Indians had "further alienated themselves from important sources of supernatural power by abandoning their burial rituals" (1982:106). There is no doubt that this epidemic and ones that followed had a demoralizing and disruptive effect, yet the pattern from the sites discussed in this chapter clearly shows that increasing numbers of grave goods were the rule rather than the exception throughout the 17th and into the 18th century.

3. I owe my initial insight to the reading of Salisbury's excellent work on the interaction between Indians and the English, viewed through their conflicting world views. He defines *manitou* as the

> manifestation of spiritual power, a manifestation that could occur in almost any form. . . . It enabled its adherents to accommodate traditional religion to changing circumstances. . . . Rather than rejecting that which was unknown, they welcomed it and sought to come to terms with it. Thus Algonquian horticulturalists had made the transition from a hunting-oriented culture without experiencing a radical discontinuity in world-view, and thus hunters and farmers alike would seek in the same way to accommodate themselves to the more abrupt changes accompanying European colonization. (1982:39)

However, Salisbury fails to recognize its real potential, namely, as the key to understanding how these groups—which were decimated by disease and warfare, confined to ever smaller reservations, heavily indoctrinated and inundated with European material culture and ideological concepts—managed to emerge, redefine themselves, and persist to the present day.

4. For a discussion of mortuary ritual in southern New England in prehistoric times see Snow (1980) and Gibson (1980).

5. At the Titicut site in Bridgewater, Massachusetts, 23 burials representing 26

individuals were excavated by members of the Massachusetts Archaeological Society under the direction of Dr. Maurice Robbins (1959). Information from Robbins' report on 19 graves representing 23 individuals was used for this chapter. Robbins's date of 1500–1620 is based on circumstantial historical evidence that the site was abandoned before the arrival of the Pilgrims in 1620 and on the presence of some European materials such as copper and the pipe stem.

6. The West Ferry site in Jamestown, Rhode Island, is on Conanicut Island in Narragansett Bay. In 1966–67, controlled excavations were carried out under the direction of Dr. William S. Simmons on behalf of the town (Simmons 1970). Tradition places the summer village of the Narragansett sachem Canonicus on the island in the early 1600s. In 1637 Roger Williams and Henry Vane purchased rights to cut hay and graze sheep on the island from Canonicus and Miantunnomu, the joint sachems of the Narragansett. Later the English rights to the island were disputed and the island was repurchased in 1660 by the English. The final agreements stipulated that the remaining Narragansett were to leave the island, thus providing a possible terminus ante quem for the use of the cemetery. After the King Philip's War, historic records again show some Indian occupation of the island (Simmons 1970:35–39).

7. See Bowden (1981:96–133) for a useful overview of Protestant missions in the northeast. In addition, a number of researchers discuss conversion on a group-by-group basis in southern New England. See, for example, Simmons (1983) on the Narragansett conversion during the Great Awakening, Ronda (1981) and Simmons (1979) on the conversion of the Martha's Vineyard groups in the 17th century, and Morrison (1974) and Brenner (1980) on the Massachusetts praying towns.

8. The Burr's Hill site was located in Warren, Rhode Island, on a gravel bank above the Warren River. Sowwams, the main village of the Wampanoag sachem Massasoit, was also in Warren. Massasoit's son Metacomet, better known as King Philip, had his main village, Paukunnawkett, to the south, on Mount Hope Neck in Bristol, Rhode Island. The cemetery may have been used by both villages. The European items found in the graves indicate that the cemetery was in use from ca. 1650 to 1720. Some of the Wampanoag who survived the King Philp's War were living near Burr's Hill in the late 1600s and early 1700s.

9. The Pantigo site was located 2 miles east of Easthampton on the southern shore of Long Island. The site was excavated in 1917 by archaeologists from the Museum of the American Indian (Saville 1920: 75). Saville concludes that the cemetery was begun ca. 1660 during a smallpox outbreak among the Montauk (1920:71–72). Two English coins, both dated 1728 and recovered from the same grave, provide a terminus post quem for the cemetery, which may have been in use up until 1750.

10. For a comprehensive reconstruction from ethnohistorical sources of the traditional cosmology of these groups see Simmons (1986:37-64).

11. For a discusion of Puritan cultural bias toward Indian religion and way of life see Simmons (1981).

12. A period of separation followed the burial for the relatives of the deceased. Those in mourning, especially the women, "kept their faces blackt with coal mixt with grease" and any singing, dancing, or wearing of fine clothing was prohibited (Occum [1761] 1809:109). The Wampanoag and Massachusett renewed the period of mourning annually "with a blacke stiffe paint on their faces" (Wood [1638] 1967:104). A celebration or feast marked the reintegration of the mourners into the community of the living, which made society whole once again.

13. *Chepeck*, meaning "the dead," is derived from *cheppi* meaning "it is separate or apart." *Chippeu*, which comes from the same root, means "he is dead," or
more literally "he is separated/he separates himself/or the separated" (Trumbull
1903:22). The dead are separated from the living, the souls separate from the body
and the dead are never spoken of by name. They are referred to according to their
status in life—for example, *chepassotam*, "the dead sachem," or *chepesquaw*, "the dead
woman," as someone who is apart, gone away or separated (Trumbull 1903:98,22).
Chepewssin was the northwest wind among the Narragansett; among the
Massachusett *wutchepwosh* represented the east wind (Trumbull 1903:250).

14. *Mauchautom* referred to "the dead man," but literally translated meant "he
has passed away"; the prefix *maw* meant "he is gone" (Trumbull 1903:243).
Kitonckquei also referred to someone who had died and literally meant "life goes,"
from *keteaonk*, "the life," and the formative of the verb to go (Trumbull 1903:37).
One other term used by John Eliot in his translation of the Bible— *nuppuk*, "the
dead" and *nuppoo*, "he dies"—may not have been the preferred way to speak of the
dead (Trumbull 1903:242).

The concept of the soul among eastern Algonquians had a dual quality; Roger
Williams was the only observer to record this dualism for southern New England
groups (Hultkrantz 1953:73–83,130; Williams [1643] 1973:193–94). The soul—
called *cowwewonck* in Narragansett and *koueonk* in Massachusett—resided in the
head or brain and traveled at death to Cautantowwit or wandered abroad to plague
the living. This soul could leave the body more or less at will often while someone
slept and was closely identified with the personal identity of the individual.

The second type of soul, *michachunk*, was described as having an affinity to "a
word signifying a looking glass, or cleare resemblance" (Williams [1643] 1973:194).
The meaning of *michachunk* is also associated with *nashauonk*, or breath, which denoted breath of life or the spirit (Trumbull 1903:326, 229). Words for both concepts
of the soul also appear in the Massachusetts and Wampanoag vocabularies.

15. The words for grave, earth, mother, and planting corn are all derived from
the same root, *ohke*. The word for grave, *weenohke*, comes from the word *ohke/aukee*
meaning "ground" or "earth" (Trumbull 1903:270). *Ohke* more precisely meant
"that which produces or brings forth as in the animate object *ohkas*, the bringer
forth, the mother" (Trumbull 1903:250). *Okasu*, meaning "a mother," is derived
from the same root as *ohke*, the earth, which is also found in terms and phrases associated with planting and sowing. "He sows" or "he plants" is *ohketeau* and "to plant
corn" is *aukeeteaumen* (Trumbull 1903:325). The linguistic evidence suggests that the
southern New England groups had a concept of earth-mother, although there is no
mention of this in the ethnohistorical sources according to William Simmons (personal communication 1987). It seems clear, however, that these groups thought of
the ground in which one planted corn, buried the dead, and from which all plants
grew, as earth-mother.

16. W. H. Trumbull has traced the etymology of the Algonquian words *manit*
and *manitou:*

> *Manit* is a noun, or more exactly a verbal used as a noun; . . .
> *Manitooo* or *Manitou* means "Manit is," or "It is Manit." . . .
> [However] the verb-form was so often used by the Indians that it
> has been very generally mistaken for the primary name-form, and

almost universally adopted as such by Christian missionaries. (1870:335–36)

The "m" is not part of the root *anit*, which is derived from a verb meaning to "be more than," "to surpass," "to exceed" (Trumbull 1870:336). Trumbull continues:

> Used as a substantive, *anit* signifies, "that which is more than," "passes beyond," or "exceeds," the common or the normal. It does not connote life, or spiritual existence, or any moral attributes; for one of its most common uses is in the sense of "corrupt," or "rotten." *i.e. more than* ripe—past or *gone beyond* its natural or proper state . . .Restoring now the indefinite and impersonal prefix, we have for the primary meaning of *Manit*, "somebody who, or something which goes beyond, exceeds, or is more than the common or normal"; something extra-ordinary, or preter-natural (not, necessarily, super-natural) . . . [And for] *Manit-ooo* or *Manit-ou*, "He (or it) is preternatural, or transcends common experience." (1870:339–40)

Cautantowwit or variously *Kehtanit* is a compound of *"Kehte* 'chief,' 'greatest,' and *anit"* (Trumbull 1870:336). Sampson Occum noted that among the Montauk, "Cauhluntoowut . . . signifies one that is possessed with supreme power" ([1761] 1809:108–109). Other names for deities also incorporated the root *anit*.

17. The exact location of King Philip's grave, if indeed he was ever buried, is not mentioned in the historical accounts of his death and beheading in 1676. Simmons collected a story from a Narragansett source that gives conflicting accounts of where King Philip's head may be buried. Some maintain that his head is buried under the doorstep of the Leonard family homestead in Taunton, Massachusetts. "Indian tradition disputes history, and there are those who believe it, that the great sachem's head is buried between Taunton and Mt. Hope, and no one knows its resting place. Tradition says that every three generations the ghost of Philip walks abroad, and reveals to a medicine man this spot" (Simmons 1986:140–41).

REFERENCES CITED

Axtell, James
   1981   *The European and the Indian Essays in the Ethnohistory of Colonial North America.* New York: Oxford University Press.

Bowden, Henry Warner
   1981   *American Indians and Christian Missions.* Chicago: University of Chicago Press.

Bragdon, Kathleen Joan
   1981   *"Another Tongue Brought In:" An Ethnohistorical Study of Native Writings in Massachusett.* Ph.D. diss. Brown University.

Brenner, Elise M.
1980   To Pray or to Be Prey: That Is the Question: Strategies for Cultural Autonomy of Massachusetts Praying Town Indians. *Ethnohistory* 27(2): 135–52.

Durkheim, Emile
1965   *The Elementary Forms of the Religious Life.* New York: The Free Press.

Gennep, Arnold van
1960   *Rites of Passage.* Chicago: University of Chicago Press.

Gibson, Susan G. (ed.)
1980   *Burr's Hill, a Seventeenth Century Wampanoag Burial Ground in Warren, Rhode Island.* Haffenreffer Museum of Anthropology, Studies in Anthropology and Material Culture 2.

Gookin, Daniel
[1674]   *Historical Collections of the Indians in New England.* Towtaid.
1970

Hodder, Ian
1982a   *Symbols in Action.* New York: Cambridge University Press.

1982b   *Symbolic and Structural Archaeology.* Cambridge: Cambridge University Press.

Hultkrantz, Ake
1953   *Conceptions of the Soul among North American Indians.* The Ethnographic Museum of Sweden, Monograph Series Publication no. 1. Stockholm.

Johannsen, Christina B.
1980   *European Trade Goods and Wampanoag Culture in the Seventeenth Century.* In *Burr's Hill,* ed. Susan G. Gibson. Haffenreffer Museum of Anthropology, Studies in Anthropology and Material Culture 2.

Kellaway, William
1961   *The New England Company 1649-1776.* London: Longmans.

Mayhew, Experience
1727   *Indian Converts: Or Some Account of the Lives and Dying Speeches of a Considerable Number of the Christianized Indians of Martha's Vineyard, in New England.* Samuel Gerrish, London.

Mayhew, Matthew
1694   *A Brief Narrative of the Success Which the Gospel Hath Had, among the Indians.* Boston: Bartholomew Green.

Morrison, Kenneth M.
    1974   "That Art of Coyning Christians:" John Eliot and the Praying Indians of Massachusetts. *Ethnohistory* 21: 77–92.

Morton, Thomas
    [1632]   New English Canaan. in *Tracts and Other Papers: Origin, Set-*
    1838   *tlement, and Progress of the Colonies in North America.* Vol. 2. Washington, D.C.: Peter Force.

Occum, Sampson
    [1761]   An Account of the Montauk Indians, on Long Island. *Massachusetts His-*
    1809   *torical Society Collections,* ser. 1, 10: 105–11.

Robbins, Maurice
    1959   Some Indian Burials from Southeastern Massachusetts, part 1. *Massachusetts Archaeological Society Bulletin* 20(2): 17–32.

Robinson, Paul A., Kelley, Marc A., and Rubertone, Patricia E.
    1985   Preliminary Biocultural Interpretations from a Seventeenth-Century Narragansett Indian Cemetery in Rhode Island. In *Cultures in Contact,* ed. William W. Fitzhugh. Anthropological Society of Washington Series. Washington: Smithsonian Institution Press.

Ronda, James P.
    1981   Generations of Faith: The Christian Indians of Martha's Vineyard. *William and Mary Quarterly* 38(3): 369–94.

Salisbury, Neal
    1982   *Manitou and Providence Indians, Europeans, and the Making of New England, 1500–1643.* New York: Oxford University Press.

Saville, Foster Harmon
    1920   A Montauk Cemetery at Easthampton, Long Island. *Indian Notes and Monographs,* Musem of the American Indian, Heye Foundation 2(3).

Shepard, Thomas
    [1648]   The Clear Sun-Shine of the Gospel Breaking Forth upon the
    1834   Indians in New England. In *Collections of the Massachusetts Historical Society* 4, 3d ser., pp. 25– 67.

Simmons, William S.
    1970   *Cautantowwit's House.* Providence, R.I.: Brown University Press.
    1979   Conversion from Indian to Puritan. *New England Quarterly* 52:177–218.

1981   Cultural Bias in the New England Puritans' Perception of Indians. *William and Mary Quarterly* 38:56–72.

1983   Red Yankees: Narragansett Conversion in the Great Awakening. *American Ethnologist* 10(2): 253– 71.

1986   *Spirit of the New England Tribes Indian History and Folklore, 1620–1984.* Hanover, N.H.: University Press of New England.

Snow, Dean R.

1980   *The Archaeology of New England.* New York: Academic Press.

Trigger, Bruce

1985   *Natives and Newcomers.* Montreal: McGill-Queen's University Press.

Trumbull, James Hammond

1870   On the Algonkin Name "Manit" (or "Manitou"), Sometimes Translated "Great Spirit." *Old and New* 1: 337–42.

1903   *Natick Dictionary.* Smithsonian Institution, Bureau of American Ethnology Bulletin no. 25. Washington, D.C.

Van der Donck, Adriaen

[1656]   A Description of New Netherlands. *New York Historical Soci-*
1841   *ety Collections* Ser. 2, 1:125–242.

Wagner, Roy

1981   *The Invention of Culture.* Chicago: University of Chicago Press.

Whitfield, Henry

[1652]   Strength Out of Weaknesse. In *Collections of the Massachusetts*
1834   *Historical Society* 4, 3d ser. pp. 149–196.

Williams, Roger

[1643]   *A Key into the Language of America.* Detroit, Mich.: Wayne
1973   State University Press.

Winslow, Edward

[1624]   Good News from New England. Abridged. *Massachusetts*
1832   *Historical Society Collections,* ser. 2, vol. 9, pp. 74–104.

Wood, William

[1638]   *New England's Prospect.* Research and Source Works Series
1967   131, American Classics in History and Social Science 2. New York: Burt Franklin.

PART III

The Archaeology of the
Georgian Worldview and the
18th-Century Beginnings
of Modernity

The 18th century is probably the most celebrated period of American history today, particularly the years associated with American Independence. Schoolbook history moves swiftly from the Pilgrims to the Salem witch trials to the French and Indian War to the American Revolution. In such histories, the French and Indian War is only of use as a prelude to the Revolution. Modern Americans continually try to link today with the Founding Fathers, for a wide variety of purposes (see Wallace 1986), and they root as many contemporary values as possible in the values of the American Revolution.

However, not everyone agrees that the American Revolution was the most important thing that happened in 18th-century America. Deetz, for one, challenges this popular idea and is praised for doing so by Schlereth (1982: 49). Deetz is, of course, the author of his own revolution within historical archaeology, a revolution based on his use of Henry Glassie, structuralism, and the idea of the Georgian worldview. Owing at least in part to the charisma of Deetz and the provocativeness of the idea of the Georgian worldview, the 18th century has been the focus of a great deal of American historical archaeology. But the Georgian worldview has hardly replaced the American Revolution as a key factor in American history. Rather, this worldview, with its striving for balance, order, symmetry, segmentation, and standardization, transcends the political sphere and provides insights into the patterns of thought of both the leaders of the Revolution and those who fought the battles. Understanding the patterns of thought and the givens of daily life is particularly important in the light of Rhys Isaac's (1982) suggestion that the largest challenge faced by the leaders of the Revolution was not getting it started but getting it stopped before it toppled them for the same reasons that it pushed the English out. As 18th-century political ideology the Georgian worldview must have been a very sensitive instrument, for those under its sway were able to determine just how much segmentation and stratification was vital to the emerging American social and economic system and how much was detrimental to it. Deetz would argue, in accordance with the structuralist emphasis on underlying patterns of thought, that the same ideas that the Founding Fathers used to organize postrevolutionary American society were used by thousands of ordinary Americans to organize, on a much smaller scale, their daily lives.

Despite the seeming accuracy of the Georgian worldview as a characterization of 18th-century life, its predictive value, and the integrative power of the structuralist paradigm, a recurring criticism of Deetz's work—one leveled at almost all structuralist anthropology from Levi-Strauss on down—is that it is not testable and not replicable. Many archaeologists have marveled at Deetz's insights while complaining that he provided no game plan for going out to do likewise. To many it seemed as if the only possible research strategy was to go out and collect corroborative data, that is, more examples of the Georgian worldview to pile up next to Deetz's.

The next four chapters demonstrate that there are, after all, productive ways to study the archaeology of the Georgian worldview and to do archaeology using that idea. The essays by James Deetz and Mark Leone extend the idea of the Georgian worldview into ever more areas of material culture and suggest ways of measuring it. They work at the conceptual level, while Barbara Little and Ann Palkovich demonstrate how Deetz's concept may be applied to archaeological problems. Little uses Georgian ideas to organize and connect data from a single archaeological site, and Palkovich uses them both to explain an archaeological site and to examine the possibility that the Georgian worldview, as an idea in 18th-century society, was at times rejected.

The idea of the Georgian worldview, brought into historical archaeology by Deetz, is now a well-used intellectual tool, and structural anthropology is no longer the "still controversial" school of thought it was when Deetz began drafting the essay that appears in this volume. Nonetheless, Deetz provides important details for understanding his use of structuralism. In addition, he pushes the idea of the Georgian worldview and structural shifts toward that mode of thinking deeper into the material world of 18th-century Anglo-America. An example of the former is a provocative discussion of the whitening of gravestones, dishes, and houses that occurred at about the same time. The structural paradigm allows Deetz to move beyond thinking of these things as things and to focus on whiteness, as an idea. By focusing on such ideas, Deetz brings the human mind into material culture studies in a way that he has virtually pioneered for historical archaeology. An example of the latter contribution, pushing the idea of the Georgian worldview farther than ever before into the material world, is his discussion of the decoration of plates as having a role in their marking or not marking the Georgian way of thinking.

Deetz's essay is also important because it contains two responses to the charge that his work is not replicable or extendible. The first, as already mentioned, is that Deetz has discovered Georgian and non-Georgian values for variables previously considered irrelevant to the study of the operation of the Georgian mind-set. The second is his suggestion that a careful accounting, at the local level, will show the spread of this new way of thinking; his discussion of the Salem witch trials offers a brief, suggestive example.

Leone's essay is clearly based on Deetz's work and extends it in at least two important ways. Using data from Annapolis, Maryland, Leone takes up Deetz's challenge to investigate the penetration of the Georgian way of thinking at the local level and does so with the expectation that, in addition to the kind of variation from town to town that Deetz noted in New England, there will be evidence for variability in the acceptance of these ideas in a single locale, across social classes, across occupations, and across the various aspects of daily life. As tools for measuring such microvariation, Leone introduces a range of artifact types that demonstrate the use of Georgian ideas as well as a technique for analyzing plate-rim sizes to determine the degree of Georgianness at the level of the ceramic assemblage. All of this detail is significant because it not only demonstrates new measures of the Georgian worldview, but also moves another step forward in archaeological interpretation. Deetz tells us what the Georgian worldview is; Leone tells us what it is good for. Leone contends that the set of ideas we call Georgian are also the ideas used to organize industrial labor in the United States in the 18th and 19th centuries. Whatever else it may be, the Georgian worldview is, according to Leone, the order of modern capitalism, and this is a part of what provides historical archaeology with a vital connection to life today. Leone also hits head-on the knotty problem of the American Revolution and, by way of Rhys Isaac (1982), suggests the complexity of the position of its leaders and the elegance of the solution available through Georgian ideas. A subsidiary benefit of Leone's economic argument is that it also points to linkages between Georgian ideas and early 18th-century life, a period of American history more poorly understood than the second half of the century but, as Leone's data from Annapolis show, an intimately connected prelude to the Revolutionary era.

In contrast to the essays by Deetz and Leone, those by Little and Palkovich concentrate on particular archaeological sites. Little's essay is less explicitly about Georgian ideas than any of the others in this section, but it makes as much use of the concept as any of the others. Little is concerned with the analysis of the Jonas Green printshop site in Annapolis. She has at her disposal both the archaeological record of at least 70 years of printing carried out by three generations of the same family and also a nearly intact set of issues of the *Maryland Gazette,* which was produced on the site and was one of the principal products of Green's printing business. Just as Deetz sees the same structure behind the whitening of gravestones, plates, and houses in late 18th-century Anglo-America, Little finds in the widely varied classes of material culture (from ceramics to the pages of the *Gazette*) a measure of balance, order, symmetry, and segmentation, and is able to determine the degree of correlation between shifts in various classes of material culture. Among the contributions of her study, at least from the perspective of the history of printing, is her presentation of a series of variables in newspaper layout (e.g., the number of columns and the presence/absence of printed lines between columns, stories, sections, and advertisements) and elements of grammar (e.g., the signification of words of emphasis and proper nouns as well as the use of the short "s" and quotation marks) that indicate Georgian ways of thinking. Little's conclusion is that the result of shifts in all of these variables is a newspaper that was much more standardized and segmented at the end of the 18th century than it was at midcentury. Following the lead of Beaudry (1980, n.d.) and others (Potter 1984), Little treats the documentary record with the kind of analytical sophistication usually reserved for the below-ground archaeological record.

Little's second important contribution is her use of Mary Douglas's taxonomy of social constructs based on "group" and "grid" or collective and individual behavior (Douglas 1966, 1978). Douglas suggests that all social behavior has both individual and group aspects and that the two are *not* mutually exclusive. This means that social analysis need no longer be based on a simple continuum ranging from individual to group behavior, but can employ a four-box matrix—in which each box represents one of the four possible combinations of strong and weak, individual and group orientation—to better approximate the complexity of human behavior. Little uses this idea to add another level of sophistication to the series of mediations that Deetz says characterize the shift to the Georgian mind-set and to respond to the challenge issued by both Deetz and Leone to find ways to use the Georgian worldview as an analytical tool at the local level.

Palkovich's essay dives into an issue hinted at by Deetz and discussed by Leone: the penetration of the Georgian worldview. If this way of thinking did not simply impose itself on people but did enter society differentially, if its penetration was based on its acceptance by individuals, groups, or classes, then that admits the possibility of its rejection, too. It is easy to forget, when we find evidence of the ideas we call Georgian in the 18th century while living in a modern world underpinned all around by such ideas, that both our history and the history of these ideas could not have been a smooth and even progression from then to now.

Palkovich discusses what the rejection of the Georgian worldview looks like architecturally through the archaeology of the Morris Pound House. At the same time, she shows what to do with data that don't fit. The archaeologically excavated foundation indicates that this house was close to, but not exactly symmetrical. Such data can be handled in two ways. One can assume that the builder intended a fully symmetrical house and simply was not able to build one, because of poor tools, techniques, or what have you, and thus that the deviation from Georgian ideas was accidental. In other words, the idea behind the house was of the mind-set. Alternatively, one can do what Palkovich does: She demonstrates that the builders of the house were sufficiently competent to make the house fully symmetrical, and suggests that they did not, on purpose. She calls this a subtle rejection of Georgian ideas and those associated with them, subtle because the deviations in the house are large enough, she argues, to be intentional but small enough not to be blatant or antagonistic. Whether or not Palkovich is correct—the final verdict awaits more detailed historical research and analysis of other archaeological data from the site—her essay points out the need for close analytical attention to the antitheses of the Georgian worldview as discoverable archaeologically. This will not only help us better understand the thought and lives of 18th- and 19th-century Americans, but will also shed light on the Georgian worldview itself, by showing us its edges and the things standing in opposition to it. This is an important step because it helps us to see the Georgian worldview as a dynamic entity and not some immobile cultural monolith.

REFERENCES CITED

Beaudry, Mary C.
   1980   *Folk Semantic Domains in Early Virginia Probate Inventories.* Ph.D.
           diss., Department of Anthropology, Brown University, Providence.
   n.d.   *Documentary Archaeology.* Cambridge: Cambridge University Press.

Douglas, Mary
   1966   *Purity and Danger: An Analysis of Concepts of Pollution and Taboo.*
           London: Routledge & Kegan Paul.
   1978   *Cultural Bias.* Royal Anthropological Institute of Great Britain and
           Ireland, Occasional Paper Number 35.

Isaac, Rhys
   1982   *The Transformation of Virginia, 1740–1790.* Chapel Hill: University
           of North Carolina Press.

Potter, Parker B.
   1984   Digging in the Sunday Paper: A Study of Seasonality as Reflected in
           Newspaper Advertising. In *Toward an Ethnoarchaeology of Modern
           America,* ed. Richard A. Gould, pp. 37–50. Research Papers in An-
           thropology, Department of Anthropology, Brown University,
           Providence.

Schlereth, Thomas J.
   1982   *Material Culture Studies in America.* American Association for State
           and Local History. Nashville:

Wallace, Michael
   1986   Visiting the Past: History Museums in the United States. In *Present-
           ing the Past: Essays on History and the Public,* ed. Susan Porter
           Benson, Stephen Brier, and Roy Rosenzweig, pp. 137–61. Phila-
           delphia: Temple University Press.

CHAPTER 6

Material Culture and Worldview in Colonial Anglo-America

JAMES F. DEETZ

Frozen in time and embedded in the American landscape is the track of our collective existence, material culture. It holds the promise of being more democratic and less self-conscious in its creation than any other body of historical material. Many scholars have observed that documents written by and concerning a minority of past peoples fail to provide the broadest possible view of the American experience from the 17th century to the present. Although relatively few wrote, and what was written captured the personal biases of the recorder, in theory almost every person who lived in Anglo-America left behind some trace, however slight, of their passing. Perhaps a personal possession, now broken and buried, or a line of postholes that mark the vanished boundary of someone's immediate world, or a gravestone tilted by time but still speaking to us across the centuries, or something as humble as the remains of a meal consumed and forgotten—it is all there, and we cannot disregard it.

Yet material culture is difficult to interpret, is sometimes hard and expensive to recover, and is subject to a number of research methods, many of which have conflicting goals. Scholars committed to the scientific school of historical archaeology see material culture as a source of patterns that enable one to define "covering laws" or "law-like statements" that have great predictive power (South 1977). If culture is patterned, the reasoning goes, then the concomitant pattern in its product—the built environment—might allow us to predict patterns on the basis of a more restricted body of data. The patterns in question are quantitatively derived. For example, the Carolina pattern, which is said to typify 18th-century English colonial material culture in parts of the Southeast, is a statement of the relative frequency of the number of etically imposed categories. The particular frequency of groupings such as *kitchen, personal, architectual, arms, clothing*, and so on sets the Carolina pattern apart from other patterns also derived by counting the artifacts retrieved from excavated sites. Proponents of this approach are openly scornful of those whom they label particularistic, claiming that they seek no regularities in the material record that might advance explanation, and those they call humanistic, claiming that they lack the rigor to produce controlled repeatable results. Although I would agree that a particularistic approach to material culture will not likely produce results that have explanatory power beyond the context of the immediate data set, the work of Ivor Noël Hume (1970) is of profound importance to those of us who work with the material culture of colonial America. Noël Hume not only has given us the most complete description and identification of the universe in which we all labor, but more than any other scholar has constantly stressed the relationship between documents and objects and the importance of knowing the history of the artifacts that we encounter in our research. His concern with documentary sources contrasts sharply with the approach of the scientific school, which holds that documents are of secondary importance and indeed are often a source of error better ignored.

In view of the widespread disagreement on both the means and the ends of material culture studies, it is legitimate to ask just what purpose such inquiry serves, and what is the greatest contribution it can make to our understanding of the past. If we are referring to material culture in its broadest definition—as that part of the physical world that we shape according to a set of cultural plans—one of the major benefits of studying material culture is that it provides access to the minds of those responsible for creating it in the first place. Any object, whether a house or a cut of meat, can be given any of a wide variety of forms, yet the range of variation will be narrow within any given culture. It is this consistency that underlies the concept of type in archeology, and shared artifact form is clearly and unquestionably the reflection of shared thought, not only about what is appropriate, but about what is unacceptable. One can look at any number of gravestones in the cemeteries of 17th- and early 18th-century New England and with rare exception encounter an endless parade of winged skulls. Here and there, a cherub will appear. If we know enough about the culture of the time and note whose grave the cherub stone marks, even this seemingly deviant form of design can be explained. Fifty years later, the cherub design has usurped the death's head and thus provides clear evidence of the replacement of one set of collective ideas and preferences with another. To paraphrase Henry Glassie, objects do not change, but ideas do.

To reduce this thought to an essential absurdity, one could sit and stare at a hall-and-parlor house for a century, and except for inevitable deterioration, it would not change one jot, much less transform itself into a house with a central entrance hall. Yet in less than a century, the houses studied by Glassie in the Virginia Piedmont underwent such a transformation. More precisely, the concepts that gave rise to the houses changed radically. Although this may seem to belabor the obvious, a great deal of thought devoted to material changes seems to assume *object* transformation without any concern for the underlying cause of such change (i.e., the alteration of thought) or for the way people perceive their world and their place within it and how that place can be secured by shaping it physically to provide comfortable accommodation.

The causes of the transformation of specific sectors of the physical world—be they gravestones, dishes, clothing, or houses—seem relatively easy to identify but may be difficult to explain. To say that tastes, values, or simple preference changed and produced a new form merely points to a cause and an effect, but does not explain what activated the causes (e.g., why did tastes change?). A more powerful explanatory tool might be found in the still controversial school of structural anthropology, which has incurred the distrust of many social scientists, who charge that it is nonpositivist and thus cannot be subjected to scientific methods of proof, and that it has little predictive value. Yet structuralism holds the promise of providing an explanation for change in the physical world in toto, of explicating relationships between changes in seemingly unrelated categories of material culture, and of relating these transformations to changes in attitudes and worldview. Fortunately, our path to such understanding has been pioneered; it falls to us to follow up by sharpening and extending the focus of our inquiry.

From Henry Glassie's application of Levi-Strauss's anthropological structuralism in *Folk Housing in Middle Virginia* we learn how to extend this method to other times and other places. What Glassie has done for the folk builder of the Virginia Piedmont can be shown to have relevance equally for the 17th-century New England husbandman and the 19th-century Irish coal miner on the California frontier. The method functions well as a mediation between the quantitative but overgeneralized approach of the scientific historical archaeologist and the richly descriptive but theoretically timid work of those of a more particularistic bent. Perhaps its greatest value lies in the possibility that it may be shown to have predictive value after all, since the paradigm developed for 18th-century Virginia folk builders both fits the New England data and suggests new explanations for some changes in New England material culture. In turn, the degree to which such a fit between the Virginia paradigm and New England data can be effected serves further to strengthen the credibility of the original proposition.

In simplest terms, structuralism holds that human thought is organized and functions according to a universally shared complex of oppositional structures that are mediated differently by different cultures, or by the same culture at different times. Although such a proposition is unprovable—we may or may not think in binary terms—it may provide a model that has heuristic value. As Glassie states, "At least binary thinking has aided in theory building" (1975:20). The fifteen oppositional structures employed by Glassie and their mediation are more than sufficient to accommodate the data to be examined here. Many of them are but variants of the underlying broad opposition between culture and nature, and since material culture is the prime mediator between people and the natural world, this comes as no surprise. These oppositional pairs are believed to structure subconscious thought and thus to affect all of human behavior as it is seen at the observable particularistic level. Accordingly, similar changes taking place in the same direction and at the same time in otherwise unrelated sectors of culture are attributable to changes in the nature of the mediation of underlying oppositional structures. For example, the shift from many colors to white seen not only in houses but also in gravestones and ceramics at the end of the 18th century might result from the strong mediation of the complex-simple opposition in the direction of simplicity, and the strong mediation of the opposition between artificial and natural in the direction of artificiality. Rather than seek an explanation of why houses, or gravestones, or dishes are made white by the century's end, we should look for an explanation of the underlying shift in mediation of the oppositional structures in question.

Whiteness becomes the main object of interest, not the artifacts that exhibit it, and the reason for whiteness in one part of the material culture of early 19th-century Anglo-America is most likely the reason for it in others. Glassie sees the whitening of houses as a further remove from nature: "The nearly inevitable whiteness of the nineteenth . . . century farmhouse not only marked a contraction of the traditional palette (simplicity) and the most abrupt possible separation from the natural tans, greens, and clay-reds that environed it, but also . . . it was a democratizing sign." The same can be said for gravestones; toward the end of the 18th century, New England gravestones were carved from a variety of colored stones—green, brown, tan, grey, and red. Likewise, ceramics, whether imported or domestically produced, were made largely in the same varied and more natural colors seen in houses and gravestones (before the last quarter of the 18th century). It could be argued that economic or technological causes account for color preferences at different times, but a closer look at the facts suggests that this was not so. In the case of ceramics, glazes of sufficient clarity to produce whitewares were available on the continent at least by the late 16th century, as attested by north Italian marbled slipwares and Wanfried wares. Furthermore, the Surry whitewares show a body as white as earlier cream-colored earthenware. If the glaze and body of these types had been combined, they would have produced an earthenware as light in color as Wedgwood's celebrated creamware, yet almost two centuries passed before such creamware came out. In the 1760s Wedgwood was producing clouded wares and greenwares on a light body, but the unpopularity of the greenwares cut short their life and precipitated the subsequent production of creamware. Pure white ceramics in the form of tin-enameled wares and oriental porcelain were also present in the ceramic assemblage of the 17th century, but, significantly, were never central to foodways, either as vessels for social functions or as containers for drugs or ointments. White or light-colored utilitarian ceramics first appeared with the development of Staffordshire stonewares in the middle of the 18th century in a significant variety of forms. Near complete whiteness of the ceramic assemblage was achieved by the 1780s after the immensely popular pearlwares were introduced in the 1770s.

Marble replaced multicolored slates and other stones in the manufacture of gravestones over most of New England at about the same time that white pottery was achieving universal acceptance. The first marble markers date to the 1780s, and by the first decades of the 19th century, white gravestones became quite popular. In this case, the trend from the complexity seen in multiple materials—slates, schist/sandstones—to simplicity, as typified by marble, is a clear example of the mediation of the complex-simple opposition, paralleling the change in ceramics from multiple colors and multiple decorative techniques. Marble, or at least some form of white stone, could have been used earlier. Some of the very early cemeteries in Boston have a few gravestones dating to the 17th century made from a white, sandlike material, but they obviously never became popular. Throughout the 18th century, multiple natural colors were the rule. Yet within the space of about 30 years—roughly a generation—white gravestones became the normative form. Taken in isolation, this change might be attributed to the relative ease of carving marble (if this is indeed the case) or to improved transportation making marble quarries more accessible. Viewed against the changes in ceramic colors, and Glassie's discussion of the shift to white away from more diverse and natural colors in houses, these explanations seem particularistic, weak, and possibly off the mark.

This rather lengthy discourse on the "whitening" of America has been offered both as example and as a point of departure. For if similar shifts in color preference in at least three unrelated sets of material culture indicate a mediation toward a more cultural and artificial structure, what other changes in material culture accompany this mediation in a consistent way, and what might this tell us about the way colonial Anglo-Americans viewed each other and the world in which they lived?

Glassie's diagram of the paradigmatic structure of the mind of a Middle-Virginia architect (see Figure 6.1) illustrates the mediation of the 15 oppositional structures as it occurs in the Virginia Piedmont during the late 18th and early 19th centuries. For each pair, the earliest dominant opposition is shown, as well as the direction of change from 1760 on. The related architectural features are also indicated, so that the diagram suffices to illustrate change in building form for the purposes of this discussion. If the paradigm is extendable, in time and space, what manifestations of the pairs and similar mediations might be isolated from both contemporary and earlier New England data? From the numerous strongly suggestive examples, rapid change seems to have occurred during the last quarter of the 18th century, at almost the same time that similar changes were being worked on Virginia folk building. These changes coincide with the boundary between the second and third periods of material culture history outlined in *In Small Things Forgotten* (Deetz 1977) and extend the explanation of this critical watershed in the development of American material culture.

The change from death's head to cherub in the later 18th century might well be a reflection of the mediation between intellect and emotion, owing as much to this as to a fundamental change in Puritan orthodoxy. The death's head symbol and accompanying epitaphs are powerful emotional devices, in contrast to the more ethereal angel, which is more consistent with an intellectualized belief system. The same change also relates to the natural-artificial opposition, which is

Figure 6.1: Glassie's diagram of the paradigmatic structure of the mind of a Middle-Virginia architect. Source: *Glassie (1975:161).*

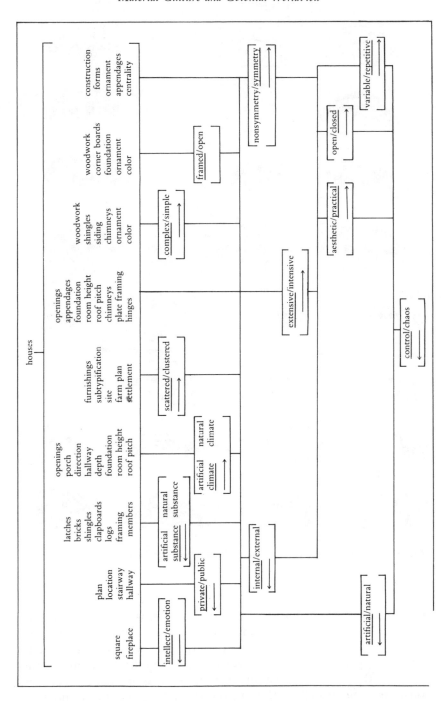

Figure 6.2: Spirit faces from Plymouth Colony. Source: *Benes (1977).*

but a reordering of the intellect-emotion pair. A skull, with or without wings, is still a part of the human body, a natural element. Angels on the other hand are artificial to the extent that they are the creation of the intellect, and although nature invests us with a skeleton, we invest ourselves with a soul. The curious transitional "soul images" (Ludwig 1966) or "spirit faces" (Benes 1977) that are so prevalent in mid-18th-century rural New England seem to be a mediation caught dead-center, visual puns that owe as much to their intended viewers as to their creators for their symbolic value (Figure 6.2). Their appearance in the more quiet backwater of rural New England could be attributed in part to a slower-paced change in those areas, slow enough to permit the flowering of a style caught between opposites. Certainly in the urban centers of New England, the mediation of the intellect-emotion structure could be effected more efficiently, since the alternative styles were immediately available to carvers and public alike, and change was proceeding at a more rapid rate.

Other manifestations of the artificial-natural opposition might be seen in trash disposal, the finish applied to the backs of gravestones, and butchering methods. In the 17th and earlier 18th centuries, household wastes were for the most part scattered around the houselot. Various preexisting depressions might have been filled with trash, but no conscious effort seems to have been made to provide discrete pits for refuse. Such a disposal method acknowledges the natural quality of debris, and to spread it over the landscape is to reunite it with the world from which it came. The later 18th-century method of disposal is quite different as it sets trash apart from the environment through careful disposition in pits excavated expressly for the purpose. That this change is not a function of increased settlement density is shown by its occurrence at about the same time in rural and urban locales alike. As a reflection of the separation of society from the natural world that typifies changes in later 18th-century attitudes, it can be seen as structurally identical to the manner in which the folk builder viewed the materials from which he constructed his houses, and the gravestone carver, his raw material. Glassie suggests that the squaring of timbers and burning of brick (a natural substance as clay) reflects the denial of the origin of these structural materials in nature; in like manner the complete smoothing of the backs of slate gravestones denies their origin in the parent vein of stone. Such finish work does not seem to be simply a matter of economics. Before the 1760s stones of all sizes and cost, from the simplest lightly carved markers to elaborate custom-made stones with family coats of arms, were finished lightly on the reverse, if at all. By the end of the 18th century, the most modest stone had the back smoothed as flat as the front, smoother than the most elaborate and expensive examples of a century before.

If smoothing the back face of a gravestone denies its origin in the natural world, the careful sawing of an animal's carcass into discrete segments accomplishes a similar result. The change from chopping to sawing in Anglo-American butchering techniques is also a late 18th-century occurrence, although saws suitable to such work had been in existence for centuries. A chop or round steak, flat on both sides and showing the effect of highly controlled sectioning contrasts sharply with a joint of meat removed from the carcass with a few hacks of an axe. Sawing also permits "portion control" and can be related to a parallel trend toward individualism of material accessories in the last decades of the 18th-century.

Such individualism signals "the point at which the face-to-face community dies" (Glassie 1975:190). This important statement is based on observed changes in vernacular housing in a tiny area of Anglo-America. How much more powerful it becomes when we realize that it might derive as well from other aspects of material culture over much of 18th- and 19th-century Anglo-America. Tied to the intensive-extensive and public-private oppositional structures, the shift from corporate communal organization to lonely individualism is reflected in many aspects of the material world. The spectacular increase in the amount of ceramics "needed" to serve a single family (Deetz 1972), the appearance for the first time of chairs in sufficient number to seat each individual member of the household, the trend toward individual burial plots and eventually family cemeteries, and the appearance of more private space within houses of the same approximate size—all tell us that the old communal order was in disarray. Glassie puts it succinctly:

> The physical environment . . . provides the stage upon which cultural options are sorted out, rejected, accepted and ordered into a particular cultural logic. The cultural logic is not a free-will philosophy, however. Architectural thinking is bound to thinking about non-architectural matters, so that any theory explaining architecture in solely architectural terms may be somewhat correct, but it can never be enough. The social, economic, political, and religious conditions of life in Middle Virginia changed. People adapted to those changes, developing new modes of thought, and the things they did, the artifacts they made, manifested the changes that had taken place in their minds. (1975:189–90)

The shift from extensive to intensive structures, manifested in housing by a virtual contraction of the house within itself, is paralleled by the withdrawal of individuals from each other, and material culture provides one means to this end. Having one's own plate from which to consume one's own portion of food while seated separately and probably in a designated place underlines one's separation from others, in contrast to earlier practices of communal consumption of dishes that were not as amenable to "portion control." Mediation in the direction of intensiveness is also seen in epitaphs. As the 18th century passes, more and more epitaphs were written in the third person. The older "remember me" gave way to "in memory of" him or her. The deceased no longer spoke to the community from their graves, but were silent and talked about. This change not only signaled an intensive withdrawal, but a mediation of the public-private opposition toward privacy as well.

Glassie suggests that the opposition between extensive and intensive is joined in thought to the opposition between complexity and simplicity (1975:151). Perhaps individualism was joined to a trend toward anonymity. Lacking the external support provided by the older corporate order, people may have felt reassured by remaining somewhat unnoticed, and simpler, less elaborated forms of material culture could assist in that. The framed-open opposition was being mediated toward openness at this time, as evidenced by the shift away from contrasting trim in house painting. Identical changes can be seen both in ceramics and in gravestone decoration. Throughout the 18th century, borders on gravestones became less elaborate. Borders several inches in width, richly decorated with fruit, faces, leaves, spirals, and stars, gave way to narrow borders with simple bands of decoration. By 1800, even these borders have disappeared, and the inscribed surface of the stone is smooth and unelaborated to the edge. Plates show an identical transformation (Figure 6.3). The marleys of mid-18th-century plates are wide and set off from the center by elaborate design. The most complex and most popular was the dot, diaper, and basket design seen on both stonewares and Whieldon clouded wares. This design and the barley pattern are by far the most frequently encountered archaeologically, and both consist of panels of decoration dividing the marley into sixths. The later "Queens shape" of earlier creamware retains the panels, but they are no longer filled with design. Following this style, the "Royal" pattern suggests the panels only in the shape of the rim, and both feather-edged creamware and shell-edged pearlware have only a narrow border of decoration on a plate essentially circular in outline. Such changes of course were not being made on ceramics *in* America, since the types in question were manufactured in England; yet they reflect both English and American preferences. To explain this transformation simply as a result of industrial mass production seems also inappropriate, since much of it had occurred prior to the full industrialization of the Staffordshire potteries. More lavishly decorated but less popular transfer printed wares were also being produced, and later "Victorian" ceramics were highly embellished, but in a different manner, largely through shape elaboration.

Ceramics, cuts of meat, gravestones, and houses are but a small part of the material universe of early America. That they figure so large

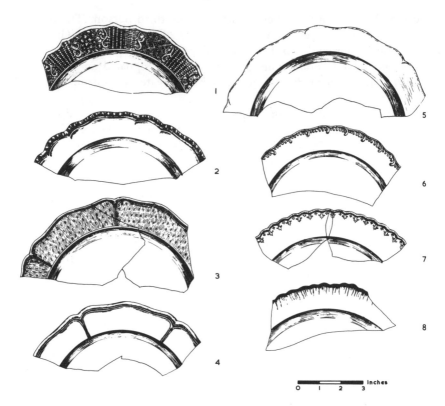

Figure 6.3: The evolution of English plate rims from white saltglaze to pearlware, ca. 1740–85. 1. Dot, diaper, and basket pattern, saltglaze. 2. "Bead and reel," saltglaze. 3. "Barley" pattern, saltglaze. 4. Queens shape, creamware. 5. Royal pattern, creamware. 6. Feather-edged creamware. 7. Spearhead, creamware. 8. Shell-edged pearlware. Source: *Noël Hume (1969).*

in this discussion is simply due to the fact that they are among the few categories of material culture that exist both in sufficient quantity and with adequate context to permit both the chronological and quantitative control needed to move toward any kind of explanation. Certainly a structural analysis as attempted here is, as Glassie says of his work, "at its most controlled, an essay in probabilities, and at its least controlled, and act of pure courage" (1975:117). Yet to suggest that *any* relationship exists between a white house and a rectangular trash pit, between a gravestone with an unfinished back and a haunch of beef chopped from the carcass, between a death's head design and a brown and yellow slipware posset pot, or between "sacred to the memory" and a shell-edged pearlware plate is the kind of "essay in probabilities" that I find personally satisfying. Perhaps it is better to chance being wrong in an interesting way than right in a dull one. Let us assume at least a limited credibility of this excursion through things and thoughts and consider the implications. If the distancing between person and person and between people and nature reflects the replacement of one order, one worldview, with another, then a careful accounting of change in the material world from community to community might tell us just when this shift occurred on a local level. Such insights in turn might help to illuminate or at least support conclusions drawn from other sources. Boyer and Nissenbaum's (1974) masterful analysis of the events that led up to the witchcraft trials in Salem and their explanation of those tragic events have their reflections in the little cemeteries that dot the Essex County landscape. One need travel only a few miles from the coast, and the designs that are to be seen on the 18th-century gravestones are a world apart from those in the coastal towns of Salem, Ipswich, and Marblehead. As late as the 1770s, the old stylistic tradition persisted; the influences from Boston, which completely transformed the designs of the coast, hardly penetrated inland. Almost a hundred years after 20 people were put to death in Salem, towns like Rowley were still looking into the past, yet Ipswich only a few miles distant had long since espoused the new decorative tradition of cherubs and portraits. Angel and spirit face look past each other, only a few miles apart in space, but a century apart in time.

Such a marked difference in mortuary art in contemporary communities forms the basis of a research design that would call for the excavation of the house sites of the most conservative faction in Salem Village, and compare them with their contemporary progressive counterparts in Salem Town. Any number of interesting hypotheses could be framed, following the model outlined here, and support of these hypotheses would in turn make our little exercise in probability all the more profitable, and the probability of its precision higher. If such an approach is in any way valid, the promise of bringing countless numbers of people into our accounting of the American past is significantly enhanced. Not only can we look at the material remains of figures who were insignificant in a traditional "historical" sense but were members of the dominant society; we might also see others—Afro-Americans, recent immigrants, Native Americans—as possessors each of a cultural tradition that had its own structural rules and that changed in an ordered and culturally sane way. The slaves who lived in the quarter at St. Simon's Island studied by Otto (1977), the free black occupants of Parting Ways (Deetz 1977), Welsh and Irish miners who dug coal from the

Diablo fields in Northern California (Emerson 1981), or Chinese laborers in northern Nevada (Marshall 1980)—all had their own rules for organizing their lives, and these rules are underlain by a structure peculiar to that culture. Change in their culture, when it occurs, is not a one-way street of acculturation, but rather, to quote Glassie yet one more time, a matter of drawing the new, alien form "through the structures in the folk . . . mind" (1975:89). A cow bone, excavated from the 19th-century coal mining town of Somersville, California, shows one end neatly sawed, the mark of the market butcher who delivered meat to the town, and the other end chopped with an axe or cleaver, evidence of a different tradition and of structure that in its various mediations sets apart its possessors from the other inhabitants of that multi-ethnic community.

In the last analysis, the study of material culture holds great promise, and happily is young enough to accommodate a diversity of approaches. The particularism of those who labor long and hard to relate objects to individuals and to instill an honest respect for the complexities of the historical record, the scientific archaeologists who rightly insist on the importance of controlled quantification, and the humanists who know that numbers can at times burden the soul—all have their place in our collective efforts. I hope that historians will be tolerant of our beginning efforts, although we are sometimes pompous, sometimes wildly off the mark, and all too often dull and pedantic, for the stakes are high, and from these efforts will emerge a more human, democratic view of the American experience. To know where we have been may not help us in where we are bound, but to know where *all* of us have truly been cannot be a bad thing to know.

REFERENCES CITED

Benes, Peter
1977   *The Masks of Orthodoxy*. Amherst: University of Massachusetts Press.

Boyer, Paul, and S. Nissenbaum
1974   *Salem Possessed*. Cambridge, Mass.: Harvard University Press.

Deetz, James
1972   Ceramics from Plymouth, 1620–1835; The Archaeological Evidence. In *Ceramics in America* (Winterthur Conference Report, 1972), ed. Ian Quimby. Charlottesville: University of Virginia Press.
1977   *In Small Things Forgotten*. New York: Doubleday, Anchor Books.

Emerson, Matthew
    1981   Progress Report of Somersville, California. *Society for Historical Archaeology Newsletter,* 14(1):30–31.

Glassie, Henry
    1975   *Folk Housing in Middle Virginia,* Knoxville: University of Tennessee Press.

Ludwig, Allan
    1966   *Graven Images.* Middletown, Conn.: Wesleyan University Press.

Marshall, Howard
    1980   *Buckeroos in Paradise.* Washington, D.C.: Library of Congress.

Noël Hume, Ivor
    1969   *A Guide to the Artifacts of Colonial America.* New York: Alfred A. Knopf.

Otto, John
    1977   Artifact and Status Differences—A Comparison of Ceramics from Planter, Overseer, and Slave Sites on an Antebellum Plantation. In *Research Strategies in Historical Archaeology,* ed. Stanley South. New York: Academic Press.

South, Stanley (ed.)
    1977   *Research Strategies in Historical Archaeology.* New York: Academic Press.

CHAPTER 7

The Georgian Order
as the Order
of Merchant Capitalism
in Annapolis, Maryland

MARK P. LEONE

This chapter attempts to deal with two questions that arise in the work
of Glassie (1975) on folk housing and Deetz (1977) on New England
material culture. First, why do changes in material culture appear in one
place before others? And, second, how are changes in material culture,
which are taken by Glassie and Deetz to reflect changes in ways of
thinking, tied to material conditions? Another way to put these questions is how can such changes be sorted out chronologically, and what
was their local effect?

    To deal with these questions and to make them sensible archaeo-
logically, I found it useful to paraphrase both Glassie and Deetz in such
a way that the effort of this chapter springs from and adds to their
work. Glassie's work is pivotal to Deetz's, in the latter's opinion.
Glassie studied about a hundred houses dating from the late 18th and
early 19th centuries in Louisa and Goochland counties, Virginia. This
area is also called Middle Virginia since it is well west of the Tidewater
area of Chesapeake Bay and east of the Appalachian Mountains. The
houses are all farmhouses, many of them looking very much alike,
leaving the viewer with the question: Just how alike are they, and
why?

    Henry Glassie wrote a "grammar" for these houses, a set of rules
for combining doors, windows, latches, and chimneys and also sizes,

shapes, and juxtaposition of rooms. He used the grammar to account for most of the variation among the houses and to order that variation by predicting which elements went with which, as a builder made decisions in the course of planning and putting up a house. The grammar may or may not have been written down; however, it was not a copybook architectural formula. The rules were explicit and precise, involved measurements, and, obviously, were widely shared. The point of using a grammar on the part of the builders, who were in all likelihood the owners and farmers as well, was to produce a house that expressed how they saw life, neighbors, work, the rest of society, and their relation to the land and that allowed them to live with those values realized.

Glassie concluded that the houses showed a tendency to become more private, used materials whose nature was modified, contained fewer decorative elements, and featured the intellect over emotion (e.g., they were painted white as opposed to bright, warm colors, or were painted white as opposed to weathering naturally). Taken as a whole, these tendencies and others reflected an increasing emphasis on the look of the outside of a house, as opposed to the inside or the fit between the two. Glassie concluded that the houses expressed and allowed greater control over postrevolutionary circumstances in Middle Virginia, which were becoming chaotic or out of control.

James Deetz was concerned with whether the same cognitive pattern could be found in colonial New England. He attempted to examine a much wider range of data, over a much longer period of time, using dishes, butchering techniques, chamber pots, mugs, gravestones and epitaphs, the framing of houses, their room placement, facade form, materials, and colors, to show that, in New England between 1660 and 1800, a corporate way of life was replaced by individualism, just as had happened in Middle Virginia.

By looking at and creating a scheme for describing changes in the ranges of material culture, Deetz showed that the culture that emerged in New England was intellectually rather than emotionally oriented, was private, used artificial or refined substances, was more oriented to internal matters, and became increasingly subdivided so that society could maintain control (Deetz 1977:37–43). The question remains, control over what?

I strongly agree with Deetz that all the domains of material culture that he mentions—and likely many more—bespeak a mental structure or worldview. However, he does not tell us what affects the rate by which the worldview of Georgian material culture spreads, why it affects some communities and not others, and why some items are affected by the new way of looking at the world before others. In addition, I depart from Deetz in looking at the recursive or active quality of material culture. People express their lives in the things surrounding them, and in that expression and use, daily life is reproduced and brought into existence each day and each generation. Therefore, knowledge of the local context of use and meaning is essential if we are to understand the material culture and the mental order that made it.

Many of the data below from 18th-century Annapolis, Maryland, are economic statistics presented as local context for understanding the appearance of some items and their social purpose. I want to define the local context as part of a system of colonial, merchant capitalism, with the understanding that an economy organized to make a profit may involve all the aspects of a culture. Therefore, the rate of appearance of items may be tied to the penetration of merchant capitalism and crises within it. When capitalism is seen not as an economic system but as a culture, it may be possible to avoid violating the coherence of a cognitive and structuralist interpretation of material culture so fruitfully created by Glassie and Deetz.

No one has yet questioned whether Tidewater Maryland, including Annapolis, was devoted to producing a profit within the scheme of European and British colonization. Annapolis in the 17th and 18th centuries was one of hundreds of small tobacco ports along the Chesapeake Bay and the hundred and fifty rivers that flowed into it. These ports and their associated tobacco and wheat-growing plantations, using first indentured and then slave labor, were an integral part of the London/Glasgow/Continental/Caribbean/African trading network. Although that trading, merchant-backed, colonizing system has always been understood as an early part of emerging European capitalism, there are some things that have not been so clear. What part of the contemporary culture was a function of capitalism and what was not? How did capitalism grow, spread, develop, eliminate, absorb, and subordinate its populations? How did capitalism actually operate on the ground—that is, in people's daily lives—and expand and deal with its many contradictions, which were in turn produced by its ever greater possibilities for profit for some people? These are the final versions of the questions I have been asking all along, and their purpose is to demonstrate what Glassie and Deetz may contribute to an understanding of capitalism.

We can begin to address some of these questions by examining the dynamic pattern of wealth holding in Annapolis, as reflected in data on the redistribution of the wealth held at death in the city between 1690 and 1775 (Table 7.1). I have assumed that probate inventories, made by law at the death of a property holder and representing all the material and real wealth of the deceased, describe enough of a population to construct a view of the pattern of wealth. Probate inventories do not exist

TABLE 7.1

The Percentage of Wealth Held by Wealth Groups in Annapolis, Maryland

Year	Group I		Group II		Group III		Group IV		Total Wealth and number of inventories	
	%W	%P	%W	%P	%W	%P	%W	%P	Wealth	Pop
1689–99	28	75	0	0	72	25	0	0	£ 321	4
1700–09	8	46	14	23	51	23	21	8	£ 2175	13
1710–22	5	38	18	42	21	13	56	8	£ 8444	40
1723–32	2	30	7	30	13	21	78	18	£41769	33
1733–44	3	37	8	27	12	16	77	20	£19804	51
1745–54	3	48	4	13	7	13	86	26	£15292	31
1755–67	2	26	7	34	7	15	84	25	£32673	53
1768–77	2	30	8	43	5	13	85	20	£17697	30

Note: Group I, estates valued between £0 and £50; Group II, estates valued between £51 and £225; Group III, estates valued between £226 and £1000; Group IV, estates valued over £1000. %W = percentage of wealth; %P = percentage of population.

Source: Russo (1983), adapted by Shackel (1987).

TABLE 7.2

City of Annapolis Population

Year	Estimate	Year	Estimate
1704	272	1720	400
1705	272	1723	520
1706	311	1726	588
1707	331	1728	642
1708	333	1730	678
1709	330	1740	746
1710	326	1755	875
1711	324	1760	951
1712	319	1764	989
1714	329	1768	1,071
1715	340	1775	1,299
1716	383	1782	1,152
1717	389	1783	1,280[a]

[a]The figure for 1783 is from an official census.

Source: Walsh (1983).

for the entire population. These were not made for slaves, who constituted a third of the city's population at virtually any time, or for poor whites, poor free-blacks, most women, or anyone who lived, but did not die, in the city. (See Table 7.2 for data on the population of Annapolis from 1704 to 1783.)

The four wealth-holding groups used here were constructed (Russo 1983: 3; Shackel 1987: 65) by examining statistical breaking points in the curve of accumulated wealth. They are statistical categories; that they had social definition can probably be taken as a given, but the definition is as yet undescribed.

Two events in the data of Table 7.1 highlight changes in the use of material culture. The first is the dramatic realignment of wealth between 1690 and 1730. During this 40-year period (a little more than one generation), the wealth held at death by the poorest group in the city dropped from 28 percent to 3 percent. Of the two middle groups, the second went from 14 percent to 7 percent, and the third wealth group went from controlling three-quarters of the wealth to controlling 13 percent. Before Annapolis was made the capital of Maryland in 1694, it had no unusually wealthy residents. Between 1700 and 1730, this fourth wealth group grew to 18 percent of the population and gained control over 78 percent of the wealth held at death. Thus, this first event consisted of the rapid rise of a relatively small, very wealthy group of people (see Table 7.1 for the changing distribution of people between the wealth groups) and the simultaneous decrease in the wealth of a large part of the population. This reorganization of wealth must, it seems to me, be taken as an event of sufficient scope that it caused changes in how people thought and lived. It had to be accommodated.

The second noteworthy event in Table 7.1 is the continuation of the trend just described, but at a slower pace up to and through the Revolution. By 1775, the wealthiest group controlled 85 percent of the wealth held at death, whereas the first, second, and third wealth-holding groups held 2, 8, and 5 percent, respectively. What allowed the trend to continue without effective challenge, and why, in the face of their ever-increasing wealth, did the wealthiest in the city defend, sponsor, and lead the American Revolution in Maryland, since that was an act of treason to the established order?

The hypothesis I propose is based on these two socioeconomic events and the intervening years, 1730 to 1760:

Event 1: Between 1710 and 1730, clocks, scientific instruments, and musical instruments were introduced and used to show that newly aggregated wealth was legitimate because its possessors understood natural law through direct observation, which justified both hierarchy and individualism. Natural law was thought to be invoked by and observed directly through clocks, scientific instruments, and musical instruments.

Event 2: During the period from about 1730 until well into the 19th century, sets of cups, plates, knives and forks, chamber pots, toothbrushes, reading materials, and dozens of other domains helped to create what E. P. Thompson (1967) described as work-discipline for the 19th century. This term refers to the internalized set of rules that when used, create the self-maintaining individual. This individual produced and reproduced according to a standard and is the chief way in which capitalist society maintained stability. Work-discipline was achieved through eating habits, personal cleanliness, and reading and speaking habits.

Event 3: By 1760–65, landscape architecture and architecture itself were used to create the dual illusion that their builders or owners could reproduce the laws of nature and, in so doing, could convince others that the owners had or deserved the power that they were actually soon to seek in leading the Revolution. The gardens and homes were statements of wishes rather than statements of fact.

These are the three parts of the hypothesis that attempts to deal with the arrival, rate of spread, and local meaning of material culture associated with one modern pattern of thought known as Georgian: a pattern of thought that falls, I argue, within capitalism.

Clocks, scientific instruments (globes, spyglasses, compasses, barometers, thermometers, and telescopes), and stringed musical instruments are normally taken as signs of established wealth, the logic being that they play so minor a role in the needs of daily life or the maintenance of wealth that they are bought after more essential things and are used for leisure. These items first appeared in Annapolis between 1710 and 1730, the very time that wealth was being concentrated in fewer hands, and they were owned by all but the poorest wealth groups. They showed up long before the city's traditionally described age of wealth.

The production and use of all the clocks, scientific instruments, and—I argue by association—the musical instruments were part of the interest in natural philosophy.

> In the seventeenth century [in England] such instruments were generally made either by scientists themselves or by makers under their supervision. The general commercial market [including the American colonies] lay rather with such instruments as quadrants, sectors, sundials, or nocturnals. The eighteenth century saw instruments such as the orrery, the air-pump, and electrical generator made for a retail market—for the lecturer-demonstrators, for educational establishments or, increasingly, for interested amateurs. This market was consciously fostered by makers such as George Adams, or Benjamin Martin, who disseminated both the natural philosophy, through books and lectures, and the instruments for its practice . . .
>
> Many of the manufactured optical instruments had functions similar to the instruments of natural philosophy, so far as the interested public were concerned. The microscope was not a research tool in the eighteenth century, but rather, an amateur's instrument, used to peruse the wonders of the invisible natural world. Telescopes too were often manufactured to satisfy amateur interests; [they] reinforced a vision of the natural world precisely managed by mathematical principles. (Bennett 1985:7)

An assumption of the machinelike character of the natural world enhanced the significance of mechanical instruments in its investigation, and these instruments entered the public scientific domain through [public] experiments. (Bennett 1985:6)

A much larger public was hungry to own such objects for pleasure, amusement, instruction, as status symbols, as things of beauty, or in pursuit of hobbies (droves of Georgians loved keeping records of the weather and so would purchase high-quality thermometers and barometers). (Porter 1985:3)

Clocks, watches, scientific and musical instruments, I am arguing, are a part of the Georgian conceptual order that Glassie and Deetz have already so successfully defined. That order segregates, subdivides, stresses the intellect and the individual and focuses on order and control. The associated items of precision appeared in Annapolis among a number of wealth-holding groups at a time when the social order was experiencing a dramatic change: where wealth was once held relatively equally among different groups, it was now held unequally.

The items that began to appear in the city (and the meaning of which in Britain has been cited above) are likely to have been used in two ways. First, since time (clocks, sundials), sight (telescopes, compasses, spyglasses, microscopes, globes, sextants, quadrants), and sound (musical instruments, sheet music) can be basic cultural divisions of nature, these items were used to observe, study, order, and rationalize natural phenomena. Second, the rules, etiquette, regulations, and routines that it took to use them introduced mechanical or cultural divisions into everyday life and modeled daily life's activities on the mechanically precise rules of the clockwork universe. Some of the items of the Georgian order appeared in Annapolis very early, but were accompanied by a social realignment in which equality gave way to hierarchy. This realignment was so drastic that it might be expected to have been challenged by the newly impoverished. Instead, the middle wealth groups, even though they were being impoverished, fiddled and stargazed along with the rich. What did this achieve?

One answer may be found in the intention and use of the Nicholson plan of 1694. A city plan for Annapolis as Maryland's capital

was well suited to the topography of the site and expanded the total area of [Annapolis] to twice the original size. . . . Its more dramatic elements, the two circles, the radiating streets . . . plac[ed] public buildings in newly opened areas forc[ing] accompanying business and residential development. . . . Investment in city lots in Annapolis, situated as it was in a tobacco producing region, almost certainly was promoted not by an expectation of profits linked to export services but by the value of the lot itself, which in a permanent capital would be certain eventually to rise in value while temporarily providing . . . rental income. (Baker 1986:193, 195)

The land investment activity . . . was pronounced enough . . . [that] in 1708 "most of the Lotts in the Said Towne and Porte are Ingrossed into three or four Peoples hands to the great Discouragement of the neighbors who would build and Inhabitt therein could they have the opportunity of taking up Lotts". (Baker 1986:195, n. 12)

The period 1695–1730 saw the town law defined, patterns of commercial development clearly established, and all essential services supplied. Public and private interests had progressed to the point that the town could accommodate future growth and residents could live in reasonable harmony and safety. (Baker 1986:199)

Three points emerge from these remarks. Annapolis was situated on hills, and the Nicholson plan placed the statehouse and state church each on its own hill, placed a circle around each with spokelike streets radiating from the circles, thus capturing vistas to the centers of power from throughout the town. This was a baroque vision of the world that managed the principles of optics for political purposes. Mapping and surveying instruments achieved this end. Second, lots were precisely surveyed and recorded and frequently rerecorded, since there was great value in land speculation. Thus, the plan and its surveying satisfied political and commercial interests. Third, the plan and survey established hierarchy in three dimensional space, used precision to do so, allowed profit to flow from its operation, and provided the appearance of being rational and efficient at the same time, since it provided as the quotation indicates, for the future, for harmony, and for safety.

I suggest that the order initiated was thought to be natural and thought to have been discovered by one's own instrument-aided hand, in the heavens or some other part of the natural world. The order—whether or not it was in sight, sound, or time—was ideological, not cognitive, and contained a misrepresentation of the material relations ordinary humans were in (Althusser 1971). The order operated on individual habits expressed daily. It misrepresented the material relations among ordinary humans by placing social reality where it did not exist, since it placed heirarchy and in equality in the laws of nature.

In Annapolis between 1710 and 1730, the social reality behind disparate wealth and the disappearance of an earlier reality of more evenly distributed wealth may not have been perceived as a manifestation of the new order, which was taken to be an order of nature. However, it is not yet clear whether people saw hierarchy or individualism, with the latter's right to succeed and fail spread out differentially in the town, as the natural order. But my hypothesis suggests that clocks, globes, and violins revealed a natural hierarchical precision, which in turn was the root of and model for a new order.

Consider now how the order of unequal wealth was sustained. The order involved craftsmen, merchants, plantation owners, officials of the state, skilled professionals such as lawyers and doctors, women, slaves, renters, small property owners, and wage workers. Home or craft industry existed in Annapolis (Baker 1986)—for example, William Reynolds made hats, Jonas Green printed, John Shaw made furniture, and William Ferris worked with silver—and each industry used indentured servants, slaves, apprentices, and members of the family in the labor. The city had one or more ropewalks, windmills, brickyards, breweries, and tanyards, many warehouses, and many, many shops. It did not have factories in the sense of those that developed in nearby Baltimore in the 19th century, but there was some mass production, wage labor, rent, mortgaging, credit, debt, speculation, and profit. We may be able to see in these people how an order of inequality was successfully taught, learned, and reproduced, after it had been introduced between 1700 and 1730. I use table manners and reading/listening to illustrate how the work-discipline was established and show that some of the items of the Georgian order appeared during this process.

The inventories in Table 7.1 for the nearly half century between 1730 and 1777 reveal several classes of artifacts associated with eating: matched sets of plates, sets of cups and saucers, knives, forks, and sets of cutlery. Sets of plates first appear in the period 1710 to 1730 and continue to be present but do not increase in popularity to the 1770s, the last decade for which probate inventory data have been tabulated. The same is true of sets of cups and saucers. But knives, forks, and sets of cutlery behave differently. They start to proliferate in the period 1710–30, and from 1740 to the end of the 1770s they are adopted by over 40 percent of the poorest people, as well as by virtually everyone with means. Taken together, these items are the individual place settings that Deetz argues represent the hallmark of the Georgian mindset in New England. Knives and forks were used by 1709 in Annapolis, and sets of dishes for eating and sets of cups for drinking by 1732. These items spread to a substantial portion of all wealth groups in the city in the middle decades of the 18th century.

Cutlery of any sort is rare in the archaeological record of the 20 or so sites excavated in Annapolis since 1981. But broken dishes are extremely plentiful. Three archaeological sites were compared for increasing use of sets of dishes with different sizes and shapes, which we believe argue for rationalized eating habits. A formula constructed by Paul Shackel (Leone, Potter, and Shackel 1987:289) was used to measure this phenomenon. These three sites—the Victualling Warehouse, the Hammond-Harwood House, and the Thomas Hyde House—represent a middle-level wealth site and two upper-wealth sites, respectively. We argued that as foodways—butchering, cooking, segregation of foods by dishes in a course and courses from one another—were adopted, the different functions would appear archaeologically as variation in plate size. And more and more size variation would be expressed within fewer and fewer ceramic types. Ceramic type is the closest we can get to the modern notion of a set of dishes. We found a substantial increase in the use of matched sets (which also had pieces for different functions) from 1775 to 1810 and an enormous increase by the middle of the 19th century. Inventories show the initial use of sets of dishes and a multiplicity of functions within them by the 1720s, but the three archaeological sites show the same pattern only by 1760–70. There could be many reasons for the discrepancy, but the cause is not clear now. Even so, habits serving as a model for work-discipline appear in Annapolis by 1720 if inventories are used and by 1760 if archaeological remains are used.

Between the inventories and the archaeology we see the beginning, not the maturity, of a "restructuring of working habits—new disciplines, new incentives, and a new human nature upon which these incentives could bite effectively" (Thompson 1967:57). It is Braudel (1979:203–209) who points out that manners, guides to etiquette, including rules at the table, are coincident with the rise of capitalism. Each place at the table should measure the width of a chair. By the 17th century in Europe, the number of courses to be served, the changing of plates at the end of each course, and replacement of napkins after every two courses were all prescribed. The etiquette that accompanied the sets of dishes found in the inventories and found archaeologically in Annapolis—and that had spread deeply throughout all wealth groups by 1775 and characterized virtually all members of all social groups except free, property-owning blacks by 1850 (Shephard 1987)—internalized work-discipline. Just as proper behavior advertised a person's willingness to be a wage worker and served as an incentive for an employer to hire him or her, the discipline learned from dining etiquette created the rules of new order at home from childhood on. I argue that dining etiquette is one of the ways work-discipline was created and sustained.

In addition, knives, forks, and sets of dishes used by everybody communicate, as Deetz has said, a notion of the individual as the central fact of social life: "We are talking about the ideological domination of individuals and this requires the prior ideological creation of antecedent, autonomous selves. . . . Given the individual, ideological domination is the forms of manipulation of selfhood which allow the reproduction of the capitalist social [order]" (Barnett and Silverman 1979:68). E. P. Thompson explains,

> As soon as actual hands are employed[,] the shift from task orientation to time labor is marked. . . . Those who are employed experience a distinction between their employer's time and their "own" time. (Thompson 1967:61)

> In 1772 . . . education [was seen] as . . . training in the "habit of industry"; by the time the child reached six or seven it should become "habituated, not to say naturalized to Labour and Fatigue." . . . Schools as "a spector of order and regularity," [teach children to] "become more tractable and obedient, and less quarrelsome and revengeful." Exhortations to punctuality and regularity are written into the rules of all the early schools. (Thompson 1967:84)

> In all these ways—by the division of labour, the supervision of labour, fines, bells, and clocks; money incentives; preachings and schoolings; the suppression of fairs and sports—new habits were formed, and a new time-discipline was imposed. (Thompson 1967:90)

> What we are examining here are . . . greater synchronization of labour and a greater exactitude in time-routines [and] these changes as they were lived through in the society of nascent industrial capitalism. (Thompson 1967:80)

With this brief and preliminary analysis we can begin to see that Georgian material culture appears to coincide with one of the first crises in an urban setting, one stemming from the lopsided accumulation of substantial amounts of capital, and the simultaneous loss of it by others, their neighbors. The individual place setting and the culture it represented and helped to sustain began and continued to spread and deepen its influence in Annapolis unimpeded by style shifts and major social changes, such as the Revolution. The ideology represented by the place setting celebrates the self as an autonomous individual. This is the central notion that was absorbed by the wealthy and the not so wealthy. Judging by the popularity of the items that compose the place setting according to inventories and archaeology, almost all of the wealthy and between a fifth and a third of the poorest property owners as well were influenced by this idea by 1770.

The goal of the etiquette associated with these dining items was self-realization or personal fulfillment (Barnett and Silverman 1979:68). The penetration of the ideology of individualism and its notion of self-realization, in an urban setting, involved "getting people to do what they 'must' do. . . . Control or domination is evident in the necessity of choices ideologically given in a contractual form. These are 'choices' only given the idea of empty substance [a pliable person] and the possibility of self-realization through performance [either through work or the presentation of self as consumer]. . . . Such performances are simply necessary to commodity production and consumption" (Barnett and Silverman 1979:69). The nearly 50 years between 1730 and 1777 were years of both progressively unequal wealth holding and of the partial penetration of capitalism throughout Annapolis. The use of the place setting, as one kind of performance among many (time keeping/punctuality; razors/personal appearance; chamber pots/elimination in private) is one of the ways the autonomous self who learned to perform within the framework of a social contract was sustained. This process demonstrates how unequal wealth could be continually generated and held without violent resistance in a capitalist setting. Thus we can see not only the context of the spread of early time-discipline, but also how important its associated items were.

Two trends are now clear in the era 1730–70 in Annapolis: One is the increasingly unequal distribution of wealth; the other is the partial, not the complete, spread of modern dining habits as a form of work-discipline. If such habits, or etiquette, do make a worker punctual and self-disciplined, then only a part of the population of Annapolis was affected or absorbed by 1770. It was largely absorbed by 1830 and completely absorbed by 1860. This means that part two of the hypothesis is only partly confirmed, and it remains to be seen whether the archaeological absence of uniform dining might be a clue to resistance to a profit-making system by some people.

Food preparation, service, eating, and disposal were only some of the ways used to introduce the routines that create work-discipline. Reading and listening also played a part in the spread of the new way of thinking and doing things. The word, particularly the printed word, may be used to eternalize its context and content (Carravetta 1984). Neither spoken language nor printed language is absolute, but when words from the past are used to present remnants from the past as though recovered, the values encoded are not merely represented, but are made to appear eternal. Spanos (Carravetta 1984) argues that appearing to quote a critical remnant from another time or a view from another place communicates a panoptic view, a universal ability to understand across times and spaces, which creates the idea of universal vision. This is in contrast to the actuality of haphazard, partial views that may actually appear to be chaotic. Spanos further argues that through the printed word, its content, and form, there is the possibility of political incarceration because the use and order of words comes to be fixed, including the definition of temporality.

One of the most important of all colonial newspapers, the *Maryland Gazette,* was printed in Annapolis weekly from 1745 by Jonas Green, a master printer. After his death in 1765 members of his family continued printing. An extensive analysis of this newspaper and the archaeologically recovered remains of the Greens' shop by Barbara J. Little (1987) and the students working with her shows that, during the middle decades of the 18th century, citations of fabulous events cease and the regular citation of historical events seen as precedent appears (Coleman and Johnson 1985). This, together with the increase in citations urging decisions be made on the basis of evaluating the merits of cases, are clues to the arrival and spread of a way of citing the past to make it look alive and thus both comprehensible and, potentially, universal. The upshot of this was to reduce the disorder inherent in the remnants of the past and to connect the present and the past in a way that appeared evolutionary, natural, or inevitable.

By 1745, the rules for printing were so firmly in place that only a few changes were made by the 1770s (Harris 1986). One was the use of quotation marks around the body of a quotation rather than at the beginning of every column line of the quotation. In addition, the news was segregated from letters and from advertisements; more columns and more horizontal dividers were used. All these changes represent the introduction of more rules, greater rationalization of printed space, and the segmentation of information by more firmly fixed categories. In other words, they represent the appearance of Deetz's Georgian order and Braudel's early capitalism in print and thus its extension into time, other cultures, and grammar. Annapolis was largely illiterate in the 18th century, and we can imagine that the newspaper was read aloud to many. How the order and its impact were retained when heard is not known; nor is it clear that oral give and take altered the impact of the new order. Even so, we do know that reading aloud occurred in taverns, the center of social life for people of virtually all classes. Reading in such a context may have carried with it a set of peers to enforce reactions, timing, meaning, chronology, and other disciplinary markers.

A second crisis in Annapolis after the period 1730–65 or so helped lead to the American Revolution. In the struggle of the Revolution, merchant capitalists in Maryland triumphed, and afterward some became much more powerful politically; some became industrial capitalists. The crisis was a complex one. Leading up to it were English laws that increasingly compromised the trading capacities and ambitions of colonial merchants and investors. Isaac points out that "in a slaveholding society personal independence was a supreme value, and a man forced into client status was invariably degraded" (1982:145). Reduction to client status had been going on in Annapolis since 1700.

> If the consolidation of property in the hands of influential [office-holders] and wealthy merchants was pronounced enough to be remarkable in 1708, it was even more striking a decade later. [By] 1718 . . . the planter/gentry/officials own[ed] forty-two percent of the [city]. Merchants and professionals held twenty seven percent and craftsmen twenty nine percent. . . . The largest part of land held by craftsmen was in the "Newtown" area. By 1740 only four of these twenty lots were still in the hands of the artisan class for whom they had been specifically intended. In other areas of the city only about half the craftsmen-owned land in 1718 remained in that status in 1740. Tradesmen still worked and lived on this same land, but fee-simple title had passed to provincial officials and merchants who leased it out. In 1740 their [officials, merchants] combined percentage of the town land stood at seventy percent and remained at this level until the Revolution. (Baker 1986:196)

The progress of this impoverishment of the middle and lower classes was disguised on the one hand by a general increase in overall income and was accommodated on the other by the culture of mercantile capitalism, the daily self-disciplining of the newly created individual who saw himself or herself as a natural phenomenon. But by the 1760s, despite a near monopoly over wealth, the wealthy's control over power—the law, courts, church, and appointed offices—had become a serious problem. In fact, given the Tuesday Club's parody of the British king and court in Annapolis in the 1750s (Breslaw 1975), the pressures of the growing crisis may have appeared even earlier.

Isaac (1982:152-153, 156-157), who has described and analyzed the same crisis in Tidewater Virginia, notes that in local terms (which I suggest apply to Annapolis as well) the problem consisted of incomplete institutions. Courts operated without the use of precedent, were thus subject to expediency, and produced a widespread sense of help-lessness. The Anglican church had no authority aside from what civil government gave it, and the resulting moral vacuum made it a part of the established order. The crisis that developed by 1765 put the local rich in the middle, and increasingly alienated them from those they had impoverished, on the one hand, and from the government, on the other, which threatened more taxes, including trading restrictions, while blocking access to Parliament and the courts. The crisis just de-scribed produced a twofold reaction in Annapolis between 1760 and 1775. The impression was created by wealthy people, who were in-creasingly threatened, that in order to demonstrate understanding of the laws of nature, particularly those involving sight, natural laws could be made to operate in concrete, sometimes experimental, settings. The rules of perspective in architecture and in landscape gardening, when expressed as the great city houses, the classic Georgian homes with their inevitable formal landscapes, were intended as witnesses to an ability to observe and copy nature accurately. Second, the implications of these homes and landscapes were to convince people that a rational social order based on nature was possible and that those with such ac-cess to its laws were its natural leaders. This hypothesis is offered to show how the crisis of power and its relationship to wealth were han-dled in Annapolis before they were handled by violent conflict.

A series of formal gardens was built or rearranged in Annapolis from the mid-1760s to the Revolution. There were at least a dozen gar-dens, but no certain count has been made. Many survive today as frag-ments; two are nearly intact, and one has been accurately restored by way of archaeology. I consider the reliable data on three of these gar-dens: the Paca, Ridout, and Charles Carroll of Carrollton gardens. Many, but not all, gardens in Annapolis looked like these three. These varied from 2 to 4 acres, were all constructed on a slope, were oriented to a view, and were green gardens featuring trees, shrubs, and lawn more than flowers. They utilized elements of English early Georgian gardens, which emphasized solid rather than plane geometry. The house was the centerpiece of the plan, and, so far as I can tell, every great house in the city of Annapolis had a garden accompanying it, and most of these were terraced or falling gardens.

All the gardens were designed with at least one main prospect, usually from the center top of the terraces. Some of the rules for han-dling sight as found in the three pertinent Annapolis gardens follow. These rules are derived from Philip Miller (1733), Batty Langley (1726), and Stephen Switzer (1742); these works were all published in London, but were available in Annapolis and the southern colonies.

Terrace walks . . . it is very well known . . . to be a small Bank
of Earth, laid out and trimmed according to Line and Level, being
necessary for the proper Elevation of any Person that walks
around his Garden, to view all that lyes round him. . . . A seat [is]
of No Value without them.

Avenues . . . terminate in a Prospect. . . . As for such Avenues to Woods or Prospects etc. they ought not be less than sixty
foot in breadth [width], and . . . as to such Avenues that lead to a
House, they ought to be as Wide as the whole Breadth of the Front
[of the house]. . . .

On parterres, or level divisions of ground:

As to the Proportion of Parterres[,] an Oblong or Long Square is
accounted the most proper Figure for a Parterre; because by the
rule of Perspective, or the natural Declension of the visual Rays in
Optics, a long Square sinks almost to a Square, and an exact
Square appears much less than it really is; therefore a Parterre
should not be less than twice as long as it is broad [wide]. . . .

As to the breadth of a Parterre, it is to take its dimensions
from the Breadth of the Front of the House: If it be not above a
hundred Feet, 'twill be too narrow; and if the Front be two hundred Feet the Parterre must be of the same Breadth.

Some do not approve of making Parterre's very broad, because it makes 'em appear too short; when nothing is more pleas-
ing to the Eye, than a contracted, regular Conduct [walk] and
View, as soon as a Person goes out of an House or Building: And
a forward, direct view is the best, whether it be either a Parterre
or Lawn, or any other open Space, either two, three, or four-fold
to the Width: And for that Person, those Designs may justly be
disapproved by which the Nobleness of the View is marred at the
immediate Entrance into the Garden, the Angle of Light being
broken and confused. (Miller as quoted in Lockwood 1934:5–7)

A landscaped volume required the rules of perspective. A volume was
to produce a sense of harmony and awe. The next quotation is from
Stephen Switzer, whose *Ichnographia Rustica* (1718) was almost as popular in the southern colonies as Miller's books.

'Tis in the Quiet Enjoyment of Rural Delights [meaning a garden,
probably including a wilderness garden . . . that . . . are dispell'd
. . . Vapours . . . and . . . Hypocondraison. . . . 'Tis there [the
garden] Reason, Judgment, and Hands are so busily employed, as

to leave no room for any vain or trifling thoughts to interrupt. . . . And 'tis from the Admiration of these [the thoughts while in a garden] that the Soul is elevated to unlimited Heights above, and modell'd and prepared for the sweet reception [of what] Omniscience has created. (Switzer as quoted in Lockwood 1934:5).

To paraphrase all this: Gardens in England, from early Georgian times on, were to be built according to the skillful use of the rules of perspective; in England, they frequently carried a particular message, such as individual liberty, through their iconography (Rorschach 1983:1–7) and were to so engage a visitor's emotional reaction by entertaining the eye through the illusions and allusions in them, that the message appeared to have a more real existence by being copied in nature. Such, copying could, of course, occur only if the rules were assumed to exist in nature in the first place. The connection between the iconography and nature was created by sustaining the "happy enjoyment of Felecities" that help "clear the oppressed Head" of "Vapours" and "terrors," in other words, through the manipulation of the emotions.

Does any of this happen in Annapolis? It does between 1765 and the end of the Revolutionary era. In the Paca, Ridout, and Carroll gardens, the manipulation of sight by handling volume is clear and direct. The Paca Garden's topography is an archaeologically valid reconstruction made in the 1960s and 1970s. The Ridout garden is known to be largely intact; certainly its central section is, although any surviving garden will likely have been altered as landscape styles changed. A map of this garden was made in 1984 by archeologists Joseph Hopkins (1986) and Nigel Holman. The Carroll Garden is known to be altered, but is also largely intact. A map of this garden was made in 1986 by archaeologists William Roulette (1986) and Eileen Williams under the direction of Paul A. Shackel.

The Paca Garden had been destroyed and buried early in this century. The Ridout garden is largely there, still in the hands of the family that built it. The Carroll garden was begun at an as yet unestablished date, and assumed its present form between 1770 and 1774, as described in letters (Edie 1987) between Charles Carroll of Carrollton and his father Charles Carroll of Annapolis. Since the mid-19th century, the garden has been attached to a Redemptorist rectory and Roman Catholic Church, but has always been used as a garden. All three gardens have enough of their 18th-century contours and fabric to be fairly trustworthy illustrations of late 18th-century gardening in Annapolis.

The Paca and Ridout gardens cover about 2 acres, the Carroll garden between 3 and 4 acres. The Paca and Ridout gardens fall 16 feet, the Carroll garden 24 feet. Paca, Ridout, and Carroll each have five parterres and four falls. The Paca, and probably the Ridout garden, had wildernesses at their lowest points; the Carroll garden has over 600 feet of waterfront forming an open and varied view.

Each garden has a broad upper terrace longer than the house, and this top parterre is one of the principal places from which the garden was to be viewed. In Paca and Ridout, the garden then descends to parterres that become narrower. In the Paca Garden the descent is to terrace two, 80 feet wide; terrace three, 55 feet wide; and then terrace four, 40 feet wide. In the Ridout garden, terrace three is 44 feet wide. This is the first one visible from the viewing point. Terrace four is 35 feet wide. Then there is a broad bottom land that probably had a stream running through it and that opened up to a view of the harbor in the 18th-century. The Carroll garden's uppermost terrace varies from 100 feet to 50 feet in the areas where one has a view to the water. Terrace two is 30 feet wide, terrace three is 40 feet wide, and terrace four is 50 feet wide. The narrowing bottom planes of the Paca and Ridout gardens were used for city gardens built in limited spaces. When a view was to appear to be extended beyond its natural limits, a rapidly descending plane was used to make a distant object appear more distant than it was. Carroll's bottom plane goes from 30 to 40 to 50 feet, reversing the order of Paca and Ridout, thus also reversing the visual illusion and appearing to pull distant objects closer, whereas the others pushed them further away. Viewed from the water entry, however, rapidly narrowing planes going uphill made the Carroll House appear to be further and higher, thus producing the same ennobling impact as at Paca and Ridout, but from a different spot.

Eighteenth-century garden books also recommended that lines converge on a focal point. A short garden, for example, could be made to appear longer by planting the sides of paths, the edges of beds, or rows of shrubs or trees in converging rows, not in parallel lines. This produced the effect of greater distance than was there. Using plants with lighter green leaves on the edges and ends of a vista also was recommended to produce the same result.

> That all walks whose lengths are short, and lead away from an
> Point of View, be made narrower at their further Ends than at the
> hither Part; for by the Inclination of their Sides, they appear to be
> of a much greater Length than they really are: and the further End
> of every long Walk, Avenue, etc. appears to be much narrower
> than that End where you stand.
>   And the Reason is, that notwithstanding the sides of Such
> Walks are parallel to each other, yet as the Breadth of the further
> End is seen under a lesser Angle, than the Breadth of that Part

where you stand, it will therefore appear as if contracted, altho'
the Sides are actually parallel; for equal Objects always appear
under equal Angles, Q.E.D. (Langley 1726:196)

In the Ridout garden, the central ramp survives. There were to be rows
of shrubs along the paths in any garden, and in the Ridout garden planting beds survive. The current beds are important because they show
how, by reducing the distance between the pairs of beds and then by
making the beds themselves narrower, the principle of foreshortening
noted by Batty Langley was employed. Even though the central walk
does not narrow, its adjacent beds do and thus they heighten the illusion of a walk with narrowing sides; as a result, the garden seems
longer than it is because distant objects appear to be further away than
they actually are.

I have suggested that the results used in garden layout, which employed rules of vision or optics to display principles of perspective,
were found in at least three Annapolis gardens. But after these gardens
were built, *how* were they used? We know that they were not private,
and we know that their purpose was realized largely by walking
through them, sitting in them, or sometimes bathing, eating, or playing cards or other games in them. There is an extensive correspondence
that survives about American gardens of the colonial era and after Independence. McCubbin and Martin (1984) serve to show the details, correspondence, and stock of comparisons generated by the continuous
flow of visitors to these gardens. Given the enormous number of 18th-
century gardens up and down the British-American East Coast, some
sampling of which is to be seen in the staggering survey published in
Gardens of Colony and State, (Lockwood 1931, 1934), a parade of visitors
seem to have been ever present in them. This apart from the whole host
of servants, slaves, and family members who used them for practical
purposes, for they were filled with outhouses, sheds, storage houses,
dairies, baths, fences, food patches, walls, canals, greenhouses, hot-
beds, and pavillions.

In Annapolis, the surviving limited correspondence shows Paca's
garden to have been among the best in the city full of noticeable gardens
(Paca-Steele 1987). Carroll, the Signer, paid considerable attention to
gardens (Edie 1987) on several of his plantations and clearly intended
the garden to be impressive. The enormous parterres in the Carroll
garden are up to 300 feet long and are breathtaking even now.

Thus far I have not mentioned horticulture, but have described
landscape architecture. The same garden books set out information on
plants, with names, origins, and family relationships. They state growing conditions, and so on. Frequently this is done with advice on how

to copy or follow the work of famous experimental scientists on evapo-
ration, heat transfer, acidity, and other topics. But duplicating the rules
of perspective and following horticultural principles appear in fact not
to have been actually experimental. They were, as Porter (1985:3)
and Bennett (1985:6–7) have said, to serve as amusement, instruction,
and as status symbols. The many instruments used in association with
gardens, the abundance of experimental work recommended for gar-
deners, the many scientific instruments found in Paca's Annapolis inventory, and the fact that others of his rank kept records of their gardening observations, all suggest that the gardens were regarded as the
place to observe and duplicate the precision of the clockwork universe.
They were places to observe and to demonstrate an ability to duplicate
the laws of nature.

By the late 18th century, society too was regarded as a natural phenomenon, and an Annapolitan like Charles Willson Peale (Richardson
et al. 1983) performed hundreds of experiments and built an entire natural history museum in Philadelphia in order to argue that by observing the laws of nature one could build a new society according to more
natural rules and thus establish a more perfect social form.

Gardens, I believe, were meant to be demonstrations, like scientific
demonstrations, of the rules of nature observed and duplicated. They
were intended to be public experiments. Although they certainly *were*
public, they were not experiments in the scientific sense. They likely
were attempts to show that their builders understood the natural, and
thus the social, order. Because the building of falling gardens involved
optical illusions in Annapolis using the natural principles of optics and
occurred roughly between 1765 to 1779, because they were built by
parvenues like Brice; by Paca, who married his wealth; or by disfranchised men like the Catholic Carroll, and because many of these same
people sponsored the Revolution, the gardens may represent their last
effort to mask their growing political powerlessness and to argue for
power for themselves as men who could mediate between natural law
and a new natural society.

That is to say, "the temptation to build solidly and durably is
strongest among the *nouveau riche*. The more rapidly the fortune has
been got, the greater he feels the obligation upon him to erect brick or
stone monuments of a perpetual sort. . . . The rich lawyers and planters who built the stately mansions which may still be seen at Annapolis
and in the lower counties of the western and eastern shores [of Mary-
land], nearly all got their fortunes between 1745 and 1790" (Scharf as
quoted in Lockwood 1934:121). Paca, Ridout, and Carroll are not usually thought of as nouveau riche, but the point can be seen if we think
of their gardens as expressions of social and political insecurity. Since

wealth does not automatically mean power, and since the wealthy in Maryland were becoming less politically secure after 1750, we may link the older and newer rich through their simultaneous expressions of attempted control in the immediate prerevolutionary era.

Most of the homes just mentioned were accompanied by descent or falling gardens, and these are expressions of control. There were several possible garden styles to choose from and a great variety of alternative elements within the larger traditions. The Rennaissance garden was usually flat, had walls around it, had geometrically even divisions, little or no ornamentation, and, like the garden at Bacon's Castle in Northern Virginia (Luccketti 1987), contained mostly vegetables. These flat, enclosed gardens contained few possibilities for perspective views. The restored gardens of Williamsburg are of this type and show that early 18th-century gardens there were not planned with perspective in mind. Note, however, that the politically insecure Governor Spotswood of Virginia (Sanford 1987) built the falling garden at his country estate at Germana during this period. The fully developed natural or wilderness garden, dependent entirely on curvilinear geometry, was available as a model from the early 18th century in England. This form was not adopted widely in Maryland and Virginia until the 1750s; thus, it is possible to see that in garden form one style was chosen from many for reasons involving the larger social context. Falling gardens could show effective command over natural law and demonstrate the larger political competence of disfranchised yet determined builders.

To summarize, the first telescopes, clocks, and other scientific instruments appeared in Annapolis in the period when wealth in the city first became unequally distributed, that is, between 1710 and 1730. They may have served to argue that the world was both orderly and hierarchical. They may have supported the argument that the new world of individual merit and independently derived wealth was copied from nature. This is a form of ideology that says that society has to be the way it is because society follows what can be observed in nature.

By the 1760s, local hierarchies were again threatened and used control over optical illusions to sustain the ideology that nature had put them in charge and that their understanding of it should sustain that position. The ideology of naturalizing the hierarchical conditions of social life through landscape architecture was the last effort of a planter-merchant class before it adopted the much stronger argument of individual and personal freedom that it enshrined in the Declaration of Independence, the Constitution, and the Bill of Rights. The ideology of personal freedom as embedded in nature and divinity served to create the appearance of a link between much larger numbers of people across classes, that is, between rich and not-so-rich whites.

It is no accident that Paca refused to support the Constitution until the Bill of Rights was added. By then he had sold his Annapolis house and garden and was popularly elected Governor of Maryland. Charles Carroll had moved his wealth to Baltimore and was one of Maryland's first two U.S. senators. These men continued to garden, but depended not on a naturalizing ideology substantialized through them, which said an unequal social order was derived from nature; rather, they now depended on a masking ideology—personal liberty—which represented the partial as universal and the conflict-ridden as coherent.

The groundwork for this successful change in ideologies depended on the idea of the individual, just as Glassie and Deetz have argued. The archaeological record and the inventories show over and over that a rule-directed performance replaced an organic, family-framed, seasonally defined existence. Out of the period 1730–70 emerged the liberty-requiring individual, who was what he or she could do. It was this ideology of merit, performance, and contract that required the idea of personal freedom, and this was stronger because of 50 years of "practice." That ideology created the link between Paca and Carroll on the one hand, and all the others, on the other, who saw themselves as "like" them.

I believe 18th-century Annapolis is clearer now because several elements of its life have been juxtaposed: (1) Wealth held at death and the realignment of wealth over time and (2) the speculation in land for income, with the consequent reduction of propertied groups to renter status, occurred at the same time that (3) Enlightenment-based natural scientific observation and experimentation appeared in the city. Hierarchy appeared and continued, (4) accompanied by modern manners adopted by those new to renting and wage earning, and all in the context, that was ultimately to become violent, of (5) individual liberty as a natural right.

Rule-grounded housing created orderly living. Georgian cooking and eating habits appeared in Annapolis too, just as Deetz and Glassie showed for New England and Virginia, respectively. Orderly living arrived first among the rich, but in any one place occurred quickly among the poorer as well. The context of use of these items is now clearer and the context of rapid spread is clearer too, I hope, yet without using vulgar assertions of simple material cause.

Deetz and Glassie bound their data neither by time nor by class. And my own illustration is very local. In its local focus, it is also less general and less powerful for that reason. For where is this local pattern outside Annapolis? We already know it is retarded in the parishes around Annapolis (Shackel 1987: 144-229). Southern Maryland has data adequate to make a case (Kulikoff 1986). These would ground the pattern of Georgian symmetry and individualism in local context and serve to show that the Georgian mind-set can arrive and spread as a way of thinking that expresses itself in and realizes itself through material items, which reflect inequality and how inequality is made productive or resisted.

ACKNOWLEDGMENTS

An earlier version of this essay was presented to the Anthropological Society of Washington in 1985. I am grateful to the officers and membership of the society for the opportunity to present it and to organize the 1984–85 program. Most of the research reported here was supported by Historic Annapolis, Inc., which has been generous with its help but which does not necessarily agree with my opinions or interpretations. Lois Green Carr, Lorena Walsh, and Jean Russo have provided open access to their research and have helped generously at every opportunity. James Deetz has always been interested in the research. Barbara Little, Parker Potter, and Paul Shackel have provided data, analyses, reactions, and assistance of every kind. Rhys Isaac provided a friendly and cogent critique, which was central to revising the essay and furthering the research in general. My wife, Nan Wells, always listened with a keen and sympathetic ear.

REFERENCES CITED

Althusser, Louis
    1971   Ideology and Ideological State Apparatuses. In *Lenin and Philosophy,*
            trans. Ben Brewster, pp. 127–86. New York: Monthly Review Press.

Baker, Nancy T.
    1986   Annapolis, Maryland 1695–1730. *Maryland Historical Magazine*
            81(3): 191–209.

Barnett, Steve, and Martin Silverman
    1979   *Ideology and Everyday Life.* Ann Arbor: University of Michigan
            Press.

Bennett, Jim
    1985   The Scientific Context. In *Science and Profit in 18th-Century London,*
            pp. 5–9. London: Whipple Museum of the History of Science.

Braudel, Fernand
    1979   *The Structures of Everyday Life: Civilization & Capitalism 15th-18th
            Century.* Vol. 1. New York: Harper & Row.

Breslaw, Elaine
 1975 The Chronicle as Satire: Dr. Hamilton's "History of the Tuesday Club". *Maryland Historical Magazine* 70(2): 129–148.

Carravetta, Peter
 1984 An Interview with William Spanos. *Critical Texts* 3(1): 10–27.

Coleman, Simon, and Matthew Johnson
 1985 *Exploratory Analysis of the Layout of the Maryland Gazette.* Paper on file, Dept. of Anthropology, University of Maryland, College Park.

Deetz, James F.
 1977 *In Small Things Forgotten.* Garden City, N.Y.: Anchor Books.

Edie, Andrea
 1987 Charles Carroll of Carrollton Research Project. Ms. on file, Historic Annapolis, Inc. Annapolis.

Glassie, Henry
 1975 *Folk Housing in Middle Virginia.* Knoxville: University of Tennessee Press.

Harris, Tery
 1986 *Grammar and the "Maryland Gazette" as Reflections of the Georgian Mindset in Eighteenth and Early Nineteenth Century Annapolis.* Paper on file, Department of Anthropology, University of Maryland, College Park.

Hopkins, Joseph W. III
 1986 A map of the Ridout Garden, Annapolis, Maryland. Ms. on file, Historic Annapolis, Inc. Annapolis.

Isaac, Rhys
 1982 *The Transformation of Virginia, 1740–1790.* Chapel Hill: University of North Carolina Press.

Kulikoff, Allan
 1986 *Tobacco and Slaves: The Development of Southern Culture in the Chesapeake, 1680–1800.* Chapel Hill: University of North Carolina Press.

Langley, Batty
 1726 *New Principles of Gardening.* London: Bettsworth and Batley.

Leone, Mark P., Parker B. Potter, Jr., and Paul A. Shackel.
 1987 Toward a Critical Archaeology. *Current Anthropology* 28(3):283–302.

Little, Barbara J.
1987   Ideology and the Media: Historical Archaeology of Printing in
        18th-Century Annapolis, Maryland. Ph.D. diss. State University
        of New York at Buffalo. University Microfilms, Ann Arbor.

Lockwood, Alice G. B.
1931,   *Gardens of Colony and State.* Vols. 1, 2. New York: Charles
1934   Scribner's Sons.

Luccketti, Nicholas
1987   The Castle Gardens: An Archaeological Excavation of a Late
        17th-Century Garden at Bacon's Castle, Virginia. Paper given at the
        Society for Historical Archaeology, Savannah, January.

McCubbin, Robert P., and Peter Martin
1984   *British and American Gardens in the Eighteenth Century.* Williamsburg,
        Va.: Colonial Williamsburg Foundation.

Miller, Philip
1733   *The Gardener's Dictionary.* London: Printed for the author.

Paca-Steele, Barbara
1987   The Mathematics of an Eighteenth Century Garden. *Journal of Gar-
        den History* 6(4): 299–320.

Porter, Roy
1985   The Economic Context. In *Science and Profit in 18th-Century Lon-
        don,* pp. 1–4. London: Whipple Museum of the History of Science.

Richardson, Edgar P., Brooke Hindle, and Lillian B. Miller
1983   *Charles Willson Peale and His World.* New York: Abrams.

Rorschach, Kimerly
1983   *The Early Georgian Landscape.* New Haven, Conn.: Yale Center for
        British Art.

Russo, Jean
1983   Economy of Anne Arundel County. In Annapolis and Anne Arun-
        del County, Maryland: A Study of Urban Development in a To-
        bacco Economy: 1649–1776; ed. Lorena S. Walsh. Ms. on file, His-
        toric Annapolis, Inc. Annapolis.

Roulette, William
1986   Map of the Carroll Garden, Annapolis, Maryland. On file, Historic
        Annapolis, Inc., Annapolis.

Sanford, Douglas
1987   Governor Spotswood's Garden in Germana, Virginia. Paper deliv-
        ered at Conference on Landscape Architecture, University of Vir-
        ginia, September.

Shackel, Paul A.

    1987   A Historical Archaeology of Personal Discipline. Ph.D. diss. State University of New York at Buffalo. University Microfilms, Ann Arbor.

Shephard, Steven J.

    1987   Status Variation in Antebellum Alexandria: An Archaeological Study of Ceramic Tableware. In *Consumer Choice in Historical Archaeology,* ed. Suzanne M. Spencer-Wood, pp. 163–98. New York: Plenum.

Switzer, Stephen

    1742   *Ichnographia Rustica.* Printed for J. and J. Fox, and B. and B. Barker et al. London.

Thompson, E. P.

    1967   Time, Work-Discipline, and Industrial Capitalism. *Past and Present* 38: 56–97.

Walsh, Lorena S.

    1983   Anne Arundel County Population. In Annapolis and Anne Arundel County, Maryland: A Study of Urban Development in a Tobacco Economy: 1649–1776, ed. Lorena S. Walsh. Ms. on file, Historic Annapolis, Inc. Annapolis.

CHAPTER 8

Craft and Culture Change
in the 18th-Century Chesapeake

BARBARA J. LITTLE

This gentleman is of a middle Stature, Inclinable to fat, round-faced, small lively eyes, from which, as from two oriental portals, incessantly dart the dawning rays of wit and humor, with a considerable mixture of the amorous lear, in his countenance he wears a constant smile, having never been once seen to frown; his body is Thick and well-set, and for one of his make and stature he has a good sizeable belly, into which he loves much to convey the best vittles and drink, being a good clean knife and forks man.

> Alexander Hamilton on
> Jonas Green (in Land 1981:194)

Last Thursday Morning departed this Life, Mrs. ANNE CATHARINE GREEN, relict of the late Mr. Jonas Green, Printer to the Province; and on Friday Evening her Remains were decently interr'd in Saint Anne's Churchyard: She was of a mild and benevolent Disposition, and for conjugal Affection, and parental Tenderness, an Example to her Sex.

> *Maryland Gazette*
> March 30, 1775

An inventory of the goods and chattels of Frederick Green late of Anne Arundel County deceased . . . April 27, 1811 William S.

Green, administrator; Ridgely Weems, John Munroe, Creditors;
Richard H. Harwood, James Green, Henry Green, Relations.
Maryland Hall of Records
Anne Arundel county
probate inventories 1811

Feature 54 is the exterior builders' trench for the south wall of the
latest phase of the printshop structure. Most of the artifacts, including printers' type, a piece of transfer-printed pearlware, a
wrought nail, and quahog shell, come from the upper portions of
the trench fill. The brick and mortar fragments found at the bottom of the trench are construction debris.
Crosby and Little (personal
communication)

In the search for meaning, whether in the past or in the present, connections provide a thread with which any individual weaves together understanding. Connections are made not only by tying bits of data and
impressions together, but also by intertwining them onto the warp provided by one's worldview and ideology. This process of creating
meaning is no less true of the archaeologist or the historian who works
with bits of data that mean very little outside of their various contexts.
The historical archaeologist must make the above exemplified documentary and archaeological, impressionistic and objective evidence into
some kind of whole cloth. The range of these often isolated portraits of
people and things from the past suggests that connections among them
need to be created if any sense is to be made of them.

Both historians and archaeologists have recently begun to seek new
meanings in the past. Stone (1979) and Miller and Tilley (1984) observe
major changes in attitudes about the central subject matter of history
and archaeology, respectively. Certain members in each discipline have
turned their attention toward making the past human, toward understanding that ideas, ideology, and choices of the participants in the past
are not strictly determined but are also determinants. "The historical
record has now obliged many of us to admit that there is an extraordinarily complex two-way flow of interactions between facts of population, food-supply, climate, bullion supply, prices, on the one hand,
and values, ideas, and customs on the other. Along with social relations of status of class, they form a single web of meaning" (Stone
1979:8).

There is a move to put people like those introduced at the beginning of this chapter back into (pre)history. That move is in part a reac-

tion to the same concerns about complexity in each discipline. Miller and Tilley (1984:2) suggest that this change of attitude stemmed from dissatisfaction with the following aspects of the new archaeology: the uncritical acceptance of positivism; the stress on functionalism and adaptation to environment; the behaviorist emphasis on biological directives; the disdain for approaches that emphasized social relations, cognition, or ideology; the lack of consideration of the present social production of knowledge; the emphasis on stability and lack of attention to conflict; the reduction of social change to an effect of external factors; and the belief that quantification is the goal of archaeology. Stone was disillusioned with the new history for similar reasons. Ironically, Stone states that one reason for the reaction to the "new history" is that anthropology has replaced sociology and economics as the social science exerting the most influence in history.

More recently Ian Hodder (1986) has gone beyond a critique of processual archaeology and has begun to explore the potential of post-processual archaeology. Hodder's approach not only includes the individual and the present context of knowledge, but also emphasizes past context and the meanings of material culture. I attempt to touch upon each of these four factors in this chapter.

My goal here is to be consciously present oriented and past oriented. I consider craft and look for connections and meanings among the things that may have impinged both upon craft and craftsfolk and upon the modern study of craft. I would be guilty of making too many connections if I allowed my past orientation to be as broad as "craft." Thus, I focus on printing as it was carried out by the Green family in the 18th and early 19th centuries in Annapolis, Maryland. Although my subject is printers, other artisans and community institutions provide a context for a partial historical reconstruction of the Green family and its social milieu. I attempt to show a small part of the complexity of the family members' lives, mainly as printers, but also as parents, spouses, masters, and public servants. This task consists of connecting specific bits of archaeological and documentary data on the Greens and the site of their print shop and home, and of connecting this highly particularistic synthesis with a broader cultural context understood through secondary sources and created through theory.

The orientation to the present, which I address first, is served by reacting to the fragmented treatment of craft in the discipline of history. Historical archaeology fragments the study of the past in a different way from history, but the reasons for the separation are the same. This fragmentation has its roots in the very period of time that this study investigates. The same process that obtained in the 18th century affected the lives of the Greens and affects our lives today. By considering how the fragmentation of our scholarship originated, we may find a way to make connections between the present and the past.

THE FRAGMENTATION OF CRAFT STUDIES IN HISTORY

Historian's studies of craft fall into three types based on area of concentration: product, work process, and worker (Schlereth 1984). In an analysis of the historiography of craft, Schlereth was able to classify the ways in which historians have tended to study craft. Those who have emphasized the product have tended to celebrate the art rather than the artisan and therefore appeal to an antiquarian interest. (The categorization comes from scholarship dating back to the late 19th century and continuing today.) Schlereth points out that several scholars also consider technique when studying the product. Schwind (1984), Brownell (1984), and Ward (1984), for example, connect products with the methods of their manufacture. This type of work is part of a "new" field of study, decorative arts history.

The second category of craft study is concerned with craft processes and emphasizes tools, skills, and working conditions. Schlereth points out that much of this research has been considered part of economic history, folk-life or ethnographic studies, or the history of technology (1984:47) and that it tends to be prevalent in museum settings.

The third category concentrates on the persons involved in craft: the individuals, their social roles, and social institutions. Carl Bridenbaugh's *The Colonial Craftsman* (1950) is one of the earliest examples of studies in this category. Much labor history of the 19th century also fits here. An example of this in printing history is the work on the mechanics associations and labor unions of printers. For example, Rosemont (1981) details an 18th-century labor dispute among printers.

As Schlereth emphasizes, historiographical reality is not as compartmentalized as his categories suggest. His three divisions are not mutually exclusive; indeed, they are intimately connected. The study of artifacts leads directly to the study of techniques, which cannot but lead to the study of labor relations and shop organization; these subjects are in turn linked to economic and political roles of artisans as community members. This historiographical fragmentation is clearly not a "natural" division dictated by the way craft was organized. Even though there are historians whose work straddles one or more of these categories, Schlereth's division is enlightening by the very fact that he was able to create it.

It is fair to ask why craft studies should be fragmented in this way when social history aims at holism and connections. Hobsbawm (1971) argues that social history cannot be treated as a specialization like traditional economic history because its subject matter cannot be isolated: Social aspects cannot be separated from other aspects. There are separations anyway. Hobsbawm identifies in the social history of the 1960s six topics still being addressed in various degrees of specificity: (1) demography and kinship, (2) urban studies, (3) classes and social groups, (4) mentalité and culture, (5) transformations of society such as industrialization and modernization, and (6) social movements and phenomena of social protest. Craft studies that concentrate on the artisan as a person could fit into any of these categories as well as others, such as biography. "Work culture" is part of the process of a craft but work technique is largely left out of social and labor history. Artifacts are almost completely invisible in social history. The point is that not just craft studies are fragmented in the way Schlereth suggests. Social history in general separates who people are from what they do and from the objects that surround them. There are two main reasons for this. One has to do with why artifacts are seldom considered in history. The other, which I discuss first, with the uses of history.

Compare the separation of artifact from labor from person with the separations in historical scholarship and publicized history that Potter (1986) has observed for Annapolis. Through ethnography, he has attempted to discover how history is created and used in the city. Potter argues that history often functions as ideology in the Marxist sense. That is, history serves to conceal and mask conflict-ridden relationships. In Annapolis, the fragmentation of history serves this purpose. Black history is separate from white history; the 18th century is separate from the 19th century; the history of the Naval Academy is separate from the history of the city. Potter suggests that these fragmentations of history stem from the political needs of white Annapolitans. The "Golden Age" of the 18th century is presented as important history because the city seeks to portray itself as important today as the city was in colonial days. This portrayal masks the city's economic decline that lasted through the 19th century into the 1950s. The fragmentation of history avoids historical connections that could be read as conflicts between black and white and between the Naval Academy and the city.

There seems to be a similar political motivation for the historiographical separation of produced artifact from labor process from person. It is not in the interests of people who make a profit from mass production to teach a history that makes connections between people and what they produce. The unification of occupation and identity is missing for most workers in a capitalist economy in which labor is alienated. Instead history separates the person into component parts and does not recognize any connections between a craftsperson and tools or trade. The connection is made only when quality and pride in work are being sought or imposed. Then, the history of the proud American craftsman is invoked to make present-day workers feel degenerated unless they take pride in assembly line work and seek to ensure its quality. The separation of person from life work is projected into the past in order to establish the long roots of the fragmentation and therefore give it legitimacy and a sense of inevitability.

This is the same process that Potter has described in his ethnography of history in Annapolis. The roots are the same a well. Before we can find the roots of this fragmentation in the past and show how this process affected the lives of the Greens as printers of Maryland, we must set out a few organizing principles. The meaning of goods must be discussed to show how they can reenter history. A model that uses goods and their creative nature must be developed for interpreting changes that occur in goods, particularly in the 18th century. The model I use is based on Mary Douglas's model of cultural bias and on Leone's approach to the study of emerging capitalism using Deetz's and Glassie's observations.

THE MEANING OF GOODS

Historical studies of the United States seldom use artifacts for anything except illustration. This lack of interest in the material world stems from a poor understanding of the roles that goods play. Although some historians, like Schlereth, use artifacts extensively for interpretive clues, this is not the norm. This state of affairs has recently been criticized in several quarters.

There are some recent promising studies of the meanings and uses of goods in both social history and American studies. Such work includes that of T. H. Breen (1986), Jackson Lears (1981), and Wayne Craven (1986). Braudel (1979), for example, masterfully demonstrates the primacy of everyday life and of the material in the process of history. Among others, Mary Douglas (1966, 1978; Douglas and Isherwood 1979) and Amos Rapoport (1982), who discusses material "behavioral cues," provide the framework for assigning meaning to goods and for understanding that material objects and categories are not only created by us but also create us.

In her book *Purity and Danger* (1966), Douglas demonstrates that all categories are culturally created. Even the physical environment, which is often thought of as fixed and restrictive, is classified, understood, and used in particular ways to meet social and cultural needs. In her more recent work Douglas has continued to emphasize human metaphorical understanding of goods as markers of cultural categories. Goods act as an information system. There are no goods without meaning, according to Douglas. "Even the choice of kitchen utensils is anchored to deep preconceptions about man and nature" (1979:73). Members of a society endow goods with value as category markers. Goods act to elicit and stabilize consensus about cultural categories and about value and thereby make and maintain social relationships through the information system. In this way, the universe of goods and of people is made intelligible and controllable (Douglas and Isherwood 1979).

Once we recognize this universal imposition of cultural categories, we begin to see that the search for meaning through the study of past culture should include the analysis of material goods and environment and that ideology may be discovered in material culture. This is no surprise at all to many archaeologists who have been at work interpreting symbols and ideology through archaeological data (for example, Hodder 1982a, b; Miller and Tilley 1984; Miller 1985). This approach may be hard to accept for those historians who have been blind to many of the possibilities of studying material culture.

Ideology, material culture, social context, and social change must all be linked together. In attempting to make this link, I have used Douglas's deceptively simple but powerful taxonomy of social contexts and concomitant cosmologies, which she introduced in 1966 and presented more fully in 1978. Recognizing that both individualism and group behavior are always present in any social group, Douglas constructed a two-dimensional graph for mapping degrees of "grid" and of "group." Grid measures the rules of interaction to which individuals are subject. Where grid is high, individuals are strongly controlled by rules, and where grid is low, individuals tend to transact freely. The group axis measures the strength of group identity. Figure 8.1a presents a graph taken from Douglas's book *Cultural Bias*. She writes, "Most anthropologists (and others) have assumed that the shift from status to contract goes in step with the breakdown of corporate groups, as if the increase of individual freedom could only be traded against decrease in group strength. I am trying to present a less impoverished view of social change" (1978:7).

If one wanted to characterize an entire society and ignore its complicated internal structure, then a linear model of the kind Douglas seeks to supplant would be adequate. Figure 8.1b illustrates such a model. Douglas prefers to examine the behavior and beliefs of the individuals who make up society, as well as the characteristics of the soci-

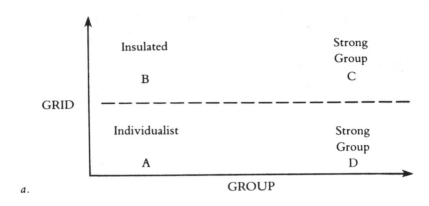

a.

b.

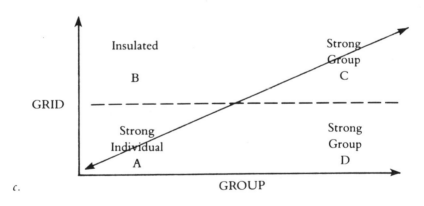

c.

Figure 8.1: Graphic representations of societal taxonomies. a. Douglas's four types of social environment. Source: Douglas (1978:7). b. Linear model of cultural types. c. Relationship between Douglas's and linear models. Grid is a relative measure of the explicit rules to which individuals are subject. Group is a relative measure of the strength of group identity.

ety that molds its members. Archaeologists and historians who are looking for meaning in the past by making people their subject matter could do worse than to consider her work seriously.

Douglas's model is rich enough that the space here does not allow me to recap the implications and predicted cosmologies for each type of social context. The central point to note is that this model defines cosmology as a set of distinctive values and a belief system that follows from a particular social environment as necessary for the legitimation of actions taken within it (Douglas 1978:53). I take the terms *worldview* (as used by Deetz 1977) and *ideology* to be roughly synonymous with this definition of cosmology.

As Douglas suggests, worldview is not a singular phenomenon equally shared by all individuals. Within various subsets of a culture, people have differing perspectives that may change at various rates and in varying directions, depending upon catalysts from other groups in the culture. It seems logical that groups in Douglas's system may split along boundary lines associated with distinctions such as rural/urban, rich/poor, and female/male, but this assumption should be considered hypothetical for the time being.

Douglas formulates relatively few hypotheses about the characteristics of material culture to be found in each of the four extreme positions on the graph. She gives enough other conditions so that it is possible, by combining her work with the observations of Deetz (1977), to outline some expectations about the changes occurring in Anglo-America in the 18th century.

Deetz's (1977, 1983) work provides us with a substantial baseline from which to work in putting material culture into a model of cultural change. I need not summarize here his influential and familiar book *In Small Things Forgotten* (1977), except to emphasize that he argued that changes observed in material culture reflect a change in worldview, notably from the medieval communality to the Renaissance-born emphasis on the individual. The emergent worldview is named "Georgian." This sort of observed change toward individuality is similar to that represented in Figure 8.1b. This is a change from a strong group/strong grid toward a weak group/weak grid. Deetz's insights can be enhanced by considering all four quadrants of Douglas's taxonomic graph. Figure 8.1c illustrates a combined view of Deetz's and Douglas's models.

In 1983 Deetz identified a number of structural oppositions that rest on the underlying opposition of control/chaos: intellect/emotion, private/public, artificial/natural, clustered/scattered, extensive/intensive, simple/complex, framed/open, and symmetry/nonsymmetry (1983:32). He proposed that in colonial America a switch occurred by the late 18th century. Worldview came to emphasize the characteristics suggested by the first word in each pair as it changed from an earlier form that had emphasized the second. Material culture reflects this change. Ceramics, foodways, mortuary markers, and music exhibit changes for switchovers within each opposition. Architecture also reflects these changes (Deetz 1977; Glassie 1975).

Each of these oppositions relies on categorization of thoughts and behaviors. If taken to be unidirectional and assigned to a particular time and place, all of these oppositions may be subsumed under another opposition whose components are even more clearly culturally determined: appropriate/inappropriate. None of the switchovers would have taken place if they had not been influenced by a changing valuation of appropriateness. This opposition explicitly condemns what must be its earlier half, just as the behaviors and the material culture associated with each "appropriate" category must supercede what is to be left behind as inappropriate and, in structuralist terms, is no longer "good to think." Changes in what is appropriate are signals and results of a changing worldview.

The political and economic impetuses for altering ideologies are forces that must be explicated if we are to approach an understanding of cultural change. Mark Leone (1984, 1985) has extended Deetz's idea of Georgianization and has postulated its economic and political bases in emerging capitalism. In Leone's view, the individual is created as a wage laborer through segmentation of time, of work from domestic life, of space, and of social position through adherence to particular rules of behavior. This separation of people from each other and from their work is part of the social relations necessary for industrial capitalism to emerge and develop. This is the same separation that leads to the fragmentation of social history. Georgianization is said to be both a product and a producer of capitalism. It places increasing emphasis on the individual through segmentation (public to private; scattered to clustered) and on symmetry. Segmentation should be observable in the separation of work from domestic life, in the division of labor within work, and in the characteristics of artifacts. According to Deetz (1977), symmetry should be observable within artifacts and between their parts, as in architecture, and between people and goods, as in a one-to-one correspondence between persons and plates, say, or chamber pots. Symmetry between goods refers to a standardization of goods that renders all individuals of a type identical. Culturally defined symmetry and standardization should also develop between individuals, and therefore some form of an ideal of republican egalitarianism should develop with an emphasis on access to goods and to perceived rights in a one-to-one relationship.

Meanings of goods can be explicit or implicit. The Georgian house with symmetrical and segmented facade and floor plan might be explicitly understood as a sign of wealth and social standing and as a place for deference. It might be implicitly understood as a natural outgrowth of the way people "ought" to live: separating eating from sleeping from playing cards and private daily life from public life. A set of decorated pearlware dinnerware might explicitly confer a message of status for its owner. The organization of the ceramics into a matched set implicitly declares that segmentation and standardization (of dinner and diner) are desirable and natural. Similarly a newspaper might be explicitly understood as carrying political propaganda for the American revolutionary patriots and implicitly understood as a natural amenity of civilization: a regularly issued, regularly sized sheet laid out in logical sections that are well differentiated.

The grid-group chart shows this Georgian worldview becoming dominant in much the same way that Deetz's work in New England did. Figure 8.1b is a simple model of this change to a Georgian worldview. Figure 8.1c shows this overall change with the grid-group system. In Douglas's model a society can be generally characterized as belonging to some quadrant of the graph, but more specific segments of the society can be characterized as existing elsewhere on the graph. If we consider segments of society, we can identify an exploitive, entrepreneurial group, possibly wealthy, urban and male, moving into the weak grid/weak group quadrant where individuals transact relatively freely and have few group restraints. In Annapolis, these are the merchants, shop owners, and possibly the governmental elite. Other exploited groups, possibly those whose members are poor, rural (or urban) and female, move into the strong grid/weak group area, which Douglas (1978:7) describes as holding insulated individuals who have little group support but are bound by many rules that govern their transactions with other individuals. These are the people who are created as wage laborers in a system of emerging capitalism.

The material manifestations of the new ideological, social, and economic way of life should exhibit the broad characteristics that Deetz has identified (1977, 1983). The material culture adopted and used by specific economic, ethnic, age, and gender categories should exhibit differences that would place them in the grid/group graph somewhere off the main line of change.

At this point, we need to ask how industrial capitalism emerging from mercantile capitalism affected printing and other crafts. Can we see evidence for increasing segmentation and symmetry in printing products, processes, and people in 18th-century Annapolis? Before we can tackle this question, we must look at the available data.

THE DATA BASES

The Jonas Green Print Shop site is located in the historic district of the city of Annapolis, Maryland. Members of the "Archaeology in Annapolis" project excavated the site as part of the University of Maryland's summer field school for four seasons, from 1983 to 1986. The Greens' home and shop occupied the same city lot from the 1730s to at least 1780 and possibly until 1811. Greens lived in the house until 1847. The house occupied by the Greens still stands. Enough of the details of the building are exposed to give us an idea of the evolution of the structure as it was modified during the course of the 18th century. The deepest parts of the foundations of the print shop were uncovered in what is now the backyard of the house. The kinds of materials recovered are in general what one expects from a site that has been domestic for at least 250 years: There is a great quantity of ceramics and glass; there are buttons, marbles, pins, toothbrushes, bricks, nails, and so on. Since this was an operating print shop for many decades, a great deal of printers' type is also associated with this domestic material. Many examples of the imprints produced at the site fortunately survive. The newspaper printed by the Greens has proved a useful resource as both document and artifact. Documents pertaining to the Greens and their house and shop are also relatively abundant.

At the time of writing, excavation and analysis are still in progress and therefore any conclusions for the site as a whole would be tentative. Only a small part of the archaeologically recovered material is analyzed in this discussion. A sample of the ceramics recovered during two of the four excavation seasons is analyzed using a technique developed by Paul Shackel (1987). This technique is demonstrated in Leone, Potter, and Shackel (1987), who argue that segmentation of tasks, standardization of products through mass production, and standardization of behavior through rules of etiquette became entrenched in Annapolis during the 18th century.

They also argue that a greater variety in sizes and types of dishes measures segmentation of people during a meal and the segmentation of foods within a meal. This segmentation is also an indirect measure of the processes at work in the 18th century. The formula developed uses the variation of ceramic types and sizes to quantify the variability and changing segmentation represented by the ceramics. The formula, (Type-Size/Type times Size = Index) yields an index value that can be compared between time periods and sites. Type is the number of standard ceramic types; Type-Size is the number of sizes of each type represented; Size is the number of different sizes present. Ceramics used are plates or rims of plates that can be measured to obtain plate diameter.

TABLE 8.1

Measure of Tableware Variation

Type		Size (inches)			
	5	6	7	8	9
Porcelain				x	
Pearlware			x		x
Whiteware	x				x

Note: Type = 3; Type-Size = 5; Size = 4;
$(5/3)(4) = 20/3 = 6.67$.
Source: Leone, Potter, and Shackel (1987).

Table 8.1 demonstrates the technique. Low variability would yield an index of 1.0. Higher indices mean more variability. The upper limit depends upon the assemblage.

The plate rim fragments analyzed from the Jonas Green site represent three phases of the later occupation of the site. The earliest contexts determined for the site so far exhibit a terminus post quem (TPQ) of pearlware and a mean ceramic date of 1784. This is Phase IV. Phase III has a TPQ of pearlware and coal and a mean ceramic date of 1782. The third and last phase discussed here is Phase II, which has a TPQ of whiteware and a mean ceramic of 1793. The results of the ceramic analysis (see Table 8.2) indicate increasing segmentation in table settings as the index rises.

Although the index of plate size variability does increase markedly and quickly after 1780, a measure of segmentation in the printer's household remains elusive for the earlier part of the century. While the site is known to have been occupied from 1745 at the latest, it appears that much of the early deposit is covered, destroyed, or thoroughly mixed by house additions and other landscape alterations of the 18th, 19th, and 20th centuries.

If excavated ceramics are unable to help determine changing segmentation in the earlier printers' lives, perhaps the type itself can tell us something of standardization in the process of printing. The excavated type, dated by matching to the newspaper, by archaeological context, and by technical attributes, ranges from the 1750s to the 1870s. (There are no historical data to explain the presence of this late 19th century type.) Standardization was sought in type body size, type height, space

TABLE 8.2

Ceramic Index of Variability for the Jonas Green Site

Type	Size					
	4	6	7	8	10	12
Phase II: 1820 to mid-19th century[a]						
Slip combed						X
White salt glaze			X			
Creamware				X	X	X
Pearlware		X		X		X
Whiteware						X
Porcelain		X				X
Phase III: 1810–1820s[b]						
Tin glaze earthenware	X					
Creamware		X				
Pearlware					X	
Porcelain			X	X		
Phase IV: 1780 to early 19th century[c]						
Creamware		X				
Pearlware		X				

[a]TPQ = whiteware; mean ceramic date = 1793; number of dated sherds = 1,184; number of plate rim sherds = 28. Type-size = 11; Type = 6; Size = 5; (11/6)(5) = 9.17.

[b]TPQ = pearlware and coal; mean ceramic date = 1782; number of dated sherds = 201; number of plate rim sherds = 7. Type-size = 5; Type = 4; Size = 5; (5/4)(5) = 6.25.

[c]TPQ = pearlware; mean ceramic date = 1784; number of dated sherds = 1118; number of plate rim sherds = 4. Type-size = 3; Type = 2; Size = 2; (3/2)(2) = 3.

Ceramic index of variability for Phase II = 9.17; for Phase III = 6.25; for Phase IV = 3.0.

height, and chemical composition, none of which became definitively more standard through this time period. Type height and chemical composition were already standard before the period of study. Space height remained variable throughout the period. An increase in the number of body sizes supports the expectation of segmentation. The details and causes of the variation are complicated and interesting (Little 1987), but are not the focus of this chapter. I suspect the variation has more to do with the peculiar nature of printing and with centuries of Western culture change than with changes specific to the 18th century. Some of the more focused changes appear in an examination of the products of the press as artifacts.

This study is also concerned with unexcavated artifacts. Documents are an essential part of historical archaeology. Often these are accepted at face value for the information they contain, even though the meaning of the recorded information is not obvious. I have trusted the information in the documents that I have used to assemble information about the Greens.

The Maryland Hall of Records has been my main source of primary records, which include administrative and testamentary bonds that are part of probate records, land records, militia records, tax assessments, merchant order books and correspondence, court judgments, levy books, and certificates of freedom. Probate inventories are a major source. These are inventories of all the goods owned by a head of household upon death. In spite of possible problems in the accuracy of reporting and biases in sampling (e.g., Main 1975), these documents provide precisely dated lists of material possessions. Histories of printing and histories of Annapolis have been useful secondary sources. Nancy Baker's (1984) study of Annapolis craftsmen from 1695 to 1776 provides a local basis for comparing the place of different Greens in the community.

The newspaper printed by the Greens themselves has been useful as a source of historical detail. The paper has the advantage of time depth, precise dating, and regularity of issue. It was published weekly with few lapses from 1745 to 1839 and for most of its life was the only paper published in Annapolis. The *Maryland Gazette* has been used as both document and artifact. Every document is indeed an artifact and, as Wolf (1984) points out, is subject to a great deal of interpretation. In the case of the newspaper, the content is taken to have a more explicit meaning, both today and at the time of publication, than the form and the layout of the paper that delivers its meaning in a much more implicit manner.

The form of the newspaper as artifact is analogous to style in other artifacts, particularly building facades and floor plans since these may be analyzed as two-dimensional spaces. The newspaper can be described in terms of symmetry and segmentation by measuring the presence, absence, and relationship of carefully chosen items. In this way, the newspaper can be analyzed for its role as an artifact reflecting and reinforcing the Georgian order.

Coleman and Johnson (1985) analyzed 322 issues of the *Maryland Gazette* printed between 1745 and 1814. An average of just under 10 issues per year for 33 years was sampled. They recorded information for 28 questions on each issue. Although there is temporal variation in the answers to most of these questions, the meaning of some of the variation is uncertain. Five of the characteristics of the paper are discussed

TABLE 8.3

Presence (+) and Absence (−) of printed lines in the Maryland Gazette

Year	Columns −	Columns +	Stories −	Stories +	Sections −	Sections +	Advertisements −	Advertisements +
1745	x		x		x[a]			x
	x		x			x		x
	x		x		x			x
1750	x		x			x		x
					x			
						x		
1755		x	x		x			x
		x	x			x		x
		x	x		x			x
1760		x	x			x		x
		x	x			x		x
		x	x			x		x
1765		x	x			x		x
		x	x			x		x
		x	x			x		x
1770	x		x			x		x
	x		x			x		x
1775								
	x		x			x		x
	x		x			x		x
1780								
1785	x		x			x		x
	x		x			x		x
	x		x			x		x
1790								
	x		x			x		x
	x		x			x		x
1795								
1800								
	x			x		x		x
1805	x			x		x		x
1810								
		x		x		x		x
		x		x		x		x
1815		x		x		x		x

[a]This is schematized; there is variation between issues within any single year through 1758.

here: (1) number of columns, (2) printed lines separating columns, (3) printed lines separating sections of the paper, (4) printed lines separating stories in the paper, and (5) printed lines separating advertisements. The overall increase from 1745 to 1814 in the separation by printed lines by columns, sections, stories, and advertisements indicates increasing segmentation within the layout of the paper. In the 1750s the number of columns increases from two to three and the presence of lines separating sections of the paper becomes consistent rather than sporadic; these changes indicate standardization among issues. More lines separate stories in the paper after the Revolution. By the early 19th century there are five columns and there are lines separating components of each of the four categories examined. Table 8.3 illustrates changes in the last four items. Within each column an "X" indicates either the presence or absence of printed lines separating columns, stories, sections, or advertisements. Gaps in data are blank on the chart.

Harris (1986) selected grammar rules from four printer's manuals published in 1683 (Moxon), 1755 (Smith), 1808 (Stower), and 1818 (Van Winkle). She searched for adherence to these rules in the *Maryland Gazette* from 1745 to 1825 in an evenly spaced 5 percent sample of 157 issues. Of the 22 chosen rules, 8 showed variation over time. These are best thought of as four pairs of two rules each, since the rules in each set are grammatically related and tend to covary. These rules are (1) words of emphasis are placed in italics (from Moxon), (2) words of emphasis are placed in small capitals (from Moxon), (3) proper nouns are set in italics (from Moxon), (4) proper nouns are set in large capital/lowercase format (from Smith), (5) the short "s" is used only when it is the last letter in a word (Smith), (6) the long "s" is used unless it is the last letter of the word (Smith), (7) quotation marks are carried in every line of a paragraph (Smith), and (8) quotation marks are carried only at the beginning of every paragraph (from Stower).

It is hard to judge the meanings of these grammar rules for standardization. What is the most clear here is the way that adherence to the rules changes, rather than the content of the rules themselves. Table 8.4 provides a count of the number of switchovers between adherence and nonadherence that occur within particular time periods. The first set of rules begin to show serious variation in 1771 and continues to show variation through 1816. The second set of rules shows some initial variation and then becomes consistent. The third set of rules is consistent until a sudden switch in the early 1800s. Like the second set, the last set shows initial variation and then becomes consistent after 1776. Whatever the grammer itself means, the standardization evident in the second and fourth set and the quick and orderly switch in the third set support the expectation of an increasingly standardized newspaper.

TABLE 8.4

Switchovers in Adherence to Grammar Rules

Rule No.	1745–50	1758–64	1771–76	1780–87	1795–1802	1809–16	1823–25
n=	21	24	18	26	28	29	11
1	3(14)	0	12(67)	8(31)	10(36)	8(28)	0
2	0	0	7(39)	8(31)	10(36)	6(21)	1(9)
3	8(38)	1(4)	6(33)	0	0	0	0
4	2(9)	0	0	0	0	0	0
5	0	0	0	0	0	5(17)	0
6	0	0	0	0	0	5(17)	0
7	10(48)	11(46)	8(44)	0	0	0[a]	0
8	10(48)	8(33)	2(11)	0	0	0[a]	0

Note: n = number of issues per time period. Table gives number of switchovers between adhering and not adhering to a particular rule; numbers in parentheses denote the percentage of possible switchovers given the number of issues examined.

[a]The actual counts for these time periods are higher (14 percent and 7 percent, respectively), but are both due to the quotation of earlier literature.

The kinds of changes evident in adherence to certain grammar rules are similar to the kinds of changes seen in the layout of the newspaper. The variation shown in the first set of rules is also seen in the presence of lines printed between columns. The change from initial variation to consistency in the second and fourth sets of rules is also observable in the pattern of lines between sections. The quick switch of the third grammar rule set is also evident in the lines between individual stories. There is not a grammar analog to the consistent presence of lines between advertisements in the paper unless issues before 1745 are taken into account. These are issues of the *Gazette* printed by William Parks in Annapolis from 1728 to 1734. In the other three categories examined, Park's *Gazette* exhibits the same pattern as the early Green papers. The fact that lines between advertisements are absent in Parks however indicates a quick and complete switchover at an early point in time.

The following historical reconstruction is used to demonstrate social roles and changing printer roles in the 18th and early 19th centuries.

The artifacts are interpreted as media that reinforce the increasing segmentation within the broader society as it shifts from high grid/high group to low grid/low group.

PRINTING IN THE CHANGING SHAPE OF ANGLO-AMERICA

Given the expected general changes in material goods and what they represent and the available data, it is time to return to the people who were introduced at the beginning of the chapter. Since the process of printing with a common handpress did not change much for centuries, the basic tools and operations remain constant for all of our actors (Wroth 1938; Silver 1965). There were two operations: composition and presswork. The compositor set the type into a composing stick and then into the galley of the press, where it was secured and proofed. Corrections in the form were made by the compositor, although he or she may or may not have done the actual proofreading. Presswork was done by two laborers who divided the tasks of inking the type and pulling the press. Any particular individual could learn both operations, but each skill could be assigned temporarily or permanently to particular workers. Presswork required physical strength, whereas composing required coordination and was aided considerably by literacy. The number of workers in a shop varied according to the number of presses, the amount of work, and what the master printer could find and afford. Whatever their number, workers were interdependent and needed to trust and rely on one another. The nature of the work made this inevitable: A slow and inaccurate compositor kept a press operator from working and from being paid, and a poor press worker delayed the operation of the entire shop.

The technical requirements of printing therefore create some limitations for the organization of labor. They also have some effect on the characteristics of printing type, since some degree of standardization is necessary to ensure adequate impressions. The size of imprints was limited by the power of the handpress. Some choices in layout were doubtless influenced by the equipment available, both within the printing industry and within individual shops.

It is only relatively recently that social historians have rediscovered printing and printers and have begun to examine these in a social context. Stephen Botein (1975) has looked at the business strategies and occupational self-image of colonial printers before and after the American Revolution. Briefly, this is Botein's position: Before the political turmoil of the Revolutionary era, printers were diversified in their trade.

Beside his primary trade, a printer would often also be a shopkeeper, a postmaster, and possibly a government clerk. The content of newspapers might also be called diversified. Because there was so little business available, a printer had to try to attract all customers by offending none. Censorship (other than official government censorship) took the form of refusal to print vehemence from any one point of view. In this way newspapers were kept noncontroversial. The occupational image of printers was one of avowed neutrality. As "meer mechanics" they could espouse neutrality if accused of supporting the wrong side. When political agitation started in the 1760s, many printers tried to maintain claims to neutrality, but found it impossible to do so. Specialization of opinion, whether patriot or loyalist, became necessary under the threat of violence and of lost business. Newspapers became vehicles of controversy and propaganda. The self-image of printers changed: Instead of thinking of themselves as mere mechanics with neutral interests, they began to see themselves as men of principle with important political responsibilities. The consequences of this were, of course, changes in the content of newspapers. Content became politicized.

Judging from the papers' increased political potential, it would seem that the emerging American ruling class was making an effort at hegemonic control through newspaper content as a mechanism for propaganda. The ideological value of newspapers in their nonpoliticized phase before the Revolution is also probable. Although Botein suggests that printers are making business decisions in their political strategies, they must have been responding to more than economic carrots. They were following an ideologically determined role. In cities where there was business enough to support competing printers before the 1760s, the trade line was still one of neutrality. It was clearly in the interest of that contemporary governing class to support printers who produced noncontroversial newspapers that pretended, justifiably or not, to give both sides of any issue without portraying conflict.

Both before and during the Revolutionary era, I suspect that newspapers were supportive of the controlling class. Newspapers came to mean something new, however, with their highly visible use in revolutionary agitation. The medium became politically explicit. The changing role of printers, as creators of newspapers and other print media, paralleled that of the newspapers. The Greens began moving within the grid/group system along with the whole society, as it moved toward the low grid/low group, but they also moved as printers, as individuals. Their social roles should have changed in response to the changing society. The newspaper printed by the Greens should reflect the values and worldview of the family and of the parts of society they represent. These views include not only the political details of revolutionary partisanship, but also the more basic cultural ideals of a communality giving way to individuality.

It is difficult to predict how specific social positions will move along the grid and group axes described above as the whole society moves. The implications of standardization and segmentation for social roles are not obvious. Specialization of professions should increase as the division of labor within the community increases. Artisans who formerly identified with his or her art may become alienated, although this may not be obvious until industrialization. This relationship might be visible in relative statuses attached to a particular craft and its practitioners. The Greens seem to be rising in social status and identifying with the wealthy upper middle class. This class should move toward low group and low grid, where individual autonomy and the possibility for profit are high. If it is true that the status of an artisan is connected to the social importance of his or her art, then as the newspaper becomes a political and social force, the status of its printers should also rise. The following synopsis of the family's history illustrates its position in Annapolis.

Jonas Green and his wife Anne Catherine Hoof Green came to Annapolis from Philadelphia in 1737. Jonas was responding to a call for an official printer to the colony, a post he retained until his death. He began publishing the newspaper in 1745. Beside being a printer, editor, and publisher, Jonas was the postmaster and a shopkeeper. Jonas's career fits in well with Botein's scenario. Although he did not completely avoid controversy in his newspaper before the revolutionary era, Jonas did explicitly avoid controversy when it threatened to get out of hand as it did in the Chase paper wars during the Stamp Act controversy (Strawser 1962). Jonas Green printed a series of exchanges between the traditionalist Daniel Dulany and the more radical Samuel Chase. Green finally refused to print any more replies from Chase for fear of offending Dulany, even though Chase offered to indemnify the printer against all charges.

Jonas Green's self-image is difficult to judge. The archaeological verdict is not yet in on whatever self-presentation of wealth or status Jonas was trying to convey through his possessions. The ceramic assemblage measure of segmentation described above dates from 1780 to the mid-19th century and therefore does not include either Jonas's or Anne Catherine's lifetime, but only those of their children and grandchildren.

Baker (1984) notes that from 1731 to 1759, a period that covers most of Jonas's 30 years of printing in Annapolis, activity was increasing for most craft groups in the city. Many craftsmen were diversifying their income, largely through the purchase of indentured labor. Servants are indicated in Jonas's probate inventory, but their specialities are not listed. Occasional advertisements in the *Gazette* offer bookbinding services by traveling artisans working at the print shop. The provision of several services at the combined print shop and post office seems to have been the extent of Jonas's economic diversification. At this time, the social status of many craftsmen was rising as they began performing civil services. However, Jonas was unusually successful in his social endeavors. Before 1776, mayors, aldermen, and vestrymen were almost exclusively from the gentry and professional classes (Baker 1984), but Jonas became both a vestryman and alderman. He was also a member of the Tuesday Club, a social club for gentlemen, which admitted him in 1748.

The *Maryland Gazette* that Jonas started in 1745 is an artifact that fits the Georgian characteristics of standardization and segmentation simply because it was a regularly issued publication with a standard four-page format and a minimal degree of segmentation within the paper between the advertisements and the items that preceded them. During Jonas's lifetime the number of columns in the paper increased from two to three. This created a more segmented facade. Increasing standardization is also reflected in the consistent use of printed lines to divide sections of the paper from each other. Adherence to the first two sets of grammar rules increased in the 1750s.

Anne Catherine took over the printing business upon her husband's death in 1767. She printed under her own name, then in partnership with her son William until his early death. In spite of William's and later her son Fredrick's partnership, it was Anne Catherine rather than one of her sons who was named official printer to the colony of Maryland. As Botein expects, content of the newspaper became politicized as the *Maryland Gazette* became a patriot paper. Throughout the revolutionary era, the *Gazette* publicized news so as to support the revolutionary effort (Skaggs 1964).

Judging from Baker's research (1984), there are not many changes in Annapolis craft to distinguish the period 1760–76 from the preceding 30 years. The luxury trades boomed with the lifting of certain trade restrictions after 1765, but printing may not have responded directly to those changes. Because political considerations such as the provision of a market of bureaucrats continued to favor service-oriented trades, printing was encouraged. Baker identifies the ingredients for a successful workshop in this period, which were the same as those established earlier in the century: owned or leased premises, diversified income, and investment in bonded labor. After her husband died, Anne Catherine Green bought the land that Jonas had leased. She also had bonded servants in her probate inventory, but their skills are unknown. She was not postmaster, but she apparently ran a shop. There are no indications that itinerants were available for bookbinding. The extent of her diversification is not known, but seems to have been less than that of Jonas.

It is hard to judge the changes in Anne Catherine's newspaper since she was in charge of it for only eight years. These eight years are not crucial in the changes in adherence to three of the four sets of grammar rules. The first set of rules begins to vary greatly in influence during this time and continues to do so throughout the 18th century. Most of the segmenting lines that Jonas used were kept. The lines between columns were eliminated. It was found that white space between columns can be as effective a dividing line as printed lines. Horizontal white space is less likely to be used to segment because it tends to waste more space than vertical white space. The meaning of the presence or absence of printed vertical lines is therefore ambiguous.

Baker has only a few comments to make about the craft environment in Annapolis after the Revolution. The city went into economic recession and by 1800 was much the same as it had been in 1730. Annapolis was and again became a small retail market town with a stable population, adequate housing, and little or no industry (Baker 1984).

Frederick Green took over the printing business and house from his mother when she died in 1775 and proceeded to become a very wealthy man in Annapolis. According to wealth assessed in the 1783 tax record, Frederick ranks in at least the top fifth of the city's population (Papenfuse 1975:140). Frederick Green's probate inventory contrasts sharply with those of his parents in the number and variety of items that are associated with Georgianization. Leone and Shackel (in press) and Shackel (1986) have written about a particular etiquette that behaviorally separates classes and also enforces standardization of individuals. Frederick's probate lists 10 of the 14 leisurely dining items that Shackel (1986) has identified as being associated with the Georgian worldview. Neither of his parents had more than two of these, even though Jonas was relatively wealthy and was certainly upwardly mobile.

By the early 19th century, Frederick's newspaper began to exhibit more segmentation through the use of printed lines to separate stories. Otherwise there was not much change in the layout represented by the items analyzed here. By 1780, two of the four sets of grammar rules were being followed consistently and that was the case at least through 1825. Adherence to the first set of rules in Table 8.4 does begin to vary until the 1770s and continues to vary until the 1820s. The remaining set of grammar rules exhibit a sudden switch from the use of the long "s" to the short "s."

In the excavated ceramics and the index of segmentation discussed above, two of the phases represented archaeologically record changes in Frederick's tenure as head of the household. Segmentation of the table is indicated by a doubling in the ceramic index, from 3.0 to 6.25, within a decade or two. Segmentation is also shown by the leisurely dining items mentioned above.

Frederick's son Jonas took over in 1811 when his father died. This Jonas no longer lived in the same house or printed in the same shop as his father or grandfather had. In a town struggling economically, Jonas went bankrupt and his goods were auctioned at a sheriff's sale in 1841. He died in 1845, six years after he stopped printing the 94-year-old *Gazette* . Lines reappeared between columns in the newspaper after 1811. The first set of grammar rules finally stopped being followed sporadically. Segmentation of the table continued to increase. By the middle of the 19th century, the ceramic index had risen to 9.17. This may not directly reflect on the life of Jonas Green the grandson, since he did not live in the house. However, other Greens did live in the family home and were also participating in a segmented way of life.

Through the 18th and early 19th centuries, the printers were moving into a position of low grid/low group. Jonas and his son Frederick competed successfully, although Jonas Green the grandson failed. Their newspaper was also exhibiting characteristics of increasing standardization and segmentation that indicate this documentary artifact was part of the developing Georgian ideology.

The structural role of the newspaper as a whole has been suggested. Characteristics of the paper's layout and content may be analyzed in terms of increasing standardization with the idea that rules of standardization are being communicated and consumed as appropriate rules. That is, standardization is becoming good to think. It is not surprising that material culture communicates ideology or cosmology in different ways, depending upon the social context of the audience. The acceptance of or reaction to these messages by different segments of 18th-century society is unclear, but the messages themselves can be distinguished.

Demand for newspapers rose dramatically as newspapers became vehicles of controversy and propaganda. The number of newspapers in the American colonies doubled between 1763 and 1775 (Davidson quoted in Botein 1975:41). There was a dramatic increase in what we now consider "news." Printers, without benefit of new technology, become involved in the mass production of news. This occurred at about the same time that Josiah Wedgwood began to mass produce creamware in England.

There may be a connection between these two types of mass-produced artifacts. They are both in the position of demonstrating, truthfully or not, an ideal symmetry between people and goods. A symmetry or equality between individuals is implied. For some segments of society, particularly the low grid/low group individuals who transact freely among themselves, there is a real potential for obtaining these symmetries. For other groups in society—for example, the high grid/low group or insulated individuals—the symmetry implied by these goods is little more than a ruse, a concealment of the limited potential for obtaining an ideal symmetry.

CONCLUSION

The search for meaning in historical archaeology leads us into historiography (and its anthropological counterpart) and into past events and interpretations. Each path leads to understanding from a slightly different, but related perspective. If people in our past and present and their ideologies and lifeways are to be understood, then we must look for connections between past and present as well as connections within each.

The archaeologist should be and has been particularly concerned with relationships among material objects, including documents, and with social contexts and ideologies. I have attempted to initiate a model for cultural developments that takes seriously the influences of each. One necessary assumption adopted by increasing numbers of archaeologists—and by no means invented here—is that material culture does more than reflect social reality; it creates it. Material culture is used by various segments of society in attempts to control, react to, and resist categories and their implications. The control of categories and of the markers of appropriate/inappropriate is cultural hegemonic control.

The work of Mary Douglas, James Deetz, and Mark Leone provides a framework for understanding cultural change in the 18th- and 19th-century Chesapeake. The Greens were moving toward a position of low grid/low group, partly because of the product they created. Issues of the *Maryland Gazette* have been examined for subtle changes that might reveal increasing standardization as an indication of an emerging Georgian, or capitalist, ideology. The family that printed the newspaper also began participating more fully in a way of life influenced by the same ideology. There is evidence for this both in the way their table was organized and in the social roles they played as printers. Although not examined here, the organization of labor at the print shop and the physical organization of the house and shop also responded to this larger cultural impetus. It is clear that the product, process, and people of the printing craft had real and discernible mutual influence.

The craft of printing was changing within a complex historical context of broad cultural values and specific political values. Individuals, acting according to many expectations and desires, responded to messages in their material environment. Through their behaviors, consumer choices, and manufacture of goods, they created messages for others to decipher. During the 18th and 19th centuries, aspects of the Greens' lives were changing toward increasing segmentation and standardization. These changes paralleled those occurring in the mainstream of their cultural context. To understand the complexities of that context, we also need to study the behaviors and choices of individuals who resisted change or who attempted to establish alternative categories. Such comparisons will enhance the usefulness of Douglas's social taxonomy as well as our understanding of cultural complexity and change and the roles of material culture in each.

ACKNOWLEDGMENTS

I am grateful to Mark Leone for discussions about the ideas in this chapter and for endless encouragement. Thanks to Mark Leone and Parker Potter and to Ezra Zubrow, Paul Shackel, Samuel Brainerd, Diana Kehne, and the ASW reviewers for comments on the drafts. I am indebted to Matthew Johnson and Simon Coleman for coding data on the layout of the newspaper and to Teresa Harris for the information on grammar use in the *Gazette*.

REFERENCES CITED

Baker, N.
   1984   An Overview of Masonry Crafts in Annapolis, Maryland
           1695–1776. Prepared for the International Union of Bricklayers and
           Allied Craftsmen. On file at Historic Annapolis, Inc.

Botein, S.
   1975   "Meer Mechanics" and an Open Press: The Business and Political
           Strategies of Colonial American Printers. In *Perspectives in American
           History*, ed. D. Fleming and B. Bailyn, pp. 127–225. Vol. 9. Cambridge, Mass.: Harvard University.

Braudel, F.
1979   *Civilization and Capitalism, 15th–18th Century.* 3 Vols. New York: Harper & Row.

Breen, T. H.
1986   The Meaning of Things: The Consumer Culture of 18th Century America and the Coming Revolution. Paper presented at Winterthur Museum conference "Accumulation and Display: The Development of American Consumerism 1880–1920," Winterthur, Delaware. November, 7–8, 1986.

Bridenbaugh, C.
1950   *The Colonial Craftsman.* Repr. 1961. Chicago: University of Chicago Press.

Brownell, C. E.
1984   Latrobe, His Craftsmen, and the Corinthian Order of the Hall of Representatives. In *The Craftsman in Early America (Winterthur)*, ed. I. Quimby, pp. 247–272. New York: W. W. Norton.

Coleman, S., and M. Johnson
1985   Exploratory Analysis of the Layout of the *Maryland Gazette*. Paper on file with the Department of Anthropology, University of Maryland, College Park.

Craven, W.
1986   *Colonial America Portraiture.* Cambridge: Cambridge University Press.

Crosby, C., and B. Little
        In preparation: Jonas Green Print Shop site report. On file Department of Anthropology, University of Maryland, College Park.

Deetz, J.
1977   *In Small Things Forgotten.* New York: Doubleday.
1983   Scientific Humanism and Humanistic Science: A Plea for Paradigmatic Pluralism in Historical Archaeology. *Geoscience and Man* 23:27–34.

Douglas, M.
1966   *Purity and Danger: An Analysis of Concepts of Pollution and Taboo.* London: Routledge & Kegan Paul.
1978   *Cultural Bias.* Royal Anthropological Institute of Great Britain and Ireland Occasional Paper no. 35. London.

Douglas, M., and B. Isherwood
1979   *The World of Goods.* New York: Basic Books.

Glassie, H.
1975   *Folk Housing in Middle Virginia.* Knoxville: University of Tennessee Press.

Harris, T.
1986   Grammar and the *Maryland Gazette* as Reflections of the Georgian Mindset in 18th and Early 19th Century Annapolis. On file with the Department of Anthropology, University of Maryland, College Park.

Hobsbawm, E.
1971   From Social History to the History of Society. *Daedalus* 100(1):20–45.

Hodder, I.
1982a   *Symbols in Action, Ethnoarchaeological Studies of Material Culture.* Cambridge: Cambridge University Press.
1982b   Theoretical Archaeology: A Reactionary View. In *Symbolic and Structural Archaeology,* ed. Ian Hodder, pp. 1–16. Cambridge: Cambridge University Press.
1986   *Reading the Past, Current Approaches to Interpretation in Archaeology.* Cambridge: Cambridge University Press.

Land, A.
1981   *Colonial Maryland, A History.* Millwood, N.Y.: KTO Press.

Lears, J.
1981   *No Place of Grace.* New York: Pantheon Books.

Leone, M.
1984   Interpreting Ideology in Historical Archaeology: The William Paca Garden in Annapolis, Maryland. In *Ideology, Power and Prehistory,* ed. D. Miller and C. Tilley, pp. 25–35. Cambridge: Cambridge University Press.
1985   Class Formation in Eighteenth-Century Annapolis, Maryland. Paper presented at the American Anthropological Association meetings, Washington, D.C.

Leone, M., P. Potter, Jr., and P. Shackel
1987   Toward a Critical Archaeology. *Current Anthropology* 28(3): 286–302.

Leone, M., and P. Shackel
In Press The Georgian Order in Annapolis. *The Maryland Archaeologist.*

Little, B. J.
1987   *Ideology and Media: Historical Archaeology of Printing in 18th Century Annapolis, Maryland.* Ph.D. diss. State University of New York at Buffalo.

Main, Gloria L.
1975   Probate Records as a Source for Early American History. *William and Mary Quarterly.* 3d ser., vol. 32: 89–99.

Miller D.
1985   *Artifacts as Categories: A Study of Ceramic Variability in Central India.* Cambridge: Cambridge University Press.

Miller, D., and C. Tilley
1984   *Ideology, Power and Prehistory: An Introduction.* In *Ideology, Power and Prehistory,* ed. D. Miller and C. Tilley, pp. 1–15. Cambridge: Cambridge University Press.

Moxon, J.
1683   *Mechanick Exercises on the Whole Art of Printing.* Reprint 1978. New York: Dover Publications of Oxford University 1962 Edition (ed. H. Davis & H. Carter).

Papenfuse, E.
1975   *In Pursuit of Profit, The Annapolis Merchants in the Era of the American Revolution 1763– 1805.* Baltimore: Johns Hopkins University Press.

Potter, P.
1986   Ideology in History and the Search for the Past in Annapolis, Maryland. Paper presented at the Society for American Archaeology meetings, New Orleans, La.

Rapoport, A.
1982   *The Meaning of the Built Environment, a Nonverbal Communication Approach.* Beverly Hills, Calif.: Sage Publications.

Rosemont, H. P.
1981   Benjamin Franklin and the Philadelphia Typographical Strikers of 1786. *Labor History* 22(3): 398–429.

Schlereth, T.
1984   Artisans and Craftsmen: A Historical Perspective. In *The Craftsman in Early America (Winterthur),* ed. I. Quimby, pp. 34–61. New York: W. W. Norton.

Schwind, A. P.
1984   The Glassmakers of Early America. In *The Craftsman in Early America (Winterthur),* ed. I. Quimby. New York: W. W. Norton.

Shackel, P.
1986   The Creation of Behavioral Standardization and Social Segmentation in Anglo-America. Paper presented at the Northeastern Anthropological Association meetings, Buffalo, New York.
1987   The Archaeology of Social and Behavioral Segmentation in Colonial and Early America. Ph.D. diss., State University of New York at Buffalo.

Silver, Rollo
1965   *The American Printer, 1787–1825*. Charlottesville: University Press of Virginia.

Skaggs, D. K.
1964   Editorial Policies of the Maryland Gazette 1765–1783. *Maryland Historical Magazine* 59: 346.

Smith, J.
1755   *The Printer's Grammar*. Reprint 1965. London: Greig Press.

Stone, L.
1979   The Revival of Narrative: Reflections on a New Old History. *Past and Present* 85: 3–24.

Stower, C.
1808   *The Printer's Grammar*. Reprint 1965. London: Greig Press.

Strawser, N.
1962   Samuel Chase and the Annapolis Paper War. *Maryland Historical Magazine* 57: 177-95.

Van Winkle, C.
1818   *The Printer's Guide, or An Introduction to the Art of Printing*. Reprint 1981. New York: Garland.

Ward, B. M.
1984   Boston Goldsmiths, 1690–1730. In *The Craftsman in Early America (Winterthur)*, ed. I. Quimby, New York: W. W. Norton.

Wolf, S. G.
1984   Documentary Sources for the Study of the Craftsman. In *The Craftsman in Early America (Winterthur)*, ed. I. Quimby, pp. 17–33. New York: W. W. Norton.

Wroth, Lawrence C.
1938   *The Colonial Printer*. Portland, Maine: Southworth-Anthoensen Press.

CHAPTER 9

Asymmetry and Recursive Meanings in the 18th Century
The Morris Pound House

ANN M. PALKOVICH

Precision and symmetry (Deetz 1977:111) are acknowledged as two important concerns reflected in the material culture of 18th-century America. Clocks, scientific instruments, and perspective landscaping as well as land surveys and population censuses were developed, improved, or took on a new importance after 1700 (Leone 1987, in this volume; Richardson, et al.). A similar concern with order is noted in the switch from vernacular styles to "academic" traditions in buildings, furniture, and pottery (Deetz 1977:111–113). A major thrust of symbolic, structural and critical archaeology today is the search for the underlying meanings of such patterns in the archaeological and material records. These approaches reveal the ways in which observed past economic, environmental, social, and other patterns—as well as our own cultural constructs that create and interpret these patterns—mask the manipulation of symbols and meanings.

Deetz (1977, in this volume) and Glassie (1975) have made important contributions to our understanding of the archaeological record, particularly the material culture of the 18th century. As Leone (1986) has noted, their approach is one variety of cognitive archaeology. Derived from structuralism, it compares and arranges diverse phenomena or data to reveal underlying patterns. Cognitive explanations are then offered to account for the unifying themes of these patterns. For example, both Deetz (in this volume) and Glassie (1975:190) note that during the 18th century the emphasis shifts from community to individualism, as observed in the change from open, single-room houses to compartmented, halled houses, and from common eating vessels and utensils to individual place settings (however, see Zuckerman 1977). Precision and symmetry prevail in the developing Georgian mind-set. Glassie notes that, even when a strict adherence to bilateral symmetry seems to be violated in houses, it is preserved at another level—it is expressed through architectural "competence," that is, a set of "grammatical" rules that through repetition restate the orderliness of symmetry.

A shortcoming of this cognitive approach has been its lack of concern for the recursive quality of the patterns identified. That is, little attention is given to how such patterns form, why they disappear, and how symbolic elements are used and manipulated by past societies (Leone 1986:425). Shifts from one underlying cognitive pattern to another are presented in historical sequence and may serve to indicate how the present distorts the past through imposed categorization. Yet the past is still seen as a panorama rather than the product of any dynamic symbolic interplay.

Paradoxically, a second shortcoming of the cognitive approach lies in its major virtue, that is, its search for underlying coherence. The strength of the structuralist approach in archaeology is that it compares seemingly unlike objects and categories of objects, accommodating the search for underlying themes and meanings that may not be made apparent by other analytical approaches. Unfortunately, this search for themes tends to override the significance and meaning of variation inherent in the archaeological record. Binford (1983, 1984, 1986), Gould (1980; Gould and Watson 1982), Wylie (1985b), and others have shed new light on contemporary archaeological issues (such as the use of analogy in archaeological interpretations) by documenting unaccountable variations in the archaeological record, variously defined as anomalies (Gould 1980), ambiguities (Binford 1983:68, 1984:17, 1986:472 –75), or dissimilarities (Wylie 1985b). Although argued from different standpoints, the basic idea is to note the point of mismatch either between concordant lines of reasoning that lead to incongruous conclusions or between the premises developed theoretically and the empirical evidence—and then to evaluate the mismatch as the next potential element of inquiry, rather than automatically dismiss it as extraneous bias or error.

Careful analysis of variations in the archaeological record may have an equally important contribution to make to critical archaeology, particularly in the light of nihilistic conclusions of cultural relativism so oftcn reflected in symbolic archaeological interpretations (Wylie 1985a; Leone 1986). By using the idea of recursivity essential to critical archaeology (Leone 1986:426) to evaluate discrepancies from expected underlying patterns, researchers may be able to reveal how action, structure, and meaning may have served as dynamic elements in symbolic interplay. A brief and preliminary example from the recent excavations at an 18th-century village in Northern Virginia may serve to illustrate the point.

EIGHTEENTH-CENTURY COLCHESTER

The beginning of the 18th century was a period of transition in Northern Virginia from frontier settlements to an established system of agrarian production and trade. Until the early 1700s, efforts to establish towns along major waterways had been largely unsuccessful in this area, despite the favorable incentives legislated by a series of English "port acts." Between 1707 and 1719, however, land adjacent to most major navigable waterways had been chartered in land grants and settled. New land grants began to be issued for inland areas. Fields cleared for agricultural production in these new inland tracts created a need for convenient shipping points to promote the tobacco trade. As a result, new roadways and ferry crossings were encouraged. The Tobacco Act of 1730 reestablished a warehousing and inspection system (Hening 1821:VI, 331), and, of course, the inevitable duties and taxes were all quickly instituted (Sprouse 1975:9–11).

Ferry crossings were a key element to the budding transportation network. A ferry on the Occoquan River, informally established by the Mason family in 1684, had been formally authorized by court order in 1691. By the early 1700s, this Occoquan ferry had become part of the heavily traveled north-south route—the Old Post Road—between Philadelphia and Williamsburg (Sprouse 1975:7). Although the Mason family owned the ferry concession (Hening 1821:V, 252), it did not own the adjacent tract of land, which remained in disputed ownership until it was sold in 1746 by Elizabeth Luke to John Graham. The 351 1/2-acre tract was sold again by Graham in 1753 to Peter Wegener.

Wegener, impressed by the success of the towns of Dumfries and Alexandria, chartered in 1749, immediately petitioned the Virginia General Assembly to grant a charter for a town to be founded on his newly acquired property. The enabling act was granted soon after, stating, "a town on the Occoquan . . . would be very convenient for trade and navigation, and greatly to ease the advantage of the frontier inhabitants" (Hening 1821:V, 396). The charter also specified that the town

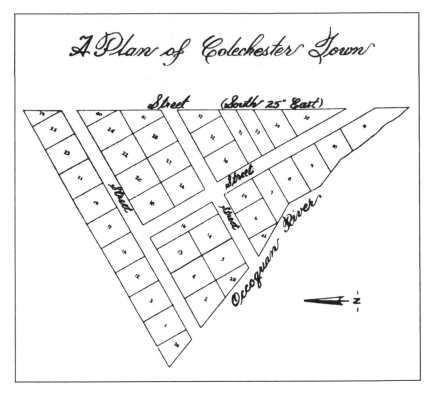

Figure 9.1: Town plan of Colchester, 1754. Source: Sprouse (1975:17).

was to be established on a triangular 25-acre tract at the southern tip of Wegener's land and was to include the Mason family ferry within its boundaries. Surveyed in 1754 and named Colchester, the town was divided into 42 lots (Figure 9.1). The initial sale of the lots took place in 1756 (Sprouse 1975:19–22).

Like other towns founded in the mid-18th century in Northern Virginia, Colchester's economic activity centered around its tobacco warehouses. Tobacco was big business for England; its production increased in the Chesapeake region from 20 million pounds in 1700 to roughly 100 million pounds by 1775. The Tobacco Act of 1730 closely regulated the inspection and sale of tobacco hogsheads from public warehouses located primarily in these newly founded towns along major rivers. These warehouses served as the central economic and social focal points throughout the 18th century in Virginia and Maryland.

Tobacco notes of transfer were even recognized as legal tender (Sprouse 1975:55–58).

Colchester reached a commercial zenith around 1785. In 1762, a petition to move the public warehouses from Occoquan to Colchester was granted. Warehouses were soon built on three Colchester lots (Figure 9.1; Lots 7, 8, and 29). The tobacco trade boomed at Colchester; auditor's records note £282 in tax revenues were collected between 1781 and 1783 at 5 shillings per hogshead (Virginia State Auditor's Ledger 179; Account of Duty on Tobacco, Colchester Warehouse 1771–1789; Accession 28; Virginia State Library). However, shifts in agricultural production in Northern Virginia from tobacco to wheat led to a rapid decline in trade from Colchester by the 1790s. Activity at the public warehouse waned, and it was closed after 1805 (Sprouse 1975:58).

Despite its notable though short-lived success in the tobacco trade, there was never great economic interest or financial investment in Colchester. Of the original 42 town lots, only a third sold at the initial sale. Only 26 lots were ever built on or improved. The economic success of Colchester depended solely on the tobacco trade and the ferry crossing. With the decline in local tobacco production and subsequent shift in economic interest to the upstream town of Occoquan—not to mention the silting of the river at Colchester, improved inland road systems, and the building of a bridge that reduced the importance of the ferry crossing and of the Old Post Road through Occoquan—the importance of Colchester as a trade and transportation center rapidly declined. By 1817 only 7 lots still had taxable structures (Sprouse 1975). The area soon returned to wilderness and farmland and became recognized merely as a map location rather than a viable town. Because Colchester reverted to farmland, portions of the 18th-century town were preserved archaeologically, undisturbed by 19th-century urban development.

The mid-18th-century boom in new English town charters and economic activity no doubt had a significant impact on the patterns of material culture in Northern Virginia. This period in the mid-1700s was marked by a notable change in architectural styles, as well as stylistic influences on other aspects of colonial American material culture (Deetz 1977:37–40). By about 1760, the Renaissance influence on English material culture was transplanted throughout the colonies. The expressions of this "Georgian" architectural style quickly supplanted the indigenous vernacular, regional Anglo-American cultural developments that Deetz dates from roughly 1680–1760.

Colchester was founded just as the Georgian influence was beginning to be felt in Northern Virginia. Colchester's only extant 18th-century building (currently called the Fairfax Arms) does not strictly

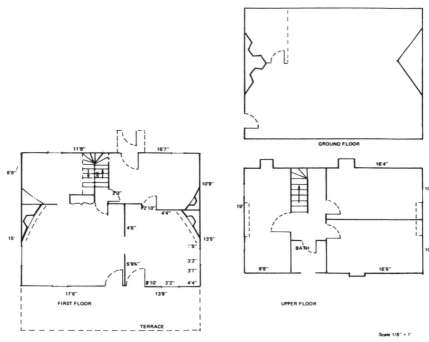

Figure 9.2: Recent floor plan of the Fairfax Arms. Source: Sprouse (1975:142).

adhere to Georgian architectural rules—for example, two asymmetrically placed front doors open directly into large rooms (Figure 9.2). Yet elements of precision and symmetry characteristic not of the preceding vernacular structures but of Georgian houses—such as symmetrically placed fireplaces—are present and suggest a level of conformity to the new Georgian standards of architectural competence (see Glassie 1975). The prescriptions of the Colchester town charter clearly suggest that larger, symmetrical houses were to be built (Hening 1821:VI, 396). It would seem that these prescriptions also indirectly sanctioned Georgian house styles as the socially accepted architectural standard.

THE MORRIS POUND HOUSE

Recent archaeological investigations at Colchester (Palkovich 1984, 1985) have revealed a previously unrecorded, intact 18th-century house foundation. This foundation, built of locally available slate, was uncovered immediately adjacent to the Old Post Road (now called Old Colchester Road), within the boundaries of 18th-century Lot 18. Pieces of Rhenish blue stoneware and Dutch earthenware found within the upper debris of the foundation date it to the 1760s. This closely corresponds with the available historic documents, which indicate that a structure was built on Lot 18 during this period.

Stone foundations dating to the mid-18th century in Northern Virginia have the architectural qualities of good focus and good visibility (Deetz 1977:94). Good focus means that the size and shape of aboveground structures are clearly represented in the stone foundations and also that the placement of fireplaces and porches is evident in the foundation footings and posthole patterns. Good visibility means that these foundations, whether constructed of readily available stones or manufactured brick, usually are well preserved. Conclusions regarding architectural competence—specifically, the size, shape, and symmetry of a structure—may be confidently based on the structural elements retained in these house foundations. The principles or "rules" of construction thus apply to foundations as well as above-ground construction in this case. That the size, shape, symmetry, and workmanship of the foundation were probably matched in the above-ground structure may be assumed from the competence evident in the Fairfax Arms in Colchester (Sprouse 1975:142). A similar correspondence likely also existed between the foundation on Lot 18 and the structure that once stood above it.

In 1758, the Colchester property (Lots 18 and 26; see Figure 9.1) was purchased for £12 by Morris Pound, a German immigrant, who planned to establish a vineyard on the land. He built the recently rediscovered structure on Lot 18 and cleared both properties for his vineyard. What little is known about Pound comes from a letter sent by George Mason III to Charles Grayson, Daniel French, George William Fairfax, Spence Grayson, Thomson Mason, Benjamin Grayson, and George Washington (Rutland 1970:44–45). The letter was eventually signed by these individuals as a loan agreement. Pound mortgaged his lots at Colchester to them for £118 in an attempt to save his financially floundering vineyard. In 1762, Benjamin Grayson alone was deeded the lots, Pound apparently defaulting on his loan probably as a result of his failed enterprise. (Recent soil analyses indicate that the high clay content of the soil on Pound's lots rendered his property completely unsuitable for grapevines; Palkovich, 1985). Court records show Pound resided in Colchester until his death in 1770 (Topper 1983).

As required by the town charter for Colchester, Pound's original deed states that Pound, his heirs, or assigns shall erect, build and finish on each of said lots one house of brick, stone or wood well framed of the dimensions of 20 feet square, 9 feet pitched at the least or proportionally thereto with a brick or stone chimney and place the same according to the direction of the Trustees within 2 years after the date thereof. (Fairfax County Library, Deed Book 1758, 633)

Property was to revert to the town trustees for resale if this improvement was not made. In a letter dated October 1759, George Mason noted,

Maurice Pound a Native of Germany having setled at Colchester in the said County about three years since on two Lotts which he purchased (*one of which he has improved according to Law*) and planted a Vineyard on them; during which time he has lived at his own Expence without any profit from his Vineyard and having been much retarded in his Undertaking by these two last dry summers, & *having one of his Lots yet to save by the building of the legal Improvements.* (Rutland 1970:44–45, emphasis added)

Pound had apparently met the legal requirement stated in the deed by building a structure on one of his lots by 1759, eventually defaulting on his loan but not on the original deed stipulation.

A curious discrepancy was revealed when the foundation of the Pound House was fully exposed. A foundation at least 20 feet square was expected, but the structure initially appeared to be only 12 feet square. Once loose stones were cleared and the interior walls were clearly delineated, the foundation turned out not only to be small, thus violating an explicit stipulation of the lease, but also asymmetrical, placing the house in violation of both the lease and the prevailing architectural competence (see Figure 9.3; compare, in particular, the 12-foot east wall dimensions with the 10-foot 4-inch west well dimension; Palkovich 1985). Likewise, the 18th-century Fairfax Arms, while exceeding the mandated size requirement, is notably asymmetrical (Figure 9.2; North Wall ... 28'1", South Wall 31'2"; East Wall 24'2", West Wall 22'2"; Sprouse 1975:142). One is led to wonder why. Why, at a time when precision and architectural competence were emphasized, do these structures violate both explicit and implicit, unconsciously held cultural rules? What do these discrepancies reflect about the 18th century?

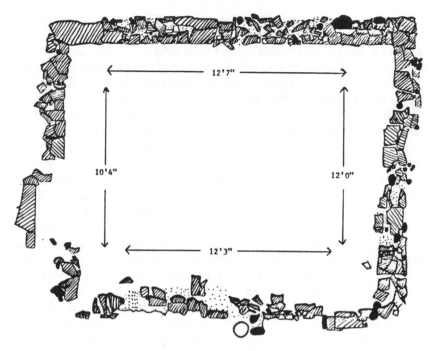

Figure 9.3: Slate foundation of Morris Pound House.

ANALYTICAL VIEWS

A positivist analysis might dismiss the variations or discrepancies in the structures at Colchester as sloppy workmanship or simply substandard construction and perhaps attribute them to the economic limitations of the owners. However—and this is key—examination of the interior walls of the Pound House and Fairfax Arms foundations shows that careful attention was paid to their construction. Irregularities inherent in the building materials project to the outside of the structures. The interior walls are straight, smooth, carefully built—and irregular in their dimensions. Arguing that the stylistic evolution of house forms in the 18th century had not yet been completely adopted at Colchester tells us very little. Simply concluding that an incomplete transition in construction style is being observed does not explain why these structures could violate well-known rules of construction and still be considered to legally meet deed requirements.

A cognitive analysis of these structures might suggest that the observed discrepancies represent a transition, that the new mind-set of precision and symmetry had not yet been fully infused in all aspects or levels of the observable material culture or had not yet been adopted by all participants. These houses would be ungrammatical or incompetent in Glassie's terms, and thus, in a sense, would also be viewed as sloppy. If variations and internal inconsistencies are ignored in favor of overriding patterns, a move encouraged by cognitive analysis, the importance of empirically observed discrepancies in these structures becomes lost.

If one considers the recursive quality of the discrepancies presented by the Pound House, analysis of them may lead to meaning. Rhys Isaac's book, *The Transformation of Virginia: 1740–1790*, provides some insights for us. Viewing action, structure, and meaning as dynamic elements in a symbolic analysis, Isaac suggests that social, economic, and political domains in the second half of the 18th century were used symbolically by the landed gentry to secure their authority and stabilize their position in the social order. Whereas Isaac focuses on the differences between Anglo-American and Afro-American traditions during the 18th century, similar but more subtle discrepancies are evident between the social power and authority of the planter elite and the social and economic deference of the common planters.

It is not surprising that the only documentary information available about Morris Pound is contained in legal records—deeds, court records, and loan agreements. Court days and legal proceedings played a unique and central role in 18th-century Virginia (Isaac 1982:88–94). In a society that was still largely illiterate and dependent on oral tradition, the courts served as the primary vehicle by which the landed gentry defined, exercised, and consolidated its authority.

The authority of the landed gentry also lay in the attributes of gentility and, particularly, in demonstrating one "possessed the means of personal independence" (Isaac 1982:131). Proper deportment, attire, manners, and education were deemed requisite. However, a true gentleman also demonstrated his financial means and independence through, in essence, domination: "The means that secured independence to the gentleman fixed the dependence of others upon him" (Isaac 1982:132). Although Isaac notes that such subjugation was most clearly expressed by slave ownership and indentured servants, it is clear that a similar though more subtle master-servant dichotomy existed between the landed gentry and common planters. Unable to support himself after several unprofitable years, Pound submitted to financial subjugation and mortgaged his property to a group of "gentlemen." Shortly thereafter, he lost his property and appeared periodically in the court records as the defendant in a series of debt cases until his death (Topper 1983). Pound's livelihood and future were determined by his indebtedness and subsequent court proceedings.

The power of the landed gentry in the 18th century was partly expressed through its control over the destinies of others. George Mason's original benevolent letter and offer of financial assistance to Morris Pound reflects Mason's independence and role as a "gentleman" (Isaac 1982:132). The litigation of Pound's debts defined his role as a "servant"; his appearance in the documentary record reflects the interests of the dominant "gentlemen" and was determined by the extent to which his debts continued to be a liability to his benevolent benefactors.

The authority, power, and dichotomy of "master-servant" that were negotiated socially and legally seem likely to have been reflected in patterns of material remains. The distinctions between Anglo-American and Afro-American material culture are often said to reflect both the actual differences in cultural traditions between European white and African black and also the need to actively create different explanations of European white and African black origins and futures to justify the social order in the 18th century (Deetz 1977; Isaac 1982:306). The sharp differences in cultural domains and the master-slave dichotomy between Anglo-Americans and Afro-Americans left distinctive material patterns. The differences among various interrelated European cultural traditions transplanted in 18th-century America, however, took on a different order of expression, despite sometimes having a structure similar to that of Afro-American/Anglo-American relations.

The discrepancies of size and symmetry seen at the structures in Colchester may reflect one way in which the "master-slave"—or perhaps more subtly the "dominant-dominated"— dichotomy was expressed. Adherence to the "rules" and conventions of appropriate house forms was essential to the landed gentry; it was part of what provided the physical expression of their power and authority (see Leone 1987). For the common planter, like Morris Pound, the "rules" and conventions of appropriate house forms provided a role for him in the Anglo-American social order, but at the same time sharply bounded the limits of his rights and authority. Gunston Hall, George Mason's home, is the epitome of precision, symmetry, and orderliness as prescribed by the budding Georgian mind-set of the 18th century. At a glance, the Pound House and the Fairfax Arms *appear* symmetrical from outside and at a distance, when in fact they aren't. The elegance and refinement seen in Gunston Hall are missing; the strict adherence to stylistic rules is not carried through in these Colchester structures. However, the careful workmanship they exhibit suggests that their discrepancies in size and the asymmetry are not necessarily the result of economic limitations, but could be symbolic manifestations. If Pound and the builders of the Fairfax Arms could have built symmetrical houses, but did not, the slight asymmetries of their houses could represent a subtle, symbolic rejection of the local hierarchy, one that was visible to them and to careful observers but one that was not blatant enough or inflammatory enough to cause social damage. Pound's social, political, economic, and legal subjugation were necessarily visibly negotiated within the Anglo-American domain of the 18th century, and may possibly be observed by us today as cultural prescriptions not quite met, be it Pound's house or his legal obligations.

This observation, if it is correct, is an example of the recursive quality of some of the discrepancies that may be observed in the archaeological record. The discrepancies and variations we observe do not necessarily reflect errors, poor workmanship, economic differences, environmental variations, or poor archaeological preservation. These discrepancies may be material representations of a past society's symbolic negotiations of meaning. The asymmetries of the Pound House suggest that other subtle discrepancies may exist in the archaeological record.

Obviously a single, slightly cockeyed house is only a beginning. Yet it is a tantalizing start. One must keep in mind that simply identifying category-by-category mismatches between our theoretically constructed expectations (say, precision and symmetry for the 18th century) and our empirical observations (the Morris Pound House) misses the point of recursiveness in a critical analysis. How the individual discrepancies fit with each other is what allows us to suggest what people in the past used to negotiate meanings symbolically and how these individual elements were integrated. The asymmetry of Pound's house, and by extention, this preliminary analysis, is not enough. The way in which Pound's appearance in the documentary record was determined, and by whom, adds another piece to the picture. Additional analyses could consider the spatial arrangements of other structures and debris on Pound's property, the varieties and kinds of pottery, glassware, and utensils that he discarded, and his use of available foodstuffs—but the point would not be to learn how many buildings Pound could afford to build, or the dates of occupation of his house, or what he chose to eat. Rather, these data, in a critical analysis, could reflect the ways in which he negotiated his role as a common planter and could suggest the extent to which different material elements recovered archaeologically embody these negotiated 18th-century meanings and symbols in Northern Virginia.

By exploring the ways in which the recursive quality of the past is observable archaeologically, we avoid empty relativistic conclusions (Wylie 1985a). This approach has the potential to free symbolic analyses of the archaeological record from what has been a seemingly necessary and inherent dependence of such interpretations on historical documents. Discrepancies or ambiguities identified make fundamentally different contributions to archaeological interpretations. Ambiguities as championed by Binford (1986:472–75) enable archaeologists to define universal archaeological signatures and thus to establish uniformitarian laws. For Binford, meaningful interpretations of human behavior and patterns of culture in the past as well as comparisons of various aspects of the archaeological record itself can then be based on such laws. In critical theory, ambiguities or discrepancies also serve as a focal point of the analysis. However, the identification of ambiguity, coupled with the idea of recursivity, provides an opportunity to examine how meanings were actively negotiated. Discrepancies or ambiguities used in critical theory are one means of examining the dynamic quality of the past and the ways in which actions, meanings, and symbols lent integrity to the fabric of these past cultures.

REFERENCES CITED

Binford, Lewis
    1983   *Working at Archaeology*. New York: Academic Press.
    1984   *Faunal Remains from Klasies River Mouth*. New York: Academic Press.
    1986   In Pursuit of the Future. In *American Archaeology: Past and Future*, ed. David Meltzer, Don Fowler, and Jeremy Sabloff, pp. 457–459. Washington, D.C.: Smithsonian Institution Press.

Deetz, James
    1977   *In Small Things Forgotten*. Garden City, N.Y.: Anchor Books.

Glassie, Henry
    1975   *Folk Housing in Middle Virginia*. Knoxville: University of Tennessee Press.

Gould, Richard
    1980   *Living Archaeology*. Cambridge: Cambridge University Press.

Gould, Richard, and Patty Jo Watson
    1982   A Dialogue on the Meaning and Use of Analogy in Ethnoarchaeological Reasoning. *Journal of Anthropological Archaeology* 1: 355–81.

Hening, William
　　1821　　*The Statutes at Large: Being a Collection of All the Laws of Virginia*
　　　　　　 . . . 13 Vols. Richmond, Va.: J. G. Cochran.

Isaac, Rhys
　　1982　　*The Transformation of Virginia: 1740–1790.* Chapel Hill: University
　　　　　　 of North Carolina Press.

Leone, Mark P.
　　1986　　Symbolic, Structural and Critical Archaeology. In *American Archae-
　　　　　　 ology Past and Future,* ed. David Meltzer, Don Fowler, and Jeremy
　　　　　　 Sabloff, pp. 415–438. Washington, D.C.: Smithsonian Institution
　　　　　　 Press.
　　1987　　Rule by Ostentation: The Relationship between Space and Sight in
　　　　　　 Eighteenth Century Landscape Architecture in the Chesapeake Re-
　　　　　　 gion of Maryland. In *Method and Theory in Activity Area Research,*
　　　　　　 ed. Susan Kent, pp. 604–633. New York: Columbia University
　　　　　　 Press.

Palkovich, Ann M.
　　1984　　*The Eighteenth Century Village of Colchester: 1982–83 Field Seasons.*
　　　　　　 Anthropology Program, George Mason University, Fairfax, Va.
　　1985　　*The Eighteenth Century Village of Colchester: 1985 Field Season.* An-
　　　　　　 thropology Program, George Mason University, Fairfax, Va.

Richardson, Edgar P., Brooke Hindle, and Lillian B. Miller
　　1983　　*Charles Willson Peale and His World.* New York: Abrams.

Rutland, Robert (ed.)
　　1970　　*The Papers of George Mason. Vols. I–III.* Chapel Hill: University of
　　　　　　 North Carolina Press.

Sprouse, Edith
　　1975　　*Colchester: Colonial Port on the Potomac.* Fairfax County, Va.: Fairfax
　　　　　　 County Office of Comprehensive Planning.

Topper, Linda
　　1983　　Colchester and Its People, 1746–76. Manuscript on File, Depart-
　　　　　　 ment of Sociology/Anthropology, George Mason University.
　　　　　　 Fairfax, Va.

Wylie, Alison
　　1985a　 Putting Shakertown Back Together: Critical Theory in Archaeol-
　　　　　　 ogy. *Journal of Anthropological Archaeology* 4: 133–47.
　　1985b　 The Reaction against Analogy. In *Advances in Archaeological Method
　　　　　　 and Theory,* Vol. 8, ed. Michael Schiffer. New York: Academic
　　　　　　 Press.

Zuckerman, Michael
　　1977　　The Fabrication of Identity in Early America. *William and Mary
　　　　　　 Quarterly* 34: 183–214.

PART IV

Nineteenth-Century
Plantation Slavery
and Its Aftermaths

In the general introduction to this book we raised the issue of the political content of archaeology, or at least its political context. In that essay we suggested that the impending celebration of the Columbian Quincentennial in particular and the archaeology of Spanish colonization in general are to some extent products of growing Hispanic political power in Florida and the Southeast. Similarly, as Native Americans have gained a stronger political voice, they and their allies have made the reburial of Native American remains and the repatriation of Native American religious objects enormously important political issues within American archaeology, the visibility of which extends far beyond the boundaries of the discipline. In view of this situation, the apolitical nature of a large majority of the historical archaeology of black America is particularly striking. It is beyond the scope of this brief introductory essay to hypothesize as to why Afro-American archaeology is so apolitical, but we can provide several examples of this apoliticality and its consequences.

When we refer to Afro-American archaeology as being apolitical, we refer to two characteristics. First, in archaeological treatments of slavery there is rarely much discussion of the pervasive and all-encompassing domination of one group of people by another, that is, by definition, slavery. In reading much of Afro-American archaeology one tends to forget that the subject is often people owned by other people. Second, even more rarely do these treatments consider the contemporary social context of plantation archaeology and the social value of studies of slavery. Unasked is the question Who benefits from such studies? This lack of attention to politics, past or present, is not just an omission; it has consequences.

For example, in Otto's otherwise excellent work on Cannon's Point Plantation (Otto 1984), he begins by laying out as one of his research designs a consideration of the quality of slave life. He presents the arguments on both sides and frames archaeological questions about the composition of slave diet and the nature of slave housing. There are two problems here. First, "quality of life" ends up being judged on a caloric basis or in terms of square feet of living space per person or in some other way that is anything but a native point of view and contains neither passion nor a call to conscience. "Quality of life" becomes a measure of how much work an owner could extract from a slave. Second, the very act of entering into the debate of whether slave life was good or bad is a step toward avoiding the far more important fact that whether slave life was good or bad was largely controlled by white owners and overseers.

A second example of the apoliticality of Afro-American archaeology can be found in Kelso's study of Kingsmill (Kelso 1984). Kelso's first chapter, which is entitled "Above Ground," contains three sections: "Context," "Things," and "People." The principal discussion of slaves and slave life is placed in the section called "Things," whereas the white owners and planters are discussed under the heading "People." This may have the tendency to perpetuate inadvertently relations of domination and subordination that Kelso has no intention of endorsing.

In defense of Otto and Kelso, whose work we admire, we have used some fairly conventional techniques from literary criticism and other disciplines to read between the lines of two major contributions to historical archaeology. We do not question their value to the field. Further, there is no question that the intentions of Otto and

Kelso are clearly opposed to the messages that may be in their subtexts. And that is just the point. Otto and Kelso are apolitical. However, a central issue with which each must contend in his data and in modern America—namely, the relations between white and black Americans—is unavoidably political, and often hotly so. Given the nature of such an issue, it is often just when we think we have spared our research from becoming ensnarled in it that we can see it surface inadvertently; in this case, 19th-century categories have been carried up into the present. Our point is that avoiding the issue on the surface does not necessarily mean avoiding the issue, and it is easy to see harm done by uncontrolled and unintended messages below the surface. We do not necessarily urge archaeologists to be more political, only more conscious of the subtle political meanings of their work.

In the essays that follow, both Charles Orser and Theresa Singleton avoid some of the difficulties encountered by Otto, Kelso, and so many other archaeological commentators on slavery and black life, including Handler and Lange (1978) and Geismar (1982). Orser attends to the pervasive inequality of slavery by understanding slave life through a theory of power. A focus on power is one way to avoid the narrow perspective that usually accompanies attempts to answer the quality-of-life question. Singleton is attentive not only to the physical and social realities behind the rhetoric of emancipation—and thus does not lose sight of the political context of quality of life—but also to the contemporary use of the products of plantation archaeology in museum settings. Making museum settings an object of study is the way to avoid Kelso's misstep, when he neglected the fact that how something is said is often a part of what is communicated, or in more familiar terms, the fact that the medium is often a part of the message. In these ways, both Orser and Singleton attempt to place plantation slavery and its aftermaths in a larger social, economic, and cultural context.

Orser's approach is to understand plantation slavery as a special case of capitalist production and then analyze both slavery and postbellum Afro-American life using Nowak's (1983) version of historical materialism and theory of power. In Nowak's scheme, class struggles may take place in each of three "momentums," or spheres of social life: the economic, the political, and the ideological. Also important to Nowak is the Marxian concept of alienation. From this perspective, Orser evaluates various postbellum land-tenure systems in terms of ownership of the means of production and the right to divide the products of agricultural labor. By making land-tenure the primary variable in understanding postbellum Afro-American life, Orser is able to understand just why the living conditions and social positions of free blacks after 1875 so closely resembled antebellum slave life. Further, this analytical decision allows him to make a strong case for the importance of studying the patterning of architectural features; they are the archaeological signatures of land-tenure systems and as such constitute primary evidence for the exercise of social power. (One rule for locating slave quarters, reported by Orser, is that they be far enough away from the main house to be inoffensive but close enough to allow supervision of slaves by their masters. This tension between distance and proximity is similar but not identical to the tension implicit in seeing Afro-Americans as participating in but being separate from early 19th-century American society.) Orser's analysis of Millwood plantation is a demonstration of the value of land-tenure and economic power as organizing concepts for the understanding of late 19th-century Afro-American life in the American South.

Singleton, like Orser, moves to place understanding of 18th- and 19th-century Afro-American life in a broader cultural context, while maintaining the integrity of Afro-American culture. The scope of the data in her study is broader; she focuses not on a single plantation, but on a stretch of the Southeastern coast from North Carolina to northern Florida that was characterized by large plantations worked by hundreds of slaves. In addition, the temporal focus of her essay is broad, covering the period from 1740 until 1870. This time-depth is important because it allows Singleton to describe three distinct phases in the changing material culture and material conditions of slaves and newly emancipated blacks. The 18th century is characterized by the highest frequencies of Africanisms in all realms of material culture, and presumably, everyday slave life. (Although Singleton does not make this claim, it may be that allowing African cultural patterns to persist was a strategy employed by the white gentry to reconcile the glaring contradiction in the fact that men who owned other men wrote with conviction that "all men are created equal." Perhaps the extreme "otherness" that slaves were allowed to exhibit was used as justification for excluding them from the rhetoric of independence.) Singleton characterizes 19th-century slaves as living in a material world dominated by European-American material culture, from the forms of houses they lived in to the kinds of dishes they ate from. Finally, the material record of early postbellum Afro-American life suggests to Singleton that after emancipation the conditions of black life were even worse than before. Evidence for this includes considerable amounts of salvaged and reused construction materials, subsequent substandard construction and faunal remains indicating a diet heavily dependent on nondomestic sources of food. Singleton's essay, as well as Orser's, helps us understand that it is necessary to look below the surface of the rhetoric of emancipation, and that once we do, we will likely find that there was a significant difference between legal statutes and the economic, social, and physical reality, that is, the lives lived by newly freed blacks.

Singleton's essay concludes with a discussion of the contemporary social context of plantation archaeology and the potential uses to which the material evidence of slavery may be put. She has detected a trend away from considering slavery a taboo subject in museums and sees museums as understanding that slavery is a part of the American past that should not be ignored. This trend is all to the good, but we should pay careful attention to the political meaning of the lifting of this taboo. Does it mean that American museums are willing to take on serious considerations of past and present relations of inequality between black and white Americans, or does it mean that some museums consider American slavery and its consequences a dead issue and therefore safe to exhibit? The answer to this question is important and will come from paying attention not just to what is said in museum exhibits, but also to how slave life is presented. This is the issue we raised above regarding Kelso's Kingsmill book, and the principle is the same, the medium is a part of the message. A sophisticated examination of museum exhibits about slave life is the way to determine whose interests are served by such exhibits. Do they deaden and distance the black experience and serve to separate contemporary blacks from their slave ancestors, or do they make the history of slavery a usable past for American blacks? Answers to these questions are worth seeking because even powerful data like Orser's and Singleton's are also fragile, and they are so because any kind of radical information presented in the context of a conservative paradigm risks being used to support the assumptions that lie behind the conservative position.

REFERENCES CITED

Geismar, Joan
   1982   *The Archaeology of Social Disintegration in Skunk Hollow: A Nineteenth-Century Rural Black Community.* New York: Academic Press.

Handler, Jerome, and Frederick Lange
   1978   *Plantation Slavery in Barbados: An Archaeological and Historical Investigation.* Cambridge: Harvard University Press.

Kelso, William M.
   1984   *Kingsmill Plantations 1619–1800: Archaeology of Country Life in Colonial Virginia.* New York: Academic Press.

Nowak, Leszek
   1983   *Property and Power: Towards a Non-Marxian Historical Materialism.* Dordrecht, Holland: D. Reidel.

Otto, John
   1984   *Cannon's Point Plantation 1794–1860: Living Conditions and Status Patterns in the Old South.* New York: Academic Press.

CHAPTER 10

Toward a Theory of Power
for Historical Archaeology
Plantations and Space

CHARLES E. ORSER, JR.

In 1955, geographer Merle Prunty wrote an article that has become widely used in plantation studies. In it Prunty argues that plantations continued to exist after 1865 and that they had a strong spatial aspect throughout their existence. Prunty also states that plantation settlement and "power-management relationships" were interrelated. Although Prunty takes power-management to mean cultivating power—provided first by slaves, then by mules, and finally by tractors—his idea has merit if a different meaning of "power" is employed. If the technological meaning of power is replaced with a more social meaning that refers to relations of power between plantation inhabitants, another perspective can be introduced into the study of plantation spatial organization. Archaeologists are particularly well suited to provide data pertinent to this study because of their ability to recover physical evidence about housing and housing arrangements. The purpose of this chapter is to explore a perspective that is useful for studying the more social aspects of "power" in general and plantation "power" in particular and to illustrate its application at one plantation site.

A CRISIS IN HISTORICAL ARCHAEOLOGY

During the late 1960s and early 1970s, Western scholars began to reevaluate the perspectives, methods, and intentions of their disciplines. In the United States, this self-evaluation was precipitated by, among other things, the civil rights movement, a developing recognition of worldwide human rights, and an understanding of the modern world's political complexities, perhaps most aptly demonstrated by the war in Vietnam. Anthropologists were not immune to this self-examination and many began to wonder how they might make their disciplines more "relevant" to the world around them (Copans and Seddon 1978: 14–15). Many anthropologists started to question their role in perpetuating imperialism, racism, and colonialism (Gough 1968; Caulfield 1974; Willis 1974; Leacock 1982).

This new attitude was slow to develop in historical archaeology, but some archaeologists did turn their attention to the "common" members of society, just as many historians were doing. In plantation archaeology, this change meant shifting one's focus from the plantation big houses to the slave quarters. Thus, in the past few years, archaeologists have provided abundant information about slave housing and the material culture used in the daily life of slavery (Fairbanks 1974, 1983; McFarlane 1975; Otto 1975, 1984; Singleton 1980, 1985a). In addition, some historical archaeologists have turned their attention to the descendants of plantation slaves—plantation tenant farmers (Adams 1980; Anderson and Muse 1982; Orser 1985a, 1986b, 1988; Orser and Holland 1984).

The central concern of historical archaeology may have changed, but little effort has been put into developing a sound theoretical basis for the new approach, despite the debates occasioned during the formalization of historical archaeology (South 1968). This lack of explicit theorizing obtains even though at least one prominent archaeologist realized a few years ago that historical archaeology should be in the forefront of theory building in archaeology (Binford 1977:13). That this has not been the case, or that its practitioners have not produced a unified way in which to examine the past, constitutes a serious crisis in the field.

Much of the research conducted in historical archaeology to date might best be termed "eclectic." As a philosophy, eclecticism mandates no clear commitment to any particular theoretical orientation, and eclectics are free to change their epistemology as the situation seems to warrant (Harris 1980:287–314). However, rather than being openminded and versatile, eclectics usually have a "scattershot" approach to

the problems they study (Price 1980:155), and instead of providing ontological depth to their analyses they are unable to collate their endeavors in a clear and consistent manner.

The many formal definitions of historical archaeology offered
since the field was first recognized attest to its eclecticism and inner theoretical turmoil. At one extreme, J. C. Harrington (1952:336) defines
historical archaeology as a sort of history that is concerned with the excavation and study of sites that are judged, within the dominant national ideology, to have been associated with significant events or per-
sonages from the past. At the other extreme, ethnologist Bernard L.
Fontana (1965:61) defines historical archaeology in relation to Native
Americans and classifies historic-period sites according to their degree
of "Indianness."

These and other views of historical archaeology proposed during
the critical time of the early development of the field served not to define and to identify the future scope, direction, and purpose of historical archaeology, but only to confuse and to obstruct the development of
a sound epistemological outlook. Nonetheless, within this confusion—
this so-called crisis of identity (Cleland and Fitting 1968)—a proper
course for historical archaeology was proposed.

Robert Schuyler (1970:84) argued that historical archaeology is
"the study of the material remains from any historic period," whereas
"historic sites archaeology" is the study of the material remains associated with the expansion of European culture into the non-European
world since the 15th century. Accordingly, historic sites archaeology
focuses on the study of the rise and development of European mercantile capitalism, nationalism, and the technological changes wrought by
the Industrial Revolution. In this definition of "historic sites archaeology," Schuyler identifies the proper subject of historical archaeology—
capitalism and capitalist development and growth. This view was
expressed later by Leone (1977), another prominent historical archaeologist, but the field did not come of age until Russell Handsman (1985:6)
described its subject matter as "power, commodities and capital, class
struggle and resistance, hegemony and masking," in other words,
problems associated with capitalism.

When capitalism becomes widely recognized as the proper focus of
historical archaeology, its practitioners will be freed from the reifica-
tion so commonplace in the formal, academic disciplines. Historical archaeologists will no longer be concerned with such artificial categories
as "history" and "anthropology" and will not worry about which category best describes their research. Historical archaeologists will be
able to examine capitalism and its various components—colonialism,

imperialism, industrialization, class struggle, and social formation—as historical subjects that are neither properly "history" nor "anthropology," but both.

One explicitly theoretical way in which historical archaeologists might study the development of capitalism in North America and seek to assign meaning to the material remains of capitalist communities is provided in historical materialism. Historical materialism is particularly well suited to the archaeological study of the past.

HISTORICAL MATERIALISM AND HISTORICAL ARCHAEOLOGY

The philosophical doctrine of materialism contains a complex set of ideas that have generated considerable scholarly debate (Matsumae 1975; Aronowitz 1981; Giddens 1981). Many different kind of materialism exist today (Harris 1980:29–76, 141–64; Nonini 1985), but perhaps the most well-known form is the historical materialism of Karl Marx.

Historical materialism, or the materialist conception of history, is a philosophical outlook based on the proposition that "the mode of production of material life conditions the general process of social, political, and intellectual life" (Marx 1970:20–21). This mode of production, although its exact meaning is not always agreed upon, includes most of the tangible human actions and items produced in daily life. The relations of production are those social relations created for a particular mode of production. These relations include the division of labor and the economic class structures. Society changes when a conflict arises between the mode of production and the relations of production (the relations of ownership and the division of labor).

The strength of Marx's historical materialism lies in (a) its insistence on sound historical research, (b) its emphasis on production of human action over human thought and the "inevitable forces of history," and (c) the concept that the economic foundation of society necessarily engenders social relations and that the economic, political, and ideological segments of society cannot be separated. Although some commentators have misinterpreted Marx's views about the role of the economic foundation of society, believing that he took the economic base to be the determining element of social life (caused by a mistranslation of Marx's preface to A Critique of Political Economy [Rader 1979:14–15]), historical materialism is clearly not economic determinism. As Engels (1974:294) stated, "If somebody twists this [the materialist conception of history] into saying that the economic element is the *only* determining one, he transforms that proposition into a meaningless, abstract, senseless phrase." By the same token, to reduce Marx's historical materialism to mere technological determinism, as Leslie White (1959) and his archaeological followers have done, is to grossly oversimplify Marx's thesis (Carver 1982:61–62, 93–94; Miller 1984: 174–95).

In any case, historical materialism provides an excellent theoretical framework for archaeological research (Kohl 1981:108–12), particularly for studies of the historic past. Historical archaeologists can make use of historical materialism for at least three reasons. First, historical materialism offers extensive concepts and insights that are just now being explored in depth by archaeologists (Spriggs 1984a; Trigger 1984b), even though at least one prominent archaeologist examined them earlier (Childe 1947, 1951, 1979). Second, a tradition of using historical materialism in the formal disciplines of history (Fox-Genovese and Genovese 1983; Genovese 1984) and anthropology (Bloch 1975, 1985; Godelier 1977), two disciplines inextricably tied to historical archaeology, is developing at a fast pace. And third, historical materialists and historical archaeologists concentrate on the same kinds of societies: modern, literate, capitalist ones. Thus, historical materialism is a directly relevant philosophical doctrine around which to organize ideas for historical archaeological interpretation.

One problem, however, is the way some scholars choose to view the doctrine. Historical materialism represents a complex body of thought that cannot be comprehended easily or quickly, since so much of its voluminous literature is labyrinthine and contradictory, but many scholars make little effort to untangle it and eschew it outright because of its revolutionary character and contemporary socialist associations. Concern over linking archaeology and politics, especially totalitarian socialism, through materialism, has been expressed by Mark Leone (1982:757), who has received sharp criticism for his view that the political side of Marxism must be excluded from archaeology (Spriggs 1984b:7n.). Leone's stance, however, is consistent with that of Childe (1947:71–72) and is forged from experience. It may have been true, as Engels said during his graveside eulogy, that Marx was "before all else a revolutionary" (Foner 1983:39), but to claim that historical materialism is lifeless without "its revolutionary practice" (Thalheimer 1936:185) is too extreme. The explicit use of historical materialism in archaeology may be "revolutionary," but not necessarily in a political sense. For that matter, all archaeology is "political" to some extent (Trigger 1984a), but American historical archaeologists would gain nothing in their research efforts by allying themselves with contemporary Marxist-Leninist politics. However, archaeologists practicing within such regimes have great insights to offer Western archaeologists that must not be ignored because of political ideologies (Klejn 1977; Trigger 1978).

This point hinges on a somewhat subtle but important distinction between the terms *Marxist* and *Marxian*. In most contemporary contexts, Marxist refers to one who believes in the political ideas of Marx, Engels, and Lenin, mainly militant communism. Marxian, on the other hand, refers to one who finds value in historical materialism as a methodology and in Marx's philosophical or socioeconomic concepts and views of history (Maquet 1984:2). Most research by Western archaeologists using Marx's concepts can be considered Marxian. Conversely, such studies written by Soviet archaeologists might be considered Marxist, but not necessarily so.

Particularly important in this regard is the research of Polish social philosopher and historical materialist Leszek Nowak (1983). Nowak's version of historical materialism is a Marxian critical theory that reflects both his socialist education and his opposition to the "inhuman nature" of modern socialism. (For comments on the historical context for this sort of attitude, see Ash [1983]). For Nowak, the importance of Marx's work lies not necessarily in his ideas about the past, but in his method of inquiry, best exemplified perhaps in *Capital* (Marx 1967). (A similar conclusion has been reached by American philosopher Daniel Little [1986].)

As a scholar living under Soviet totalitarianism, Nowak sees classical Marxism as a mystification of reality, used to keep rulers in power. Thus, in line with Marxian dialectics, an old theory must be replaced with a new one. This theory must be a theory of power. Once formulated, this theory can be used to study all kinds of social formations, past and present (Orser 1987).

NOWAK'S HISTORICAL MATERIALISM AND THE THEORY OF POWER

Nowak (1983:137) believes that a refined theory of power must be built because this aspect of social life is "the weakest point of Marxian social theory." Also believing that historical materialism is useful, he builds this theory on the classical Marxian model of society that contains three "momentums" or spheres of social life: economic, political, and ideological. (Ideology is used here simply to refer to ideas, concepts, and beliefs [i.e., culture] rather than in the sense of false ideas devised to conceal economic or political interests [Rader 1979:42].)

Nowak defines the classes in each momentum on the basis of the allocation of the material forces of society. In keeping with a dialectical view of social life, Nowak maintains that a class struggle occurs within each momentum. In the economic momentum, the struggle is waged between direct producers (those who work) and owners (those who own); in the political momentum, the struggle occurs between citizens (those who are ruled) and the disposers of the coercive forces (those who rule); and in the ideological momentum, the struggle occurs between the faithful (those who listen) and the disposers of the means of production of consciousness (those who preach) (Nowak 1983:174). These struggles have an identical structure. Each struggle only appears to be different in any given time and place because of a different historical development. In any case, the underlying reason for the struggles, at least as far as the superordinate classes are concerned, is the same in every case: to increase their own power, or influence, over others.

The concept of "alienation," central to Marx's conception of history, is also central to Nowak's social formulation. Although this concept has many different meanings within contemporary Marxian thought (Schacht 1970; Ollman 1971), Nowak uses the term to refer to the difference between what direct producers, citizens, and the faithful expect from owners, rulers, and spokesmen by right of their labor, loyalty, and belief and what they receive. In the economic momentum, the "alienation of work" is the difference between the economic needs of the direct producers and the capital they receive from the owners. This idea is similar to Marx's notion that alienation in the workplace is "an historically produced evil" (Rader 1979:103). "Civic alienation" refers to the autonomy the citizens expect to receive versus what they are actually granted. (The struggle in the ideological momentum is less well formulated by Nowak [1983:177].) Class struggles occur, then, when the gap between what the subordinate class receives versus what it expects to receive becomes so wide that it is unbearable. For Nowak, like Marx, revolution occurs when oppression and debasement make people feel estranged from the human condition they have a right to expect (Marx and Engels 1956:51). However, Nowak's revolution comes not at the end of the cycle, as is the classic Marxian idea, but in the middle, when the oppressed still have the ability and strength to fight.

Within each momentum, a balance can be reached so that the acts of disobedience by the subordinate classes do not escalate into full-scale revolution. In the economic momentum, for example, the owners keep the variable capital (received by the direct producers for their labor) high enough so that the producers do not organize against them; at the same time, the surplus value (profit) for the owners is kept high enough so that they do not feel the need to change the way in which commodities are produced in order to increase their profits. In the political momentum, the balance is more easily struck because mass citizen action can be avoided either by keeping the political alienation so low that the citizens are not interested in revolting, or by keeping the repression so high that the citizens suffer "declassation" and find overt action to be impossible. For Nowak, interned in December of 1981 when martial law was declared in Poland, this more severe sort of balance is characteristic of the Soviet Union and its totalitarian satellites.

The important point is that, even though the struggles are structurally identical, the struggle in the economic moment differs markedly from that in the political moment. In the economic moment, when the level of economic alienation is too low, the owner's interest is compromised. Workers in extreme poverty are not able to fight the owners, no matter how much they might desire to do so; at the same time, the surplus capital that goes to the owners is small. In the political moment, the situation is different because a completely subjugated citizen "is perfect raw material for a ruler" (Nowak 1983:146). When the citizens are so disfranchised that resistance seems impossible, the control of the ruler becomes total. Revolution generally does not occur when people are totally oppressed.

SPACE AND POWER

Nowak does not mention it, but his concept of power can include space and the use of space. In fact, the interrelation between space and power provides a key to the archaeological study of the past.

Archaeologists have been interested in spatial analysis for years, and many sophisticated models have been proposed and used in the analysis of past settlements (Hodder and Orton 1976; Crumley 1979). Many of these studies have focussed on the ecological, religious, and economic determinants of settlement (Trigger 1968; Clarke 1977), on the assumption that the composition and distribution of settlement provides physical information about social relationships (Trigger 1967:151). Recently, it has been found that power relations also can be identified in the spatial arrangements of past settlements (Renfrew 1984, 1986).

Not long ago, anthropologist Edward T. Hall (1963:1003; 1969) identified a field of investigation called "proxemics," which he defines as the study of "the interrelated observations and theories of man's use of space as a specialized elaboration of culture" whose subject matter is "the distance between men in the conduct of daily transactions, the organization of space in his houses and buildings, and ultimately the layout of his town." Hall demonstrated that many different kinds of space—visual, auditory, olfactory, and tactile—exist.

Refining this idea, noted scholar Henri Lefebvre (1979) argued that space is a social product that cannot be explained by reference to the environment, human nature, or even culture. Rather, space has its own reality within the existing mode of production. Thus, although the use of space is culture-specific, as Hall maintained, space is also intrinsic in the way in which the material world is produced. For Lefebvre (1979:287–89), space has at least four functions: it acts as a means of production, it is an object of consumption, it intervenes in class struggle, and it is a political instrument. Concerning the last function, Lefebvre (1979:288) states that space is administratively controlled and policed and is allocated according to a hierarchy that corresponds to the social classes within a mode of production. In other words—to borrow a term from another researcher (Donley 1982)—the use of space includes "house power."

The archaeological task of recognizing past material manifestations of power relations is decidedly difficult (Miller and Tilley 1984). Years of research are needed before a firm understanding of the relationship between power and archaeological remains will be attained. Nonetheless, plantations seem to provide a perfect arena in which to begin the search.

THE SOUTHERN PLANTATION IN NOWAK'S TERMS

Scholars do not agree on an exact definition of the word *plantation* (Orser 1984:1), but a usable definition would indicate that a plantation is a capitalist kind of agricultural organization in which a number of laborers produce a certain crop under the direction of others (Mintz 1959:43–44). The definition must also include the idea that plantations contain a special set of social and spatial relationships (Orser 1984:1–2, 1985b; Prunty 1955:460).

On an antebellum plantation, the planter (owner) exerted economic control over his slaves. Not only were the slaves personally owned, they were also the direct producers. They had to produce enough capital to provide both for the planter's family and for their own families (through the planter). Slaves experienced significant civic alienation as planters exerted political control over them. When southern sugar, rice, and cotton became major money crops, planters grew concerned, not just about production, but also about the production of surplus labor itself (Marx 1967:236). Planters used this surplus labor to purchase luxury items symbolizing their wealth and power. As the planter's ability to purchase luxury items increased and as the slaves were forced to work harder, the gap between planters and slaves grew wider. Economic and political alienation was high as planters were gaining wealth through the labor of their slaves, while denying slaves all access to substantive power. The existence of violent slave revolts, nonviolent slave desertions (Aptheker 1964, 1968; Cheek 1970), and the retention of certain Africanisms in material culture (Ferguson n.d.; Singleton 1980) indicate that many slaves had not given the situation up as hopeless. With the end of the American Civil War in 1865, the United States entered what Marx called its "revolutionary period" (Marx and Engels 1937:277). This "revolution" was supposed to transform the South from a slaveholding society to one wherein freed slaves, who would receive "40 acres and a mule," would become small farmers. This change in land tenure did not materialize, and the plantation system continued to operate in the South (Raper 1936; Woofter et al. 1936; Langsford and Thibodeaux 1939; Ransom and Sutch 1977; Orser 1986a).

Although southern plantations continued to exist after 1865, the relations between the owners and the direct producers were of a different nature, even though the individuals involved were often the same. The classes maintained relatively the same economic relationship they had before the war (owners and direct producers), but the social relations that existed between them were different in that the plantation owners were now landlords and the direct producers freed tenant farmers. The result was sharecropping, debt peonage, and summary dismissal from the plantation, all of which would have been impossible before the Civil War (Fields 1982, 1983). Thus, the "antebellum plantation mode of production" was not identical to the "postbellum plantation mode of production."

Black plantation farmers, like most southern blacks, did make some political gains during the decade immediately following the war. By 1875, however, they had lost most of them, as landowners managed to reconsolidate their collective power as autocratic "rulers" (Zinn 1980:193–205). Again disfranchised, this time by terrorism rather than by overt bondage, plantation agriculturalists were cemented further into their new social position: Although "citizens," they were unable to decrease their civic alienation, except through the actions of short-lived tenant farmer unions and occasional strikes (Grubbs 1971; Schwartz 1976).

On postbellum plantations, the power relations between owners and direct producers were reflected in their tenure relationships. Ideally, barring racism and discrimination, the alienation of the tenant was supposed to decrease as he moved up the "agricultural ladder" (Spillman 1919), a hierarchy that was used to rank farmers according to the arrangement they were able to make with a landlord. Wage laborers, who occupied the lowest position on the agricultural ladder, did not own land, tools, or work animals, and simply worked for a wage. Sharecroppers also did not own the means of production, and as far as southern courts were concerned (Applewhite 1954; Woodman 1979), were merely wage laborers who accepted a share of the crop in the place of wages. Share renters owned their own tools and animals and supplied part of the fertilizer, but their landlords supplied the rest of the fertilizer and owned the land. At the top of the ladder, but below independent owner-operators, were the standing renters and cash renters who owned their own animals and tools and paid the landlord rent in the form of a set amount of crop (in the case of the standing renter) or money (in the case of the cash renter).

The ownership of the means of production and its attendant power was what distinguished plantation landlords from tenants. The greater power of landlords was manifest, in one way, by the landlord's legal right to divide the crop. Southern courts maintained that when landlords owned the means of production, they also owned the crop and had the right to divide it. Thus, sharecroppers did not own the crop they had worked so hard to produce. According to the Supreme Court of North Carolina in 1874, for instance, the sharecropper, "although he has, in some sense, the possession of the crop, it is only the possession of a servant, and it is in law that of the landlord." On the other hand, standing renters and cash renters owned the means of production and had the right to divide their own crops. The same court maintained that when the standing or cash tenant "pays a share of the crop for rent it is he that divides off to the landlord his share, and until such division the right of property and of possession in the whole is his" (Hargrave 1905:8–9). The direction in payment, then, from the landlord to the tenant or from the tenant to the landlord, signaled power.

The ownership of the means of production and the power that was attached to it also were indicated in the plantation's spatial organization. Large antebellum plantations normally took the form of a clustered settlement. The planter's house was usually at the center of the estate within a cluster of support and service buildings that included carriage houses, servants' quarters, smokehouses, and sheds. Another cluster contained the field slave quarters, the overseer's house, the slave hospital, the slave nursery, and other support structures. This settlement pattern, described by many contemporaries (Ball 1837: 137–40; Trowbridge 1866:483–84; Avirett 1901:35–42) and often mentioned by former slaves (Rawick 1977–79), has been referred to as the "Ante Bellum Plantation Occupance Form" (Prunty 1955:463–66).

The antebellum plantation spatial plan was designed to put the workers near their workplaces (Orser and Nekola 1985). Field slaves generally lived near the fields, house slaves lived near the planter's home, and overseers lived between planters and slaves. However, a strong message of power also resided in the settlement form because the clustered pattern was designed to enable planters and overseers to maintain surveillance over their slaves. For example, in speaking of the "proper" placement of slave quarters in colonial Louisiana, A.S. Le Page du Pratz (1975:381) said that "prudence requires that your negroes be lodged at a proper distance, to prevent them from being troublesome or offensive; but at the same time near enough for your conveniently observing what passes among them." The distance between slave quarters and planter's houses was quite variable (Orser 1988:87–88), but the idea expressed by Le Page du Pratz probably represented prevailing planter attitudes.

The clustered settlement pattern of the plantation was dismantled after the Civil War. This change is consistent with the idea that settlement is an inherent aspect of the mode of production. Thus, after the war, many former slaves moved out of their slave quarter cabins in search of their own land and houses. When it became painfully clear that emancipation did not necessarily mean economic independence, many freedmen returned to plantation life. Some freedmen did not leave their plantation homes at all simply because they had nowhere to go (Orser 1986c).

One of the experimental land tenure arrangements used immediately after the war in South Carolina, at least, had a distinctive kind of settlement. This system, called the squad system, was a share collective composed of kin-related former slaves (Shlomowitz 1979, 1982). Squad members lived in clustered settlements, as they had as slaves, but at some distance from the landlord. So, although they were still living in closely spaced houses, they were not under the direct, constant supervision of the landlord (Orser 1986b).

After about 1875, when the tenancy system started becoming institutionalized and the experimental systems were largely abandoned, another settlement change occurred on southern plantations. To be practical economically, tenancy required that each farmer live near his fields. On at least one plantation, tenants who continued to live in the slave quarters had to walk a mile to their fields (Barrow 1881:832). To alleviate this sort of problem, the settlement pattern of tenancy was modified to place tenants in individual houses all across a plantation (Campbell 1879:142). Most freed slaves were happy to accept this arrangement because it took them out of the quarters forever and gave them some measure of freedom over their lives. This settlement form has been termed the "Post Bellum 'Fragmented' Occupance Form" (Prunty 1955:467–82).

This information about plantation organization and settlement can be used in conjunction with the ideas of Nowak and Lefebvre to formulate the following assumptions: (1) plantations contained at least two gross classes of people (owners and direct producers), (2) the social relations created between these classes permitted the owners to dominate the direct producers, and (3) these power relations should have material correlates that will be exhibited, among other ways, spatially. These assumptions can be used to examine the nature of the spatial correlates at Millwood Plantation in Abbeville County, South Carolina.

POWER RELATIONS AT MILLWOOD PLANTATION

Millwood Plantation, one of the only two postbellum cotton plantations ever studied in detail by historical archaeologists, provides an excellent site at which to study the archaeological manifestations of plantation power relations. Millwood was created in 1834 on the Savannah River in Abbeville County, South Carolina. Cotton was the major crop cultivated by the 195 slaves who lived there in 1860. Many of these slaves continued to live on the property after the Civil War, and in 1867 the planter made a squad arrangement with seven of them. These seven were responsible for farming a particular piece of the plantation with their hired squad laborers (Orser 1986b). Perhaps by 1870, but certainly by 1875, the squad arrangement was abandoned for a fixed renting system. About 95 tenants remained on the property until the 1920s (Orser, Nekola, and Roark 1987).

Thus three separate modes of production—slavery, the squad system, and tenancy—can be identified at Millwood Plantation. Ideally, each is temporally distinct, but they could, and did, appear simultaneously. For example, before 1865, when the slave mode of production operated, an undetermined number of white tenant farmers also lived at Millwood.

Even though Millwood Plantation was occupied and operated from 1834 until the late 1920s, the 33 building foundations visible in 1980–81 probably reflect, in the main, the spatial arrangement of the last of the three plantation modes of production. That is, the probability is high that the arrangement of buildings at the site reflect its most recent occupation. Although some of the foundations may well be antebellum in origin, no clearly antebellum archaeological deposits were located during the fieldwork. The paucity of these materials undoubtedly relates to natural processes—the severe erosion of the Southern Piedmont—and probably also to behavioral processes—yard cleaning and the other daily activities of the postbellum plantation inhabitants, people who were not concerned with the preservation of the earlier deposits. Artifacts of antebellum date were found in the postbellum deposits, but no pristine antebellum deposits of any sort were located. Still, of all possible kinds of material culture, housing may be one of the most lasting. Postbellum plantation inhabitants could have swept away all of the artifacts found around their homes quite easily, but they may have been more reluctant to dig up the foundation of an old building unless they intended to recycle the materials. Antebellum buildings probably were used after 1865, but without clear antebellum deposits, the buildings at Millwood cannot be positively dated to the slave mode of production.

To circumvent the problems caused by the lack of archaeological visibility of the slave mode of production, this analysis focuses on the tenant mode of production, roughly from 1875 to the 1920s, and 10 building foundations. Artifacts collected from these foundations derive from the postbellum period, and the assumption is made that the inhabitants of the buildings represented by the foundations operated within the tenant mode of production.

The structures to be considered are Structures 1, 2, 8, 10, 11, 17, 19, 23, 27, and E (Figure 10.1). Each contained at least one fireplace hearth or a central chimney support and so are judged to have been used as dwellings. Census data suggest that, with the exception of Structures 1 and 8, all of these buildings were inhabited by freed slaves from Millwood Plantation (Orser, Nekola, and Roark 1987).

If Lefebvre's (1979:286) idea that space is appropriated at least in part according to "the relations of production, namely, the division of labor and its organization," then it can be assumed that a correlation might exist between house size and position on the postbellum agricultural ladder. Landlords would be expected to live in larger houses than wage hands. This logic makes sense today, because the relations of production operating in the South during the late 19th and early 20th centuries are not temporally far removed from those of today.

The foundations under examination indeed were different sizes. These foundations can be arranged in descending order of square feet available (Table 10.1). The largest foundation is Structure 1 and the smallest are Structures 11 and E. Independent historical, oral, and pictorial information suggests that Structure 1 was the home of the white plantation landlord, that part of Structure 2 was the home of his longtime black servant (the remainder of the building was apparently used as a kitchen), and that Structure 8 was the home of the white resident manager. Former plantation tenants suggested that Structures 17, 19, and 23 had been tenant farmer homes, even though Structure 23 probably was used also during the squad mode of production (Orser 1986b).

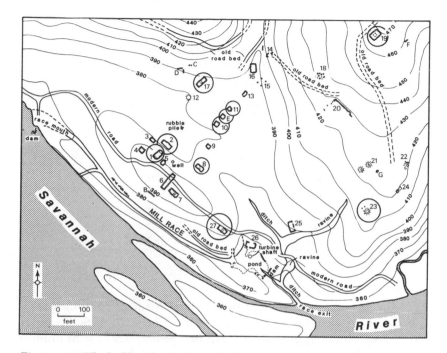

Figure 10.1: *The building foundations at Millwood Plantation, 1980–81. The buildings examined are circled.*

The evidence that Structures 10, 11, and E were wage hand dwellings is circumstantial but plausible. The strongest evidence stems from their size, shape, and uniformity. They appear slightly larger than slave dwellings (323.1 and 370.6 square feet), whose generally "recommended" size was between 288 and 320 square feet (Collins 1854:423). Archaeological research has substantiated that many slave cabins were built within this range (Ascher and Fairbanks 1971:8; Ehrenhard and Bullard 1981:33; Otto 1984:38). Even though these foundations bear a strong resemblance to slave cabins, photographic evidence makes it quite clear that they were occupied in the 1870s. In addition, census materials indicate that in 1879, when the landlord was 81 years old, his 5-acre farm yielded one bale of cotton, 20 bushels of cow peas, 10 cords of wood, and seven pounds of fleece (U. S. Census 1880). This agricultural production was most certainly obtained through the labor of wage hands. Wage hands were commonly housed in former slave cabins in the years immediately after 1865 (Rawick 1977–79, 7(2):778, 8(3):1347; Killion and Waller 1973:55).

327

TABLE IO.I

*Square Footage of Foundations
with Occupant Association*

Square feet	Structure	Possible occupant
897.0	I	Landlord
743.0	27	Millwright
630.0	19	Tenant
546.0	17	Tenant
498.0	2	Servant
370.6	10	Wage hand
323.1	11	Wage hand
323.1	E	Wage hand

The largest foundations at the site were Structure 6 (which measured 1,580.0 square feet) and Structure 21. The walls of Structure 21 could not be located, but its two large, double fireplace hearths implied that the building had been quite large. The size of these dwellings indicates, perhaps, that they were inhabited by the plantation owner. Local oral tradition holds that the owner moved from Structure 6 to Structure 1 sometime after the death of his wife in 1844 (Orser 1988:204–6). The large size of Structure 6 makes this interpretation possible. Structure 21 may have been used as a squad dwelling in the period from 1867 to about 1870, but it also may have been the landlord's first home at the plantation when his slaves were busy clearing it in the early 1830s. Unfortunately, this supposition cannot be confirmed, and the reason for the large size of Structure 21 remains a mystery. (The size of Structures 8 and 23 could not be determined because their walls could not be located.)

On a plantation, as in all of society, it can be hypothesized that the differences in house size probably related to economics. The landlord could provide the money for the construction of a large house for himself, and smaller houses for his employees. However, the landlord's ability to build his employees' houses also indicated his power over them. The disfranchised direct producers, who were required to live on the plantation, lacked the political strength to demand better housing and the economic strength to provide their own. Thus, size of house can be viewed as a physical manifestation of plantation power.

House size, however, is not the only factor to reveal power relations; equally important should be the location of houses within a plantation landscape. A plantation's landscape is a bounded universe with clear limits. To be someone's tenant required living on his or her land. As such, the spatial arrangement of plantation housing should reflect power relations to some degree.

It can be expected, given the plantation's primary economic function, that plantation houses were located closest to the work places of their inhabitants. Thus, the millwright, in Structure 27, lived near the mill pond and the mill building (Structure 26), and the landlord's servant lived near the landlord. However, what may be more indicative of power relations are the relationships between the individual buildings themselves. In other words, the relationships between the buildings should have carried a social meaning created to reflect, among other things, the power relations enacted within the dominant mode of production at the plantation.

To test this idea, the linear distances between the foundations (as measured from the center) were calculated for the 10 foundations and recorded in a symmetrical matrix (Table 10.2). These measurements make it possible to argue that plantation power relations did have spatial correlates.

The significance of these distances can be illustrated when those pertaining to the major tenure groups at the plantation—landlord, manager, wage hands, and tenants—are graphically represented (Figure 10.2). The major tenure groups are arranged down the left side of the chart and the distance of the homes of the other workers are arranged along the horizontal lines. By examining this chart, the distance between the houses can be quickly recognized.

The distances on the first two lines, those of the landlord and manager, represent a pattern that may be a reflection of the power relations enacted at the plantation. In both cases, the wage hands, millwright, and servant were closest whereas the tenants were furthest away. The proximity of one tenant dwelling (Structure 17) to the landlord's house may be misleading, because the building may not have been inhabited during the landlord's life. The landlord died in 1889 and an informant who once lived in Structure 17 said that she did not live there before 1910. It cannot be determined whether this dwelling was inhabited before 1910 (Holland n.d.).

Interestingly, the same informant suggested that she may have moved to Structure 19 after leaving Structure 17. If this statement were true, the distance and direction of the move would most certainly convey a meaning. This meaning, however, may reflect only indirect power considerations. After the death of the landlord in 1889, local whites began to use the plantation as a camping ground. When camping

TABLE 10.2.

Distances between Foundations Associated
with Plantation Inhabitants (in feet)

	Landlord	Manager	Servant	Wage	Wage	Wage	Millwright	Tenant	Tenant	Tenant
Landlord (1)	—	170	50	265	340	300	390	340	970	850
Manager (8)	170	—	160	185	260	220	260	340	860	680
Servant (2)	50	160	—	215	285	250	400	270	920	830
Wage (10)	265	185	215	—	80	40	410	180	710	680
Wage (11)	340	260	285	80	—	40	470	160	635	670
Wage (E)	300	220	250	40	40	—	440	160	675	675
Millwright (27)	390	260	400	410	470	440	—	585	970	570
Tenant (17)	340	340	270	180	160	160	585	—	705	825
Tenant (19)	970	860	920	710	635	675	970	705	—	695
Tenant (23)	850	680	830	680	670	675	570	825	695	—

there, whites stole garden produce from those tenants who still lived at the plantation, particularly those near the camping area in the vicinity of Structure 1. When Structure 17 was destroyed by fire sometime between 1910 and 1925, its inhabitants decided to live far away from the camping area. In one respect, then, this move may demonstrate another kind of power, the dominant power of whites in southern society, rather than strict plantation power relations.

The homes of the wage hands appear in a central location within the site, and the tenants' homes are not as far away as they were from the landlord and manager. This centrality is probably both a function of economics (i.e., of being close to the workplace, the landlord's farm), but probably also a function of power (i.e., being close to those who would supervise them). The very real difference between working for wages and working as a tenant were summarized well by tenant farmer Ed Brown when he said: "You couldn't join in the fun if you was on wages and your time belong to the bossman" (Maguire 1975:44). When the crop was laid by, Brown's landlord made his wage hands haul logs, cut ditches, clean fence lines, and work in the sawmill. Brown reinforces a generally accepted supposition, that landlords held more power over their wage hands than over their tenant farmers. This distinction has been expressed beautifully in fiction as well (Perry 1986:8–11).

The two tenant homes, one of which may have been used by one of the squad families (Orser 1986b), appear furthest away from the landlord's dwelling. However, because the landlord had died before these dwellings probably were occupied by tenants, the most important "power" distance was probably to the manager's residence. Of course, for the squad family, the most significant distance in terms of power would be to the landlord's house. In the case of the tenants in Structures 19 and 23, the increase in elevation may have been as important as was the distance. Both dwellings were located on hills above the landlord's and manager's houses. Structure 23, the possible squad dwelling, was located on a hill overlooking the Savannah river and Structure 19 was on the highest point of the entire archaeological site. If the tenants in Structure 17, in fact, had moved to Structure 19, then its placement may be even more revealing.

In actuality, the dispersement of tenants at Millwood Plantation was much more significant than is apparent at the archaeological site. Those tenants who stayed at the plantation were dispersed throughout the 10,000-acre estate as far as 4 miles or more from the landlord's and manager's houses (Orser and Nekola 1985). This important settlement distribution is only partly apparent at the 32-acre archaeological site, in the distances between the tenant dwellings (Structures 19 and 23) and those of the landlord and manager (Structures 1 and 8).

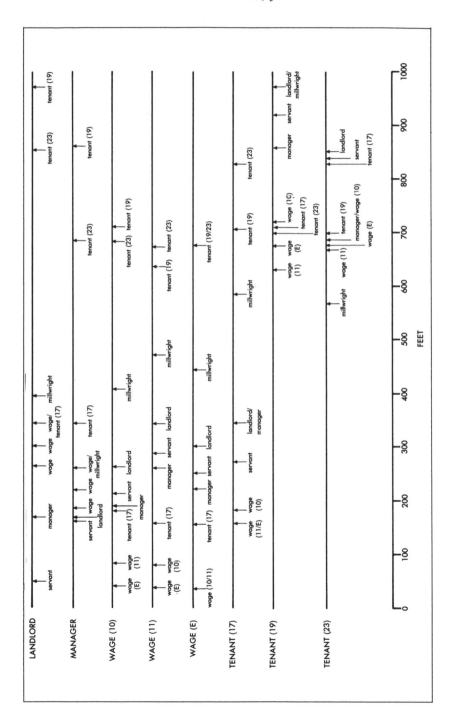

CONCLUSION

The current state of knowledge about the physical remains of plantations and the new direction in historical archaeology mean that much research needs to be done before archaeologists will be able to assign plausible meanings about power to past remains. Such assignments will not be easy to make in any case. On antebellum plantations, the very workers were owned as property and the relations of production included obvious domination (Little 1986:43; Marx and Engels 1970: 44–45). In the postbellum period, domination was no less real, and the task will be equally difficult because of the variations in tenure. Obstacles can also be expected in the study of what may be the most important period of all, the transition between slavery and tenancy (Singleton 1985b, also Chapter 11 this volume; Orser 1986c), because of the difficulty of clearly identifying artifacts owned by freed men and women. Moreover, the freedmen continued to occupy slave cabins on many plantations, and at emancipation freed slaves did not turn in all of their "antebellum" artifacts for new "postbellum" ones. The artifacts used in 1860 were probably not all that different from those used in 1867, but the social relations of 1867 were far different from those of 1860. This problem of distinguishing between slavery and freedom in the material culture of Afro-Americans, or as it has been called, the "gray area in the identification of slave and free contexts" (Singleton 1985b:291), will continue to be a major concern of plantation archaeologists over the next few years. However, perhaps the most fruitful line of investigation will be plantation housing.

This chapter does not offer concrete answers about the correlation between the relations of power and the modes of production enacted at southern plantations. Rather it provides a helpful perspective and an outline for future research, both on and off plantations. Archaeologists will not be able to attach meanings of power to the material remains they study without a perspective that is sensitive to such meanings.

Historical materialism and Nowak's theory of power hold tremendous potential for historical archaeologists. Regrettably, it will not be easy to adapt these powerful tools to historical archaeological research, and the task will not become any easier in the immediate future. For now, historical archaeologists can try to experiment with these ideas and contribute to them, because only through such creative activity

Figure 10.2: Graphic representation of distance measurements between selected foundations at Millwood Plantation.

will historical archaeology acquire the credibility it deserves. These goals are worthwhile and important. Historical materialism represents a vibrant and exciting philosophy for exploring the past, and historical archaeologists must follow their colleagues in sociology, history, political science, and philosophy into this realm. If left behind, historical archaeology will never assume an important place in the search for knowledge and meaning.

ACKNOWLEDGMENTS

I would like to thank Mark Leone for his ideas, assistance, and patience during the preparation of this chapter. I also would like to thank Mary Lee Eggart of the Louisiana State University, Department of Geography and Anthropology Cartographic Section, for preparing the figures, and my wife, Janice, for typing and editing the manuscript. The Millwood Plantation research was conducted under contract number C-54042(80) funded by the United States Army Corps of Engineers, Savannah District, and administered by the Archaeological Services Branch, National Park Service, Southeast Region, Atlanta.

REFERENCES CITED

Adams, William H. (ed.)
　　1980　　*Waverly Plantation: Ethnoarchaeology of a Tenant Farming Community*. Atlanta: Heritage Conservation and Recreation Service.

Anderson, David G., and Jenalee Muse
　　1982　　The Archaeology of Tenancy in the Southeast: A View from the South Carolina Lowcountry. *South Carolina Antiquities* 14: 71–82.

Applewhite, Marjorie Mendenhall
　　1954　　Sharecropper and Tenant in the Courts of North Carolina. *North Carolina Historical Review* 31: 134-49.

Aptheker, Herbert
　　1964　　Negro Slave Revolts in the United States, 1526–1860. In *Essays in the History of the American Negro*, pp. 1–70. New York: International Publishers.
　　1968　　Slave Guerrilla Warfare. In *To Be Free: Studies in American Negro History*, pp. 11–30. New York: International Publishers.

Aronowitz, Stanley
　　1981　　*The Crisis in Historical Materialism: Class, Politics, and Culture in Marxist Theory*. New York: Praeger Press.

Ascher, Robert, and Charles H. Fairbanks
  1971   *Excavation of a Slave Cabin: Georgia, U.S.A. Historical Archaeology*
          5:3–17.

Ash, Timothy Garton
  1983   *The Polish Revolution: Solidarity.* New York: Charles Scribner's
          Sons.

Avirett, James Battle
  1901   *The Old Plantation: How We Lived in Great House and Cabin before
          the War.* New York: Tennyson Neely.

Ball, Charles
  1837   *Slavery in the United States: A Narrative of the Life and Adventures of
          Charles Ball, A Black Man.* New York: John S. Taylor.

Barrow, David Crenshaw
  1881   A Georgia Plantation. *Scribner's Monthly* 21: 830–36.

Binford, Lewis R.
  1977   Historical Archaeology: Is It Historical or Archaeological. In *Histor-
          ical Archaeology and the Importance of Material Things,* ed. Leland Fer-
          guson, pp. 13–22. Special Publication 2, Society for Historical Ar-
          chaeology. Columbia, S.C.

Bloch, Maurice (ed.)
  1975   *Marxist Analysis and Social Anthropology.* New York: John
          Wiley and Sons.
  1985   *Marxism and Anthropology.* Oxford: Oxford University
          Press.

Campbell, George
  1879   *Black and White: The Outcome of a Visit to the United States.* London:
          Chatto and Windus.

Carver, Terrell
  1982   *Marx's Social Theory.* Oxford: Oxford University Press.

Caulfield, Mina Davis
  1974   Culture and Imperialism: Proposing a New Dialectic. In *Reinventing
          Anthropology,* ed. Dell Hymes, pp. 182–212. New York: Vintage
          Books.

Cheek, William F.
  1970   *Black Resistance before the Civil War.* Beverly Hills, California:
          Glencoe Press.

Childe, V. Gordon
  1947   *History.* London: Cobbett Press.

1951   *Man Makes Himself.* New York: Mentor Books.
1979   Prehistory and Marxism. *Antiquity* 53: 93–95.

Clarke, David L.
    1977   Spatial Information in Archaeology. In *Spatial Archaeology,* ed.
            David L. Clarke, pp. 1–32. London: Academic Press.

Cleland, Charles E., and James E. Fitting.
    1968   The Crisis of Identity: Theory in Historic Sites Archaeology. *The
            Conference on Historic Site Archaeology Papers* 2(2): 124–38.

Collins, Robert
    1854   Management of Slaves. *DeBow's Review* 17: 421–26.

Copans, Jean, and David Seddon
    1978   Marxism and Anthropology: A Preliminary Survey. In *Relations of
            Production: Marxist Approaches to Economic Anthropology,* ed. David
            Seddon, pp. 1–46. London: Frank Cass and Company.

Crumley, Carole L.
    1979   Three Locational Models: An Epistemological Assessment for An-
            thropology and Archaeology. In *Advances in Archaeological Method
            and Theory,* ed. Michael B. Schiffer, 2: 141–73. New York: Aca-
            demic Press.

Donley, Linda Wiley
    1982   House Power: Swahili Space and Symbolic Markers. In *Symbolic and
            Structural Archaeology,* ed. Ian Hodder, pp. 63–73. Cambridge:
            Cambridge University Press.

Ehrenhard, John E., and Mary R. Bullard
    1981   *Stafford Plantation, Cumberland Island National Seashore, Georgia: Ar-
            chaeological Investigations of a Slave Cabin.* Tallahassee: Southeast Ar-
            chaeological Center.

Engels, Frederick
    1974   Engels to J. Bloch in Konigsberg. In *On Historical Materialism: A
            Collection,* compiled by T. Borodulina, pp. 294–96. New York: In-
            ternational Publishers.

Fairbanks, Charles H.
    1974   The Kingsley Slave Cabins in Duval County, Florida, 1968. *The
            Conference on Historic Site Archaeology Papers* 7:62–93.
    1983   Historical Archaeological Implications of Recent Investigations.
            Geoscience and Man 23: 17–26.

Ferguson, Leland
    n.d.   Struggling with Pots in Colonial South Carolina. In *Inequality in Everyday Life: The Material Culture of Domination and Resistance*. ed. Robert Paynter and Randall H. McGuire. Oxford: Blackwell Press.

Fields, Barbara J.
    1982   Ideology and Race in American History. In *Region, Race, and Reconstruction: Essays in Honor of C. Vann Woodward*, ed. J. Morgan Kousser and James M. McPherson, pp. 143-177. New York: Oxford University Press.
    1983   The Nineteenth-Century American South: History and Theory. *Plantation Society in the Americas* 2:7–27.

Foner, Philip S. (ed.)
    1983   *Karl Marx Remembered: Comments at the Time of His Death*. San Francisco: Synthesis Press.

Fontana, Bernard L.
    1965   On the Meaning of Historic Sites Archaeology. *American Antiquity* 31: 61–65.

Fox-Genovese, Elizabeth, and Eugene D. Genovese
    1983   *Fruits of Merchant Capital: Slavery and Bourgeois Property in the Rise and Expansion of Capitalism*. Oxford: Oxford University Press.

Genovese, Eugene D.
    1984   *In Red and Black: Marxian Explorations in Southern and Afro-American History*. Knoxville: University of Tennessee Press.

Giddens, Anthony
    1981   *A Contemporary Critique of Historical Materialism*. Vol. 1: *Power, Property and the State*. Berkeley: University of California Press.

Godelier, Maurice
    1977   *Perspectives in Marxist Anthropology*. Cambridge: Cambridge University Press.

Gough, Kathleen
    1968   Anthropology: Child of Imperialism. *Monthly Review* 19(11): 12–27.

Grubbs, Donald H.
    1971   *Cry from the Cotton: The Southern Tenant Farmers' Union and the New Deal*. Chapel Hill: University of North Carolina Press.

Hall, Edward T.
    1963   A System for the Notation of Proxemic Behavior. *American Anthropologist* 65: 1003–26.
    1969   *The Hidden Dimension*. Garden City, N.Y.: Doubleday and Company.

Handsman, Russell G.
    1985   Thinking about an Historical Archaeology of Alienation and Class
            Struggle. Paper presented at the Annual Meeting of the Society for
            Historical Archaeology, Boston.

Hargrave, Tazewell L. (rep.)
    1905   Harrison v. Ricks. *North Carolina Reports* 71: 5–11.

Harrington, J.C.
    1952   Historic Site Archaeology in the United States. In: *Archaeology of
            Eastern United States,* ed. James B. Griffin, pp. 335–44. Chicago:
            University of Chicago Press.

Harris, Marvin
    1980   *Cultural Materialism: The Struggle for a Science of Culture.* New York:
            Vintage Books.

Hodder, Ian, and Clive Orton
    1976   *Spatial Analysis in Archaeology.* Cambridge: Cambridge University
            Press.

Holland, Claudia Croy
    n.d.   "Everything on the Land was Yours Except that Bale of Cotton":
            The Archaeological Manifestations of a Share Renter's House on a
            Cotton Plantation in the South Carolina Piedmont. Unpublished
            manuscript in the author's possession.

Killion, Ronald and Charles Waller (eds.)
    1973   *Slavery Time When I was Chillun Down on Master's Plantation: Inter-
            views with Georgia Slaves.* Savannah, Ga.: The Beehive Press.

Klejn, Leo S.
    1977   A Panorama of Theoretical Archaeology. *Current Anthropology* 18:
            1–42.

Kohl, P. L.
    1981   Materialist Approaches in Prehistory. *Annual Review of Anthropology*
            10: 89–118.

Langsford, E. L., and B. H. Thibodeaux
    1939   Plantation Organization and Operation in the Yazoo-Mississippi
            Delta Area. United States Department of Agriculture. Technical
            Bulletin 682. Washington, D.C.: Government Printing Office.

Leacock, Eleanor Burke
    1982   Marxism and Anthropology. In *The Left Academy: Marxist Scholar-
            ship on American Campuses,* ed. Bertell Ollman and Edward Vernoff,
            pp. 242–76. New York: McGraw-Hill.

Lefebvre, Henri
  1979   Space: Social Product and Use Value. In *Critical Sociology: European Perspectives,* ed. and trans., J. W. Freiberg, pp. 285–95. New York: Irvington.

Leone, Mark
  1977   Foreword. In *Research Strategies in Historical Archaeology*, ed. Stanley South, pp. xvii–xxi. New York: Academic Press.
  1982   Some Opinions about Recovering Mind. *American Antiquity* 47: 742–60.

Le Page du Pratz, A. S.
  1975   *The History of Louisiana.* Ed. and trans. Joseph G. Tregle, Jr. Baton Rouge: Louisiana State University Press.

Little, Daniel
  1986   *The Scientific Marx.* Minneapolis: University of Minnesota Press.

McFarlane, Suzanne B.
  1975   The Ethnoarchaeology of a Slave Community: The Couper Plantation Site. Master's Thesis, University of Florida.

Maguire, Jane
  1975   *On Shares: Ed Brown's Story.* New York: W. W. Norton.

Maquet, Jacques
  1984   Diffuse Marxian Themes in Anthropology. In *Marxian Perspectives in Anthropology: Essays in Honor of Harry Hoijer 1981,* ed. Jacques Maquet and Nancy Daniels, pp. 1–10. Malibu, Calif.: Undena.

Marx, Karl
  1967   *Capital: A Critique of Political Economy.* New York: International Publishers.
  1970   *A Contribution to the Critique of Political Economy.* Ed. Maurice Dobb, New York: International.

Marx, Karl, and Frederick Engels
  1937   *The Civil War in the United States.* Ed. Richard Enmale, New York: International Publishers.
  1956   *The Holy Family or Critique of Critical Critique.* Moscow: Foreign Languages Publishing House.
  1970   *The German Ideology.* Ed. C. J. Arthur, New York: International Publishers.

Matsumae, Shigeyoshi
  1975   *Materialism in Search of a Soul: A Scientific Critique of Historical Materialism.* Tokyo: Tokai University Press.

Miller, Richard W.
   1984   *Analyzing Marx: Morality, Power and History*. Princeton: Princeton
            University Press.

Miller, Daniel, and Christopher Tilley
   1984   Ideology, Power, and Prehistory: An Introduction. In *Ideology,
            Power, and Prehistory*, ed. Daniel Miller and Christopher Tilley, pp.
            1–15. Cambridge: Cambridge University Press.

Mintz, Sidney W.
   1959   The Plantation as a Socio-Cultural Type. In *Plantation Systems of the
            New World*, ed. Vera Rubin, pp. 42–49. Washington, D.C.: Pan
            American Union.

Nonini, Donald M.
   1985   Varieties of Materialism. *Dialectical Anthropology* 9: 7–63.

Nowak, Leszek
   1983   *Property and Power: Towards a Non-Marxian Historical Materialism*.
            Dordrecht, Holland: D. Reidel.

Ollman, Bertell
   1971   *Alienation: Marx's Conception of Man in Capitalist Society*. Cam-
            bridge: Cambridge University Press.

Orser, Charles E., Jr.
   1984   The Past Ten Years of Plantation Archaeology in the Southeastern
            United States. *Southeastern Archaeology* 3: 1–12.
   1985a   Artifacts, Documents, and Memories of the Black Tenant Farmer.
            Archaeology 38(4): 48–53.
   1985b   What Good is Plantation Archaeology? *Southern Studies: An Inter-
            disciplinary Journal of the South* 24: 444–55.
   1986a   The Death of the Southern Plantation: A Legend for Modern Ar-
            chaeology. Paper presented at the Annual Meeting of the Society
            for American Archaeology, New Orleans.
   1986b   The Archaeological Recognition of the Squad System on
            Postbellum Cotton Plantations. *Southeastern Archaeology* 5: 11–20.
   1986c   Out of Slavery: The Material Culture of Freedom. Paper presented
            at the Annual Symposium on Language and Culture in South Caro-
            lina, Columbia.
   1987   Plantation Status and Consumer Choice: A Materialist Framework for
            Historical Archaeology. In *Socio-Economic Status and Consumer Choice:
            Perspectives in Historical Archaeology*, ed. Suzanne Spencer-Wood, pp.
            121–37. New York: Plenum Press.
   1988   *The Material Basis of the Postbellum Tenant Plantation: Historical Ar-
            chaeology in the South Carolina Piedmont*. Athens: University of Geor-
            gia Press.

Orser, Charles E., Jr., and Claudia C. Holland
1984   Let Us Praise Famous Men, Accurately: Toward a More Complete
        Understanding of Postbellum Southern Agricultural Practice. *South-
        eastern Archaeology 3:* 111–120.

Orser, Charles E., Jr., and Annette M. Nekola
1985   Plantation Settlement from Slavery to Tenancy: An Example from a
        Piedmont Plantation in South Carolina. In *The Archaeology of Slavery
        and Plantation Life,* ed. Theresa A. Singleton, pp. 67–94. Orlando,
        Fla.: Academic Press.

Orser, Charles E., Jr., Annette M. Nekola, and James L. Roark
1987   *Exploring the Rustic Life: Multidisciplinary Research at Millwood Plan-
        tation, a Large Piedmont Plantation in Abbeville County, South Caro-
        lina, and Elbert County, Georgia.* Report submitted to the National
        Park Service. Atlanta, Ga.

Otto, John Solomon
1975   Status Differences and the Archaeological Record: A Comparison of
        Planter, Overseer, and Slave Sites from Cannon's Point Plantation
        (1794–1861), St. Simons Island, Georgia. Ph.D. diss., University of
        Florida. Ann Arbor, Mich.: University Microfilms.
1984   *Cannon's Point Plantation, 1794–1860: Living Conditions and Status
        Patterns in the Old South.* Orlando, Fla.: Academic Press.

Perry, George Sessions
1986   *Hold Autumn in Your Hand.* Albuquerque: University of New Mex-
        ico Press. (Originally published in 1941)

Price, Barbara J.
1980   The Truth Is Not in Accounts but in Account Books: On the Epis-
        temological Status of History. In *Beyond the Myths of Culture: Essays
        in Cultural Materialism,* ed. Eric B. Ross, pp. 155–80. New York:
        Academic Press.

Prunty, Merle C.
1955   The Renaissance of the Southern Plantation. *The Geographical Re-
        view* 45: 459–91.

Rader, Melvin
1979   *Marx's Interpretation of History.* New York: Oxford University
        Press.

Ransom, Roger L., and Richard Sutch
1977   *One Kind of Freedom: The Economic Consequences of Emancipation.*
        Cambridge: Cambridge University Press.

Raper, Arthur
1936   *Preface to Peasantry: A Tale of Two Black Belt Counties.* Chapel Hill:
        University of North Carolina Press.

Rawick, George L. (ed.)
    1977–79 *The American Slave: A Composite Autobiography*. Westport, Conn.:
        Greenwood. 41 vols.

Renfrew, Colin
    1984   *Approaches to Social Archaeology*. Cambridge, Mass.: Harvard Uni-
        versity Press.
    1986   Peer Polity Interaction and Socio-Political Change. In *Peer Polity In-
        teraction and Socio-Political Change,* ed. Colin Renfrew and John F.
        Cherry, pp. 1–18. Cambridge: Cambridge University Press.

Schacht, Richard
    1970   *Alienation*. Garden City, N.Y.: Doubleday.

Schuyler, Robert L.
    1970   Historical and Historic Sites Archaeology as Anthropology: Basic
        Definitions and Relationships. *Historical Archaeology* 4: 83–89.

Schwartz, Michael
    1976   *Radical Protest and Social Structure: The Southern Farmer's Alliance and
        Cotton Tenancy, 1880–1890*. New York: Academic Press.

Shlomowitz, Ralph
    1979   The Origins of Southern Sharecropping. *Agricultural History* 53:
        557–75.
    1982   The Squad System on Postbellum Cotton Plantations. In *Toward a
        New South: Studies in Post-Civil War Southern Communities,* ed.
        Orville Vernon Burton and Robert C. McMath, Jr., pp. 265–80.
        Westport, Conn.: Greenwood.

Singleton, Theresa A.
    1980   The Archaeology of Afro-American Slavery in Coastal Georgia: A
        Regional Perception of Slave Household and Community Patterns.
        Ph.D. diss., University of Florida. Ann Arbor, Mich. University
        Microfilms.
    1985a   (ed). *The Archaeology of Slavery and Plantation Life*. Orlando, Fla.: Aca-
        demic Press.
    1985b   Archaeological Implications for Changing Labor Conditions. In
        The Archaeology of Slavery and Plantation Life, ed. Theresa A. Single-
        ton, pp. 291–307. Orlando, Fla. Academic Press.

South, Stanley (ed.)
    1968   Historical Archaeology Forum on Theory and Method in Historical
        Archaeology. *The Conference on Historic Site Archaeology Papers* 2(2):
        1–188.

Spillman, W. J.
    1919   The Agricultural Ladder. In *Papers on Tenancy*. Office of the Secre-
        tary of the American Association for Agricultural Legislation, Bul-
        letin 2, pp. 29–38. Madison: University of Wisconsin.

Spriggs, Matthew
  1984a   (ed.). *Marxist Perspectives in Archaeology*. Cambridge: Cambridge
          University Press.
  1984b   Another Way of Telling: Marxist Perspectives in Archaeology. In
          Marxist Perspectives in Archaeology, ed. Matthew Spriggs, pp. 1–9.
          Cambridge: Cambridge University Press.

Thalheimer, August
  1936   *Introduction to Dialectical Materialism: The Marxist Worldview*. Trans.
          George Simpson and George Weltner. New York: Covici-Friede.

Trigger, Bruce G.
  1967   Settlement Archaeology: Its Goals and Promise. *American Antiquity*
          32: 149–60.
  1968   The Determinants of Settlement Patterns. In *Settlement Archaeology*,
          ed. K. C. Chang, pp. 55–70. Palo Alto, Calif.: National Press.
  1978   No Longer from Another Planet. *Antiquity* 52: 193–98.
  1984a   Alternative Archaeologies: Nationalist, Colonialist, Imperialist.
          Man 19: 355–70.
  1984b   Marxism and Archaeology. In *On Marxian Perspectives in Anthro-
          pology: Essays in Honor of Harry Hoijer 1981*, ed. Jacques Maquet
          and Nancy Daniels, pp. 59–91. Malibu, Calif.: Undena.

Trowbridge, J. T.
  1866   *The South: A Tour of Its Battlefields and Ruined Cities*. Hartford,
          Conn.: L. Stebbins.

U.S. Census
  1880   Manuscript Census, Agricultural Schedule, James Edward Calhoun.
          Magnolia Township, Abbeville County, South Carolina.

White, Leslie
  1959   *The Evolution of Culture*. New York: McGraw-Hill.

Willis, William S., Jr.
  1974   Skeletons in the Anthropological Closet. In *Reinventing Anthropology*,
          ed. Dell Hymes, pp. 121–52. New York: Vintage Books.

Woodman, Harold D.
  1979   Post-Civil War Southern Agriculture and the Law. *Agricultural His-
          tory* 53: 319–37.

Woofter, Thomas J., Jr., Gordon Blackwell, Harold Hoffsommer, James G.
Maddox, Jean M. Massell, B. O. Williams, and Waller Wynne, Jr.
  1936   *Landlord and Tenant on the Cotton Plantation*. Works Progress Ad-
          ministration, Division of Social Research, Monograph 5. Washing-
          ton, D.C.: Government Printing Office.

Zinn, Howard
  1980   *A People's History of the United States*. New York: Harper and Row.

CHAPTER II

An Archaeological Framework for Slavery and Emancipation, 1740–1880

THERESA A. SINGLETON

As the archaeological study of slavery matures into a well-established research interest, synthetic discussions of these data become necessary to determine what these findings are and why they are important. Recent efforts have assessed the state of the art and offered directions for future research (Fairbanks 1984; Orser 1984; Singleton 1985b). But, what still appears to be missing are frameworks that can provide a context for understanding archaeological data from a particular site. Unfortunately, the preoccupation with identifying artifact patterns has often resulted in little more than comparing and contrasting archaeological resources, with little explanation as to why particular similarities or differences occur. One possible avenue to a better understanding of these artifact patterns is to view them through time and to understand the historical processes that may have influenced artifact distributions.

This essay explores the archaeological data derived from numerous sites in the coastal area of the southeastern United States and interprets them within a chronological sequence that spans a period of approximately 140 years. This discussion begins with the flowering of coastal plantation society in the mid-18th century and ends with the early years following emancipation in the third quarter of the 19th century. At least three periods are discernible throughout the 140 years: colonial slavery (1740–90), the spread of slavery (1790–1861), Civil War and Emancipation (1862–80).

My specific interest is two processes of change that affected Afro-American material life in this period. The first began taking shape after the Revolutionary War when antislavery fervor forced southern defenders of slavery to adopt reforms that resulted in a social order that may have suppressed an African heritage in material expressions. The other change occurred after emancipation and was manifested in the ways in which ex-slaves responded to new circumstances.

The coastal southeast provides an appropriate testing ground for viewing slavery and emancipation through such a framework. Historically, one of the heaviest concentrations of slaves existed along this coastal strip, which extends approximately 30 to 40 miles inland from Cape Fear, North Carolina, to the St. Johns River in northern Florida. Since the initial testing of slave sites undertaken by Charles H. Fairbanks in the late 1960s, this region, has become the most intensively studied area in slave archaeology (Figure 11.1) and is producing a growing body of archaeological data that spans the years from the colonial period to the reorganization of labor after emancipation.

Archaeologists working on coastal plantations, however, have seldom viewed entire coastal areas as one large plantation region, because of localized variations in artifact distributions between sites in South Carolina and Georgia. Although these variations help to explain intersite patterns, a study of the broader context promises to shed light on larger trends in the material cultures and cultural processes.

ENVIRONMENT AND BRIEF HISTORY

The term *coastal southeast* refers to all the lands of the coastal plain affected by the influence of the tide, or tidewater. This includes the barrier islands that border on the open ocean and extends to the point where extensive areas of pine forests begin to occur. The tidewater, a diverse environment rich in plant and animal resources, consists of several habitats: beach and dune area, estuaries composed of a maze of salt marshes, tidal creeks, and sounds; highlands of oak and hickory forests; freshwater marshes; and cypress swamps of the river deltas. During the 18th and 19th centuries, most of the cypress swamps were cleared and reclaimed for rice cultivation.

A colonial plantation economy emerged primarily from the cultivation of rice introduced to South Carolina in the 1690s. Rice culture required a sizable cash investment and numerous slaves and therefore was restricted to a few wealthy planters. Black slaves soon outnum-

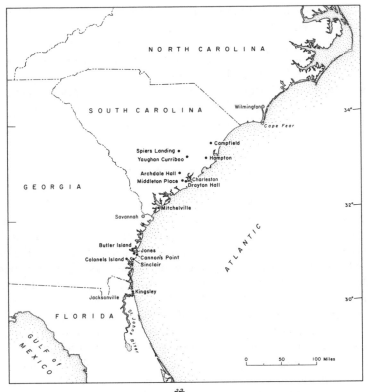

Figure 11.1: Map of the coastal Southeast showing sites referred to in text.

bered whites in the area, and this factor accounts for the dense slave population. The successful production of indigo in the 1740s and the procurement of a British bounty in 1748 gave this colonial plantation economy an added boost. Indigo, a plant used to make blue dye, enjoyed an assured market with the British textile industry (Weir 1983:146).

The Revolutionary War brought disastrous setbacks to the coastal plantation economy. The bounty on indigo formerly received from the British government ceased and the exportation of rice declined. Prosperity was restored, however, with the successful introduction of sea island (long-staple) cotton in 1780s. Like rice, it too was a labor-intensive crop as it was a special variety of cotton that required more care in cultivation, harvesting, and packing than short-staple cotton grown elsewhere in the southern United States. Unlike short-staple cotton, the sea island cotton was produced for a more specialized market and it commanded higher prices. Many rice planters acquired land and equipment for cotton culture and produced both crops. By the mid-19th century, these planters were enjoying sizable profits and had expanded their operations southward to include all of coastal Georgia and the northern tip of Florida and northward to the southern tip of North Carolina (Clifton 1978:xvii– xvii). The devastating effects of the Civil War made it impossible to revive either the cotton or the rice culture in the postwar years (Singleton 1985:293).

ARCHAEOLOGICAL RESEARCH AND PROBLEMS

The objective of the archaeological research undertaken at slave and freedmen sites is to interpret material aspects of past Afro-American life and culture that are not readily apparent from written or oral historical sources. A major focus of this research has been to examine the extent to which an African heritage prevailed in the slave and later material culture. A secondary interest in understanding the ways in which slaves survived the rigors of day-to-day life arose because there were insufficient data to document African influences in Afro-American life. This secondary interest has provided detailed information on topics such as the existence of a pottery tradition, building technologies, food procurement techniques, culinary practices, household equipment, and personal possessions. Such topics have received little or no attention in the historiography of slavery and emancipation.

Early archaeological investigations in coastal Georgia and northern Florida were undertaken to provide material evidence of an African heritage. In both coastal Georgia and South Carolina, a distinctive Afro-American tradition flourished in the decorative arts, language, cuisine, and music because of the high concentration of blacks that lived in relative isolation from whites. The goal of the archaeology was to uncover evidence of the origins of this tradition. Unfortunately, no identifiable evidence of African-influenced traits was uncovered from these excavations (Fairbanks 1984:2).

New data are emerging from sites in South Carolina, although the evidence of an African heritage from purely archaeological sources is still quite fragmentary. African influences in slave material culture are seen in slave housing from two mid-eighteenth-century sites and a folk pottery tradition. The housing (discussed in greater detail below) appears to have incorporated an African building technology consisting of mud-walled structures, possibly with thatched roofs (Wheaton, Friedlander, and Garrow 1983; Wheaton and Garrow 1985). Leland Ferguson (1980) has suggested that the manufacture and use of locally made folk pottery, termed colonoware, reflects an Afro-American tradition. This low-fired, unglazed earthenware resembles pottery produced by historic Indians, like the Catawba, who are still producing pottery today. However, recent studies of colonoware have tentatively differentiated between Catawba ware and the colonowares that were presumably produced by Afro-Americans (Wheaton and Garrow 1985:248–51). Fragments of this pottery are numerous at South Carolina plantations and make up a sizable proportion of slave assemblages. More recently, Ferguson (1985) has suggested that colonoware may represent not only the influence of African or Afro-Caribbean potting techniques on a localized craft, but perhaps the preservation of African foodways and symbolic system.

At present, colonoware is the only artifact associated with Afro-American life that persistently occurs at plantation sites. Along the South Carolina-Georgia coast, however, it has only been found at sites in South Carolina and is virtually absent from plantation sites in Georgia. This difference in distribution is as yet unexplained.

What was initially perceived as a secondary goal of slave archaeology—namely, the recovery of detailed information on the everyday life of slaves in their quarters—has met with greater success than the search for material evidence of an African past. Details of housing, diet, foodways, and household implements not only help to fill the gaps in the written record, but also have the potential to significantly reshape thinking on certain aspects of slave life. For example, the archaeological studies of slave subsistence have demonstrated that slave diet was made nutritious through slaves' own food collecting efforts, which enabled the slave population to increase itself through natural means (Gibbs et al. 1980; Reitz, Gibbs, and Rathbun 1985:184–85).

Evidence of food preparation within individual cabins, as opposed to centralized kitchens, firearms, and writing equipment contradict the abundant narrative history of slavery. Traditional interpretations of slavery based on a variety of written sources indicate that slaves' meals were prepared for them at one central plantation kitchen, that slaves were forbidden access to firearms and were not provided with opportunities to learn how to read and write. The archaeological data recovered from slave quarters present alternative interpretations of these issues. For example, in nearly all of the slave dwellings excavated to date, substantial evidence of charred bone, cast iron kettles and cauldrons, serving and storage vessels suggest that large quantities of food were prepared in individual cabins, not in a central kitchen. In fact, no archaeological evidence of a central plantation kitchen has been identified. This finding is significant because it suggests that slaves prepared their food to suit their own tastes, perhaps incorporating aspects of traditional West African cuisines. It was unlawful for slaves to possess firearms and for anyone to teach slaves to read and write in most of the slave states. Yet archaeological investigations have repeatedly uncovered gun parts, lead shot (presumably used for hunting), and graphite pencils among slave quarters debris. Obviously these laws were not always enforced.

Such findings have led both archaeologists and historians to reassess slave life and to suggest that slaves did not passively accept the material conditions provided for them by their owners, but actively sought to improve their lives whenever possible. For example, one historian has proposed that slaves along the coastal reaches of South Carolina and Georgia may have experienced a limited amount of autonomy (Morgan 1982). Under the task labor system, which was used extensively in the production of coastal staples, all field hands were classified as full, three-quarter, half, or quarter according to the amount of work they could perform. When a task was completed, the slave was finished for the day, and at certain times of year tasks could be completed by mid-afternoon. Slaves could and did use the time after work to hunt, fish, cultivate gardens, and sell handicrafts. These activities gave them the opportunity to acquire goods such as livestock, produce, and wagons (Morgan 1982, 1983). Archaeological investigations of slave quarters provide tangible evidence to document the extent to which the task labor system operated.

In the remainder of the chapter I look at selected data derived from the archeology of slavery and emancipation and attempt to interpret the impact of economics, ideology, and historical events on the development of slave and ex-slave life in the coastal southeast. I also briefly comment on the contribution of archaeology to the study of Afro-American life and culture. The period under discussion begins in 1740, the date when slavery and plantations flourished in the South Carolina low country. This is also the earliest date for which archaeological artifacts have been uncovered in the region. The period ends with the early years of emancipation, during which slaves became free labor, but had not yet been reorganized into tenant farmers or sharecroppers.

COLONIAL SLAVERY, 1740–1790

Slavery was legal in South Carolina from the time the colony was founded in 1670. Most of the earliest slaves arrived with their West Indian masters, who came to South Carolina expecting to produce a commercial crop, like sugar, as they had done in the Caribbean (Weir 1983:172–73). Once planters developed exports that could be produced on a large scale, the demand for slaves grew rapidly. By 1708, half of the population, exclusive of Indians, were black. By 1720, the population ratio in many areas of the coast might have been seven to eight slaves to every white person (Wood 1974:142–50). These ratios remained fairly constant throughout the rest of the colonial period.

This "black majority" supplied more than labor in settling the frontier and transforming it into a prosperous plantation society. Slaves also functioned as cultural agents in helping their white owners adapt to the new environment. Africans brought with them two essential assets: Those who came from malarial climates brought with them the sickle-cell allele, a genetic trait that produces a partial but heritable immunity to malaria. This biological trait permitted Africans to work in many swampy areas where most whites could not. Africans also brought skilled knowledge of rice growing, cattle-raising, woodworking, and boat management (Wood 1974:74). Particularly important was their knowledge of rice growing, which was outside the experience of the English and literally made possible this plantation society.

West African culture was thoroughly woven into the daily lives of South Carolinians in the colonial era. Material evidence of this influence comes from both archaeological and architectural studies. Excavations at Yaughan and Curribo, two 18th-century indigo plantations established by French Huguenot settlers, have supplied evidence of what appears to have been African-styled slave houses. The early slave quarters dating from approximately 1740 to 1790 at both plantations utilized a wall trench construction filled with carefully selected clays. Presumably the walls of the structures were constructed entirely from this clay fill (Wheaton and Garrow 1985:244).

African influences in the architecture of coastal South Carolina are also suggested in the art of the 18th century. A painting of Mulberry Plantation by Thomas Coram shows the big house and a row of slave quarters (Figure 11.2) with pyramidal roofs, which Carl Anthony (1976:11) suggests are "unmistakably African." The big house, built in 1714, seems a fusion of African and Huguenot architecture. Prints of 18th-century Charleston supply evidence that the shotgun house was introduced to the American South prior to the 1800s. This type of housing is identified with black Americans throughout the southern United States. In plan, it is composed of three or more rooms that are arranged linearly but without a hallway, and the doorway is located in the street-oriented gable end. According to folk sources, this house form is referred to as "shotgun" because a person could stand at the front door, fire a shotgun into the house, and the bullet would come out the rear door without hitting anything inside (Jones 1985:204–206). Studies of the shotgun house form in Nigeria and in Haiti have estab-

Figure 11.2: "Mulberry Plantation," by Thomas Coram. Collection of the Carolina Art Association, Gibbes Art Gallery, Charleston, South Carolina.

lished that this form is indeed an African influence in New World architecture (Vlach 1975, 1978:123–31).

In addition, high frequencies of colonoware indicate an African influence in coastal foodways. Table 11.1 shows the distribution of colonoware at several plantation sites in South Carolina. Although colonoware occurs in higher frequencies at slave-occupied areas, it also accounts for significant percentages of the total ceramics used in planter households. This finding suggests that Africans may have prepared food for the planter family using their traditional culinary techniques and thus influenced the local cuisine. Curiously, the highest frequencies of colonoware occur at early Yaughan and Curriboo, the two sites with mud-wall structures. The investigators of Yaughan and Curriboo have suggested that the high frequency of colonoware in association with African-styled housing indicates a period in which the slaves of colonial South Carolina had not yet been acculturated to European ways of satisfying their basic needs; and that the replacement of colonoware with imported wares and European-styled housing at sites dating from a later time indicates the increased acculturation of slaves (Wheaton and Garrow 1985:251–57).

It is clear that some form of culture change had occurred, but why it occurred is unclear. By the close of the 18th century, the demography of low country South Carolina was changing. Amy Friedlander has

TABLE 11.1

Relative Frequencies of Colonoware at Plantations

Site	Date[a]	Status	Number	%[b]	Reference
Early Yaughan	1740–1790	Slave	15043	89	Wheaton and Garrow (1985)
Curriboo	1740–1800	Slave	3316	87	Wheaton and Garrow (1985)
Late Yaughan	1780–1820	Slave	2545	65	Wheaton and Garrow (1985)
Hampton	1750–1865	Slave	430	74	Lewis and Haskell (1980)
Hampton	1741–1860	Planter	72	22	Lewis and Haskell (1980)
Middleton	1741–1860	Planter	3383	62	Lewis and Hardesty (1979)
Drayton Hall	1742–1860	Planter	2593	29	Lewis (1985)
Spiers Landing	1780–1830	Slave	1230	56	Drucker and Anthony (1979)
Archdale Hall	1700–1780	n.d.	130	39	Zierden, Calhoun, and Norton (1985)
Archdale Hall	1780–1880	n.d.	107	17	Zierden, Calhoun, and Norton (1985)
Campfield	1830–1880	Slave/freedmen	37	18	Zierden and Calhoun (1983)

— n.d. No data on status; that is, status could not be determined.

[a]Approximate date range of peak occupation based on both archaeological and documentary resources.

[b]Percentage of total historic ceramics recovered.

353

shown that within St. Stephens Parish, the locality of Yaughan and Curriboo plantations, the ratio of blacks to whites dropped from 11 blacks to every white person in 1790 to 6.6 blacks to every white person in 1800. From then on, the ratio of blacks to whites fluctuated, but never again reached the level of the colonial period (Friedlander 1985:220–22). At the same time that these demographic changes were taking shape, South Carolina decided to prohibit the African slave trade (which was closed from 1794 to 1803, reopened in 1803, and then finally abolished throughout the United States in 1807). This ruling restricted the supply of African-born slaves. As a result, the African influence on coastal lifeways in colonial South Carolina rapidly came to an end.

THE SPREAD OF SLAVERY, 1790–1861

The artifact patterns and demographic changes described above coincided with the beginnings of trends associated with antebellum slavery in the coastal southeast. After the revolutionary war, slavery spread throughout the South. With the invention of the cotton gin by Eli Whitney in 1793, slavery became profitable in the cultivation of short-staple cotton. In 1790, the time of the first national census, a little more than 600,000 slaves resided in the southern United States. By 1860, there were nearly 4 million slaves in this area (Owens 1976:8).

As slavery spread throughout the South, the movement to abolish it gained considerable momentum in the North. The ideals of liberty that developed from the Revolution sparked an antislavery fervor. By the 1830s, abolitionism assumed a preeminent role in the development of sectional differences between North and South (Filler 1960:10–55). Once the abolition movement captured public attention, slaveholders came to realize that slavery had to be defended or it would be undermined (Filler 1960:55).

Proslavery thought developed along many different lines, but the most widely accepted proslavery view appears to have been embodied in a reform intended "to rid slavery of its attendant evils" (Jenkins 1960:94) At the same time, slavery was defended as a "positive good" that would elevate or improve the Negro (Stamp 1956:28; Jenkins 1960:95). This reform ideology was aimed primarily at improving the spiritual well-being of slaves and in revising slave codes in order to make them more humane. How this proslavery thought may have influenced slave material life is implied in efforts to standardize slave management practices. Material improvements, particularly in housing, became a well-articulated concern. Southern agricultural journals be-

tween the 1830s and 1860s waged a determined campaign to urge planters to adopt housing standards that would protect the health and welfare of slaves (Genovese 1974:524). By the 1830s, the recommended
standard dwelling for a single family was 16 by 18 (or 20) feet, was located at least 75 feet from neighboring dwellings, and raised upon
building piers of 2 to 3 feet. It also had plank floors and large fireplaces
(Genovese 1974:524). Although such standards were often the ideal,
most slaves of the antebellum period lived in houses that approached at
least some of these criteria.

The archaeological evidence of slave housing from 19th-century
sites in the coastal southeast exhibits one or more of the above characteristics. When size could be determined, slave structures were close to
the recommended dimensions of 16 by 18 feet, and a few were larger
(see Table 11.2). Slave sites that have a significant 19th-century component or that date from the antebellum period are characterized by
higher percentages of architecture group artifacts than those of the 18th
century, as shown in Table 11.3. This artifact pattern suggests that antebellum slave houses along the coast were constructed of more permanent materials and perhaps were subject to more repair and alteration
than those of the 18th century.

This standardization of slave housing by reformers apparently led
to the suppressions of African-influenced architecture. Whether planters
consciously or unconsciously suppressed an African worldview is difficult to ascertain. Clearly, the tenor of this proslavery reform was to ed-
ucate the African both spiritually and morally to European ways. The
often-cited example of Okra, a slave from Cannon's Point Plantation on
St. Simons, Georgia, tends to support this view. Okra built a mud-
walled hut, but his owner ordered that it be torn down (Georgia
Writers Project 1940:179). Excavations at Cannon's Point revealed that
Okra's owner preferred a European-styled, two-pen cabin (Otto
1975:111–12).

Of course, not all planters were influenced by the reform. Historical descriptions of slave houses of the late antebellum period provide
evidence of plantation structures that reflect traditional African forms.
W. E. B. DuBois quoted this description of slave quarters in Florida in
1830 in his 1908 survey of African and Afro-American house types:

> The dwellings of slaves were palmetto huts, built by themselves of
> stakes and poles, with the palmetto leaf. The door, when they had
> any, was generally of the same materials, sometimes boards found
> on the beach. They had no floors, no separate apartments, except
> the Guinea Negroes built themselves after task and on Sundays.
> (1969:49).

TABLE 11.2

Comparison of Architecture/Kitchen Group Artifacts for Slave Sites

Site	Date	Kitchen		Architecture		Reference
		Number	%	Number	%	
Early Yaughan	1740–1790	18800	84.2	4480	11.82	Wheaton and Garrow (1985)
Curriboo	1780–1800	4480	79.9	965	16.65	Wheaton and Garrow (1985)
Late Yaughan	1780–1820	4439	70.7	1569	25.00	Wheaton and Garrow (1985)
Spiers Landing	1780–1830	2273	73.7	623	20.20	Drucker (1981)
Campfield	1830–1880	442	24.33	1304	71.11	Zierden and Calhoun (1983)
Sinclair	1790–1860	550	22.16	1875	75.54	Moore (1985)
Jones	1790–1860	1740	29.27	3915	65.86	Moore (1985)
Cannon's Point	1794–1861	2771	25.84	7613	70.84	Otto (1975), MacFarlane (1975)
Butler Island	1803–1860	1385	25.66	4494	67.90	Singleton (1980)

TABLE 11.3

Comparison of Antebellum Slave-Unit Dimensions

Plantation	Family Unit	Width (feet)	Length (feet)	Reference
Spiers Landing	one	15.5	18.9	Drucker and Anthony (1979:91)
Kingsley	one	12.	16.1	Fairbanks (1974:108)
Kingsley	one	8.2	16.1	Fairbanks (1974:108)
Cannon's Point	one	17	20	Otto (1975:112)
Cannon's Point	duplex	20	40	Otto (1975:111)
Sinclair	one	11.2	21	Moore (1981:152)
Butler Island	duplex	20	40	Singleton (1980:129)

There are other examples of African-style houses in the late 1840s and 1850s, such as the house built in Edgefield, South Carolina, by Tahro, a Bakongo enslaved in 1858 (McDaniel 1982:34–35). In addition, unusually small, square-shaped cabins measuring 10 by 10 feet or 12 by 12 feet suggest the use of an African floor plan (Vlach 1978:125). In this subtle way, an African heritage may have been perpetuated to fairly recent times.

These examples were exceptions, however, rather than the rule. Their existence can be explained in part by the massive importation of slaves into South Carolina in the last days of the slave trade (as many as 39,000 between 1803 and 1807; see Stampp 1956:28), and additional boatloads of slaves were smuggled into South Carolina and Georgia up to the Civil War (McDaniel 1982:34). The prevailing house form for slaves in the antebellum South most often resembled the standards recommended by reformers.

The decreasing use of colonoware may have also stemmed from slave management practices adopted in the 19th century. With the greater availability of inexpensive, mass-produced imported wares, slaves substituted imported ceramics for locally made colonoware, either by choice or through housewares supplied to them by owners. Unfortunately, the extent to which slave owners provided their slaves with ceramics and other housewares for preparing and serving food is unknown. On small plantations, discarded vessels may have been recycled to slaves. But on very large plantations discards would not have adequately served the needs of hundreds of slaves. Slaves may have received periodic provisions of ceramics. This appears to have been the case at one large rice plantation (Singleton 1980:154). Nonetheless, the gradual replacement of locally made wares with imported ones does imply that the need for slave-made ceramics had diminished.

Leland Ferguson has suggested that the substituted imported wares may have continued the same patterns of 18th-century slave foodways reflected in colonoware usage (Ferguson 1985). The predominant vessel form of colonoware, small unrestricted bowls, is replaced in the 19th century with small serving bowls, frequently termed "annular wares" (Noël Hume 1970:131). Thus, although the ceramic type changed, the function that ceramics served in Afro-American foodways was maintained.

The other artifacts of antebellum slaves in the coastal southeast display a marked degree of predictability. Like housing and imported ceramics, these artifact patterns suggest standardized provisioning practices. For example, stoneware crocks most likely functioned as containers for the storage of molasses, cornmeal, and salted meats—foods frequently rationed to coastal slaves (Allston 1858; House 1954; Phillips 1969:114–30). Faunal analyses indicate that beef and pork contributed most of the animal protein to the slave diet, but these rations were abundantly supplemented with nondomestic foods (wild birds, wild mammals, fish, and shellfish), which may have contributed as much as 40 percent of the meat to the slave diet (Reitz, Gibbs, and Rathbun 1985:184). Archaeological resources and plantation documents both suggest that some rice coast slaves occasionally received issues of tobacco, clay pipes, and even alcoholic beverages (Singleton 1980:158).

Archaeological implications that can provide some understanding of slave worldview are difficult to ascertain, because so much of slave material culture particularly in the 19th century was imposed upon slaves by Euro-American owners. Subtle possibilities, however, have been alluded to in the previous discussion. The most notable appears be in the area of foodways where the use of a traditional pottery and its later replacements in the preparation and serving of food may have permitted slaves to maintain former or to establish new culinary practices and social customs associated with food. This possibility is further supported by archaeological findings indicating that slaves prepared their own meals in their cabins. Another area where slaves may have attempted to shape their material world to suit their needs is in housing and the use of space. It seems quite likely that whenever slaves could exercise their creativity in building design they did so. The simple use of a floor plan similar to those found in parts of West Africa may well be another manifestation of slave worldview.

In summary, excavations of slave sites in the coastal southeast have permitted archaeologists to document the early African presence in the New World and the role African traditions played in shaping the material culture of plantation society. This tradition is less identifiable in the antebellum era and may have been masked by the deliberate efforts of planters to impose their standards of acceptable material conditions. Antebellum slave artifacts maintain the same pattern up to at least the Civil War, and possibly throughout most of the 19th century.

CIVIL WAR AND EMANCIPATION, 1861–1880

The coastal southeast offers a unique opportunity to study the immediate effects of emancipation and the early days of freedom. During the Civil War, Union troops occupied most of the region south from Charleston, South Carolina, to Jacksonville, Florida. Consequently, the area rapidly became a haven for the temporary settlement of "contraband" refugee slaves who escaped to Union territory (Bullard 1982:72). Moreover, the southeastern coast became the scene of two early efforts to resettle the blacks and prepare them for their eventual emancipation. One was the Port Royal Experiment, a settlement program begun in the South Carolina sea islands in 1862 by Union troops as a way to keep black laborers working for white planters. Referred to as a "rehearsal for reconstruction," the Port Royal Experiment placed black laborers on contracts with white landowners. Northerners established the work routines, the wage to be paid, and time required to complete a job (Rose 1967). Some of the freedmen settlements that developed from the Port Royal program lasted until tenancy emerged in the 1880s. The other effort, known as "Sherman's Reservation," was the establishment in 1865 of a 40-mile-wide belt of land extending south from Charleston that was reserved exclusively for black settlement. Both former slaves of the area and those escaping from the interior attempted to settle the reservation, but it lost its status in 1867. Because of it, however, many freedmen associated emancipation with ownership of land and established freedmen settlements ranging from squatters camps to substantial settlements (Singleton 1985:293).

At present the archaeological data associated with emancipation and freedmen in the coastal region are limited to two sites. Although several antebellum slave sites contain evidence of postbellum occupations (for example, Otto 1975; Hamilton 1980; Zierden and Calhoun 1983), they do not have discrete archaeological resources that date after emancipation. Instead, the post-Civil War occupation is represented by a smattering of mixed late 19th-century and antebellum artifacts. Unfortunately, this is often the case as it is often difficult, if not impossible, to distinguish between antebellum and postbellum components occurring at the same site.

The two forms of resettlement efforts described above are reflected in the two freedmen sites. A study of a freedmen village resulting from the Port Royal Experiment has recently been completed. This settlement, known as Mitchelville, was established on Hilton Head, South Carolina, in 1862 and was occupied to the early 1880s (Trinkley 1986). The Mitchelville site provides the first detailed information on early planned freedmen villages along the south Atlantic seaboard. Archaeological investigation revealed four structures, one of which was intensively excavated. The other site, at Colonel's Island near Brunswick, Georgia, was a former slave settlement that was presumably reoccupied by ex-slaves. Although it is uncertain that the archaeological resources at Colonel's Island were left by freedmen, this interpretation of Colonel's Island as an ex-slave site is based on a postbellum date of 1867 established from the construction of one of two excavated structures, historical references to the presence of contraband at Colonel's Island, and the makeshift and temporary quality of the settlement, which is suggestive of squatter camps established along the coast during the Civil War and early postwar years (Singleton 1978, 1985a).

The archaeological records of Colonel's Island and Mitchelville clearly indicate that the two sites represent two different forms of settlement associated with emancipation. As a planned freedmen settlement, Mitchelville was intended for permanent occupancy, and it contained substantial dwellings and other structures comparable to those found on plantations (Trinkley and Hacker 1986:278). Colonel's Island was apparently intended as a temporary camp as the dwellings were flimsy and haphazardly constructed from salvaged bricks and stones, oyster shells, and mud (Singleton 1985a:299–302). Differences in quantity and quality of artifacts are also evident at the two sites. Artifacts from Mitchelville suggest that the freedmen were actively participating in a cash economy and were beginning to acquire higher status items such as furniture hardware, stemmed ware, more expensive tablewares, silver utensils, and fancy jewelry than those they previously had access to in slavery, but their lives were still far from being opulent (Trinkley and Hacker 1986:268–278). The artifacts at Colonel's Island consisted of the same kinds of items typically used by slaves, but these items were found in substantially smaller quantities at Colonel's Island than those found at slave sites. Moreover, the material poverty of the Colonel's Island occupants is emphasized by objects such as a badly worn hoe blade fragment that was apparently used even after the hoe had fallen apart

(Singleton 1978:114). Such artifacts together with makeshift housing suggest that the ex-slaves of Colonel's Island were materially "worse off" in freedom than in slavery.

Food remains also show marked differences. At Colonel's Island, a diet derived from foraging is indicated, although the faunal sample was quite small. Nondomestic foods contributed 98 percent of the meat in the diet of the occupants compared with 40 percent or less at slave sites. These nondomestic foods consisted of deer, raccoon, opossum, fish, and sea turtle. Faunal analysis also suggested that the site may have been occupied briefly, or possibly on a seasonal basis from June to October (Reitz 1978:142; Reitz, Gibbs, and Rathbun 1985:173). This finding is further evidence in support of the suggestion that the Colonel's Island site was a temporary settlement occupied briefly until the occupants sought a more stable livelihood than foraging. The data for Mitchelville do not compare favorably with Colonel's Island, as 85.7 percent of the total meat at Mitchelville was supplied by domestic species pig, cow, chicken, turkey, and goose (Wilson and Wilson 1986:310). In fact, the faunal assemblage at Mitchelville does not conform to any of the faunal assemblage patterns noted for urban, rural, or slave sites on the Atlantic coast. This unique feature of the Mitchelville faunal assemblage may be related to several factors: the fact that the inhabitants enjoyed a status that they did not have before as slaves or later after the Union forces left the area, or that the inhabitants had access to wages to purchase meat segments or live animals, or that they could receive meat segments as part of the rations issued by the Union army to those employed by them (Wilson and Wilson, 1986:311).

Colonel's Island and Mitchelville present two strikingly different pictures of emancipation that provide insights into the ways ex-slaves chose to manifest their freedom. Ex-slave life at Colonel's Island was more circumscribed materially than at Michelville. Housing was inadequate and the occupants had to rely upon foraging for sustenance. But, for many freedmen, independence under these marginal circumstances was preferable to their former existence in slavery or to working with old masters under new unsettled conditions (Litwack 1979:226, 229). The archaeological resources from Colonel's Island suggest that many recently emancipated slaves had an unsettled status, whereas the freedmen at Mitchelville experienced a material standard slightly above that which they experienced as slaves. Housing was not only more substantial than at Colonels's Island but, perhaps, for the first time in their lives the occupants of Mitchelville were permitted to exercise some creativity in their building design, as the structures exhibit considerable individuality and variability in construction style and detail (Trinkley and Hacker 1986:280). The Mitchelville freedmen also had greater access to goods that they did not have access to previously as slaves. This new way of life depended upon the work and wages set in motion by the Union army, and these conditions may have persisted to some extent until the reorganization of labor in tenancy and sharecropping arrangements.

Although the archaeological data of emancipation are fragmentary, when combined with archaeology and historical descriptions, they may be used to develop testable field models that can serve as guides in identifying ex-slave sites. Unlike the predictability of slave sites, ex-slave sites are perhaps more likely to represent idiosyncratic behavior, because freedmen sites took many forms, from substantial village settlements to briefly occupied camps. This means that the archaeological resources could range from a trash pit to substantial remains. The entire range of evidence must be examined before archaeologists can hope to understand the material and behavioral changes that resulted from emancipation.

CONTRIBUTION OF ARCHAEOLOGY
TO THE STUDY OF AFRO-AMERICAN LIFE

The findings derived from slave archaeology have been slow to enter the mainstream of Afro-American history. The primary reason for this state of affairs appears to be that material culture does not generally enter the purview of most studies of slavery. The historiography of slavery has traditionally examined the institution of slavery and how it shaped the social, political, and economic development of New World societies. Such an analysis of slavery does not require the study of material culture, although archaeological studies do ultimately contribute to this discussion by providing primary data on the ways slaves shaped their lives.

In the 1970s historical studies of slavery began to emphasize "life in the quarters" as a consequence of the "new social history." The first slave archaeology was also initiated at this time. However, the social history of slavery and slave archaeology developed independently of each other, with little communication between the two groups of scholars, although some historians have cited archaeological findings (for example, see Eugene Genovese's seminal work on slave life, *Roll Jordan Roll: The World the Slaves Made*). Genovese referred to excavations undertaken by Charles Fairbanks as tangible evidence that coincided with the documentary record on slave material culture. More recently, works such as George McDaniel's *Hearth and Homes* (1982) and Charles Joyner's *Down by the Riverside* (1984) have incorporated archaeological findings of slavery.

At least three factors may account for the absence of communication between archaeologists and historians interested in slave material culture. First, archaeologists have been slow to publish their findings in a form understandable to scholars of other disciplines and in publications accessible to them. Second, few historians or other specialists knowledgeable in the literature of slavery or in other areas of Afro-American history have participated in archaeological studies of slavery. Third, there is some question as to whether the information obtained from archaeology can be more effectively derived from other kinds of evidences, such as historical descriptions, graphic sources, or oral traditions.

Most of the literature of slave archaeology remains buried in unpublished sources such as master's theses, Ph.D. dissertations, site reports, or archaeological publications of limited distribution. To date there are fewer than 10 monographs or book-length publications on slave archaeology, and these are written for archaeologists. More important than the limited distribution of literature, nonarchaeologists complain that archaeological publications are jargon-laden, overemphasize method, and frequently contain little information on actual findings and conclusions. This problem could not be resolved without a major overhaul in the way archaeologists report their findings. For example, special articles that discuss findings in relation to historical questions could be prepared for history journals.

The lack of participation of historians in archaeological research projects is another concern of the entire field of historical archaeology. In a recent article about the investigation of historic Hispanic sites, Deagan and Scardaville offer two suggestions: that historical archaeologists receive rigorous graduate training in historical research, and that a trained historian be employed to conduct the historical research for the project (1985:33). Archaeological projects are in fact beginning to employ more trained historians to conduct historical research, particularly in projects generated by contract archaeology.

Now that the study of material culture is shared by scholars of diverse fields—such as art historians, social historians, folklorists, cultural geographers, vernacular architects—the details of slave material life can be derived from a variety of resources: paintings, photographs, above-ground structures, surviving materials that are well documented, written descriptions (probate records, diaries, travelers' accounts), and oral testimonies of ex-slaves. These resources, many of which were underused until slave material culture gained attention, offer information that archaeology alone cannot provide on topics such as clothing, housing, furnishings, and craft practices. Although archaeology has been able to provide unique information on diet, house construction, settlement patterns, and personal possessions, it is not a substitute for the resources described above—nor are these resources a substitute for archaeology. Any thorough study of slave material culture must consider all potential resources.

Archaeology, however, is making an impact within public programs, particularly in museums. Within the past few years, several museums around the country have based some exhibitions and educational programs on the topic of slavery. The archaeology of slavery cannot be credited alone as the driving force for this development, but it has certainly contributed to these programs. Slavery had been a taboo topic in museums until now, because many institutions maintain that the public is embarrassed by it. Some institutions have ignored the subject because few objects made or used by slaves have survived to the present day. Archaeological studies have provided examples of authentic objects that could be exhibited or reproduced for exhibition. At the National Museum of American History of the Smithsonian Institution, excavated materials from slave sites are on display in the exhibition, "After the Revolution, Everyday Life in America." The use of archaeological materials for an exhibition on slavery, particularly at the Smithsonian Institution, signifies that other museums are likely to follow this example in the near future.

Slave archaeology appears to have had the least amount of impact within the black community, whose heritage is under investigation at these sites. Unfortunately, archaeologists have seldom reached out to these communities to include them in the investigations or to provide the results of their research in a form that is palatable to lay audiences. There are some notable exceptions, however. Afro-American archaeological projects that have involved the active participation of blacks include the Drax Hall plantation excavations in Jamaica (Douglas Armstrong 1983), the Weeksville Project in Brooklyn, New York (Bridges and Salwen 1980), and excavations at Buxton, Iowa (Gradwohl and Osborn 1984).

Within the relatively short span of 15 years, slave archaeology, in particular, and Afro-American archaeology, as a whole, have grown from modest beginnings into a specialized interest. Early studies provided only descriptive information on subsistence, but recently the research has begun to address anthropological concerns—behavioral patterns, ideology, and culture process. Scholars in other disciplines and the public at large are also becoming aware of this research. Nonetheless, archaeologists should endeavor to develop frameworks like the one suggested here for the evaluation and interpretations of archaeological data. Such frameworks would certainly hasten a wider acceptance of archaeology as a primary means of analyzing Afro-American life.

REFERENCES CITED

Allston, R. F. W.
  1858   Notes on the Management of a Southern Rice Estate. *De Bows Review* 23: 324–21.

Anthony, Carl
  1976   The Big House and Slave Quarters: Part II, African Contributions to the New World, *Landscape* 2(1): 9–15.

Armstrong, Douglas
  1983   The Old Village at Drax Hall Plantation: An Archaeological Examination of an Afro-Jamaican Settlement. Ph.D. diss., University of California, Los Angeles. Ann Arbor, Mich.: University Microfilms.

Bridges, Sara T., and Bert Salwen
  1980   Weeksville: The Archaeology of Black Community. In *Archaeological Perspectives on Ethnicity in America*, ed. Robert L. Schuyler, pp. 38–47. Farmingdale, N.Y.: Baywood.

Bullard, Mary
  1982   *An Abandoned Black Settlement Cumberland Island, Georgia*. DeLeon Springs, Fla.: E. O. Painter.

Clifton, James M.
  1978   *Life and Labor in Argyle Island*. Savannah, Ga.: Beehive Press.

Deagan, Kathleen, and Michael Scardaville
  1985   Archaeology and History in Historic Hispanic Sites: Impediments and Solutions. *Historical Archaeology* 19(1): 32–37.

Drucker, Leslie M.
  1981   Socioeconomic Patterning at an Undocumented Late 18th Century Lowcountry Site: Spiers Landing, South Carolina. *Historical Archaeology* 45(2): 58–68.

Drucker, Leslie, and Ronald W. Anthony
  1979   *The Spiers Landing Site: Archaeological Investigations in Berkeley County, South Carolina*. South Carolina Archaeological Services. Columbia, S.C.

Dubois, W. E. B.
  1969   *The Negro American Family*. Westport, Conn.: Negro Universities Press. (Reprint of 1908 version).

Fairbanks, Charles H.
  1974   The Kingsley Slave Cabins in Duval County, Florida, 1968. *Conference on Historic Sites Archaeology Papers* 7: 62–93.

1984   The Plantation Archaeology of the Southeastern Coast. *Historical Archaeology* 18(1): 1–18.

Ferguson, Leland
    1980   Looking for the "Afro" in Colono–Indian pottery. In *Archaeological Perspectives in Ethnicity in America*, ed. Robert Schuyler, pp. 14–28. Farmingdale, N.Y.: Baywood.
    1985   Struggling with Pots in Colonial South Carolina. Paper presented at the Annual Meeting of the Society for Historical Archaeology, January 14.

Filler, Louis
    1960   *The Crusade Against Slavery: 1830–1860.* New York: Harper Torch.

Friedlander, Amy
    1985   Establishing Historical Probabilities for Archaeological Interpretations: Slave Demography of Two Plantations in South Carolina, 1740–1820. In *The Archaeology of Slavery and Plantation Life*, ed. Theresa A. Singleton, pp. 215–238. Orlando, Fla.: Academic Press.

Gibbs, Tyson, Kathleen Cargill, Leslie Sue Lieberman, and Elizabeth Reitz
    1980   Nutrition in a Slave Population: An Anthropological Examination. *Medical Anthropology* 4: 172–262.

Genovese, Eugene
    1974   *Roll Jordan Roll: The World the Slaves Made.* New York: Pantheon Press.

Georgia Writers' Project
    1940   *Drums and Shadows.* Athens: University of Georgia Press.

Gradwohl, David, and Nancy M. Osborn
    1984   *Exploring Buried Buxton: Archaeology of an Abandoned Iowa Coal Mining Town with a Large Black Population.* Ames, Iowa: Iowa State University Press.

Hamilton, Jennifer M.
    1980   Early history and excavation of LeConte-Woodmanston Plantation. Master's thesis, University of Florida, Gainesville.

House, Albert
    1954   Labor Management Problems on a Georgia Rice Plantation, 1840–1860. *Agricultural History* 28: 149–53.

Jenkins, William S.
    1960   Proslavery Thought in the Old South. Gloucester, Mass.: Peter Smith. (Reprint of 1935 edition)

Jones, Steven L.
  1985   The African-American Tradition in Vernacular Architecture. In *The Archaeology of Slavery and Plantation Life*, ed. Theresa A. Singleton, p. 195–213. Orlando, Fla.: Academic Press.

Joyner, Charles
  1984   *Down by the Riverside: Slave Life and Culture in Waccamaw Neck, South Carolina.* Urbana: University of Ilinois Press.

Lewis, Kenneth E., and Donald L. Hardesty
  1979   Middleton Place: Initial Archaeological Investigations at an Ashley River Rice Plantation. Institute of Archaeology and Anthropology, Research Manuscript Series 148. University of South Carolina, Columbia.

Lewis, Kenneth E., and Helen Haskell
  1980   Hampton II: Further Archaeological Investigations at a Santee River Plantation. Institute of Archaeology and Anthropology, Research Manuscripts Series 161, University of South Carolina, Columbia.

Lewis, Lynne
  1985   The Planter Class: The Archaeological Record at Drayton Hall. In *The Archaeology of Slavery and Plantation Life*, ed. Theresa A. Singleton, pp. 35–65. Orlando, Fla.: Academic Press.

Litwack, Leon F.
  1979   *Been in the Storm So Long: The Aftermath of Slavery.* New York: Knopf.

McDaniel, George W.
  1982   *Hearth and Home: Preserving a People's Culture.* Philadelphia: University of Temple Press.

MacFarlane, Suzanne
  1975   The Ethnoarchaeology of a Slave Cabin Community: Couper Plantation. Master's thesis, University of Florida, Gainesville.

Moore, Sue M.
  1981   The Antebellum Barrier Island Plantation: In Search of an Archaeological Pattern. Ph.D. diss., University of Florida, Gainesville.
  1985   Social and Economic Status on the Coastal Plantation: An Archaeological Perspective. In *The Archaeology of Slavery and Plantation Life*, ed. Theresa A. Singleton, pp. 141–60. Orlando, Fla.: Academic Press.

Morgan, Phillip D.
  1982   Work and Culture: The Task System and the World of Low Country Blacks, 1700 to 1880. *William and Mary Quarterly* 39 (ser. 3): 563–597.

1983   The Ownership of Property by Slaves in the Mid-19th Century
        Low Country. *Journal of Southern History* 49(3): 399–434.

Noël Hume, Ivor
    1970   *A Guide to the Artifacts of Colonial America.* New York: Knopf.

Orser, Charles
    1984   The Past Ten Years of Plantation Archaeology in the Southeastern
            United States. *Southeastern Archaeology* 3(1) Summer: 1–12.

Otto, John S.
    1975   Status Differences and the Archaeological Record—A Comparison
            of Planter, Overseer, and Slave Sites, from Cannon's Point Planta-
            tion (1799–1861), St. Simons Island, Ph.D. diss., University of
            Florida, Gainesville.

Owens, Leslie Howard
    1976   *This Species of Property: Slave Life and Culture in the Old South.* New
            York: Oxford University Press.

Phillips, Ulrich (ed.)
    1969   *Plantation and Frontier.* New York: Bart Franklin.

Reitz, Elizabeth
    1978   Report on the Faunal Material Excavated by West Georgia College
            from Colonels Island, Georgia. In The Cultural Evolution and En-
            vironment of Colonels Island, ed. Karl T. Steinen, pp. 135–65. Re-
            port on file, Department of Sociology and Anthropology, West
            Georgia College, Carrollton, Ga.

Reitz, Elizabeth, Tyson Gibbs, and Ted Rathbun
    1985   Archaeological Evidence for Subsistence on Coastal Plantations. In
            The Archaeology of Slavery and Plantation Life, ed. Theresa A. Single-
            ton, pp. 163–91. Orlando, Fla.: Academic Press.

Rose, Willie Lee
    1967   *Rehearsal for Reconstruction: The Port Royal Experiment.* New York:
            Vintage Books.

Singleton, Theresa A.
    1978   Report on Historic Excavations, Colonel's Island, Glynn County,
            Georgia. In The Cultural Evolution and Environment of Colonels
            Island, ed. Karl T. Steinen, pp. 70–135. Report on File, Department
            of Sociology and Anthroplogy, West Georgia College, Carrollton,
            Ga.
    1980   The Archaeology of Afro-American Slavery in Coastal Georgia: A
            Perception of Slave Household and Community Patterns. Ph.D.
            diss., University of Florida, Gainesville.

1985a   Archaeological Implications for Changing Labor Conditions. In *The Archaeology of Slavery and Plantation Life*, ed. Theresa A. Singleton, pp. 291–307. Orlando, Fla.: Academic Press
1985b   *The Archaeology of Slavery and Plantation Life*. Orlando, Fla: Academic Press.

Stampp, Kenneth M.
1956   *The Peculiar Institution: Slavery in the Antebellum South*. New York: Knopf.

Trinkley, Michael (ed.)
1986   Indians and Freedmen Occupations at Fish Haul Creek Site (38BU805) Beaufort County, South Carolina. Research Series 7, Chicora Foundation, Columbia, S.C.

Trinkley, Michael, and Debi Hacker
1986   Historic Artifacts. In *Indian and Freedmen Occupation at the Fish Haul Site Beaufort County, South Carolina*, ed. Michael Trinkley, pp. 282–312. Research Series 7, Chicora Foundation. Columbia, S.C.

Vlach, John
1975   Sources of the Shotgun House: African and Caribbean Antecedents for Afro-American Architecture. Ph.D. diss., Indiana University.
1978   *The Afro-American Tradition in the Decorative Arts*. Cleveland: Cleveland Art Museum.

Weir, Robert
1983   *Colonial South Carolina: A History*. Millwood, N.Y.: KTO Press.

Wheaton, Thomas, Amy Friedlander, and Patrick Garrow
1983   Yaughan and Curriboo Plantations: Studies in Afro-American Archaeology. Report submitted to National Park Service Southeastern Regional Office Branch Contract Number C-5950. Soil Systems, Inc., Marietta, Georgia.

Wheaton, Thomas, and Patrick Garrow
1985   Acculturation and the Archaeological Record in the Carolina Lowcountry. In *The Archaeology of Slavery and Plantation Life*, ed. T. A. Singleton, pp. 239–59. Orlando, Fla.: Academic Press.

Wilson, Jack H., Jr., and Homes Hogue Wilson
1986   Faunal Remains. In *Indian and Freedmen Occupation at the Fish Haul Site Beaufort County, South Carolina*, ed. Michael Trinkley, pp. 282–312. Research Series 7 Chicora Foundation. Columbia, S.C.

Wood, Peter H.
1974   *Black Majority: Negroes in Colonial South Carolina from 1670 through the Stono Rebellion*. New York: Norton.

Zierden, Martha, and Jeanne Calhoun
    1983   *An Archaeological Assessment of the Greenfield Borrow Pit, Georgetown County, South Carolina.* Charleston, S.C.: Charleston Museum.

Zierden, Martha, Jeanne Calhoun, and Debi H. Norton
    1985   *Archdale Hall: Investigations of a Lowcountry Plantation.* The Charleston Museum Archaeological Contributions 10. Charleston, S.C.

PART V

The Archaeology of Industrial Capitalism and Modern America

It may be fair to suggest that the authors represented in this part of the book—Texas Anderson and Roger Moore, Robert Paynter, and Randall McGuire—have faced a greater challenge than any of the other authors in this book. This sounds absurd at first, given the difficulties Thomas had to deal with, for example, even in finding Santa Catalina. But for archaeologists of the very recent past there is a serious problem that is just the reverse of Thomas's.

The archaeological, artifactual, and architectural evidence for 19th-and 20th-century industrial America is all around us. Many of our cities, themselves built on 19th-century plans, are filled with 19th-century buildings and more than a few of us live and work in them today. Many aspects of modern American material culture, or at least the techniques and patterns of labor needed to produce them, were invented or perfected in the 19th century. Many American institutions like libraries, the universities and museums that employ many of the authors in this book, the historic preservation movement, and even the Smithsonian Institution and the Anthropological Society of Washington, publishers of this book—all of these have

19th-century origins. At one level, the problem is how to find significant meanings in yesterdays that look so much like today. There is also a deeper problem. Not only does the similarity between the present and the recent past complicate the recovery of meaning; so too does the fact that many aspects of that past are alive in our contemporary world. If we accept for historical archaeology the basically anthropological task of understanding everyday life in the past and what accounts for its structure, and if we define ideology as something that hides or masks certain underlying aspects of social reality (Althusser 1971), then archaeologists of the recent past have the job of piercing a *living* ideology. That is, the ideology we study as scholars is the same ideology we deal with as members of a society. We contend that it is more difficult to penetrate an ideology that is still serving living interests than it is to see through a dead ideology, one with no contemporary beneficiaries. It is easy to see this dilemma, wherein the similarity and the vitality of the recent past lead in several directions: to an archaeological dismissal of the "modern" portion of the 19th century, to shoddy scholarship that is little more than a tedious recitation of obvious trivialities, to scholarship that unconsciously affirms a dominant ideology, to the kind of object obsession that characterizes bad industrial archaeology, or to the three essays in this part, each of which builds upon and attempts to penetrate the familiarity of industrializing 19th-century America, producing in the process studies of broad value to historical archaeology as a whole.

The next three essays—Anderson and Moore's about houses, Paynter's about things, and McGuire's about gravestones—do not seem to share a thematic focus in the way that the essays in the preceding parts do. This is likely the result, in at least some diffuse way, of the ability of capitalism to hide its structures and operations through ideology. The connections between the subjects of these essays may be well hidden by the culture that surrounds us, but, below the surface, the integrating power of industrial capitalism connects Anderson and Moore's Ashton Villa, Paynter's bottles, and McGuire's gravestones even more tightly than the Georgian worldview held together Deetz's 18th-century plates, gravestones, and houses. In addition to all being about the products of industrial capitalism, these three essays have something else in common. Although each is theoretically different from the others, all three are characterized by a theoretical rigor and methodological integrity that come from taking the richness of the 19th-century database not as a signal that less needs to be done to analyze and interpret it, but rather, that more can be done and must be done to illuminate the 19th-century roots of 20th-century America. Each author attempts, in his or her own way, to pierce the living capitalist ideology that has helped structure his or her data and that today surrounds us all, as scholars and as citizens.

Anderson and Moore's approach to piercing this ideology is a symbolic analysis of Ashton Villa, a surviving mid-19th-century house built by a member of the Galveston, Texas, merchant elite. (Galveston is clearly not on the East Coast, the geographic focus of this volume, but Anderson and Moore's essay is appropriate for the book on the basis of the authors' convincing demonstration that Galveston entered a period of economic decline as soon as it lost its position as a point of transshipment to the East. So, although not on the East Coast, Galveston was significantly connected to the East Coast.) Anderson and Moore choose the symbolic approach for the same reasons that others in this volume, like South and Thomas, have chosen some version of the functionalist paradigm. All seek an interpretive framework with a holistic potential. In their discussions of various architectural styles, Anderson and Moore understand that they are not dealing with individual symbols, but with systems of meaning, and they carefully bear in mind that some of these meanings have considerable social and economic value. A key to their symbolic analysis is their understanding that buildings are not just shelter; architecture is a form of communication. As a further part of their acknowledgment of the economic context and meaning of style, they hint at the social use of style, its active or recursive quality, by arguing that architectural styles do not just reflect individual thoughts: they reflect, *enact*, and attempt to *influence* various versions of social reality or ideology. This sets the stage for their discussion of Ashton Villa.

In particular, Anderson and Moore focus on the make-over of Ashton Villa from a strictly symmetrical Georgian style, expressing egalitarian ideals, to a more asymmetrical Italianate style, appropriate for "merchant princes." Anderson and Moore call the Italianate style symbolic of an ideology based on social Darwinism, one that suggests that individual effort can ensure success for any person.

Whereas Anderson and Moore discuss social Darwinism by its popular names, McGuire (this volume) would argue that this use of Italianate architecture is ideology of the naturalizing sort, like his elaborate Victorian gravestones. Naturalizing ideology, unlike a masking ideology, does not try to hide social inequalities. Instead, it expresses inequalities while placing their origin or causes in some aspect of the natural world, where they are unchallengeable, rather than in the social world, where they could be challenged and even redressed. A naturalizing ideology would suggest that members of certain nationalities or ethnic groups succeed economically because they are naturally (and inevitably) inclined to do so and that members of other groups and classes fail not because of systematic (and remediable) discrimination against them but because of a natural disinclination toward the kinds of activities that would lead to success.

In addition, Anderson and Moore echo Palkovich (this volume) in an implicit way in their use of Deetz and in their suggestion that the wildly romantic and individualistic Italianate style was not just a new style, but was actually a rejection of the earlier, classically inspired styles. This constitutes their statement on the recursive nature of material culture, the idea that material culture does not just reflect thought and behavior, but also has the capacity to carry messages and influence thought and behavior. This is an idea that also informs McGuire's essay, at the end of this section.

Paynter's essay begins with an archaeological question: To what do we attribute the rapid increase in the numbers and forms of objects that form the archaeological record of the late 18th century and beyond? He rejects as too limited both idealist/diffusionist and market models, suggesting in their place class models, the major topic of his essay. Class models consider the relationships among capitalists and between capitalists and workers in the light of the capitalist's goal of making a profit. As a temporal framework, Paynter introduces three periodizations or cycles describing capitalist economic growth, business cycles (1–15 years), Kondratieffs (approximately 50 years), and logistics (200–300 years). Each cycle is characterized by a period of expansion followed by a period of contraction, and during each different relations hold among capitalists and between capitalists and workers.

A principal contribution of Paynter's essay is his delineation of archaeological signatures for various stages in the perpetual conflict between capitalists and workers. For example, the replacement of workers by machines—a shift clearly discernible in the archaeological record of both commodities *and* the means of production—is understood as a way of controlling labor costs. The ability to control labor costs is particularly important during times of market saturation because, by controlling labor costs, the capitalist can forestall the profit squeezing that usually accompanies market saturation. On the other hand, the explosion in the kinds and quantities of material goods beginning in the late 18th century is seen to represent the other principal way of protecting and assuring a profit, flooding the market. The importance of Paynter's essay lies in the fact that neither of these characterizations of 19th-century production are assumptions based only on theory, but represent a careful correlation of changes in factory production with already documented Kondratieff cycles for the 18th, 19th, and 20th centuries. Paynter gives historical archaeologists the best set of reasons yet to study the production of the goods that have become our artifacts, and his approach guarantees that such a study *cannot* become yet another sterile exercise in the history of technology. Not only is this an attractive approach because it keeps people in the picture and puts people before things, but more important this is his way of avoiding entrapment in the ideology he is attempting to study and is, as well, his method of piercing it. Finally, Paynter's essay is an important complement to Leone's Chapter 7 in that it also provides a solid economic context for Deetz's formulation of the Georgian worldview, thus inserting the potential for causality into considerations of Deetz's mind-set.

The final essay in this volume, by Randall McGuire, brings the book closer to contemporary America than any of the previous chapters. Some of McGuire's gravestones are less than 20 years old and some of his cemeteries are still used for burial. But the newness of some of his artifacts is not the only way that McGuire's essay is about the present. Even if they were not still being used for burial, many of McGuire's cemeteries would still be used by people visiting graves.

Of all the artifacts considered in the essays in this book, McGuire's gravestones are the artifacts most explicitly and unambiguously intended by their makers to have a communicative function. The communicative intent of his artifacts is perhaps one reason for McGuire's discussion of ideology, which is one of the most detailed in the book and is also one of the most important parts of McGuire's essay. In his discussion of ideology McGuire makes two key moves, each based on the complexity of the messages that constitute his dialogue with the dead, as initiated by their gravestones.

First, McGuire rejects an instrumentalist definition of ideology, which says what ideology does but not what ideology is. Instrumentalist definitions, which McGuire attributes to Althusser (1971), among others, talk about ideology as a mystification or misrepresentation of social reality in terms of its usefulness to members of dominant classes for maintaining their own privileged positions. McGuire, on the other hand, says that misrepresentation of reality is a product of all human perception, because perception is invariably selective. Thus, misrepresentation is inherent in culture. Rather than call all culturally based mystification ideology, McGuire chooses to call ideology only that part of mystification that involves relations of power.

McGuire's second important move is his use of Abercrombie, Hill, and Turner (1980) to reject the dominant ideology thesis. Instead, they suggest that the principal use of the dominant ideology is for integrating the dominant class, that the dominant ideology does not necessarily subvert subordinate classes, and that subordinate classes have their own ideologies that reject the dominant ideology.

As a result of these two moves, McGuire provides a sophisticated, systematic way of understanding the large number of gravestones he encountered, which were not directly reflective, in some mechanical way, of the socioeconomic status of the people they memorialized, a common assumption in many mortuary and other material culture studies. McGuire's definition of ideology allows him to discover things beyond class interests and interests beyond those of the dominant classes in the cemeteries he studies.

As for data, McGuire found early 19th-century cemeteries filled with relatively uniform gravestones. This, he argues, is material culture as ideology, masking the fact that there was marked inequality in the distribution of and access to wealth and power in early 19th-century Broome County, New York. In the later 19th and early 20th centuries, this uniformity disappears and is replaced by considerable variety in the size, elaborateness, and cost of memorials. McGuire argues that this is an accurate reflection of power relations. These gravestones are still ideology, but of the naturalizing kind. This kind of mortuary display was a product of the prevailing social Darwinism of the time, a doctrine that said that everyone could succeed and that people got what they deserved. By rooting this attitude in the works of Darwin, taken to be a description of the natural world, people passed off social inequalities as natural rather than socially produced phenomena. Finally, in the period between the two world wars, there was a move back toward uniformity in the cemetery. McGuire suggests that this represents a symbolic harkening back to the egalitarian ideals expressed in the early 19th-century graveyard— ideals placed in the graveyard precisely because they existed nowhere else in society. This analysis of the most modern gravestones demonstrates McGuire's understanding that modern gravestones do not exist in a vacuum but are designed and erected upon consideration of and in reference to the stones already erected, among which any new one will stand. The value of McGuire's discussion of and use of the concept of ideology goes well beyond the microdiscipline of gravestone studies.

REFERENCES CITED

Abercrombie, Nicholas, Stephen Hill, and Bryan S. Turner
1980   *The Dominant Ideology Thesis*. London: Allen and Unwin.

Althusser, Louis
1971   *Lenin and Philosophy*. New York: Monthly Review Press.

## CHAPTER 12

Meaning and the Built Environment

A Symbolic Analysis of a 19th-Century Urban Site

TEXAS B. ANDERSON AND ROGER G. MOORE

Miller and Tilley (1984:151) have underscored the need for the archaeologist to "confer meaning and significance to a world of otherwise meaningless objects." The research at Ashton Villa, with its focus on the message of the built environment, has been just such an attempt to explore the cultural context and identify the cultural themes that determined the form and content of one particular archaeological site.

Historic archaeological sites generate such an abundance of artifacts and artifact categories that research reports seldom go beyond a description of artifacts and related historical or behavioral events and processes. However, archaeologists have recently come to focus increasingly on the ideas and ideologies behind the artifacts (Childe 1964; Wobst 1977; Deetz 1978; Hodder 1982; Kus 1984; Leone 1982, 1984; Miller and Tilley 1984; Trigger 1984). The research discussed in this chapter follows this new tradition. It is important to recognize at the outset the troublesome dialectic between the objective reality of a site and the undeniable fact that it can only be known through subjective interpretation, just as Tyler (1978) has noted in regard to texts. The realization of the open and relative nature of site interpretation, however, should not lead to the assumption that all analytical frameworks are equally valid—or invalid. We seek to examine the utility of symbolic analysis through its application at a specific site.

How, then, does one justify a symbolic interpretation and what is its value for the historical archaeologist (aside from the fact that it is an exciting way to organize the research and that it provides an intellectually satisfying means for presenting the results, the interpretations)? Perhaps its most important value is that symbolically oriented analysis mandates a holistic view of the particular past under investigation. The details are recognized as parts of the whole, parts of the culture that produced and was produced by them. Understanding is enhanced because there is an explicit acknowledgment, not just of the artifacts and events, but of the ideological matrix in which they existed, of which they are representative.

In order to discover and develop the appropriate symbolic framework, it is necessary to investigate the multiple and overlapping social, political, economic, and religious settings in which the particular people played out their lives—the constituents of the societal ideology—and search for themes that will be repeated not only in social structure, "literature," or public architecture, but in the language of a letter, the construction of a home or a garden walkway, or even in the arrangement of a mirror and shelves over a mantlepiece. These themes, repeated ad infinitum within the culture, constitute representations of an ideology, perhaps one of several functioning simultaneously at different levels of the society.

For the purposes of this investigation, an intentionally generalized definition of ideology shall suffice. For example, although we are dealing with an unarguably elite site, it is not important to this study to tie the definition of ideology to concepts of dominance, coercion, and oppression. More critical is the common element expressed in the divergent views on a definition of ideology presented in Hodder's (1982:10) introduction to *Symbolic and Structural Archaeology*: "The way in which the structured sets of symbols are used in relation to social strategies depends on a series of concepts and attitudes that are historically and contextually appropriate." The content of this pervasive series of concepts or attitudes constitutes the operant ideology and is archaeologically relevant since "all material patterning is generated by symbolic structures within a cultural matrix" (Hodder 1982:10).

This study is concerned with a significant change in the pervasive ideology of the American republic, a change that was initiated within 50 years of its formation and that is clearly reflected in the material record. We examine the material consequences of the decline of an ideology, and of the ascendancy of a new one in its place: the loss of cultural relevancy and acceptance of the old ideology leads to similar changes in its referent symbolic vocabulary. The old symbols become meaningless, or they take on a new meaning to continue as reflections of the significance of the new social order.

We contend that the specific ideological transition under study is that from a democratically based, egalitarian ideal to one that permits, encourages, even glorifies the expression of social and economic inequality. Our archaeological investigation has been structured to reveal and interpret any changes in the use of form and space that reflect materially this change in social relations. The formative ideology of the United States in the 18th and early 19th centuries is viewed as one generated from a universal need to replace an irrelevant and repudiated Old World ideology, one based on control of the society and the economy by the landed aristocracy. The replacement was an ideology rationally and consciously developed, or rather redeveloped from its classical roots to accommodate the opportunities offered by a vast and undeveloped land, rich in natural resources. Its most visible material referent was an architectural vocabulary derived from emulation of its classical inspiration, one stressing (but not limited to) symmetry and homogeneity in architectural design.

The very abundance of resources and opportunities, however, sowed the seeds of the demise of the idealistic, agrarian-based, egalitarian ideology and its most visible expression, the idiom of classical architecture. Its symbols became inappropriate for the ideology of the commercial and industrial democracy that material success and equality of opportunity created in its stead.

Our investigation has confirmed that Ashton Villa, a residence still standing in the island city of Galveston on the upper Texas coast, is a material reflection of these shifts in ideology and symbolic vocabulary spanning the middle third of the 19th century. The following discussion of research undertaken at this urban estate suggests how a symbolic perspective can be developed and how its use can expand our understanding of the processes responsible for artifacts and features, the intangibles that directed the form of the tangible.

HISTORICAL BACKGROUND

Ashton Villa, built in 1859 by James M. Brown, is now owned by the city of Galveston and administered by the Galveston Historical Foundation as a house museum (Figure 12.1). The interior has been restored to approximate its appearance at the turn of the century, and the yard has been landscaped and modifications made to provide social and administrative areas for the execution of museum activities.

Figure 12.1: Ashton Villa as a house museum.

The villa stands between the bay-side wharves and modern bank-
ing houses that dominate the northern half of Galveston (physically and
economically) and the beaches, restaurants, and motels on the southern,
Gulf side of the Island. The house museum is now one of a number of
historical and natural features that draw thousands of visitors to the island city annually. In fact, as Houston, its sister city and long-time rival
50 miles away on the mainland, has come to dominate the coast economically, Galveston has become more and more dependent on tourists
for its economic well-being.

But it was not always thus. In the mid-19th century, Galveston
was well on its way to becoming the premier port on the Texas coast
and the "jewel of the Gulf," the epithet frequently applied to it at the

close of the century. Like Houston and San Antonio, it was economically and socially dominated by merchants, most of whom had recently emigrated from the North Atlantic States or from Europe. The majority of these were engaged in some sort of wholesale transaction, and, like James Brown, were frequently involved in more than one occupation (Hayes 1974). By 1870, one-half of the Texans possessing $100,000 or more in assets lived in these three cities (Wooster 1970).

In the first two decades of the 19th century the Karankawa Indians, hunting and gathering people organized in small kinship bands, still controlled the west end of the island. Their technology was no match for the pirates, led by Jean and Pierre Lafitte, who made settlement on the eastern end of the island around 1819 (Webb 1952; Hayes 1974). According to Warren D. C. Hall, who was living on the island at the time, slave trading was the principal industry during the Lafitte occupation. Although the early Anglos eventually exterminated the indigenes, as late as 1822 a few Karankawa still made seasonal use of the island. After the Lafitte group burned their own fort and left the island, at the firm request of the U.S. government, Warren Hall was by his own account the only white inhabitant on the island (Hayes 1974).

The following February, Moses Austin received a grant from the Spanish allowing him to bring Anglo-American settlers into the region. Upon the death of the elder Austin, the empressario grant was affirmed to his son Stephen F. Austin by the Mexican emperor, Iturbide. However, Galveston remained sparsely populated until 1835–36, when colonists fleeing before the invading Mexican army sought refuge there (Hayes 1974). Land developers from the East Coast had become interested in the Galveston Bay area for some of the same reasons it had attracted privateers and filibusterers: It afforded a safe harbor and a convenient port of entry for immigrants and materials (Hardy and Roberts 1910; Hayes 1974; Henson 1976). After General Sam Houston's defeat of the Mexican army of Santa Anna at nearby San Jacinto, Galveston was again declared a port of entry, this time by the Congress of the Republic of Texas instead of the Mexican government.

In the summer of 1837, Harrison Sandusky made a plat of the city, and the grid of urbanization began to be realized on the island. Although the Houston Telegraph reported that there were "fifty or sixty elegant houses" in Galveston in mid-1838, the Englishman Charles Hooten was less impressed, noting three years later that streets were either deep sand or a mire of mud. He abandoned his efforts to farm on the island when the city scavengers, roving bands of pigs, continued to harvest the few fruits and vegetables he could manage to grow in the sandy soil (Hayes 1974).

Commercial activities were more successful, and the port grew with the influx of immigrants eager to find better economic and political conditions on the American frontier. Brown arrived in 1843 with some special skills and an entrepreneurial cast of mind, ready to take advantage of the opportunities offered in the burgeoning city. Born of Dutch immigrant parents in New York, he apprenticed to a brick mason and plasterer before leaving home at age 16. Over the next six years he made his way across the South, honing his skills and accumulating considerable property (Hardy and Roberts 1910). In his first four years in Galveston he established a construction business, began to manufacture bricks at a kiln on the mainland, and opened a hardware business (Hayes 1974). His ability to assess the needs of his community and to exploit them became increasingly evident. He could now supply not only the building skills and labor force, but also the hardware and other supplies demanded by the construction boom that accompanied the tide of immigrants into the frontier (Hayes 1974; Brown Family Papers; Robinson 1981).

In 1859 Brown turned his attention to his own building needs as a father of three, owner of a thriving wholesale business, and newly elected president of the Galveston, Houston, and Henderson Railroad (Hayes 1974). Selecting four lots facing the broad boulevard that traversed the spine of the island, Brown created the three-story, red-brick symbol of his newly attained status. He chose a "look" and a label for his home that bespoke his connection with the established American elite. Brown's wife, Rebecca Ashton Stoddart Rhodes, only 16 when she married James, had left Philadelphia with her mother, Sara Moses Stoddart (later Rhodes), reportedly just after her father's death, while Rebecca was still an infant. Her great-grandfather, Isaac Ashton, had been an officer in the revolutionary war (Brown Family Papers; Philadelphia City Directories: 1825, 1833; Brown n.d.; Allgeyer n.d.). Ashton Villa, the name James and Rebecca chose for their new home, symbolized historic depth as well as aristocratic status.

As elsewhere in the South, the following decade brought hardships to Galvestonians. In spite of the opposition of some of Galveston's most prominent business leaders and Governor Sam Houston, the ordinance of secession was passed and shortly thereafter Union forces established a blockade of the port (Hayes 1974:1). Exempted from service because he was the president of a vital railroad, Brown oversaw the extension of his railway and also became a purchasing agent for the Confederacy in Mexico, the major outlet for cotton and other Texas commodities during the war (Ramsdell 1934). Although the *Galveston Daily News* reported, upon his death in 1895, that Brown had "lost heavily . . . in chattel slavery" at the close of the war, a search of the Galveston and Harris County tax rolls revealed the ownership of only the three house servants who continued to serve the family after Emancipation—a document first read to the blacks of Galveston from the second-story balcony at Ashton Villa (National Association for the Advancement of Colored People, Galveston Branch, 1980). Although tax records do indicate that Brown's worth in cash in hand and at interest declined from $31,600 to $21,600 by the end of the war, this apparent decline was a temporary setback at worst; the net profits of the railroad during his presidency were $745,532 (Galveston County Tax Rolls 1863 and 1864). After the war Brown resigned his office and resumed his wholesale hardware business (Hardy and Roberts 1910). "The rapid increase in population after the war as a result of heavy migration from the older South afforded ambitious merchants new opportunities for profit in wholesaling and retailing, particularly in hardware and grocery commodities" (Wooster 1970:25–26). Ever the canny entrepreneur, Brown traveled to Washington to take the oath of allegiance and expedite the renewal of the economically important citizenship rights he had lost during the war (Hardy and Roberts 1910).

Although the economic structure in Texas was considerably altered by the war, those hardest hit were the wealthy sugar and cotton planters who had relied on slave labor. Galveston, on the other hand, prospered. The population more than doubled between 1860 and 1870, and more wealthy men lived in Galveston County in 1870 than in any other county in Texas; among the 11 wealthiest, Brown was third, with $175,000 in real and $100,000 in personal property (Hardy and Roberts 1910; Wooster 1967, 1970). All 11 were merchants and at least 40 years old, and the majority were born on the East Coast or in Europe (Wooster 1970). These similarities suggest a powerful economic network; Brown and John Sealy, one of only two Texans worth at least half a million dollars, were also bankers, both held offices in utility and railroad companies, and both were appointed after the war to the Galveston Board of Aldermen—by a governor who wished to have influential businessmen direct the reorganization of civil and economic affairs of Texas cities (Hardy and Roberts 1910). Between 1864 and 1871, Brown, Sealy, and Henry Rosenburg (another of the 11) were vestrymen at Trinity Episcopal Church. Economic and social considerations were perhaps more important than dogma in selecting a church, and Trinity at the time attracted not only Christians of various denominations, but also some ethnic Jews (Brown Family Papers; Webb 1952; Hayes 1974).

Over the next 25 years, the Browns elaborated their social position. Their eldest daughter came to personify Galveston's belle époque, spending lavishly on art, antiques, and a resplendent wardrobe. She studied art in Europe and wintered in New York, and in the spring the social season at her favorite resort near Milwaukee never really began until Bettie Brown "made her appearance with her 16 trunks, . . . her carriage . . . liverymen . . . coachman, and horses" (*Milwaukee Journal*, 9 March 1930). The *Journal* reported that she led the grand march in "a black velvet princess gown" with a court train decorated in "solid gold" leaves, carrying "a large ostrich fan studded with pearls." Although she never married, one surviving photograph shows her on a chaise with two attentive men by her side. In another, she models the $5,000 lace coat she wore to a garden party in Vienna for Franz-Joseph. A relative of one of her father's business associates in Galveston revealed to the senior author that his great-uncle, a widower, delighted in Bettie's company in his later years and kept apartments in New York and Paris for her convenience.

James Brown and his family had been a part of the "brilliant and fashionable society . . . on the island . . . one that could hold its place with any metropolis in the country" (Graham and Newan n.d.). Galveston had been the only deep-water port on the Gulf Coast between New Orleans and Vera Cruz, Mexico. The city's drummers traveled vast territories, not only through Texas, but New Mexico, Arkansas, the Indian Territory, western Louisiana, and Mexico (Graham and Newan n.d.).

But the economic wave James Brown had ridden and directed to such heights was cresting (Menig 1975:74):

> From the moment the M, K, & T [Railroad] bridged the Red
> River, produce began to flow northward out of Texas. By 1890
> half of the cotton in North Texas went directly by rail to the East,
> rather than by way of Galveston to the sea. But even more signifi-
> cant was the inflow of manufactures and supplies of all kinds. St.
> Louis merchants, aided by cheap rail rates, greater resources, and
> vigorous promotion, quickly made heavy inroads into the trading
> territories heretofore complacently controlled by Houston and
> Galveston.

On Christmas morning of 1895, James Brown died of epithelial cancer, only shortly before economic, personal, and physical events began to crash down on Ashton Villa and the Brown family. His youngest daughter left her abusive husband a few months later and, with her three children, came back to live with her mother, sister, and grand-mother at the villa. Construction of a three-story addition to the house was scarcely complete when a massive hurricane hit the island on September 8, 1900. Because of the elevated location Brown had chosen for his home, and its raised first floor, the villa was protected from the full fury of the hurricane-driven tidal wave that smashed across the city. At dawn, looking across the broad boulevard toward the Gulf, the Brown women could see a high wall of debris that had only the night before been the homes of the estimated six thousand who had lost their lives (Alperin n.d.; Weems 1980).

A new type of municipal government (the city commissioner system) was formed to plan and direct the rebuilding of the city (Alperin n.d.). First, a massive seawall 3 miles long was built along the Gulf shore, then a canal was dredged just inside this seawall. The town was gridded with dikes, houses and other buildings were jacked up several feet, and sand dredged from Galveston Bay was brought down the canal to pumping stations. It was thence pumped through a distributary network of pipes to spread over the surface of the city (*Galveston Daily News*, 1 October 1927). Twenty-seven million cubic yards of wet sand had been pumped onto the city by 1927, thus raising its surface by as much as 9 feet at the Gulf margin (*Galveston Daily News*, 15 October 1907, 22 June 1930).

Although it was a heroic effort, neither Galveston nor the Brown family regained their former status. In 1929 the El Mina Shriners bought the villa from the youngest daughter's estate and razed some of the dependencies to construct a meeting hall/ballroom; and for the next 40 years they saved the villa from the fate of most of the mid-19th century homes that had survived the 1900 hurricane. But in the late 1960s the Shriners announced that Ashton Villa would be demolished to make way for a larger, Moorish-style temple. A group of concerned citizens saved the villa once more, raising sufficient money and furor to coerce the Shriners into selling the home to the city, and later raising additional money to refurbish the house and dependencies and to landscape the yard.

CULTURAL IMPLICATIONS OF THE BUILT ENVIRONMENT

The archaeological research at Ashton Villa tests the premise that there is considerably more to the built environment than aggregates of artifacts—the constructions—that constitute it. The built environment is regarded as a significant medium of communication. The organization of the physical space, as well as the structures themselves, provide visual reinforcement for the organization of the social structure. The built environment is more than shelter for the people who built it; it is a physical representation of the ideology that shapes the society. It repeats the myth by which they construct their lives and social order.

The earliest inhabitants on Galveston Island carried not only their stone and bone tools, pots, and baskets with them as they waded or canoed across from the mainland; they also carried the physical, as well as cognitive, frames for their shelters. The first waves of European men also carried materials to the island for their crude, dirt-floored cabins: logs brought in on sailing vessels and later on steamboats. One of Galveston's earliest entrepreneurs, Samuel May Williams, was not content to bring only materials and a mental template for his residence to the island; he and his business associate, Thomas F. McKinney, had the materials for their homes prefabricated in Maine and then shipped to Galveston. Williams knew what he wanted his home to convey, and took no chances with having the message garbled by inexperienced laborers. Phillip Tucker, who brought the S. M. Williams home in 1850, wrote in his memoirs that McKinney ordered and then supervised the construction of the identical houses (Margaret Henson: personal communication 1986).

The symmetrical organization of the doors and windows, the treatment of the front door and central hall of the Williams home were all characteristics of the dominant architectural order in the United States since the beginning of the 18th century (Davidson 1971; Henson 1976; Poppeliers 1976–77). From "about 1700 with the construction of the Wren building at the College of William & Mary, and soon after, the Governor's Palace and the Capitol at Williamsburg . . . rigid symmetry, axial entrances, and geometric proportion became the hallmarks of Anglo-American architecture" (Poppeliers 1976–77:7). This architectural form, from its florescence in the Georgian mode of the colonial period, through the Federal and then the Roman revival idioms, to the resurrection of the Greek embellishments after 1820, had given a basic homogeneity to Anglo-American structures. This time-span, varying geographically from 100 to 150 years, gave rise to "the first true horizon in American history" (Deetz 1978:284–86). In this usage, the term *horizon* signifies not only the rapid introduction of stylistic similarities across a broad geographical area, but also the corresponding spread of an explicit political, economic, or belief system.

Many factors influence the constituent parts and emergent form of cultural constructs and their subsequent transformation. As Glassie (1975:189–90) has asserted for the interpretation of structures, "Architectural thinking is bound to nonarchitectural matters, so that any theory explaining architecture in solely architectural terms may be somewhat correct, but it can never be enough. The social, economic, political, and religious conditions of life in Middle Virginia had changed. People had adapted to those changes, developing new modes of thought, and the things they did, the artifacts they made, manifested the changes that had taken place in their minds."

Until the late colonial period on the East Coast, and well into the 19th century in Texas, regional and ethnic variations marked the American-built environment. Deetz ascribes a "medieval" culture to 17th-century New England, one that was "heterogenous and asymmetrical in its cognitive aspects" (Deetz 1978:285). The architectural manifestations of a distinctly Anglo-American mind-set "had their origins in New England's urban centers" (Deetz 1977:39), but by the mid-18th century, symmetry in architectural forms had become widespread in the emerging democracy. This unity of form reflected a unity of the Anglo-American people following the War of Independence, one forcefully expressed by Fitch (1966:67):

> The Classic Revival in this country was not the subversive importation of [Thomas] Jefferson alone. . . . On the contrary, as a movement it would never have gotten to first base had not its symbolism corresponded to the needs of the dominant classes of the period and been consistent with their general outlook on the world. For, with the final adoption of the Bill of Rights, the state power had been wrested . . . from the hands of Southern slaveholders and Northern Tories who had sought to hold it. Only then was bourgeois democracy, of which Jefferson was the first great spokesman, complete and secure. The aspirations of this society were rational, expansive, optimistic, breathing confidence in Man, his native goodness and nobility, his natural rights. The desire for a truly national culture based on such concepts was a quite explicit factor of the period. In attempting to express these concepts, to concretize them into esthetic standards, it is inevitable that the nation impress them upon its buildings.

The dominant architectural form, like the government itself, was firmly rooted in classical antiquity. Classical idealism and formalism had been the source of inspiration for the basic principles underlying both this new democracy and its attendant architecture. Jefferson had seen architecture and the arts consciously employed for ideological purposes in France. He firmly believed that the construction of buildings, especially public ones, in the classical idiom would serve to inspire Americans with noble attitudes, strengthening democratic principles and boldly proclaiming them to the world (Fitch 1966:67). Jefferson made dramatic use of the architectural forms associated with the Roman Republic in the construction of the University of Virginia and of his own home, Monticello.

The subsequent recognition of the role of Greece in forming the Roman Republic led to a ubiquitous philhellenism in America. The Greek revival has been termed the culmination in the United States of this interest in classical antiquity: "Perceiving an analogy between the glories of the classic world and the bright future of the republic, equating a return to architectural classicism with a return to architectural freedom, early national Americans fastened on the Greek tradition as a proper model for their own. Starting about 1820, the Greek revival dominated a generation of American architecture . . . in every corner of the country" (Drozdowski 1972:136).

Structures as functionally disparate and geographically diverse as the Water Works in Philadelphia (1799), the Quincy Market in Boston (1825), Andrew Jackson's Hermitage (1835) near Nashville, the state capitol in Indianapolis (1835), and St. Phillips Church in Charleston (1838) were conscious copies of Grecian temples. Nicholas Biddle, one of Philadelphia's most prominent citizens, added a massive Doric portico to his 18th-century townhouse on the Delaware in 1838. He noted in his diary that "the two great truths in the world are the Bible and Grecian architecture" (Lockwood 1972:58–59).

In the early decades of the 19th century, the heterogeneous architecture of Texas reflected the ethnic diversity of its immigrants, but by 1845, when Texas formalized its union with the United States, the architecture of the new state was already symbolizing that new unity. Democracy on the frontier was heralded in town and countryside, from raised cottages like Samuel Williams's imported one on the outskirts of Galveston, as surely as from the more elaborate structures in the urban centers. In Austin, the Pease Mansion and the Governor's Mansion were among the most elegant homes in the state; however, as in most cases, the largest and most forceful examples—in both a physical and a communicative sense—were the public buildings like the Texas state capitol (1852–1854; Robinson 1981). As elsewhere in the country, the classical idiom prevailed in Texas structures of every sort: religious, academic, commercial, civic, and residential.

Change, however, was imminent and by midcentury the pendulum hypothesized by de Tocqueville (1945) had begun its long swing from egalitarian ideals to an unbridled "spirit of liberty." The Jeffersonian ideology and its classical ideals, prizing immutable rules of formal order, harmony, balance, restraint, and high-mindedness, began to lose dominance, first marked in a surge of emotional romanticism. The Greco-Roman symbols no longer fit society's mood or needs. Sir Walter Scott's bold knight venturing forth to achieve glory had captured the public spirit. While only a way station to the native American architectural eclecticism to follow, the impulse for the Gothic revival movement expressing this romanticism derived from the growing recognition of the constraints—both architectural and societal—of Greek revival (Jarves 1966:258):

Grecian architecture was a perfect, organic, disciplined whole, limited in intent, and condensed into a defined aesthetic code, outside of which it could not range without detriment to its rule of being. Gothic, on the contrary, has no settled, absolute boundaries. Its essence is freedom of choice, to the intent to attain diversity of feature. Hence it is both flexible and infinite in character, affording working room for every intellectual and spiritual faculty.

The emergent masters of the American economy soon came to recognize a need for this flexibility, "freedom of choice," and "diversity of feature." A vast frontier beckoned, new industries offered unheard of potential for economic improvement. The belief that the most "exalted positions," wealth, and success were accessible to anyone "came close to being an article of faith" (Pessen 1973:204).

Not only American ideals, but the structure of society itself was changing—in a manner that both confirmed the idealization of wealth and betrayed the myth of its universal accessibility. Society was in fact becoming less egalitarian and less agrarian. In Brooklyn in 1810 the top 1 percent of the population owned 22 percent of the noncorporate wealth; 30 years later, they owned 42 percent (Pessen 1973: Tables 5, 6). In Boston the percentage of noncorporate wealth owned by the top 1 percent increased from 29 percent to 40 percent between 1828 and 1845 (Pessen 1973: Tables 3, 4).

This pattern was also exhibited by the urban South and West; the socioeconomic elite in Galveston at midcentury "were one hundred times wealthier than their fellow citizens" (Pessen 1973:217). As noted earlier, many of the men who made up this stratum were merchants who started with rather meager assets. De Tocqueville (1945:2:171) had warned that "if a permanent inequality of conditions and aristocracy again penetrates into the world," it would be created through commerce and industry, not by a landed gentry. This prediction was realized in the emergence of a new economic ruling class, which had achieved a monopoly of control over the American marketplace.

Thus, by 1850 we can observe that the commercial and industrial success of a few Americans had created a society far removed from the vision of the founding fathers. Without access to the traditional prestige of long-term, large-scale land ownership, the mobile, urban members of the newly dominant capitalist class looked to their most visible possession, their homes, as a medium for the expression and reinforcement of their social status. They quickly began to chafe at the confined limits for the expression of that status within the classical canon. In the Greek idiom, one's home may be larger and more elegant than one's less prosperous neighbors, but the immutability of its requirements for order

391

and harmony required that any statement of individuality be suppressed.

American architecture had consequently reached an impasse by the middle of the 19th century. The fruits of capitalism had created an undeniably hierarchical society. Simultaneously, the American public had embraced the related social doctrine of rugged individualism and of universal economic opportunity. The acceptance of these doctrines helped to remove any lingering social pressure to conceal the extent of one's personal wealth. The time was therefore right for an explosion of individualism in American architecture.

Before we examine this explosion of individual expression, we should step back from an exclusively American (or even Western culture) perspective to gain some sense of the fundamental principles of artistic expression that are believed to express themselves universally within egalitarian and hierarchical societies. This search for cross-cultural universals can provide some real insights into the next direction taken by American architecture. Although there are certainly dangers in comparing American and non-Western societies, there is a greater danger in failing to consider the evidence for universal themes in the evolution of American site plans.

As we consider the possibility of an expression of cognitive universals in this nation's architecture, we must still bear in mind that Western architecture carries a rich traditional baggage of explicitly understood social meanings. We have already devoted considerable space in this essay to documenting the traditional meanings of the classical idiom as it was understood and expressed by its proponents in the early days of the American republic. However, while we consider these explicit, traditional connotations of the built environment adequate for defining its overt social message, our search for meaning should attempt, at least on a tentative basis, to go beyond the understanding of the builders. This goal becomes an all important consideration for those cases in which the builders' overt intent is unknown or poorly understood.

An effort to establish connections between art form and sociocultural conditions was formulated by Fischer (1971). This study examined elements of artistic style within a "widely distributed sample of primitive, relatively homogeneous societies" in order to test hypotheses concerning the relationship between art style and social conditions (Fischer 1971:141). Fischer (1971:143) links artistic expressions to "social fantasy":

> I assume that regardless of the overt content of visual art, whether
> a landscape, a natural object, or merely a geometrical pattern,
> there is always or nearly always at the same time the expression of

some fantasied social situation which will bear a definite relationship to the real and desired social situations of the artist and his
society.

Regardless of the accuracy of his reasoning, Fischer achieved considerable success in relating stylistic elements to the degree of development
of social hierarchy, an approach of some relevance to the current study.
He postulated two ideals of society, the "authoritarian," in which social
hierarchy is positively valued, and "egalitarian," in which hierarchy as
a principal of social organization is rejected. In the ideal authoritarian
society, security is achieved when "the relative rank of each individual
is known and is distinct from the rank of each other individual" (Fischer
1971:145). In contrast, "while differences of prestige between individuals inevitably exist, it is bad taste to call attention to them" in an egalitarian society (Fischer 1971:145). Hierarchical societies are seen to value
independence, self-reliance, and ambition, whereas egalitarian societies
stress voluntary obedience, cooperation, and the suppression of statements of individuality, personal success, and self-reliance.

The congruence between Fischer's ideal egalitarian society and
the equally idealized agrarian, democratic egalitarianism of the early
United States is obvious. There is a similar, though less explicitly formulated, congruence between the social values of hierarchical cultures
and the growing recognition and acceptance of individual achievement
and ambition in the capitalist, industrial democracy of America after
1850. Fischer's research is most provocatively relevant to the current
study when he seeks to determine if specific elements of pictorial design
can be correlated with these ideal social forms. Since research at Ashton
Villa pursues similar correlates between social ideology and architectural design elements, it is difficult to ignore the similarity of results
seen in both investigations.

Employing statistical tests, Fischer (1971:145-46) determined that
symmetry, the repetitive use of simple and homogeneous design elements, and designs that employ large areas of empty space are all significantly associated with egalitarian societies. Each of these rules of design is expressed within the classical idiom, from floor plan to facade to
landscaping. In contrast, Fischer (1971:145-46) confirms the association
of asymmetry . . . design incorporating a number of unlike elements,"
and the scarcity of empty spaces with hierarchical societies. These
features of design in fact prefigure those changes we will discover at
Ashton Villa and in American architecture as a whole in the last half of
the 19th century.

Fischer's consideration of the problem of diffusion of art styles also
bears investigation. Fischer addresses the question of why, out of a

number of neighboring potential examples, a culture might find the style of one of its contemporaries congenial, and adopt that model to the exclusion of all others. Fischer (1971:159) suggests that "similarity of social conditions, and relative order of development of these, plays a major role."

American architecture of the 18th and 19th centuries was privy to a kind of diffusion particular to societies with long literate traditions: It had as models available for possible adoption not only the architecture of contemporary societies, but also those of the entire recorded span of Western architectural tradition. In this case, Fischer's question of why one model should be selected over all others applies equally in a diachronic sense. We have already examined how and why the model of classical antiquity was selected and "revived." Selective diffusion through time again comes into play by the mid-19th century, this time with a vengeance, as there begins a wholesale rifling of the past for ideologically appropriate architectural models.

When J.M. Brown constructed Ashton Villa in 1859, he created a residence that was designed in accord with the dictates of the classical revival idiom. The home presented a bilaterally symmetrical facade and floor plan, with rooms opening off the axis of a central hallway, as well as a number of other classical features that were disclosed archaeologically. However, despite his fundamental adherence to the classical style, Brown chose to depart from it in one more important sense: The residence, though still classical at its core, was embellished with Italianate ornamentation. This style, with its low roof line and bold, overhanging eaves, elaborate support brackets, and decorative door and window treatments (Poppeliers 1976–77; Thompson 1976) has been called a "clamor of individual statement" (Davidson 1971:74). Ten years prior to the construction of the Brown house, the showy Italianate style had gained acceptance among the monied in eastern cities (Sloan 1859; Lockwood 1972).

The selection in 1859 of Italianate ornamentation for a classical home by Brown and his equally affluent neighbor, Herman Rosenburg, is seen by the authors as representative of an explicit attempt to manipulate the classical idiom to convey information about wealth and status. This tinkering within the classical framework may be characteristic of elite structures (perhaps especially on the frontier) built during the transition from Greek revival to Victorian eclecticism. In addition, it is an early example of the conscious selection of an architectural model from the past to convey a new social message of industrial wealth and prestige. As Andrew Jackson Downing, a popular 19th-century architect, wrote "the curved and flowing lines and . . . profusion of delicate ornament in relief [of the Italianate style created] a very ornate and elegant effect" (quoted in Lockwood 1972:146–47). This effect was needed by the socially ambitious in "this period of social upheaval and rapid accumulation of wealth" (Lockwood 1972).

Hence, by 1859 the social message of pure classical revival architecture was in eclipse in Galveston. Prominent men of the "frontier" like J. M. Brown were manipulating its message both to call attention to their economic prominence and to symbolize their ties to the established national elite of the East Coast. Over the next 40 years, members of the new dominant class would increasingly house their families in palatial splendor. Turrets and crenulated walls would abound in the unconstrained eclecticism of the new elite's architecture of choice. Ashton Villa, through the modification of its fabric over the next 50 years, would reflect these changes. The freedom to dominate economically had been officially sanctioned. The rugged individualist, aggressive and aquisitive, was the new cultural ideal.

If we are correct in our hypothesis that ideological change will be mirrored in changes in the built environment, then some reflection of this change should be preserved in the archaeological record. When we begin our search for the archaeological correlates of the expression of concentrated wealth and lofty social position, a fundamental archaeological implication should be apparent: change. Archaeologists are traditionally expert at the concrete recognition of stylistic changes. The employment of an ideological framework will now enable us to interpret the cultural significance of these changes by providing material implications of site organization that can be tested against the archaeological record.

ARCHAEOLOGICAL IMPLICATIONS

Early 19th-century Anglo-American sites in Texas and elsewhere in the country will typically contain sites with rectilinear structures, walkways that turn at right angles and house and site plans exhibiting symmetry and balance (Deetz 1977). On the East Coast this model should hold rather well until the early 1840s; however, sites on the frontier adhere to the model for the better part of another two decades. Deviation from this physical model should suggest ideological differences, and those differences can and should be addressed by the archaeologist.

The later, eclectic architectural model exhibits a vigorous disregard for the classical architectural canon. The message is different, and the medium is altered, not only in the structures built after midcentury, but in those built earlier that continued in use. Site plans built or adapted after this transition abound in asymmetry. A wall may suddenly bow out into a giant arc, or sprout a polygonal wing. Walkways curve, or take off at unexpected angles.

Archaeologists surveying these sites cannot expect to find conformance to a specific, formal plan. The individualism that reigned is now reflected in the architecture by the absence of adherence to any particular historical model. Indeed, the only appropriate "model" is a general asymmetry and eclecticism. The linking factors between these sites are the collapse of the classical mode and a new freedom to pick patterns and forms liberally from the examples of history.

As archaeologists look in the field for material correlates of economic inequality, we will expect to find the evidence for change first and most expansively in the industrial and commercial centers where those who control the means of production and distribution reside. The expression of exalted individuality through the abandonment of symmetrical order and through liberal borrowing and mixing of styles from the past should be evident prior to 1850 in these centers. Both field research and documentary investigations should disclose floor and site plans that are characterized by the imbalance of their constituent elements. Floor plans should have no clear axis and should exhibit considerable variation in the size and shape of individual rooms. Facades should be equally imbalanced, broken by chimneys, turrets, and other (frequently unfunctional) projections. Curves and arcs should be at least as much in evidence as straight lines in the layout of walkways.

Evidence for the transition to individualistic statements in architecture should appear at a somewhat later date in more peripheral commercial centers such as Galveston, and last of all in small centers in the rural hinterland. In fact, the local fortunes of commerce should be mappable on the basis of the appearance of these statements. A sudden florescence of Victorian architectural forms in a town of previously modest Greek revival cottages should reflect the arrival of the railroad or some other watershed event in the economic fortunes of the community.

In examining sites occupied through the 19th century, archaeologists should pay particular attention to the recognition of "transitional" forms like that of Ashton Villa. Such structures, if still standing, may now present a typically Victorian site plan and profile. This visage, however, may represent later modifications that mask a residence that was originally built in the classical tradition. The investigator, using old drawings and photos, Sanborn and bird's eye maps, and field observations, must attempt to determine if the hallmark of symmetry exists at the core of the structure. A similar effort must be made to date and group subsequent alterations to the site fabric. Attention must be paid to details of construction as revealed archaeologically; differences in brick size and color, mortar thickness, and types of masonry joining are examples of structural evidence that may be critical to understanding the modification of a structure through time.

The evidence from Ashton Villa was drawn from a conjunction of documentary and archaeological data: contemporary photographs, Sanborn Fire Insurance and other historical maps, and excavations directed by the senior author in the winter and spring of 1980.

The first phase of the development of Ashton Villa, a period in which James Brown personally planned, supplied, and supervised construction, dated from 1859 to about 1869. This phase resulted in the construction of three large red-brick structures—the main house, the kitchen/servants' quarters, and the stable/carriage house. Other features included brick perimeter and stable-yard walls, a wrought iron perimeter fence, a brick-vaulted privy, walkways, and a brick driveway. The identical, two-story dependencies on the north side of the site (the kitchen/quarters structure and the stable/carriage house) were connected by a brick arcade.

Because the rear walls of these structures directly abutted the city alley, leaving no room for a backyard, all exterior domestic activities took place in front of the dependencies and the arcade, primarily on the east side of the main house. However, a 19th-century postcard shows laundry hanging along a line on the west side of the house. Although Brown provided indoor plumbing for the family (fed by attic cisterns), excavations revealed the long-forgotten servants' privy just inside the stable-yard wall. Both the privy and the wall were unrecorded in the archival materials. Their discovery contradicted the recent, popular notion that there were formal gardens directly in front of the arcade and carriage house.

The stable-yard wall extended from the west side of the red-brick, herringbone driveway, paralleled the south stable/carriage house wall, and turned north at a right angle to connect to the southwest corner of the stable structure (Figure 12.2). The wall half-hid the outdoor privy, nestled in the corner of the stable yard, and the wall was in turn concealed by a continuous screen of bushes and trees. (Thus hidden, the wall and privy are not visible in any old photograph.)

The main house was a five-bay, bilaterally symmetrical structure with a central hallway. Floor-to-ceiling windows, utilized to make the most of cool gulf breezes during the hot summers, were perfectly balanced on each side of the exterior. However, one of these was a "faux

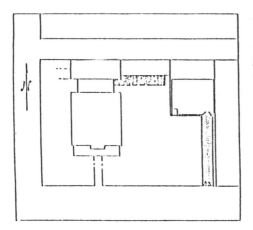

Figure 12.2: Plan showing Ashton Villa as it was designed by James Moreau Brown. Structures were placed so as to create an overall sense of balance and symmetry.

window," which provided additional interior wall space while maintaining the classical symmetry on the exterior facade.

Sanborn maps indicated that the kitchen/quarters structure was not as wide as the main house, offsetting it on the west side. Excavation results, however, once more demonstrated that the thesis of consistent bilateral symmetry during the initial phase of occupation was maintained in the actual construction. Cast iron steps to a kitchen/quarters porch (not shown on the Sanborn maps) were exposed by excavation, positioned to align perfectly with the west wall of the main house. The stable/carriage house on the east side of the site was identical in size and plan to the kitchen/quarters, maintaining the balance and symmetry of the site. Shortly after these structures were built, Brown connected the main house to the kitchen/quarters building with a vaulted-ceiling family room, extending the central hallway axis of symmetry of the main structure.

Excavations disclosed that all the original walkways were laid parallel or at right angles to the wall lines of the structures (Figure 12.2). This pattern of rectilinearity was later broken, as the original walkways were modified. The modifications followed a different model: The paths now arced or angled obliquely away from the structures. The grade-raising following the 1900 storm covered the original walks with fill. Above these original paths, new walkways were built on the fill surface. These constructions likewise were covered by more recent fill; when exposed in excavation, they were found to conform to the later, nonrectilinear model. They were also radically different in pattern and workmanship (Figure 12.3).

Typically the newer walkways were laid in simpler patterns (running bond rather than herringbone, for example) and exhibited a much lower degree of masonry skill than the work directed by J. M. Brown. The relative thickness and more careless application of mortar in the joints of these later constructions illustrate the importance of construction detail in comprehending the history of alteration at the site. In this case, the declining quality of the latest constructions also provides material verification of the declining fortunes of the Brown family after the turn of the century.

The second major phase of construction, undertaken during the last decade of the 19th century, reflected the total abandonment of the model of bilateral symmetry (Figure 12.4). Brown's daughter, Bettie, planned and supervised this work, which included the construction of a three-story, multisided wing added to the east side of the main house, a narrow high-ceilinged solarium on the west side of the family room, and a long greenhouse on the east side of the family room extending midway along the length of the arcade connecting the kitchen and carriage house. Bettie Brown also extended the carriage house forward toward the street with an offset ell, and added a third story to the structure. As mentioned above, the walkways were extended, modified, and then built anew after the grade raising. In every case, these new pathways curved or angled away from the structures. Thus, the exterior-built environment was again fully in harmony with the prevailing cultural themes.

The abandonment of the symmetrical model extended to interior fixtures: Inside the house, even the fireplaces evidence Bettie Brown's sense (conscious or not) of the communicative power of the built environment. In her own sitting room, where she often entertained, Bettie surmounted the mantlepiece with an asymmetrical arrangement of shelves and mirror (Figure 12.5).

By the beginning of the 20th century, the Brown family had become almost wholly dependent on "reputation" and the reinforcing physical symbol of their home to maintain their elite status. Bettie Brown and her siblings were not able to maintain their father's wealth or power. One son committed suicide, another died, and Bettie was no doubt hard-pressed to maintain her prestige. Indeed, late in life she appears to have abandoned her efforts, severing her ties to the elite Trinity Episcopal Church and, as a Catholic, becoming involved in charity work, especially with indigent mothers.

J. M. Brown had fully conformed to Jefferson's egalitarian ideal of architecture when he adopted its central tenets of symmetry, balance, and geometrical proportions in the floor and site plans of Ashton Villa. However, he made a tentative, incomplete departure from the model in

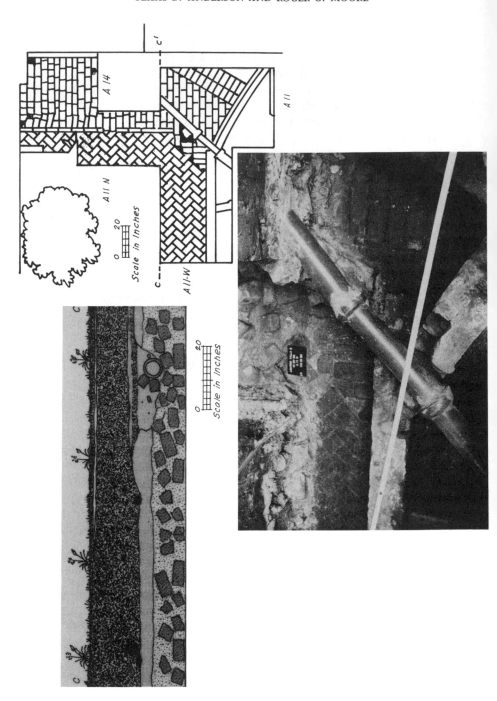

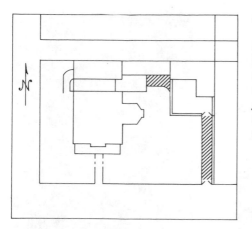

Figure 12.4: Plan showing Ashton Villa in 1899 as it was remodeled by Miss Bettie Brown. Main house has a new wing on the east side; family room has curved glass-enclosed room on west side and a greenhouse attached on the east side; carriage house and walkways were extended or altered.

utilizing Italianate embellishments. The presence of decorative elements that had already been identified for some years with the wealthy class on the East Coast presages the more flamboyant expressions of economic superiority that were to follow shortly. In her turn, Bettie Brown's wholesale modifications to the estate plan reflect the final relinquishment of the bonds of homogeneity, "modesty," and restraint that denied the existence of social hierarchy under the classical idiom.

CONCLUSIONS

Wobst (1977:324-28) has argued that stylistic messages conveyed in "visual mode" predict behavior and "broadcast the potential advantages or disadvantages to be realized" from an association. He maintains that stylistic messages "mark, maintain, and further the differences between . . . different socio-economic groups." This chapter has sought to demonstrate, by example, that symbolic interpretation of material remains—here, the built environment—is a valid and fruitful

Figure 12.3: Unit A-11. Plan and profile shows Units A-11, A-11 west, A-11 north, and A-14 (in upper corner). Profile shows section through A-11 units looking north.

Figure 12.5: Even the fireplaces at Ashton Villa reveal cognitive changes. Original symmetrical plan has been retained in the bedroom fireplace (left). However, the fireplace (right) in Miss Bettie's sitting room got an asymmetrical facelift in the late 1890s.

avenue for archaeological analysis. The study has asserted that the built environment is more than merely shelter; it is an explicit, conscious expression of communication in the "visual mode," an information system conveying meaning regarding status and reflecting prevailing cultural ideologies.

James M. Brown recreated the classical format in both his site and house plans, undoubtedly "proclaiming independence in order to promote personal freedom and individual liberty," as Leone (1984: 147–52) has argued in regard to William Paca and his garden. Brown thus placed himself, and his home, squarely within the ideology of Jeffersonian democracy. The commanding thesis of the egalitarian ideology, embodied visually in this classical architectural canon, was of restraint and denial. In order to deny that a social hierarchy existed that was incompatible with egalitarian democracy, architecture was restrained in the expression of success and social status. The abandonment of this restraint in the American culture and its native architecture is evidenced in both the life-"style" of Bettie Brown and her alterations to the Brown home; her actions in these spheres are forceful demonstrations of the transition to an era commonly known as the "Age of Excess" (Ginger 1965).

REFERENCES CITED

Allgeyer, Rebekah Brown Ratcliffe
   n.d.   Daughters of the American Revolution Application, no. 594066
          (6-048-LA). Washington, D.C.

Alperin, L. M.
   n.d.   *Custodians of the Coast*. Galveston: U.S. Army Corps of Engineers,
          Galveston District, Tex.

Anderson, Texas B.
   1985   Cognitive Structures, Status, and Cultural Affiliation: The Archae-
          ology of Ashton Villa. Ph.D., diss., Rice University, Houston, Tex.
          Ann Arbor, Mich.: University Microfilms.

Brown Family Papers
          Manuscript materials on file at the Rosenburg Library, Galveston,
          Tex.

Brown, James Moreau III
   n.d.   Brown Family genealogy compiled by James Moreau Brown III.
          Manuscript on file at the Rosenburg Library, Galveston, Tex.

Childe, V. Gordon
   1964   *What Happened in History*. Baltimore, Md. Penguin Books.

Davidson, M. B.
   1971   *The American Heritage History of Notable American Houses*. New
          York: American Heritage.

Deetz, James F.
   1977   *In Small Things Forgotten: The Archaeology of Early American Life*.
          New York: Anchor Books.
   1978   A Cognitive Historical Model for American Material Culture:
          1620–1835. In *Historical Archaeology: A Guide to Substantive and
          Theoretical Contributions*, ed. R. L. Schuyler, pp. 284–86.
          Farmingdale, N.Y.: Baywood.

Drozdowski, Eugene C.
   1972   Editor's Introduction to "Why the Greek Revival Succeeded, and
          Why It Failed," by Talbot Hamlin. In *American Civilization: Read-
          ings in the Cultural and Intellectual History of the United States,* ed.
          Eugene C. Drozdowski, p. 136. Glenview, Ill.: Scott, Foresman.

Fischer, John L.
   1971   Art Styles as Cultural Cognitive Maps. In *Anthropology and Art*, ed.
          Charlotte M. Otten, pp. 141–61. Garden City, N.J.: Natural His-
          tory Press.

Fitch, J.M.
1966   *American Building 1: The Historic Forces That Shaped It.* Boston: Houghton Mifflin.

Ginger, Ray
1965   *The Age of Excess.* New York: Macmillan.

Glassie, Henry
1979   *Folk Housing in Middle Virginia: A Structural Analysis of Historic Artifacts.* Knoxville: University of Tennessee Press.

Goeldner, P.
1974   *Texas Catalog: Historic American Buildings Survey.* San Antonio, Tex.: Trinity University Press.

Graham, S.B., and Ellen Newan (eds.)
n.d.   *Galveston Community Book.* Galveston, Tex.: A. H. Cawston.

Hardy, D. H., and I. S. Roberts
1910   *Historical Review of Southeast Texas.* Chicago: Lewis.

Hayes, C. W.
1974   *Galveston: History of the Island and the City.* Austin, Tex.: Jenkins Garrett Press. (Reprint of 1879 edition.)

Henson, Margaret S.
1976   *Samuel May Williams, Early Texas Entrepreneur.* College Station: Texas A&M University Press.

Hodder, Ian C.
1982   Theoretical Archaeology: A Reactionary View. In *Symbolic and Structural Archaeology*, ed. Ian Hodder, pp. 1–16. Cambridge: Cambridge University Press.

Jarves, James Jackson
1966   From "The Art-Idea" (1864). In *The Literature of Architecture: The Evolution of Architectural Theory and Practice in Nineteenth Century America*, ed. Don Gifford, pp. 251–69. New York: E. P. Dutton.

Kus, Susan
1984   The Spirit and Its Burden: Archaeology and Symbolic Activity. In *Marxist Perspectives in Archaeology*, ed. M. Spriggs, pp. 101–107. Cambridge: Cambridge University Press.

Leone, Mark P.
1982   Childe's Offspring. In *Symbolic and Structural Archaeology*, ed. I. Hodder, pp. 179-84. Cambridge: Cambridge University Press.
1984   Interpreting Ideology in Historical Archaeology: Using the Rules of Perspective in the William Paca Garden in Annapolis, Mary-

land. In *Ideology, Power, and Prehistory*, ed. D. Miller and C. Tilley, pp. 25–35., Cambridge: Cambridge University Press.

Lockwood, C.
1972 *Bricks and Brownstones: The New York Row House, 1783–1929, An Architectural and Social History*. New York: McGraw Hill.

Menig, D.W.
1975 *Imperial Texas*. Austin: University of Texas Press.

Miller, D., and C. Tilley
1984 Ideology, Power, and Long-Term Social Change. In *Ideology, Power, and Prehistory*, ed. D. Miller and C. Tilley, pp. 147–52. Cambridge: Cambridge University Press.

National Association for the Advancement of Colored People, Galveston Branch
1980 Letter to the general public from National Association for the Advancement of Colored People, Galveston Branch. Ashton Villa File, Rosenburg Library. Galveston, Tex.

Pessen, Edward
1973 The Egalitarian Myth and the American Social Reality in the Era of the Common Man. In *An Interdisciplinary Approach to American History*, ed. Ari and Olive Hoogenboom, vol. 1, pp. 204–18. Englewood Cliffs, N.J.: Prentice-Hall.

Philadelphia City Directory
1825 Philadelphia: Philadelphia Atheneum.
1833 Philadelphia: Philadelphia Atheneum.

Poppeliers, John
1976–77 *What Style Is It?* Washington, D.C.: Preservation Press, National Trust for Historic Preservation.

Ramsdell, Charles W.
1934 The Texas State Military Board, 1862–1865. *Southwestern Historical Quarterly* 40(2): 253

Robinson, Willard P.
1981 *Gone from Texas: Our Lost Cultural Heritage*. College Station: Texas A&M University Press.

Sloan, S.
1859 *City and Suburban Architecture*. Philadelphia: Lippincott.

Thompson, Deborah
1976 *Main Forms of American Architecture*. Camden, Maine: Down East Magazine.

Tocqueville, Alexis de
1945   *Democracy in America.* New York: Vintage Press.

Trigger, Bruce G.
1984   *Archaeology at the Crossroads: What's New. Annual Review of Anthropology.* Vol. 13, pp. 275–300. Palo Alto, Calif.: Annual Reviews.

Tyler, Stephen A.
1978   *The Said and The Unsaid: Mind, Meaning, and Culture.* New York: Academic Press.

Webb, William P.
1952   *The Handbook of Texas.* Austin: Texas State Historical Association.

Weems, J.E.
1980   *A Weekend in September.* College Station: Texas A&M University Press.

Wheeler, K.
1968   *To Wear a City's Crown: The Beginnings of Urban Growth in Texas, 1836–1865.* Cambridge, Mass.: Harvard University Press.

Wobst, H.M.
1977   Stylistic Behavior and Information Exchange. In *For the Director: Research Essays in Honor of James B. Griffin*, ed. C.E. Cleland, pp. 317–42. University of Michigan, Museum of Anthropology, Anthropological Paper no. 61., Ann Arbor: University of Michigan, Museum of Anthropology.

Wooster, R.
1967   Wealthy Texans, 1860. *Southwestern Historical Quarterly* 71:163–80.
1970   Wealthy Texans, 1870. *Southwestern Historical Quarterly,* 76(1): 24–35.

CHAPTER 13

Steps to an
Archaeology of Capitalism
Material Change and Class Analysis

ROBERT PAYNTER

One of the central problems of historical archaeology is understanding why the world's material culture exploded in the 18th, 19th, and 20th centuries into a bewildering array of new forms in vast quantities (Deetz 1973:36–37). In particular, historical archaeologists have concerned themselves with the objects of domestic life, ceramics, food, utensils, houses, and gardens, leaving the realms of work to industrial archaeologists. Among historical archaeologists the changing mentalities and sensibilities associated with the material world of domestic life have been a major research focus (e.g., Deetz 1977; Glassie 1976; Leone 1984). One approach to these past mentalities uses structural analyses to uncover the grammars for constructing senses of individuals, families, and society, coded in the things of everyday life. Another approach studies the emerging ideology of the capitalist mode of production as symbolized in the new physical world of the 18th and 19th centuries. Although these studies of the meaning of the material world of early modern North America, and its transformation to modern North America, have produced novel and intriguing insights, they by and large do not suggest what, if anything, changes in the sensibilities from the realm of capitalist work might have to do with changes in the domestic sphere.

The central focus of this chapter is to present a framework for understanding the material and organizational changes in production of the 18th and 19th centuries. The framework is general and the intent is to make sense out of the increasing volume and the increasing standardization of material culture encountered in the archaeological record. The framework is one of class analysis, and I focus in particular on the imperatives that led owners to reorganize and industrialize work, especially during the 19th century. In presenting this framework, I discuss how it is useful and provocative for studying the data and theory of historical archaeology.

I am thus concentrating on the ideas, practices, and things of the realm of work. This by no means supercedes understandings of changing ideologies that arise from studies of the material of the domestic realm. In fact, my brief illustrations will draw on these same objects and assemblages. Insights into these domestic assemblages can be gained by remembering that people spent increasing amounts of their lives working under the imperatives of the capitalist wage relation, and that the objects used in the domestic realm were increasingly produced in accordance with these same imperatives. It is my position that understandings of the domestic world might be enhanced by a better understanding of the forces affecting capitalist production. The following is thereby an offer and challenge to conduct class analyses using the data of historical archaeology, not a finished analysis. As a result, points are illustrated with reconsiderations of already familiar analyses; detailed and rich case studies are still premature.

I present my argument in three steps. First, I briefly review the traditional theories of material change and note their limitations for the task. Second I outline some of the characteristics of class models of capitalism, especially where they touch on issues of material culture and its change. Third, I consider some of the contributions historical archaeology can make to choosing between these models and stimulating the development of new ones.

MODELS OF CHANGE IN MATERIAL CULTURE

Three general approaches are used to explain material change in historical archaeology. The first, and most familiar, is the idealist approach. Idealist models consider culture to be the learned norms of a society and material culture to be the concrete manifestation of cultural templates. Change in the material culture results from change in the norms and ideals. Prominent examples of this line of argument are found in Deetz's (1977) and Glassie's (1975) studies of material change.

The second approach popular with historians of technology (e.g.

Habakkuk 1962; Temin 1971; Rosenberg 1972, 1981; Smith 1977, 1981; Ferguson 1981; Mayr and Post 1981) and some historical archaeologists, uses models of markets to account for material change. In particular, the production of material objects is said to follow the dictates of supply and demand. Culture may be reduced to an effect of attempts to maximize return, as in formalist models, or may be considered an externality that constrains the plan of the market forces in substantivist versions. Historical archaeologists (e.g., Adams 1976, 1977; Spencer-Wood 1979) have used the market approach to account for assemblage change associated with the growth and expansion of the national market.

The third approach assumes that class relations are the basis for understanding cultural and material change. Models based on this assumption posit a condition of social inequality between the controllers of access to strategic resources (such as land, tools, food, housing, clothing, and so on) and those who have to give up surplus production to gain access to these strategic resources. Change in material culture, it is argued, results from the dynamic implicit in the interactions between elites and nonelites over the production and extraction of social surplus. The central relationship affecting recent North American culture change is that between capitalists and workers. Historical archaeologists such as South (1972) and Schuyler (1970) have pointed out the importance of examining the workings of capitalism in studying the material record, although as yet only a few analysts have attempted to make detailed use of class models of capitalism (cf. Leary 1980; Leone 1984; Handsman 1985; McGuire 1985; Paynter 1985).

Each of these three approaches has its merits and its problems. A major contribution of the idealist models is the order that they have given to historical material data. Their proponents have developed the basic artifact typologies, noted the salient spatial and temporal trends, and given the discipline significant questions to answer (e.g. Noël Hume 1973; Deetz and Dethlefsen 1965; Glassie 1975; Deetz 1977). Although effective at ordering the data and raising questions, the idealist approach lacks explanatory power. That the numbers of things and their standardization increases is strongly substantiated. Why this trend occurs is generally attributed to the change to a post-Renaissance, post-Imperial, individualized culture order (Deetz 1977; Glassie 1975: 176–93). But why these factors work together, why the material world changes so drastically—these remain open questions.

Market models have been less widely applied to the archaeological record and have had less impact on questions or analytic methods. They are superior to idealist models in that they suggest conditions for technological change. Generally, qualitative and quantitative change is driven by increasing demand, which in turn arises from an increasing population that is more easily reached because of decreasing transport cost (e.g., Lorrain 1968:35; Baugher-Perlin 1982:282; Gorman 1982; Lewis 1984; Miller and Sullivan 1984:83). Supply-side problems, especially those regarding technical production—such as the use of selenium in glass decolorization (Miller and Pacey 1985:44–45) or the introduction of bottle machines in response to the need for standardized bottles for automatic filling machines (Miller and Sullivan 1984:89) —are seldom used to account for technological change. Finally, a major use of market models has been to study assemblage variation at sites of consumption (rather than production). The results have led to a better understanding of the size and scale of the modern economy (South 1972; Adams 1976, 1977; Elliott 1977; Spencer–Wood 1979; Miller 1980; Baugher-Perlin 1982:280–288; Hill 1982).

It is not so much that market theories are wrong, for in some situations changing demand and the search for optimal returns do account for technical change. Rather, their incompleteness is a problem. Explanations depending upon demand do not explain why demand increases; population growth is exogenous to the market forces, and declining transport costs are usually invoked as teleological tendencies. Production explanations explain technological change in terms of substituting technology for labor and thereby cutting costs. But, as Rosenberg (1976:109) points out, these models are theoretically incapable of explaining why the factor of labor costs, in the equilibrial firm, is the target for cost reduction. Unless this question is answered, the problem is addressed once again through exogenous factors, such as abundant land and mobile labor (Lazonick 1981:492).

In addition, an exclusive focus on the market beclouds the central issue at hand—how did the market expand itself into so many relations of daily life? Or, put another way, why did the inhabitants of North America adopt mass-produced items into their everyday world? Numerous studies by social historians abundantly confirm that other forces along with market forces affected the material life of recent North America (e.g., Merrill 1977; Henretta 1978; Clark 1979; Lemon 1980) and made the recent past different from the present. Understanding the articulation of lineal families, reciprocal communities, and imperial governments with various kinds of markets constitutes a major theoretical and empirical problem (Adams 1977:79, 86–87), one too easily ignored if only the play of supply and demand is considered (e.g., see Godelier 1977:32–51 for a general critique of this approach). In short, market forces played a major role in structuring the recent past, and market models are necessary, but they alone cannot account for the massive changes in our data.

Class models start with an assumption that surprises few anthropologists, namely that the Northwest European–North American society was stratified. Technological change results from the struggle between elites and nonelites over the perpetuation of the stratified social order. These struggles play themselves out in a number of realms, including the economy (Marx 1967), ideology (Schneider 1979; Therborn 1980; Leone 1984; Handsman 1985), politics (Szatmary 1980; Nobles 1983), society (Cott 1977), and space (Lemon 1980; Paynter 1982). As Lazonick (1981a:492) points out in his study of the adoption of self-acting mules, class models do not exclude market forces, but encompass them in a broader understanding of the economy. No widely accepted, distinctive ordering of the data of historical archaeology has emerged from these models (see Paynter 1982 for some attempts with spatial data), nor have their limits been adequately identified. In short, their major drawback is that class models have, by and large, been ignored.

The reason that class models of capitalism have been ignored and that they have recently come into vogue would make an intriguing study in contemporary ideology. In this regard, simply note that the proposition that U.S. society is capitalist is in itself controversial. The word *capitalism* is rarely used in historical archaeology to discuss the system under study, and historical archaeologists are not alone in this regard. Bowles, Gordon, and Weisskopf (1983:33) note that "few used to speak about 'capitalism' during the boom years (of the 1950s and 1960s) because most took 'capitalism' for granted. The word has since been readmitted into polite company. Magazines ask 'Is Capitalism in trouble?' Business executives worry out loud about its future." One might add, historical archaeologists hold symposiums on the subject.

This chapter is not an attempt to elaborate an anthropology of historical archaeology. In the following I argue for the role of class models as competing explanatory approaches. They should have this status because they meet two criteria of potential scientific propositions—relevance and provocativeness. By relevance I mean that class models are tightly linked to the phenomena under study, or material culture. By provocativeness I mean that there is considerable room to apply this model to material culture and that by doing so, historical archaeologists will be able to refine class models. Class models fit this scientific bill, not only an ideological one.

In sum, the full range of interpretive approaches available to social scientists and historians is not found in historical archaeology, where idealist models and diffusionist explanations are the dominant, almost exclusive means of discourse, despite the logical problems and empirical oversights implicit in their application. Market models have a greater potential for explaining the ever-growing number of objects and variations in forms, although they too easily project the relevance of market forces into the past. The least used approach identifies capitalist class relations at the heart of recent cultural and material change. Since class models have received little attention, they are difficult to assess. Nonetheless, class models are relevant to historical archaeology, as discussed in the next section. Their provocativeness is examined later in the chapter. By arguing for the logical attraction of class models, I hope to provide grounds for their use in empirical analysis in the future. Only then will it be possible to fully assess the utility of class models.

CAPITAL AND MATERIAL CULTURE

An attractive aspect of class models for historical archaeologists is the central position accorded material culture. In other theories, the material world is derivative from other, more significant aspects of culture: For structural models material culture is an imperfect replica of deep mental templates; for market-based models, material culture is a correlate of optimizing behavior. In class models, particularly of capitalism, the material world figures as specific moments in the process of accumulating social surpluses. A brief presentation of the fundamental concepts of class analysis discloses the ontological significance of the material world.

A number of different class relations may shed light on a particular society. For example, the relations between masters and slaves, between serfs and lords, and between capitalists and workers may indicate how surpluses are extracted and why society changes (Marx 1964, 1973). In each of these instances, the elite follow distinctive strategies to extract surplus from the nonelite and the nonelite use distinctive strategies to resist the extraction of surplus (Resnick and Wolf 1979). By considering domination and resistance, the analyst is able to understand the construction of ideologies, social organizations, political-economic struggles, and for our purposes, material worlds characteristic of a particular amalgam of class relations.

Of immediate interest is the relation between capitalists and workers that underlies the capitalist mode of production. This relation and the resultant model of production will help to explain how the model of capitalist relations generates a material world of ever-increasing numbers and more standardized forms of things.

Capitalists own the means of production—raw materials, tools, factories, machines—but need to hire workers to produce objects. Workers, not owning the means of production, have to sell their ability to work—labor power—to the capitalist. The capitalist pays the worker a wage, and in return the worker produces commodities that are owned by the capitalist. The capitalist sells these commodities—pearlware tea sets, gravestones, patent medicine, houses—for a profit.

The exchange of labor power for wage, the production of commodities and profits, constitutes the circulation of capital. As Harvey (1982:20) notes, "Capital . . . should be defined as a process rather than a thing. The material manifestation of this process exists as a transformation from money into commodities back into money plus profit: M-C-(M+M')." Thus, capital takes on different forms at different moments of production. First, it is money in the hands of the capitalist. Next it is the labor power of the workers, raw material (e.g., clay, wood), and tools (e.g., kilns, wheels, molds). Next, the commodities (e.g., tea sets, pans, creamers) produced by the labor power. Finally, the circuit closes as money to cover the investment plus a profit returns to the hands of the capitalist (Mendel 1962; Marx 1967:146–76; Harvey 1982:39–74; Desai 1983:64).

The logical relevance of Marx's model of capitalism for studying the material world is fairly obvious. Capital, the process implicit in the relation between workers and owners, at times takes the form of material objects. Changes in the circuit of capital necessarily change the material world. Thus, the class model of capitalism is logically applicable to the data of historical archaeology.

Insights into why material culture increases in volume and changes in form will become apparent if one considers some of the problems encountered by the capitalist. The capitalist's main goal is to realize a profit. As Marx discovered, the origin of profit is the difference between what the capitalist pays the laborer for a wage and what the product brings when sold (Godelier 1977:23; Harvey 1982:24). In short, the capitalist may pay a very low wage, because many people seek work or because mechanization has replaced workers, and then sell the commodity at a high price and realize a large profit.

However, realizing a profit is no sure thing. Two groups, in particular, stand in any individual capitalist's path: competitors and workers. Other competitors are constantly trying to cut into our capitalist's market. If they do, our capitalist is left with unsold creamers, for instance, and therefore unrealized profits. The other source of trouble is the workers, who, upon noting the discrepancy between their wage and the price their labor receives as a commodity, try to increase their wage, thereby decreasing the capitalist's profit.

Material culture plays important roles in capitalists' attempts to fend off competitors and discipline workers. One way to deal with competitors is to find a market that has no competitors. For example, one might trade previously made commodities (such as glass beads) into previously untapped markets (among Native Americans), or one might develop new commodities (such as vacuum cleaners) for people already in the market (middle-class households). This solution is reflected in the appearance of new types of material culture in archaeological deposits. The problem with this solution is that competitors may find their way into these new markets, a prospect that gives rise to a second solution for fending off competitors.

The second solution is to produce large quantities of items that are less expensive. These flood the market and take business away from competitors who are producing relatively more expensive commodities. The competitors face a crisis, as their commodities are not being transformed to money plus profit. If the competitors cannot realize a profit, they go bankrupt and leave our first capitalist without any competition. From an archaeological perspective, this solution increases the volume of objects in the material world.

One important way that the capitalist can produce cheaper commodities is to make the workers produce more. Important tactics to increase worker productivity are to divide up the work so that each worker carries out a repetitive task and to mechanize production (Braverman 1974). Mechanizing production and dividing the labor serve to increase productivity by (1) making it possible to produce more objects per worker per day and (2) standardizing the labor process so that virtually anybody can do the job. The former helps the capitalist to capture markets by increasing the volume of commodities. The latter increases the potential pool of workers, threatening the employed workers with unemployment and thereby enabling the capitalist to temper workers' demands for higher wages. Thus, mechanizing production may simultaneously defeat competitors' and labors' demands on profit. In the archaeological record mechanization and division of labor are reflected in the machinery and factories of production and the standardized commodities produced for consumption.

By penetrating new markets and producing many cheap commodities with a mechanized production process, our capitalist may achieve success, but it will only be temporary. In the world of capital, some competitor is always trying to innovate and thereby capture the market, and the work force is always looking for ways to gain a larger share of the pie. They both create a constant pressure on the capitalist to find new machinery that produces ever more commodities and increasingly disciplines the work force. The result is only temporary success and can result in a material world that virtually explodes with objects produced in standardized forms.

In sum, class models using capitalist-worker relations are logically relevant for historical archaeology. Material culture, defined as commodities produced and the means of production, is the central component of models of capitalism in that the social relations of these models alter material culture. The result is an increasing volume and changing form, which are distinctive features of the record studied by historical archaeologists.

POTENTIAL FOR A HISTORICAL ARCHAEOLOGY OF CAPITALISM

Another important reason to consider models of capitalist class relations is their provocativeness: Do they help organize our data and are our data likely to refine the models? Several benefits can be gained from studying the historical material world with class models. One of these has to do with the presence and operation of temporal processes, which are a major concern of historical archaeologists, whose task is to discover temporal processes in changing types of artifacts, in changing frequencies of types, and in changing assemblage patterns. They use such processes to interpret cultural history. Class theorists are also interested in temporal processes, as predicted by their theories of capitalist crises and studied with statistics on production and prices. The temporal trajectories of archaeologists offer information on new aspects of the political economy for evaluating class theories of the ebb and flow of capitalism. In turn, theory offers some alternative explanations for change to the limited ones presently in use.

These potential contributions can be better understood by matching some temporal patterns discussed in historical archaeology with class theories of capitalist expansion. Various periodizations have been developed by class theorists to describe capitalist growth (e.g. Research Working Group 1979; Gordon 1980; Gordon, Edwards, and Reich, 1983; Wallerstein 1984). These periodizations are usually analyzed as cyclical processes of varying duration, which makes it possible to classify them into three groups. Some, such as business cycles, last a relatively short period, on the order of 1–15 years, and are associated with overproduction that is cleared without seriously transforming the political economy. Cycles that fall in the middle range are called Kondratieffs and last about 50 years, which is long enough to see the development of new tactics for extracting and resisting the extraction of social surplus. The third group—logistics, or trend seculaire—comprises cycles on the order of 200–300 years. During these periods the dominant class relations are rearranged as are the concomitant social, political, and ideological structures supporting the class relations.

The empirical and theoretical aspects of these cycles have been studied by class theorists and neoclassical economists alike (e.g., Mandel 1975:122–39; Barr 1979; Pomian 1979; Research Working Group 1979:490–92). Many earlier theorists (e.g., Luxemburg 1951; Kondratieff 1979) hypothesized that single, economic factors are the cause of these cycles, whereas empirical workers searched for a set of symmetrical cycles, each with a uniform amplitude and period. More recent class theorists (e.g., Mandel 1975:145; Research Working Group 1979; Gordon 1980; Gordon, Edwards, and Reich 1982:26–47) still see economic factors as the driving force behind business cycles, but they posit that a variety of other factors (including demographic growth and immigration, exploration, war and political hegemony, and ethnicity and enculturation) also affect Kondratieff and logistic cycles (Held 1983; Shaikh 1983). There is generally less interest in symmetrical cycles now, as analysts are instead searching for asymmetrical periods of expansion and contraction on roughly the scales of the business, Kondratieff, and logistic cycles.

The Kondratieff and logistic cycles are particularly relevant to historical archaeology. They result from a substantial reorganization of social relations, which, when realigned generate significantly different production and consumption practices. These systemic changes in production and consumption altered the material world. Data from archaeological contexts might be analyzed with and thereby affect models explaining Kondratieff and logistic cycles. Some brief examples point to the potential for more detailed studies.

Of these two cycles, Kondratieff cycles have received the most theoretical and empirical attention. Most class theorists agree that the rise in the rate of profit signals a period of expansion (an A phase) and that decline in the rate of profit indicates a period of contraction (a B phase). Two economic forces are usually implicated in the cyclical expansions and contractions: (1) the squeeze that workers can put on profits and (2) the stagnating effects of unbridled capitalist competition (Gordon 1980:13; Gordon, Edwards, and Reich, 1982:34; Shaikh 1983). Profit-squeeze theories have been used to study the former, and overproduction/underconsumption theories to study the latter.

As noted in the preceding section, workers can demand higher wages and back up their demands with collective bargaining and strikes, thereby creating a squeeze on profits (Bowles, Gordon, and Weisskopf 1983:62–97, 122–33; Shaikh 1983:137–43). Workers can have their greatest impact during times of economic expansion and full employment for in a period of boom capitalists are unable to bring the threat of unemployment to bear on their negotiations with workers. As times get better, the capitalists' ability to realize a profit may erode,

economic booms may turn into busts, and the Kondratieff cycle continues.

Overproduction/underconsumption theories are crisis theories
that emphasize relations between capitalists (Sweezy 1942:133–236;
Shaikh 1983:137–143;Harvey 1982:190–203). According to these theories, when capitalists compete for markets, they are forced to produce
commodities. Competition is said to be a more compelling factor than
consumer demand alone in driving capitalists to expand production.
Since supply is driven by more than demand, it is possible to saturate
the market and still have capitalists turning out more and more in their
efforts to outcompete one another. The general tendency, then, will be
to overproduce commodities. However, because of the relative excess
of commodities, not all of them will be sold, and commodities will sit
on shelves. This means the same level of production need not be maintained; as a result workers will be laid off, excess money will look for
scarce investments, factories will be empty, and capitalists will fail to
realize a profit. Capitalists can use various tactics to improve their situation in periods of economic decline. For example, they can slow down
production and wait for inventories to clear, or they can eliminate inef-
ficient producers by buying them out (and thus devaluing their inventory), bring new cheap laborers into wage labor (as this devalues labor
and provides demand for labors' reproduction, a process also known as
deepening capitalist penetration), reorganize the workplace to increase
productivity, or penetrate new markets (Gordon, Edwards, and Reich
1982:19–20; Harvey 1982:190–203).

These theories on Kondratieff cycles have been used to periodize
American history. One such study by Gordon, Edwards and Reich
(1982:9) offers the following pattern for periods of expansion and contraction:

	Expansion	Contraction
1790	1820	Mid-1840s
Mid-1840s	ca. 1873	Late 1890s
Late 1890s	World War I	World War II
World War II	Early 1970s	?

Gordon, Edwards, and Reich (1982) suggest that the crises in these
cycles were resolved by altering the nature of capitalist work. Looking
at the contraction periods, the crisis of the second quarter of the 19th
century, for example, was resolved by reorganizing the work force into
factory production. The crisis of the late 19th century was resolved by
homogenizing labor, which entailed disciplining workers and mechanizing production. The segmentation of the labor market into well-

417

paid, unionized, white men and poorly paid, nonunion, nonwhite men and women was instrumental in solving the crisis of the 1930s and generating the postwar prosperity.

Two tactics for resolving Kondratieff crises—reorganizing the workplace and penetrating new markets—often involve changes in the material world. Braverman (1974:184–235) offers an extensive treatment of how technology was used to de-skill and thereby control workers in factories. The variety of forms of factory organization have clear spatial as well as technical implications, as presented in Clawson's (1980:54–70) analysis of the internal organization of factories. Studies such as these usually rely on accounts of technical and spatial relations, or on the occasionally well-preserved tool or worksite. Undoubtedly, documents and well-preserved objects reflect biases of observers' interests and preservation. Archaeological studies of workplaces, technology, and wasters should supplement these studies to disclose the variation in owners' use of objects to enforce production discipline as well as assessments of the efficacy of these tactics.

Penetrating new markets is also an important tactic for resolving overproduction/underconsumption crises. As already mentioned, this means finding whole new areas of the world in which to sell goods (i.e., expanding the market) or finding new realms of life that can make use of commodities (i.e., deepening the market). An example of the expansionary process is the export of British ceramics, textiles, and metal goods to the colonies in the 18th century. An example of the deepening process is the introduction of technology into middle- and upper-class households in the late 19th century (Hayden 1981).

Archaeological middens bear witness to the use of these two tactics, as shown in studies of the spatial distribution of the appearance of commodities (e.g., Adams 1976, 1977; Spencer-Wood 1979; Schuyler 1980). However, these studies could be expanded upon in two important ways. First, changing assemblage patterns could be linked to the existence and resolution of overproduction crises. Such studies would have to examine the timing of the replacement of folk-manufactured items by commodities and its correlation to overproduction/underconsumption crises. Second, these studies could include areas outside North America. Similar analyses could be conducted abroad (e.g., Thorbahn 1979) to investigate such questions as When do European ceramics and metal objects appear in East and West Africa, in South and East Asia? Is the initial penetration a trickle of the same "colonizing" types of artifacts, or do entire assemblages suddenly replace old objects?

There is just as much potential for archaeology to contribute to the study of the tactic of reorganizing the workplace. Marx (1967:436), for instance, notes that "it would be possible to write quite a history of the inventions, made since 1830, for the sole purpose of supplying capital with weapons against the revolts of the working-class." This could be supported with preliminary analyses of class-related changes in power generation, textile manufacture, and glass production.

Marx's suggestions have only recently gained attention in the work of historians of technology, who have applied them in systematic studies of early industrialization. For instance, Bruland's (1982) studies of the textile industry demonstrate how capitalists used technology to undermine the position of workers. Strikes often were the immediate impetus for these developments, as Richard Roberts, developer of the first effective self-acting mule noted (cited in Bruland 1982:103): "The self-acting mule was made in consequence of a turnout of spinners at Hyde [in 1824], which had lasted three months, when a deputation of masters waited upon me, and requested me to turn my attention to spinning, with the view of making the mule self-acting."

Similar profit squeezes—in the form of strikes, sabotage, and low productivity by the strong early 19th-century Union of Block Printers and the Wool Combers Union—led to the development of cylindrical calico printers and mechanized wool combing machines, respectively (Bruland 1982:110–11, 115–16). Lazonick (1981a,b,c), who has also studied the textile industry notes that the United States adopted spinning much faster than Britain. He attributes this difference to the differences in the relations between labor and management in the two countries (Lazonick 1981a:514–15, 1981b), although this interpretation is at odds with some other class theorists (1981c). In an exemplary study, MacKenzie (1984) offers an excellent review of class theories of machines along with case studies. Like the textile examples, the development of the Fourdrinier paper-making machine and moulding machines at the McCormick works can be traced to capitalists' attempts to avoid worker-generated profit squeezes (see also Rosenberg 1976; Winner 1980).

Archaeological investigations could contribute to such studies in a number of ways. For example, investigations of production sites classically describe industrialization trajectories (e.g., Rutsch and Rutsch 1975; Starbuck 1983:49,60). By carefully dating these trajectories and setting them in their labor contexts, archaeologists could shed light on the forces surrounding innovation and adoption. Similarly, the temporal redesign of factories and changing character of wastes should provide data on attempts by capitalists to reorganize the work process (Thompson 1967) and attempts by workers to resist through low productivity and sabotage (e.g., Slater 1980).

The detailed temporal trajectories that have been established in historical archaeology—such as Noël Hume's work on a variety of materials (1969), especially on ceramics (e.g., 1973); Lorrain's (1968) seminal glass trajectory; Anderson's (1968) shoe study; and so on—provide another important contribution to historical archaeology. Rarely are these trajectories explained, and yet the increasing use of molds and machines that create the temporally diagnostic attributes raise the possibility that capitalist–worker conflicts may underlie these innovations as well.

A particularly telling example comes from the North American glass industry. Historical archaeologists make use of glass, particularly bottles, in dating sites. Attributes on glass, particularly seams from molds, are evidence of the process used to produce the objects (e.g., Lorrain 1968). Three basic processes are responsible for the bulk of glass containers: free-blowing, in which human labor gathers the molten glass, mechanically forces the rough shaping of glass to its initial form, and fine finishing of the shape to its final hardened form; automatic production, in which machines gather, shape and finish the forms; and, processes that mix human labor and machine actions, exemplified by the use of molds and pressing machines. Bottles produced prior to the 19th century were predominantly made by free-blowing, and the bulk of the 20th century bottles were produced in automatic machines. The 19th century saw the development of molds, semiautomatic machines, and eventually, in the early 20th century, fully automatic machines. The fine details of these production shifts, and their traces on glassware are the subject of considerable research (e.g., Lorrain 1968; Miller and Sullivan 1984; Miller and Pacey 1985).

Although changing glass attributes are significant for addressing issues of chronology, they also raise questions about the causes of technological change. When historical archaeologists have probed this issue, they have generally relied on market explanations. For instance, Lorrain (1968:35) attributes the growing popularity of techniques, such as the use of molds in the 19th century, to "the development of mass transportation systems which opened new markets among the ever expanding and growing population." The adoption of machinery in bottle production is variously attributed to demand-side factors, such as "the increasing market for glass containers" (Miller and Sullivan 1984:83) or the need to produce standardized forms for automatic filling machines (Miller and Sullivan 1984:86), and supply-side factors, such as the high cost of labor (Miller and Sullivan 1984:89).

A strikingly different perspective is offered by Marx (1967:436). He notes that " 'The relation of the master and the men in the blown-flint bottle trades amounts to a chronic strike.' Hence the impetus given to the manufacture of pressed glass, in which the chief operations are done by machinery." The extent of labor struggles is not well documented in the literature of historical archaeology, but it could be.

For instance, there are suggestions in Miller and Sullivan's (1984) innovative, detailed, and intriguing study of the adoption and effects of semiautomatic and automatic bottle machines in North America that class processes affected the adoption of this technology. For instance, they note that the semiautomatic machines patented by Abrogast and Ashley in the 1880s met with resistance from the glassblower's unions. It took over 10 years from the time Abrogast's machine was patented for it to be used in mass production, notably, in a nonunion shop (Miller and Sullivan 1984:85). The history of the Dominion Glass Company's adoption of fully automatic machines also suggests the play of class processes. The Dominion Glass Company, formed in 1913, was the dominant glass-producing firm in Canada with a "practical monopoly" on glass production (Miller and Sullivan 1984:92). Glassware was produced by hand and by automatic machines—an unexplained mix since, as Miller and Sullivan note (1984:92), the replacement of labor by machine production for this monopoly company was not driven by the intense competition seen in the United States. This raises the possibility that the motive for adopting automatic bottle machines was to control the skilled work force. Further evidence of the uneasy relation between the glassblowers and management is the lengthy strike in the 1930s, a strike that was broken and that contributed to the demise of hand glassblowing (Miller and Sullivan 1984:92).

These examples are suggestions. Obviously, they do not substitute for a full analysis of labor relations in the glass industry. It would be important to know, for example, if mechanization was a response to the control of a recalcitrant, skilled work force at the Dominion works. It would also be important to understand labor relations at glass manufactories in the United States. Furthermore, the history of labor relations at the smaller early 19th-century glassworks needs to be probed to understand the circumstances surrounding the adoption of molds and pressing machines. Detailed studies that combine documentary research and artifact analyses, such as those by Miller and his coauthors (Miller and Pacey 1985; Miller and Sullivan 1984), clearly point the way.

Other class-related lines of production are equally intriguing, although less well studied. For instance, one might investigate the increasing use of molded ceramics (Myers 1980:32) with respect to labor relations, as well as the role of the strong shoe unions (Dawley 1976) in the changes in shoe manufacture (e.g., Mulligan 1981; Anderson 1968). These and many other chronological trajectories call attention to major changes in lines of production that have not yet been studied by class theorists. An understanding of these changes would provide an independent basis for evaluating the effect of worker-generated profit squeezes and economic crises on material change.

Kondratieff cycles are understood as the restructuring of social and political relations within capitalist relations of production. In all-encompassing crises, the reordering must extend to the manner in which surplus is produced and extracted, as in the shift from feudalism to capitalism in the Early Modern Era. The cycle associated with these general crises and their resolution is the 200–300 year logistic. It, too, is amenable to archaeological interpretation.

Various periodizations have been offered for logistics, such as the following, which was developed by researchers at the Braudel Center (Research Working Group 1979:488; Wallerstein 1979:74):

	Rise	Decline
900	1100	1450
1450	1600	1750
1750	1950	?

Feudal relations in Europe are thought to have reached their peak between roughly 1100 and 1300. The crisis of feudalism beginning in the 14th century was resolved with the development of agricultural-capitalist relations, according to some observers (e.g., Wallerstein 1974,1980), or by the domination of mercantile relations within feudal relations, according to others (e.g., Wolf 1982; more generally see Hilton 1976; de Vries 1976; Cipolla 1976). A period of European expansion often referred to as the long 16th century is followed by a period of contraction, the long 17th century (Braudel and Spooner 1967; Frank 1978:25–102; Wallerstein 1979:74, 1980:13–34). The origins of the Industrial Revolution and the establishment of British hegemony in the mid to late 18th century mark the beginnings of the present logistic (Wallerstein 1980).

With respect to the work of long-term cycles, I have noted (Paynter 1985) that the changes in broad realms of material culture identified by Deetz (1977)—the yeoman, folk, and Georgian periods—coincide with economic declines of the long 17th century and the economic rise of the long 18th century. In particular, the close of Deetz's yeoman period, ca. 1650, not only coincides with the English Revolution and a change in the climate of religious dissent, but is just about the time that the 17th-century depression penetrated Northwestern Europe, and England in particular (Wallerstein 1980:18–25). The English spun their colonies into the Atlantic economy at an unfortunate

time, just about one generation before economic conditions would decline in England, so that little control could be exercised there and little
surplus extracted. The ensuing century, Deetz's folk period, was one of
competition in the core of the European world system between England, Holland, and France for political and economic hegemony in the
world system. However, relative isolation of North American elites allowed them to accumulate surpluses outside of the tight supervision
of the central authorities in England. The resolution of the core struggles in favor of England, along with industrialization, allowed and
necessitated a renewed interest in using the colonies as a source of raw
material and as a market for manufactured commodities (e.g., Frank
1978:167–80, 190–208; Wallerstein 1980:236–41). The period in which
Britain was able to turn to the colonies coincides with Deetz's Georgian
period. Elites in the colonies who could benefit by a strengthened connection to England—exporters of raw materials and agricultural products (dependency elites)—were set against those whose ability to accumulate surpluses would decline in the face of English control—such as
shipbuilders, some merchants, early industrialists, and indebted
planters (development elites) (Schneider, Schneider, and Hansen 1972;
Frank 1978:203,208; Nash 1979; Chase-Dunn 1980; Paynter 1985).

This rough correlation leads to more specific questions about the
connection between these political economic changes and the material
changes observed in the record. For instance, what is the amount of European material culture relative to "folk" items in the folk period? How
does this vary by region and class? What was the impact of North
American elites on the material record (see Carson and others 1981 on
housing) during this period, and can the dependency and development
strategies be seen in changing domestic consumption patterns (e.g.,
Mrozowski and Schmidt 1985)? Are the material changes of the Georgian world—symmetrically designed housing, full standardized table
services, and so on—responses to labor-control problems that had been
forming in the preceding period in England? Or can these changes be
better explained by models that rely less on capitalism and more on
household, lineal family, community, and feudal modes of production
(e.g., Clark 1979; Henretta 1978; Weiss 1982)? These are as yet unan-
swered questions, but ones that would not have been asked within the
theoretical paradigm of changing mind-sets. When answers to these
class-related issues can be found, they might help explain why people
made a different sense of the world after 1650 and 1750 (e.g., Leone
1984).

A mutual concern for temporal processes clearly points to a provocative relation between class theory and historical archaeology. I suspect that when the material record is interpreted with the notions of lo-

gistics and Kondratieff cycles, the overall results will support the general trends of class theory, namely that human labor tends to be replaced by machinery and that commodities tend to expand into more and more realms of life. Moreover, such interpretations will give a richer understanding to historical archaeology's culture histories.

I also suspect that the use of archaeological material will significantly alter some important aspects of class theories. These changes will be due to the fact that what people recorded is not necessarily what they did (e.g., Bowen 1975; Schuyler 1977). We will find that the plans for projects differ from their execution (e.g., Wilson 1976), that what people owned differs from what they ate (Bowen 1975; Garrison 1985), and that generally things are more different from their images than is presently acknowledged. Historical archaeology will also challenge class theories to look at industries that have not received much attention from economic historians, but that make up the archaeological record: the ubiquitous ceramics, glass, and architectural complex. It is important to know if crises occur in these industries at the same time that they occur in the better-studied realms of textiles, small arms production, and commerce. What may be accomplished by addressing these questions with the data of historical archaeology is what has so far eluded our grasp—a reasoned evaluation of the efficacy of class models for accounting for change in the material world. A better understanding of this issue would further both historical archaeology and class theoretical approaches.

CONCLUSION

Considering the United States as a capitalist society seems a project worth taking up, in spite of the high cost of learning yet another jargon. This approach puts a set of relevant ideas on the agenda and offers explanations for change in the record that are new and provocative. The fact that it has seldom been used is not due to scientific reasons but rather to ideological ones; the use I am advocating is based on its scientific potential—its relevance and provocativeness. I fully expect that, because of the differences in the material record and the documentary record, theories of capitalism, when applied to our record, will need to be refined. Our contributions to theories of change and resultant refinements in these theories will be in the best tradition of historical archaeology—which, according to Deetz (1977), is like trying to understand where today came from.

ACKNOWLEDGMENTS

Thanks to Art Keene, Randy McGuire, Dena Dincauze, Rick Gumaer, Russ Handsman, Mark Leone, Rita Reinke, Ellen Savulis, Daniel Walkowitz, and especially Martin Wobst and Patricia Mangan. A version of this paper was read at the 1984 Annual Meeting of the Council for Northeast Historical Archaeology.

REFERENCES CITED

Adams, W. H.
  1976   Trade Networks and Interaction Spheres—A View from Silcott. *Historical Archaeology* 10: 99–112.
  1977   *Silcott, Washington: Ethnoarchaeology of a Rural American Community.* Laboratory of Anthropology, Reports of Investigations, No. 54. Pullman, Washington.

Anderson, A.
  1968   The Archaeology of Mass-produced Footwear. *Historical Archaeology* 2: 56–65.

Barr, K.
  1979   Long Waves: A Selective Annotated Bibliography. *Review* 2: 675–718.

Baugher-Perlin, S.
  1982   Analyzing Glass Bottles for Chronology, Function and Trade Networks. In *Archaeology of Urban America*, ed. R. Dickens, pp. 259–90. New York: Academic Press.

Bowen, J.
  1975   Probate Inventories. *Historical Archaeology* 9: 11–25.

Bowles, S., D. M. Gordon, and T. Weisskopf
  1983   *Beyond the Waste Land.* Garden City, N.Y.: Anchor.

Braudel, F., and F. Spooner
  1967   Prices in Europe from 1450 to 1750. In *Cambridge Economic History of Europe, IV*, ed. E. E. Rich and C. H. Wilson, pp. 374–486. Cambridge: Cambridge University Press.

Braverman, H.
  1974   *Labor and Monopoly Capital.* New York: Monthly Review.

Bruland, T.
  1982   Industrial Conflict as a Source of Technical Innovation: Three cases. *Economy and Society* 11: 91–121.

Carson, C., N. F. Barka, W. M. Kelso, G. W. Stone, and D. Upton
    1981   Impermanent Architecture in the Southern American Colonies. *Winterthur Portfolio* 16: 135–96.

Chase-Dunn, C.
    The development of Core Capitalism in the Ante Bellum United States. In *Studies of the Modern World-System*, ed. A. Bergesen, pp. 189–230. New York: Academic Press.

Cipolla, C.
    1976   *Before the Industrial Revolution.* New York: Norton.

Clark, C.
    1979   Household Economy, Market Exchange, and the Rise of Capitalism in the Connecticut Valley, 1800–1860, *Journal of Social History* 13:169–89.

Clawson, D.
    1980   *Bureaucracy and the Labor Process.* New York: Monthly Review.

Cott, N.
    1977   *The Bonds of Womanhood: "Women's Sphere" in New England, 1780–1835.* New Haven, Conn.: Yale University Press.

Dawley, A.
    1976   *Class and Community: The Industrial Revolution in Lynn.* Cambridge, Mass.: Harvard University Press.

Deetz, J. F.
    1973   Ceramics from Plymouth, 1635–1835: The Archaeological Evidence. In *Ceramics in America,* ed. I. Quimby, pp. 15–40. Charlottesville: University Press of Virginia.
    1977   *In Small Things Forgotten.* New York: Anchor.

Deetz, J. F., and E. Dethlefsen
    1965   The Doppler Effect and Archaeology. *Southwestern Journal of Anthropology* 21:196–206.

Desai, M.
    1983   Capitalism. In *A Dictionary of Marxist Thought,* ed. T. Bottomore, pp. 64–67. Cambridge, Mass.: Harvard University Press.

de Vries, J.
    1976   *The Economy of Europe in an Age of Crisis, 1600–1750.* New York: Cambridge University Press.

Elliott, S. W.
    1977   *Historical Archaeology and the National Market: A Vermont Perspective, 1795–1920.* Ph.D. diss., University of Massachusetts, Amherst. Ann Arbor, Mich., University Microfilms, Order no. 77-13, 794.

Ferguson, E. S.
  1981   History and Historiography. In *Yankee Enterprise,* ed. O. Mayr and
          R. C. Post, pp. 1–24, Washington, D.C.: Smithsonian Institution
          Press.

Ferguson L.
  1985   Struggling with Pots in Colonial America. Paper Presented in the
          Symposium of The Archaeology of Domination and Resistance,
          chaired by R. Paynter and R. H. McGuire. Eighteenth Annual
          Meeting of the Society for Historical Archaeology. Boston, Mass.

Frank, A. G.
  1978   *World Accumulation, 1492–1789.* New York: Monthly Review.

Garrison, J. R.
  1985   Architecture as Cultural Information: The E. H. Williams House.
          Paper presented in the Symposium on the Archaeology of Inequal-
          ity, at the 25th Annual Conference of the Northeast Anthropological
          Association, Lake Placid, N.Y.

Glassie, H.
  1975   *Folk Housing in Middle Virginia.* Knoxville, Tenn.: University of
          Tennessee.

Godelier, M.
  1977   Anthropology and Economics. In *Perspectives in Marxist Anthropol-
          ogy,* ed. M. Godelier, pp. 15–62. New York: Cambridge University
          Press.

Gordon, D. M.
  1980   Stages of Accumulation and Long Cycles. In *Processes of the World-
          system,* ed. T. K. Hopkins and I. Wallerstein, pp. 9–45. Beverly
          Hills, Calif.: Sage.

Gordon, D. M., R. Edwards, and M. Reich
  1982   *Segmented Work, Divided Workers: The Historical Transformation of
          Labor in the U. S.* New York: Cambridge University Press.

Gorman, F. J. E.
  1982   Archaeological Implications of a Manufacturing Industry in
          Eighteenth-Century American Cities. In *Archaeology of Urban Amer-
          ica,* ed. R. Dickens, pp. 63–104. New York: Academic Press.

Habakkuk, H. J.
  1962   *American and British Technology in the Nineteenth Century.* Cambridge:
          Cambridge University.

Handsman, R.
  1985   Thinking about an Historical Archaeology of Alienation and Class

Struggles. Paper Presented in the Symposium on The Archaeology of Domination and Resistance, chaired by R. Paynter and R. H. McGuire at the Eighteenth Annual Meeting of the Society for Historical Archaeology. Boston, Mass.

Harvey, D.
1982   *The Limits to Capital.* Chicago: University of Chicago Press.

Hayden, D.
1981   *The Grand Domestic Revolution.* Cambridge, Mass.: MIT.

Held, D.
1983   Crisis in Capitalist Society. In *A Dictionary of Marxist Thought,* ed. T. Bottomore, pp. 102–105. Cambridge, Mass.: Harvard University Press.

Henretta, J.
1978   Families and Farms: Mentalité in pre-Industrial America. *William and Mary Quarterly* 35: 3–32.

Hill, S. H.
1982   An Examination of Manufacture-Deposition Lag for Glass Bottles from Late Historic Sites. In *Archaeology of Urban America,* ed. R. Dickens, pp. 291–327. New York: Academic Press.

Hilton, R. (ed.)
1976   *The Transition from Feudalism to Capitalism.* London: New Left Books.

Kondratieff, N. D.
1979   The Long Waves in Economic Life. *Review* 2: 519–62.

Lazonick, W.
1981a   Production Relations, Labor Productivity and Choice of Technique: British and U.S. Cotton Spinning. *Journal of Economic History* 41:491–516.
1981b   Factor Costs and the Diffusion of Ring Spinning in Britain prior to World War I. *Quarterly Journal of Economics* 96: 89–109.
1981c   Conflict and Control in the Industrial Revolution: Social Relations in the British Cotton Factory. In *Essays from the Lowell Conference on Industrial History, 1980 and 1981,* ed. R. Weible, O. Ford, and P. Morian, pp. 14–32. Lowell Conference on Industrial History, Lowell, Mass.

Leary, T. E.
1980   Industrial Archaeology and Industrial Ecology. *Radical History Review* 21: 171–82.

Lemon, J. T.
1980   Early Americans and Their Social Environments. *Journal of Histori-
        cal Geography* 6: 114–31.

Leone, M.
1984   Interpreting Ideology in Historical Archaeology: The William Paca
        Garden in Annapolis, Md. In *Ideology, Power and Prehistory*, ed. D.
        Miller and C. Tilley, pp. 25–36. New York: Cambridge University
        Press.

Lewis, K. E.
1984   *The American Frontier: An Archaeological Study of Settlement Pattern
        and Process*. Orlando, Fla.: Academic Press.

Lorrain, D.
1968   An Archaeologist's Guide to Nineteenth Century American Glass.
        Historical Archaeology 2: 35–44.

Luxemburg, R.
1951   *The Accumulation of Capital*. London: Routledge and Kegan, Paul.

MacKenzie, D.
1984   Marx and the Machine. *Technology and Culture* 25: 473–502.

Mandel, E.
1962   *Marxist Economic Theory*, Vol. 1. New York: Monthly Review.
1975   *Late Capitalism*. London: Verso.

Marx, K.
1964   *Pre-Capitalist Economic Formations*. New York: International.
1967   *Capital*. Vol. 1. New York: International.
1973   *Grundrisse*. New York: Vintage.

Mayr, O., and R. C. Post (eds.)
1981   *Yankee Enterprise: The Rise of the American System of Manufactures*.
        Washington, D.C.: Smithsonian Institution.

McGuire, R. H.
1985   Elite Responses to Resistance. Paper Presented in the Symposium
        on The Archaeology of Domination and Resistance, chaired by R.
        Paynter and R. H. McGuire at the Eighteenth Annual Meeting of
        the Society for Historical Archaeology. Boston, Mass.

Merrill, M.
1977   Cash is Good to Eat: Self-sufficiency and Exchange in the Rural
        Economy of the U.S. *Radical History Review* 19: 42–71.

Miller, G.
1980   Classification and Economic Scaling of Nineteenth-Century Ceram-
        ics. *Historical Archaeology* 14:1–40.

Miller, G., and A. Pacey
  1985   Impact of Mechanization in the Glass Container Industry: The Do-
          minion Glass Company of Montreal, a Case Study. *Historical Ar-
          chaeology* 19(1): 38–50.

Miller, G. L., and C. Sullivan
  1984   Machine-made Glass Containers and the End of Production for
          Mouth-blown Bottles. *Historical Archaeology* 18(2): 83–96.

Mrozowski, S., and P. Schmidt
  1985   The Relationship of Supply and Demand to Cycles of Dominance
          and Resistance. Paper Presented in the Symposium on The Archae-
          ology of Domination and Resistance, chaired by R. Paynter and R.
          H. McGuire at the Eighteenth Annual Meeting of the Society for
          Historical Archaeology. Boston, Mass.

Mulligan, W. H.
  1981   Mechanizing the Gentle Crafts: The Introduction of Machinery into
          Lynn, Mass. Shoe Industry, 1852–1883. In *Essays from the Lowell
          Conference on Industrial History 1980 and 1981,* ed. R. Weible, O.
          Ford, and P. Morian, pp. 33–45. Lowell Conference on Industrial
          History, Lowell, Mass.

Myers, S.
  1980   *Handcraft to Industry: Philadelphia Ceramics in the First Half of the
          Nineteenth Century.* Washington, D.C.: Smithsonian Institution.

Nash, G. B.
  1979   *The Urban Crucible.* Cambridge, Mass.: Harvard University Press.

Nobles, G.
  1983   *Divisions throughout the Whole: Politics and Society in Hampshire, Co.,
          Mass., 1740–1775.* New York: Cambridge University Press.

Noël Hume, I.
  1969   *A Guide to Artifacts of Colonial America.* New York: Knopf.
  1973   Creamware to Pearlware: A Williamsburg Perspective. In *Ceramics
          in America,* ed. I. Quimby, pp. 217–55., Charlottesville: University
          Press of Virginia.

Panzieri, R.
  1980   The Capitalist Use of Machinery. In *Outlines of a Critique of Tech-
          nology,* ed. P. Slater, pp. 44–68. London: Ink Links.

Paynter, R.
  1982   *Models of Spatial Inequality.* New York: Academic Press.
  1985   Surplus Flow between Frontiers and Homelands. In *The Archaeology*

of Frontiers and Boundaries, ed. S. W. Green and S. M. Perlman, pp. 163–211. Orlando, Fla: Academic Press.

Pomian, K.
1979   The Secular Evolution of the Concept of Cycles. *Review* 2: 563–646.

Research Working Group
1979   Cyclical Rhythms and Secular Trends of the Capitalist World-Economy. *Review* 2: 483–500.

Resnick, S., and R. Wolff
1979   The Theory of Transitional Conjunctures and the Transition from Feudalism to Capitalism in Western Europe. *The Review of Radical Political Economics* 11: 3–22.

Rosenberg, N.
1972   *Technology and American Economic Growth*. New York: Harper and Row.
1976   The Direction of Technological Change. In *Perspectives on Technology,* ed. N. Rosenberg, pp. 108–25. New York: Cambridge University Press.
1981   Why in America? In *Yankee Enterprise,* ed. O. Mayr and R. C. Post, pp. 49–63. Washington, D.C.: Smithsonian Institution Press.

Rutsch, E., and M. J. Rutsch
1975   Symposium on Industrial Archaeology, 1974. Paterson, N. J. *Northeast Historical Archaeology* 4(1 + 2).

Schneider, J.
1979   Peacocks and Penguins: The Political Economy of European Cloth and Colors. *American Ethnologist* 5: 413–47.

Schneider, P., J. Schneider, and E. Hansen
1972   Modernization and Development: The Role of Regional Elites and Noncorporate Groups in the European Mediterranean. *Comparative Studies in Society and History* 14: 328–50.

Schuyler, R. L.
1970   Historical and Historic Sites Archaeology as Anthropology: Basic Definitions and Relationships. *Historical Archaeology* 4: 83–89.
1977   The Spoken Word, the Written Word, Observed Behavior and Preserved Behavior: The Contexts Available to Archaeologists. *The Conference on Historic Site Archaeology Papers* 10: 99–120.
1980   Sandy Ground: Archaeology of a Black Urban Community. In *Archaeological Perspectives on Ethnicity in America,* ed. R. L. Schuyler, pp. 48–59. Farmingdale, N.Y.: Baywood.

Shaik, A.
1983   Economic Crises. In *A Dictionary of Marxist Thought*, ed. T. Bottomore, pp. 138–43. Cambridge, Mass.: Harvard University Press.

Slater, P. (ed.)
1980   *Outlines of a Critique of Technology*. London: Ink Links.

Smith, M. R.
1977   *Harpers Ferry Armory and the New Technology*. Ithaca, N.Y.: Cornell University Press.
1981   Military Entrepreneurship. In *Yankee Enterprise*, ed. O. Mayr and R. C. Post, pp. 63–102. Washington, D.C.: Smithsonian Institution Press.

South, S.
1972   Revealing Culture Process through the Formula Concept. In *Method and Theory in Historical Archaeology*, ed. S. South, pp. 201–76. New York: Academic Press.

Spencer-Wood, S.
1979   The National American Market in Historical Archaeology. In *Ecological Anthropology of the Middle Connecticut River Valley*, ed. R. Paynter. Research Reports 18: 117–28. Department of Anthropology, University of Massachusetts, Amherst.

Starbuck, D. R.
1983   The New England Glassworks in Temple, New Hampshire. *Industrial Archaeology* 9: 45–64.

Sweezy, P.
1942   *The Theory of Capitalist Development*. New York: Monthly Review.

Szatmary, D. P.
1980   *Shays' Rebellion*. Amherst: University of Massachusetts Press.

Temin, P.
1971   Labor Scarcity in America. *Journal of Interdisciplinary History* 1: 251–64.

Therborn, G.
1980   *The Ideology of Power and the Power of Ideology*. London: Verso.

Thorbahn, P.
1979   The Pre-colonial Ivory Trade of East Africa. Ph.D. diss., University of Massachusetts, Amherst. Ann Arbor: University of Microfilms.

Thompson, E. P.
    1967   Time, Work-Discipline, and Industrial Capitalism. *Past and Present*
             38: 56–97.

Wallerstein, I.
    1974   *The Modern World-system*. Vol. 1. New York: Academic Press.
    1979   Underdevelopment and Phase-B: Effect of the Seventeenth-Century
             Stagnation on Core and Periphery of the European World-
             Economy. In *The World-system of Capitalism,* ed. W. L. Goldfrank,
             pp. 73–84. Beverly Hills, Calif.: Sage.
    1980   *The Modern World-system*. Vol. 2. New York: Academic Press.
    1984   Long Waves as Capitalist Process. *Review* 7: 559–575.

Weiss, R. S.
    1982   Primitive Accumulation in the United States: The Interaction be-
             tween Capitalist and Noncapitalist Class Relations in Seventeenth-
             Century Massachusetts. *Journal of Economic History* 42: 77–82.

Wilson, J.
    1976   *The Upper Factory Brook Sawmill Site: An Early Industrial Site in
             Middlefield, Mass.* Master's thesis, University of Massachusetts,
             Amherst.

Winner, L.
    1980   Do Artifacts Have Politics? *Daedalus* 109:121–36.

Wolf, E. R.
    1982   *Europe and the People without History*. Berkeley: University of Cali-
             fornia Press.

CHAPTER 14

Dialogues with the Dead
Ideology and the Cemetery

RANDALL H. McGUIRE

> You know if livin was a thing that money could buy, the rich would
> live and the poor would die.
>
> Traditional ballad

This line from a traditional ballad brings into focus two central points
of this paper. The first is that immortality is desirable and the second is
that power will affect how desirable things are distributed, especially if
these things can be bought and sold. Some people have sought immortality through burial and memorialization, and at different times in
human history we have witnessed great differences in the access individuals have had to such immortality.

Archaeologists have been accustomed to assuming a direct relationship between funerary investment and social status (Binford 1971;
Saxe 1970; Tainter 1978; O'Shea 1984; Bartel 1982). Many have assumed that the rich have always acquired for themselves the most
sumptuous forms of mortuary display. For these researchers the mortuary ritual, the form of burial, grave goods, and monuments directly reflect the social dimension, which is in turn a result of material relations
that determined the evolutionary level of the culture.

More recently, a growing number of researchers have rejected the
conceptualization of funerary ritual as determined and never determin-

ing and instead have located mortuary ritual in the realm of ideology (Hodder 1982; Pearson 1982; Shanks and Tilley 1982; Miller and Tilley 1984; Kristiansen 1984). They view the study of mortuary remains as a specific case in the broader study of how ideology legitimates the social order. They emphasize power and the anomalies between the powerful and the powerless in societies as an internal dynamic for cultural change. As ideology, the burial ritual does not necessarily refer to the actual relations of power in a society but to an idealized expression of these relations. The ritual acts ideologically to maintain the social order by misrepresenting the true nature of social relations. Burial ritual is therefore an active part of the negotiation and struggle between the powerful and the powerless in society.

My initial purpose in studying gravestones from the last 180 years in Broome County, New York, was to determine whether they provide a direct reflection of social stratification in the community. After even a brief examination it was apparent that in some time periods they do and in other time periods they do not. The assumption that they directly reflect the social order within a single evolutionary period clearly did not hold. More important, the answer to my initial question raised far more intriguing issues than the original inquiry.

The dead speak in the cemeteries of Broome County through the memorials that they have left behind. The dead, or their kin, raised these monuments as deliberate expressions of their ideals concerning death, class, and family. They were intended to establish and perpetuate a dialogue with the living, a dialogue that the dead hoped would reenforce the beliefs and worldview that they took to their graves. However, it was a dialogue sustained by the living, so that it took forms and directions never intended by the deceased.

The progress of this dialogue in Broome County from the 19th century to the present reveals a fundamental shift in the culture and ideology of capitalism. This shift occurred in the early part of the 20th century and it created the assumptions that we use to give meaning to our world. The shift involved a movement from mystification based on naturalization to a denial of inequalities and power relations.

IDEOLOGY

The key concept in my discussion is ideology. I use a Marxist-derived concept that is quite different from the definition of ideology commonly used in archaeology and cultural materialism (Binford 1962; White 1959). The contemporary Marxist notion treats ideology as an active component in the struggle between the powerful and the powerless, rather than a consequence of technological and social change. Most archaeological attempts to locate mortuary ritual in the realm of ideology have treated ideology as an instrumentalist phenomenon, that is, as a device that one class uses to dominate another (Hodder 1982; Pearson 1982; Shanks and Tilley 1982; Miller and Tilley 1984; Kristiansen 1984).

The cemeteries of Broome County participated in a dominant ideology that advanced one class at the expense of others, but the instrumental aspect of this ideology does not adequately account for all of the variation that occurs. In addition to being an expression of the dominant ideology, the cemetery also participated in the struggle between early 19th-century rural and urban elites and expressed the resistance of an ethnically diverse 20th-century working class to the dominant ideology.

Not all of the changes we see in the cemetery are explicable by reference to ideology and power. Many seem to relate to changes of a broader cultural nature. At the most basic level, the cemetery is about death, and the shifting representation of death in the cemetery does not directly participate in power relations. The changes in attitudes toward death parallel the shift from naturalization to denial seen in the dominant ideology and thus suggest some deeper underlying structural connection.

The instrumentalist notion of ideology gives us an incomplete understanding of what is happening in Broome County cemeteries. It fails to recognize that multiple ideologies exist in any given social context and tends to assume that all consciousness is reducible to power relations. To gain a fuller understanding, we must first analyze the theoretical concept of ideology in terms of culture, domination, and material expression.

Most analysts agree on what ideology does. That is, it masks or obscures the real nature of social relations among the members of society (Althusser 1971; Leone 1986; Gramsci 1971; Lukács 1971; Miller and Tilley 1984). This statement, however, merely defines ideology in terms of its function, and does not explain what ideology is.

If we try to move beyond a functional definition of ideology, then two meanings can be ascribed to ideology (Larrain 1983). The first of these conceives of ideology as the totality of forms of social consciousness. The second sees ideology as the political ideas connected with the interests of a class (Marx and Engels 1947). Both of these meanings are embedded in the major works on ideology and they are rarely separated (Gramsci 1971; Althusser 1971; Thompson 1963; Lukás 1971). For example, Althusser (1971) speaks of a "ruling ideology" that controls individuals through "ideological state apparatuses" and of ideology as the givens of everyday life that form consciousness. Those who emphasize the first definition of ideology tend to hold an instrumentalist view, as exemplified in Althusser's work, which has profoundly affected a number of archaeologists (Leone 1986; Handsman 1983; Miller and Tilley 1984).

The definition of ideology as the totality of consciousness essentially equates ideology with a commonly held anthropological concept of culture—that is, culture as a system that structures thought or consciousness. Culture allows us to perceive and deal with the world because it creates order through categorization. This process of categorization reduces the richness of reality into a manageable scheme, but in doing so it prevents us from understanding the whole of that richness. For example, a color wheel is a continuum of hues. We categorize that continuum into "colors" so that we can conceptualize and speak of natural phenomena. The colors that are created, however, deny us a different subdivision of the whole that would produce different colors. From this perspective, the process of perceiving the world is necessarily mystifying since it allows us some knowledge of the world only by denying us other knowledge.

Culture is neither an a priori or a flawless cognitive structure. Rather, it is created through historical processes and contains internal contradictions. It cannot have a superorganic existence; it must reside in the minds of individuals. Paradoxically, culture neither originates nor changes in the minds of individuals because it is a social phenomenon. Culture is constantly created and recreated through the interactions of individuals with other individuals, social groups, and the material conditions of life. Individuals participate differentially in these interactions and with diverse interests, so that culture is a most imperfect system differentially shared by individuals and is prone to inconsistencies and contradictions.

It is important to consider culture as something greater than ideology and to recognize that the relationship of these phenomena is historically created. The mystification inherent in perception is not limited to relations of power. Relationships of power must, however, always either consciously or unconsciously engender such mystification. Ideology therefore is that subset of culture that originates in the relationship between consciousness and power. This relationship is not given in all times and places, so that specific aspects of culture (beliefs, rituals, basic assumptions, etc.) may be ideologically loaded in one context and not in another. As Maurice Bloch's (1986) study of the Merina circumcision ritual in Madagascar shows, the forms, expression, and content of specific aspects of culture can stay amazingly constant even while the rela-

tionship between consciousness and power and the ideological consequences of this relationship may be changing radically over time.

Locating ideology within a larger cultural structure of cognition
eliminates the most simplistic reading of the instrumentalist position.
This reading would empower the ideas of the ruling class to determine
all of social consciousness. Few advocates of an instrumentalist ideology would take this extreme position, but all would see the ideas of the
ruling class as determining the relationship between consciousness and
power, and as a robust tool for controlling subordinate groups.

Abercombie, Hill, and Turner (1980) have published a critique of
what they define as the "dominant ideology thesis." They challenge
both the instrumental nature and effectiveness of ideology in affecting
social action. They argue that in most historical periods the dominant
ideology serves mainly to integrate the dominant class and that the subordinate classes reject it. They conclude that the dominant ideology is
a weak instrument because these ideologies are fractured and often contradictory. Their critique suggests that ideology engenders resistance as
well as domination and that ideology must be embedded in a larger cultural consciousness.

At the extreme, arguments like those of Abercombie, Hill, and
Turner (1980) suggest that discussions of ideology only pertain to the
actions of an elite and tell us little about how inequalities are created and
maintained. Removing ideology totally from our discourses about
power ignores the embeddedness of ideology in culture. Even in the examples given by Abercombie, Hill, and Turner (1980) it seems that the
subordinate classes do not so much reject the dominant ideology as rework it for their own ends and that ideologies of resistance share much
with dominant ideologies. Ideology as that part of culture originating
in the relationship of consciousness and power does participate in the
negotiation of social relations but not in the simple way posited in the
instrumentalist notion.

As defined here, ideology may have multiple functions in the negotiation of social relations. An ideology is both the product of, and a pre-
requisite for, a group attaining a political consciousness and as such always serves to integrate some class or portion of a class in power
struggles. In order to maintain dominance, a ruling class must be integrated by an ideology and must mystify the class's power by representing its interests as the common interests of the whole society (Marx and
Engels 1946:64; Larrain 1983:24–25). This ideology may be accepted by
subordinate classes or they may rework it into an ideology of resistance.
Conflict may result from the inconsistencies between the ideology of
elites and the ideology of subordinates, which provides the conscious

basis for resistance. Change in the ideal moves people to action, and this action transforms the reality, again challenging the ideal (Godelier 1982). Subordinate ideologies therefore may reveal power relations but, because they are cultural, they also mystify reality. Such mystification only serves to reproduce and legitimate inequalities in society if the subordinate group comes to dominate.

Dominant ideologies can mystify the true nature of social relations in at least two fundamentally different ways. They can either deny the existence of inequality or they may naturalize inequality. Ideology denies the existence of inequality by masking or hiding it. Ideology naturalizes inequalities not by denying their existence but by denying that they are social products. In the latter case, the sources for inequality are attributed to nonsocial factors such as the supernatural, personality characteristics of individuals, hormones, or genes.

Ideology does not exist just in people's heads, but has observable material and behavioral manifestations; it springs from the opacity of reality (Mepham 1979:148). Social groupings, behavior, and material objects embody ideology and give it reality. The appearances created by these things fulfill the expectations of the ideology, and through this affirmation recreate and legitimate the ideology. For example, the uniform style and size of gravestones in early 19th-century Broome County cemeteries legitimated and affirmed an egalitarian ideology that denied inequalities in the community. Individuals perceive reality differentially, depending on their own experience, so that reality is not the same for all members of society. Social relations channel this experience, and these differences are the preconditions for multiple ideologies.

The different types of mystification result from and require the manipulation of material objects in different ways. If inequalities are denied then material evidence of such inequality should be deemphasized. Any overt and visible material displays of inequality would reveal ideology to be mystification. Conversely, naturalization may entail not only the material expression of inequalities, but even the magnification of inequalities. The reality of material differences serves to objectify and validate the supposed natural origin of those inequalities.

Mystification does not result from single elements or beliefs, but from a system of elements (Mepham 1979). Burial ritual does not mystify in and of itself. It mystifies because it is part of a larger structure of beliefs and material symbols. This cultural structure includes other aspects of the ideology and aspects of consciousness not involved in relations of power. The burial ritual must maintain a minimal consistency with other rituals and material symbols and reinforce their message.

The role of burial ritual in mystification is therefore not understandable without reference to this larger system of meaning.

In studying an ideology we should seek to understand the underlying principles that structure an ideology, the divergences and contradictions within it and the dialectic through which it is created and recreated (Marx 1978). Such understanding can only be achieved in the context of a specific historical case. The dialogue that the dead of Broome County entered into with the living is an ideological discourse. This discourse brought together seemingly divergent strands of culture and ideology concerned with death, the family, and social status. By examining these strands, we can discover structural shifts in the underlying ideology and culture.

BROOME COUNTY

Broome County is in south-central upstate New York along the Pennsylvania border. Today the county includes three major towns, the city of Binghamton and the villages of Johnson City and Endicott, and has a total population of about a quarter of a million. The area was and is a manufacturing center with a variety of ethnic groups and social classes. Enough cemeteries have survived to give us a sample representing in excess of 150 years of changes in gravestones to study. The area is not so large that we cannot hope to examine it as a whole, yet contains sufficient social and historical variability to allow a consideration of ideology in the cemetery.

White Anglo-Saxon Protestants from New England and Pennsylvania initially settled the county in the late 1700s and early 1800s. The economy of the region remained rural until the mid-19th century, when Broome County began to develop as a manufacturing center. The cigar industry dominated the county during the later part of the 19th century. The manufacture of shoes gradually replaced cigars at the end of the 19th century, and by the 1920s one company, the Endicott Johnson Shoe Company (EJ), employed 60 percent of the industrial work force in the county. EJ declined in the post-World War II period, to be replaced by IBM as the principal employer in the county.

The cigar factories and EJ actively encouraged immigrant labor by bringing over 12 different ethnic groups into the community. The Irish were the first to arrive. They came as construction workers in the 1830s and through the late 19th century provided most of the labor for the cigar plants. By the end of the 19th century the Irish were rapidly joining the middle class as lawyers, shop keepers, and government workers.

The shoe industry that followed was built on the labor of the second great wave of immigrants, principally Italians and Eastern Europeans and a large-scale immigration of "native-born" Americans from the rural areas of western Pennsylvania. Italians engaged in construction lived in Binghamton and Italian shoe workers lived in Endicott. The Eastern Europeans came from many different ethnic groups and practiced different religions, which they maintained in Broome County. The largest single Eastern European group consisted of Slovaks, who were both Catholics and Lutherans. Many of the Eastern Europeans were Jewish and they became concentrated in downtown Binghamton. Jews did not enter the shoe plants, but rather worked in Binghamton's clothing industry and became small business owners.

This immigration peaked in the period between 1919 and 1922 before federal immigration laws limited it. Since then there has been some movement of Asians into Binghamton and a continued but declining chain migration of individuals from the second great wave groups. The children and grandchildren of the foreign and rural immigrants of the early 20th century continue to make up the majority of Broome County's working class, with the exception of the Jews, who have largely moved into professional, educational, and administrative occupations. Starting in the 1940s some of the Eastern Europeans attained a middle-class status through commerce, and some Italians successfully established themselves as contractors.

DATA AND METHODS

The data presented in my discussion are derived from a larger project, the Binghamton Gravestone Project, which has been in progress since the fall of 1982. The earliest grave that we have found in Broome County dates to the 1790s. Two of the earliest cemeteries in the county were destroyed in the 19th century. One was eroded away by the Susquehanna River and the second destroyed to make way for railroad yards. We generally have adequate data in our sample from the mid-19th century to 1980.

In gathering the data for the project we have attempted to build a representative sample for the entire county. This is an immense job because we would estimate there are at least several hundred thousand gravestones in the county. Up to the present time, we have collected data on over 2,000 stones from over 27 cemeteries. This sample includes family and public cemeteries in the rural areas, 5 urban protestant cemeteries, 3 catholic cemeteries (including Irish, Italians, and Slovaks), and 3 Jewish cemeteries.

In addition to collecting data from gravestones, we have examined and documented all of the family mausoleums in the metropolitan area (Roveland 1984). This study provides us with descriptive information for each mausoleum and bibliographic data on the individuals who built them.

The information gathered on the stones in the cemetery represents only half of the data available to us. We have used city directories, manuscript censuses, obituaries, other documents, and informants to identify the individuals buried under our stones. For approximately two-thirds of the stones in our sample, we know the ethnicity of the individual, occupation immediately before death or retirement, place of residence at death, and relationship to other individuals buried nearby. This information allows us to examine the linkage between the social status of individuals and how their graves are marked.

We recorded a wide variety of data for each stone. We copied down all written information exactly as it is presented on the stones. We computer coded a number of other variables, including the material of the stone, size of the stone, an estimated erection date, the formal type of the stone, the type of plot the stone is in, and of course the cemetery. Altogether, we recorded over 50 observations for each stone.

Gravestone research projects have often proceeded without an explicit and rigorous approach to the selection of gravestones for analysis. This is unfortunate as the researcher is drawn in the cemetery to the unusual and the monumental. A host of unstated and unconscious biases enter into the selection of the sample. To avoid this problem we devised a structured approach to selecting gravestones for our analysis. In cemeteries for which we had maps showing the plots, we would first stratify the cemetery by administrative subdivisions within the cemetery and then select plots for examination by use of a random numbers table. For most of the cemeteries, however, such maps did not exist or we did not have access to them. In these cases we would first subdivide the cemetery into smaller units and then randomly select stones within these smaller units. In all instances our sampling unit was the group. Having selected a stone, we would then record all of the other stones in that same group. Although we would not wish to argue that these procedures give us a fully representative sample, they do direct us to examine a wide range of variability in the cemeteries and allow us to make explicit the biases in our selection of data.

THE CHANGING FACE OF BROOME COUNTY CEMETERIES

The changes that we see in the Broome County cemeteries generally follow the same trends that Dethlefsen (1977) has projected for the entire United States. Broome County was never one of the hot spots of cultural innovation in this country so that there tends to be a slight lag in the adoption of new cemetery and memorial forms in comparison with other areas. This lag decreases through time, although even today I would judge the customs of marking graves in the county to be conservative.

The cemeteries of Broome County at the end of the 18th century and the beginning of the 19th century varied little from their New England counterparts (Tashjian and Tashjian 1974; Benes 1977; Deetz and Dethlefsen 1978). Throughout the first half of the 19th century, cemeteries were community graveyards, the property of churches or towns. Individuals gained access to the cemetery through membership in the town or the church. The graves themselves remained the property of the community and did not pass to the individual or the family. The community granted families use rights to the cemetery, and the graves were clustered in family groupings. Initially there seems to have been little systematic order to the graves, but by the second decade of the 19th century they tended to be placed in neatly ordered rows.

The earliest stones were manufactured from a dark schist, available in upstate New York and were shaped to resemble the head board of a bed (Figure 14.1). Up until the 1820s these stones were decorated primarily with some variation of the urn and willow motif. The stones commonly contained epitaphs that spoke of the rewards waiting in heaven and the escape from the suffering of this life.

The use of the urn and willow design and these types of epitaphs continued through the early 1800s, but within the first decade the form and material of the stone changed. Marble replaced schist and rectangular tablets displaced the headboard form. The marble entered Broome County in large sheets, which local craftsmen cut into tablets and carved in designs and epitaphs (Gibb 1985). In the cemetery the gleaming white tablets marked the graves of family members laid out in a row (Figure 14.2). Differences in size generally reflected the distinction between child and adult, and very little overall inequality is evident in the size and elaborateness of the stones (Figure 14.3).

Starting in the third decade of the 19th century, the form of the American cemetery began to take on a new configuration. In Boston, the start of the rural cemetery movement marks the appearance of this shift. The rural cemetery movement was a reaction to and explicit rejection of the old community cemetery (French 1975; Farrell 1980; Darnall 1983). The advocates of the movement condemned the earlier cemeteries as filthy, unhealthy, and unattractive. They argued that a more sanitary and attractive way must be found to dispose of the dead. They sought to relocate the cemetery in rural areas removed from

Figure 14.1: Bedstead gravestone with urn and willow motif.

human habitations, in parklike settings where people could picnic, walk, contemplate, and absorb the moral lessons woven into the landscape of the cemetery (French 1975).

To accomplish this goal they formed associations that established and managed the cemeteries. Individuals became members of the association by purchasing plots in the cemetery. Initially, the proponents of the movement opposed the fencing of plots and the erection of showy monuments. These objections soon faded as families converted their plots into elaborate statements about their wealth and power.

Figure 14.2: Early 19th-century family group with tablet markers.

In the 1860s a new type of cemetery, the lawn-park cemetery, appeared. It incorporated many of the features of the rural cemetery such as private ownership of plots and showy monuments. These cemeteries differed in that they did not seek to maintain a natural landscape. Rather, they emphasized human domination over the landscape by carefully modifying it to form a park. These cemeteries tended to be very commercially oriented and many were profit-making enterprises (Farrell 1980).

In 1854, the leading citizens of Broome County organized the first rural cemetery, Spring Forest, on the western edge of Binghamton. It was followed within the decade by a lower-class Protestant cemetery and a Catholic cemetery, both of which were modeled after the rural cemeteries. The next major upper-class cemetery, Floral Park, was organized as a lawn park cemetery in 1893. All subsequent major cemeteries established in the county, including those established by religious groups, were organized as associations, and by 1900 almost all of the community cemeteries were reorganized as associations, abandoned, filled up or destroyed by urban expansion. The concept of a lawn park cemetery remained the basic model for new cemeteries in Broome County up until the 1930s.

The introduction of new styles of gravestones accompanied the es-

Figure 14.3: An early 19th-century church graveyard.

tablishment of the rural cemeteries and transformed the appearance of the already existing cemeteries. From 1850 until the turn of the century, the size and variety of stones increased as families invested more and more in grave markers (Figure 14.4). In addition to headstones larger stones or family markers were also erected. The earliest form of these markers were obelisks but the variety of different forms increased until the 1880s when dozens of different forms are observed (Figure 14.5). By 1870, the materials used for memorials had begun to shift from predominantly marble to predominantly granite.

With the introduction of family markers, the family was also reorganized in the cemetery. The family ceased to rest in death side by side in a straight line. A large prominent marker, often referred to as a family marker, was erected in the center of the family plot. However, this monument was less a memorialization of the family than a monument to the family patriarch, the husband. These husband–centric markers prominently display the full name of the husband (Figure 14.6). All the names of other family members are given by their relationship to the husband (e.g., Sarah, wife of John Smith, or David, son of John Smith). In a handful of cases where the wife came from a family of

447

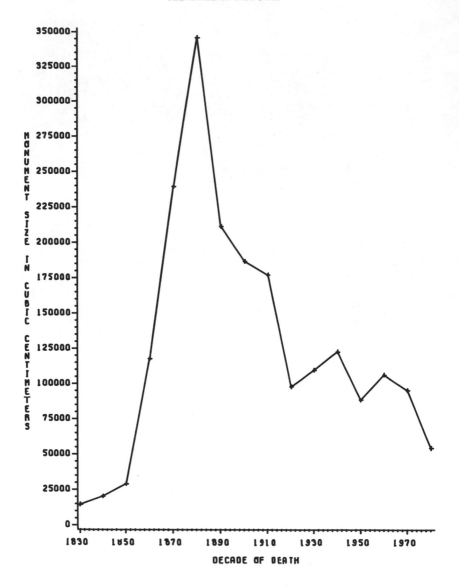

Figure 14.5: A mid-19th-century family plot with an obelisk.

greater prominence than the husband, she is listed by her maiden name. A headstone usually marks each individual grave in the plot with the generational and gender position of each person in the family (father, mother, daughter, grandfather, etc.) identifying the family member.

Today the largest and most prominent of these family plots still have low granite walls around them clearly separating them from others in the cemetery. Contemporary observers would have seen even greater segregation of families, as many plots originally were surrounded by metal fences with gates. Almost all of these have rusted away or were removed in later times to facilitate maintenance of the cemetery grounds.

The most prominent and expensive type of family plot was the family mausoleum (Figure 14.7). Sixty-two such structures occur in Broome County, and we could date and reconstruct the social position of the families that built 47 of these. The earliest family mausoleums appear in the 1880s and construction of these monuments peaks in the

Figure 14.4: A chart showing overall shifts in mortuary investment.

Figure 14.6: A late 19th-century husband-centric family plot.

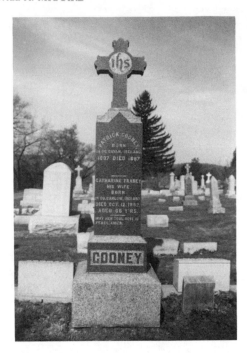

first third of the 20th century. Fourteen were built between 1900 and 1910 and 20 more in the next two decades (Roveland 1984). Protestant businessmen, manufacturers, bankers and professionals erected 18 of the 22 family mausoleums built before 1920. The remaining three were put up by traveling salesmen and an Irish business owner.

The family plots in each cemetery vied with each other for the attention of the visitor. The central marker was the focal point for the plot, catching the eye through a combination of uniqueness and size. Not all markers were (and are) successful in this competition. The mausoleums and truly monumental stones of the local capitalists capture the observer first and engage even those who do not enter the cemetery (Figure 14.8). The markers of the Protestant and Irish middle class encourage the visitor to wander through the cemetery from stone to stone to examine the differences in form and detail and to reflect on the family that erected the monument (Figure 14.9).

The late 19th- and early 20th-century family plots also exploit location both within and between cemeteries to compete for attention. In the Broome County cemeteries of this period, a definite prestige hierarchy existed between the Protestant cemeteries, which shifted over time. Within each cemetery, including the Catholic, the mausoleums and

Figure 14.7: Late 19th-century mausoleums.

largest monuments tend to cluster on the higher ground, with the lesser monuments spreading out around them.

The casual modern observer to this landscape, however, usually overlooks the scores of worker's graves found in the lower-prestige cemeteries and skirting the edges of the higher-prestige and Catholic cemeteries. These graves are marked with simple, usually marble, headstones, now grey from weathering and pollution. Even less visible to the modern observer are the scores of unmarked graves in the lowest-prestige Protestant cemeteries and along the edges of the Catholic cemeteries. Today these are visible only as slight depressions in the ground. The contemporary visitor to these cemeteries would have had better vision of these lesser graves because the marble would have been brilliantly white and less overgrown by vegetation and the now vacant expanse of unmarked graves would have been sporadically marked by bare earth overlying the most current additions to the potter's fields.

From the mid-19th century through the first two decades of the 20th, the Broome County cemetery clearly reflected the status and social position of the people who were buried in it. Archaeological assumptions concerning a direct relationship between mortuary investment and wealth or power are valid for this time. The cemetery

Figure 14.8: Late 19th-century monument of a wealthy family.

confronts the observer with marked inequalities in investment and display (Figure 14.10).

There are hints of change in this pattern during the second decade of the 20th century as overall investment in stones and mausoleums begins to decline. In the period between the world wars a renegotiation of the dialogue in the cemetery appears to be happening. Both the investment in mortuary displays and the variety of such displays decrease. Significant alterations also occur in the distribution of investment and forms within the community.

Family plots continue to be the most common form of grouping in the cemetery throughout the period between the wars. The family markers, however, become less varied and more uniform in size. They also become in effect true monuments to the family, displaying the family name only. The individual's names appear on the headstones with designations such as father, mother, or daughter (Figure 14.11). The familial relations, which earlier had been displayed secondarily to the male patriarch, assume primacy in the dialogue that the deceased wish to instigate.

The direct relationship seen earlier between mortuary investment

Figure 14.9: Late 19th-century middle-class monument.

and social position becomes confused in the 1920s and 1930s. Many wealthy and prominent Protestant and Irish families continue to put up mausoleums and three prominent Irish families erected monumental stones (two obelisks and a large Celtic cross). Some prominent families, however, begin erecting much more modest memorials. Italians and Slovaks, despite their lower social status and wealth, begin to erect prominent memorials in the 1920s and 1930s. Italian families commissioned several sarcophagi, a form of above-ground memorialization second only to mausoleums in cost. In 1938 a Slovak liquor store owner built a mausoleum costing $8,000. At the time a new, large, three-bedroom house sold for $4,000 in the county.

The overall impression of the cemetery changed greatly in the period between the wars (Figure 14.12). Substantial memorials still confronted the visitor, but they did not compete for attention as they had in the past. The decline in variety with respect to both size and form created a much more uniform appearance. The disparities evident in investment also declined so that the marked divisions of the previous period were muted or absent. Furthermore, during this time a larger portion of the burials occurred in family plots as opposed to isolated burials, as were common in the late 19th century.

One cemetery established in Broome County in 1936 radically di-

Figure 14.10: A lawn-park cemetery.

verges from the model of the lawn-park cemetery that had guided cemeteries established as late as the 1920s. Vestal Hills was built as a memorial park in which monuments were limited to standardized, flush, brass tablets (Figure 14.13). Vestal Hills reflected a national trend in memorialization, which had started elsewhere in the country in the 1920s (Jackson 1977:147). This trend emphasized a socially inconspicuous way of disposing of the dead and would dominate the later half of the 20th century in Broome County cemeteries.

Following World War II, the size and number of markers used in the cemetery declined markedly. In the 1950s the family plot quickly fell from favor, and what we have called a spouse plot became the dominant type of group in the cemetery. These spouse plots generally consisted of the burial of a husband and wife, marked by a single headstone (Figure 14.14). The decline in size, variety, and differences in investment that started in the 1920s accelerated and culminated in the postwar years.

During the late 1940s the representation of the family shifted to emphasize the relationship between the husband and wife. The couple were united forever on a single stone. Starting in the late 1950s, many stones exhibit the date of marriage in addition to the birth and death dates of the individuals. The late 1970s in Broome County witnessed a revival of epitaphs on headstones with the most common messages in-

Figure 14.11: A 1920s family plot.

volving the bond between the couple, for example "Together Forever."
Also in this time one of the popular decorative motifs was a couple
walking hand in hand into the sunset. After the war, infants were increasingly buried away from their parents in a separate nursery section
of the cemetery. Occasionally older children were buried next to their
parents, either with a separate headstone or with their name appearing
on the parents stone.

The uniformity of the interwar cemetery increased as the stones
became lower and less varied (Figure 14.15). The stones do not compete for the attention of the visitor and they communicate primarily to
the family members who come seeking them; for others they are lost in
the mass of sameness. The greatest expression of this uniformity occurs
in the memorial park and in the public mausoleums that became increasingly popular in the 1960s (Figure 14.16). In both these situations
the only thing that differentiates one burial from another is the individual name and dates on the marker. The ultimate manifestation of
uniformity, cremation, accounts for less than 5 percent of the Broome
County burials before 1980. Persons in the community working in funeral homes, cemeteries, and monument dealerships indicate that cremation is increasing markedly in the current decade and at present approaches 20 percent of all burials.

A type of mass-produced individuality has appeared on the stones

Figure 14.12: A 1920–40 period cemetery.

in the last 20 years. The relatively uniform slant and flush markers are increasingly decorated with carved symbols of hobbies and personal interests such as boats, fishermen, dogs, cars, motorcycles, and knitting needles. There has been an increased use of epitaphs with fundamentalist religious sayings, which follow expressions of marital fidelity in popularity.

In this final period, considerable deviations from the general pattern occur in the ethnic cemeteries. The Eastern European cemeteries tend to exhibit a greater investment in stones and a greater variety than the Protestant and Irish graves. The Jewish cemeteries respond not at all to the general trends but from the end of the 19th century on are characterized by medium-sized, grey granite headstones. The most striking deviation appears in the Italian stones, which are largest and most elaborately produced after the war, and often include statues (Figure 14.17). Italian families also erected all eight of the private mausoleums put up after 1940 (Figure 14.18), and one family that built a mausoleum in this period was headed by a shoeworker.

From the 1920s up to the present, the cemeteries of Broome County have not directly reflected the social stratification in the region. The distortion of the social reality is very complex. The relationships of life are not simply inverted, nor does the cemetery lose meaning in

Figure 14.13: Vestal Hills, a memorial park.

terms of the living. It should also be remembered that the modern landscape includes all of the forms discussed here. In some cases, all the
forms I have listed can be found side by side in a single cemetery. The
residents of Broome County are constantly confronted with the new
and the old in the cemeteries, and the dialogue that results is a complex
interaction between these memorials and the living.

THE CEMETERY AND THE MAKING OF IDEOLOGY

The cemeteries of Broome County were constructed as meaningful
cultural landscapes and they bring together seemingly divergent strands
of culture and ideology. In each time period, the cemeteries provided a
material form that affirmed and legitimated the dominant ideology of
the period. In the early 19th century the cemetery denied the existence
of inequalities in the community; in the late 19th and 20th century it
naturalized existing inequalities in a glorification of individual success;
and in the mid to late 20th century it denied the existence of qualitative
differences between individuals. The cemetery has been an active participant in the creation, maintenance, and recreation of these ideologies
through the perceptions of the living. Close examination of the domi-

Figure 14.14: A 1950s spouse plot.

nant ideology in the cemeteries reveals that it was often fractured by intra-elite competition and that the working classes of Broome County often reworked it to form their own ideologies.

THE CEMETERY AS AN EXPRESSION OF THE DOMINANT IDEOLOGY

The Broome County cemetery of the early 19th century arranged the dead to create the ideal community that the living could never truly attain. The boundary fence around the cemetery separated member from nonmember in death and affirmed this contrast for the living. Within the cemetery a distinction existed between husband and wife, adult and child, but not between the familial units that made up the community. The inequalities and relations of power within the community were obscured in death, denying their efficacy among the living by declaring them transitory and fleeting manifestations of this life, which were to be left behind in the better life that awaited. The cemetery created the appearance of equality among the dead and this affirmed the ideology that masked the relations of power among the living.

The cemetery also expressed the certainty of death and the promise of redemption (Saum 1975; Farrell 1980). The white stones in the

Figure 14.15: A 1950s cemetery.

churchyard were clearly visible and observed daily by the people of the community. The epitaphs speak of escaping the troubles of this world to the glories of the next. They also imply that the deceased waited on the other side to be reunited with family and loved one. For example, "Rest, Jacob, rest; When we like you have passed life's dreary journey through. We'll come and lay our weary head near thine upon the same sweet bed." The willow tree so prominently displayed on many headstones was a symbol of death and mourning, but a beautiful and inviting symbol (Linden 1980). The finality of death was also obscured, because the cemetery declared the arduous corporeal life fleeting and the true life that awaited in eternity beautiful and placid.

The late 19th-century cemeteries of Broome County are strikingly different from their predecessors. A plethora of monuments of different shapes and varying heights confronts the viewer. Massive monuments of granite, sometimes topped with marble statues, and tall obelisks dominate the visual field. The well-ordered, placid uniformity of the churchyard was replaced by a disharmonious jumble of competing images. The reality so created emphasizes inequalities in the community.

The expansion of capitalism and industrialization in mid-19th-century America brought with it an alteration in ideology, which the

Figure 14.16: A modern public mausoleum.

cemetery participated in. The new ideology stressed self-achievement and matured in the later part of the century as the doctrine of social Darwinism (Conwell 1905; Sumner 1963). The system of inequality was naturalized through reference to individual success. Success was attainable by all, and the determinants of success lay in the characteristics of individuals, thus denying the social determinants of success such as inheritance, socialization, education, and social connections (Epstein 1981:65; Sochen 1981:85). Hard work, thrift, intelligence, sobriety, cleanliness, and a little luck guaranteed success, while failure resulted from the lack of these characteristics or, more important, from their opposites—laziness, extravagance, stupidity, slovenliness, and drunkenness.

During the 19th century, the increasing separation of work and home produced by employment in the industrial sector gave rise to an ideology called the cult of domesticity. The home became a refuge for the husband from the struggle to succeed in the outside world and the women's sphere (Strasser 1982:181). To women fell the job of nurturing the husband and children and maintaining a moral environment in the face of the competitive world outside (Stowe 1865:14). To do this the women had to be protected from the corruption and immorality of the world by their husbands, who as providers and protectors exercised

Figure 14.17: Italian-American memorials of the 1960s.

a patriarchal rule of the household. In the world of commerce and work, the husband's position may have been subject to constant challenge and threat, but in the refuge of his home his authority was to be unchallenged. The dominance of the husband in the family was naturalized by allusion to biological and economic function.

Material items were not passive in the making and sustenance of this late 19th-century ideology because they provided the objective reality that made it opaque. Clear material differences delineated those who had succeeded from those of lesser character and ability who had failed. The failures lived in squalid quarters, possessed little or nothing of value, wasted what they earned on strong drink, and violated the sanctity of the home by sending their wives and children into the mines, mills, and factories. The upper- and middle-class individuals who had succeeded, on the other hand, realized that success through a conspicuous consumption of goods, homes, and labor (Veblen 1899). This middle- and upper-class consumption in turn fueled the expansion of capitalist production in consumer goods. The ideology both originated in the stark material differences between classes and perpetrated these differences.

Figure 14.18: Modern Italian-American mausoleums.

The cemetery of the mid-19th to early 20th century participated in and legitimated the ideology of Social Darwinism. The community cemetery, with its equality among the dead, was unsuited to the new developments. In the early parts of the century it was dismissed as un-clean, unsanitary, and unsightly. The rural cemetery movement of the 1830s and 1840s tried to convert the cemetery to a romantic ideal of returning the dead and the living to nature and the basic equality of individuals. The rural cemetery vested the ownership of plots in individuals, however, and the romantic ideals of equality soon gave way to a fierce competition between families, evidenced in the grandeur of their memorials. The subsequent lawn-park cemetery movement of the 1860s suffered the same transformation, as these cemeteries became "groupings of graves based on money" (Farrell 1980:124).

Despite the fact that plots were individually owned in the late 19th century, the cemeteries themselves were essentially public places. The citizens of the 19th century used them much as we now use parks for walks, outings, and meditation (Fallows 1885; French 1975; Farrell 1980). The cemetery of the late 19th and early 20th century was as much a place of the living as of the dead. The families that erected mon-uments did so knowing that they would be seen, discussed, and com-mented on. They were not private or intimate statements but very pub-lic ones. These statements were the culmination and the ultimate

462

product of the competitions for wealth and power that the family members had engaged in through their lives. The ideology of Social Darwinism was affirmed in the landscape of the cemetery, where the appearances of success and failure were as real as in life.

The primary responsibility for success in the family fell to the male patriarch and the family plot provided the final statement of his accomplishments. The memorials in the plot recreated the idealized relationships of the family. The highly visible central marker established the relations of the family to the outside world. It exalted the husband's position as provider and protector and remembered the woman's role as wife, providing the moral and material support for the husband. The kinship relations of the family were expressed on the less visible headstones that designated father, mother, son, and daughter. The family plot recreated in the cemetery the cult of domesticity that structured the middle- and upper-class family in life.

The cemetery legitimated success and reinforced the natural origins of inequality. Just as the poor in life could not glory in consumption or maintain the sanctity of their homes, so too it was in death. They often could not erect memorials or were forced to erect inferior monuments. They usually could not afford to purchase a family plot, so the family members were scattered through the cemetery and the requisite monumentalization of the cult of domesticity was absent in death, just as the reality of the cult had been absent in life. The cemeteries of Broome County in the late 19th and early 20th centuries did not declare the inequalities of life transitory and fleeting, as the earlier cemetery had, but rather pronounced them to be the natural order of things and preserved them for time immemorial.

By the beginning of the 20th century, capitalism was in crisis; that is, the operating principles of the economy were in danger of breaking down (Mandel 1978:184–92). The distinct segregation of classes, abuse of workers and labor conflict had produced the strongest and most radical militancy in the history of American labor (Amsden 1979; Guèrin 1979). Unions called not only for the improvement of working conditions but also for the establishment of a socialist economy. In 1917 the Bolshevik revolution confronted capitalism for the first time with the reality of a socialist state. Radicalism peaked in the strikes of 1919, which were brutally suppressed and the infamous "red scare" followed (Guèrin 1979).

The industry of the late 19th century had been built primarily on the expansion of the means of production (building of railroads, factories, mills, and machines) and secondarily on the production of consumer goods for the middle and upper classes (Ewen 1976:24; Mandel 1978:184–92). By the end of this century these markets had been saturated and capitalism faced a realization crisis. In order to survive, the industries of the United States had to produce far more than the existing market could consume. This crisis revealed itself in the great depression of 1893 and the falling rates of profits from the 1870s to 1900 (Mandel 1978:83, 120–21).

The resolution of this crisis lay in the introduction of mass production and the creation of a new ideology, which was both necessary to and a result of the alteration of society brought about by mass production. Mass production first appeared in 1910 when Henry Ford reorganized his auto plant as an assembly line (Chandler 1967:26–27; Meyer 1981), and the new ideology developed in the early 1920s, greatly assisted by advertising (Ewen 1976). Production did not meet the demand created by the ideology, and the new order was not fully realized until after World War II (Ewen 1976).

Mass production through the use of highly specialized single-purpose machines operated by easily trained workmen produced goods at lower cost and at astronomical rates when compared to late 19th-century production (Ewen 1976:23–24). These changes made the goods available to a wider segment of the population and the increasing numbers of semiskilled and unskilled workers became an expanding market for durable consumer goods previously purchasable only by the upper and middle classes.

Mass production also redefined the relationship between workers and capital. Whereas in the past workers had primarily been only a source of labor to capitalists, they became also a primary market for industrial production (Nelson 19745; Ewen 1976). This transformation meant that the workers needed time to consume, higher rates of pay to consume, and credit to stretch that buying power further. Capitalists expressed the new relationship in terms of a functionally integrated circle that benefited the capitalist with profits and the worker with consumer goods and exploited no one (Ford 1929:17). The new prophets of mass production blamed the conditions of the past on a deviation from the democratic principles of the country and advocated a return to the egalitarian principles that founded the nation (Carver 1926:261–62).

This new ideology did not abandon all the conceptual baggage of the past, but rather reworked it in the new context. The cult of individual success remained a central facet of the mystification. Success and failure still originated in the abilities of individuals, but the definition of success changed. Whereas previously all men had the *opportunity* to succeed in the new order, now all men could *actually attain* some measure of success. The measure of a man was no longer success or failure but the degree of success.

The new ideology both arose from and created the reality of the

1920s. The identification of success with conspicuous consumption was inherited from the past. With the spread of mass production, conspicuous consumption became possible for much of the working class. A form of commodity fetishism that had been created in the later half of the 19th century confused material things with relations of stratification (Veblen 1899). Once the availability of things changed, the illusion of a change in human relations was created. In *Middletown* of the 1920s working-class housewives allowed that classes had existed in the community in their childhood because only the rich had cars, homes, and washing machines, but now everyone had these things and only differences of degree remained (Lynd and Lynd 1929:82–83).

Just as the husband was transformed, so too was the wife. The wife became the master consumer of the family (Ewen 1976; Matthaei 1982). The new ideal gave women a public role that articulated the household with the outside world. Just as the functional integration of worker and capital were stressed, so too was the functional integration of husband and wife. This involved an ideology that denied the patriarchy of the husband and stressed the emotional bond between husband and wife (Matthaei 1982).

We see in the cemeteries of Broome County during the interwar period the renegotiation of ideology and social relations going on in the society at large. Memorials responded to the forces of mass production as advances in technology for cutting stones cheapened the memorials and increasing real wages in the 1920s widened the market for them. The marked difference between classes in the cemetery began to diminish. Many of the rich continued to erect mausoleums and large stones, but so too did families of lesser status. More and more families were able to establish family plots and these plots communicated the reconceptualization of the family. The highly visible central marker presented only the family name while the family relationships stayed on the smaller headstones.

The expansion of family plots, with family markers, to a larger segment of the population blurred the qualitative distinction between the successful and the failures creating in the cemetery the same differentiation by degree that existed in other realms of material culture such as homes and cars. The competition in memorials lost meaning as more individuals could afford elaborate memorials. Perhaps more important, those upper-class families in Broome County who maintained the consumption patterns of the late 19th century, including mausoleums and elaborate memorials were denigrated, while those that adopted less pretentious homes, life-styles, and memorials were hailed as civic leaders. These forces worked against the rich inflating the competition in the cemetery.

Following World War II, the memorialization of the dead in Broome County cemeteries no longer clearly reflected social stratification in the community, and increasingly the monuments speak to an intimate audience and not a public one. The most striking thing in cemeteries with standing memorials is the uniformity in size and form of the monuments. The monuments no longer compete with each other to draw the attention of the visitor but blend into an egalitarian mass. The distinctions between them in details of design are often highly personalized but not visible from more than a few yards away. The monument and its decoration having meaning to an intimate audience of relatives and friends who must search out the plot. Commodities or commodified activities dominate the personalized symbols and provide an identification in terms of consumption that characterized the individual. The public mausoleums and memorial gardens provide the ultimate expression of the modern cemetery. Here the uniformity is extreme and only the most careful searching locates a specific plot. In these burial places the existence of class distinctions in the community of the dead is most effectively denied. Only slight differences of degree and emblems of personal preferences remain. In the modern cemetery, the living encounter an equality in death that exceeds and validates the equality they perceive in life.

The family has virtually disappeared from contemporary Broome County cemeteries, being replaced by married couples. The vast majority of plots are spouse plots in which the couple share the same headstone and ground. In addition to the spatial association of the couple, the decoration and epitaphs on the stones glorify the couples relationship. The cemetery denies patriarchy and creates in death bonds of matrimony with the permanence that people can only idealize in life.

The shift to spouse plots is not explainable in terms of increased mobility of families or declining childhood mortality. In Broome County the spouse plot is preferred even when subsequent generations continue to reside in the community and infants or small children who die are most often buried in a special children's section of the cemetery, not with their parents. The spouse plot reflects and reinforces the conceptualization of the family as a functionally integrated union of man and woman, "Together Forever."

THE CEMETERY AS AN ACTIVE FORCE IN IDEOLOGY

The modern cemetery exists in a cultural landscape that includes the cemeteries of earlier times, and in some cases individual cemeteries include sections representing all of the trends discussed. Essentially three forms of cemetery and of memorialization existed in Broome County. The early 19th-century cemeteries belonged to communities and downplayed inequalities. The late 19th- to early 20th-century cemeteries were organized as associations and solidified inequalities in death. Finally cemeteries since World War II have denied inequalities, with memorialization becoming an intimate and personal statement to kin and friends.

In conducting my research on Binghamton cemeteries, I have been engaging also in over four years of participant observation on the death customs of Broome County. Frequent visits to the cemetery have resulted in many conversations with professionals in the funeral, memorial, and cemetery business as well as common citizens. I have presented my research to a variety of civic, church, and public school groups. We have also conducted interviews with dozens of individuals of differing faiths and ethnic backgrounds. All of this has provided me some insight into how the people of Broome County react to the memorials of each of the three periods and how the cemeteries contribute to the appearance that maintains the modern ideology.

The modern observer is constantly confronted with the contrasts between these three forms and must mediate the conflicting ideologies embodied in them. The objective reality of these cemeteries seemingly verifies the modern ideological position first advanced by reformers of the 1920s who saw the Victorian era as an aberration and linked the new order to the romantic ideals of the early United States. To the modern citizen of Broome County, the earlier churchyard cemeteries with their modest white markers appear quaint and harken to a simpler time of community and unity, which lacked the competition and conflict that mar the modern ideal of equality. The late 19th- and early 20th-century cemeteries, on the other hand, violate the modern ideology. They appear ostentatious, macabre, and aberrant. The elaborate monuments erected to attract the 19th-century observer and glorify the achievements and ideology of the deceased repel the modern visitor. The contrast between them and both the earliest and contemporary, reinforces and recreates the modern ideology in the mind of the observer.

THE CEMETERY AS OTHER THAN INSTRUMENTALIST IDEOLOGY

The changes in ideology discussed so far reflect the general trends or dominant ideology in the history of Broome County. This ideology was dominant both in the sense of it being the ideology of the elite class of Binghamton and in the sense that it is the source of most of the ideological statements made in the cemeteries. The cemeteries of Broome

County were, however, considerably more than just an ideological tool that the elite manipulated to further their dominance. The ideology of each time was differentially shared and interpreted, and the cemetery gives us access to some of these processes too. The cemeteries of Broome County figured in the conflicts between mid-19th-century rural and urban elites and in the resistance of the 20th-century ethnic working class.

In the mid-19th century the expansion of industrial production in Binghamton threatened the economic and social well-being of a rural elite who derived their wealth and position in part from rural manufacturing activities (Wurst 1986). This rural elite used the revival religion and church structure established in the Second Great Awakening, that had occurred some 30 to 40 years earlier, to solidify their identity as a group and to try and retain their position and wealth. This futile effort manifests itself in their use of Second Great Awakening symbolism on their grave markers and in their manipulation of the country cemeteries (Wurst 1986).

In opposition to the urban elites secular strategy of naturalizing class differences, the rural elite sought to perpetuate an ideology of religious centered community that denied class differentiation. The rural elite primarily erected marble tablets, in community graveyards, undifferentiated in size or form from their employees, neighbors, or kin. They decorated these stones with the symbolism of the Second Great Awakening (clasped hands, one-way signs, anchors, Bibles, wreaths, and doves) to reinforce and maintain a religious-based ideology. The symbolism rarely occurs in urban cemeteries, which were dominated by the large neoclassical and baroque monuments of the urban elite.

The use of this symbolism differentiated the rural elite from both their workers and the urban elite. The similarities in form and size between the stones of the rural elite and their workers denied the class difference that separated them, while the differences between rural and urban elite memorials defined the rural elite as separate from the urban.

The dominant ideology of a mutually beneficial, functional, relationship between capital and labor was reinterpreted and manipulated by the various ethnic groups that made up much of the Broome County working class in the 20th century (Zahavi 1983). The responses of these people to their subordinate position were both historically and culturally derived and not reducible to a simple universal process such as emulation (see Miller 1982).

The working class in Broome County organized itself for purposes of mutual support, socializing, solidarity, and resistance along ethnic lines (Clark 1986). They created their own communities, with ethnic churches, stores, associations, and markets to create the objective reality necessary to maintain an ethnic culture. The establishment and maintenance of a separate cemetery and mortuary ritual was an important component of this culture. These ethnic cultures drew on a European heritage, but the culture was recreated by class and historical experiences in America (Clark 1986). These ethnic cultures were ideological because they provided an arena separate from the dominant society in which individuals could gain power and the consciousness required for resistance to the dominant society.

The Irish use of memorialization directly parallels the dominant group with some evidence of a slight lagging emulation. The Irish never erected memorials distinctive in form from the dominant society, but rather depended on Catholic religious symbolism and a separate cemetery to distinguish themselves. As the Irish joined the middle class, they lost the sense of community, and as new Catholic ethnic groups arrived in the early 20th century their use of dominant culture forms also identified them with the broader society.

During the mid-to-late 19th century, when the Irish made up most of the Catholics in the county, they established a separate parish cemetery. A well-defined Irish community existed and ethnic solidarity provided the organizing principle for a six-month citywide strike of the cigar factories in 1890. During this time Irish graves were like early 19th-century Protestant graves, with tablets arranged in a row for a family group or scattered individuals marked by tablets. The use of older and cheaper forms of memorialization resulted from their relative poverty, while the choice of cemetery and use of Catholic religious symbols established a unique Irish identity.

In the late 19th and early 20th century, as the Irish entered the middle class they used family plots and mausoleums like middle- and upper-class Protestants. Irish investment in memorials peaked in the 1920s, about 10 to 15 years after Protestants. From World War II on there has been little evidence of a coherent Irish community in the county, and Irish graves are virtually indistinguishable from Protestant ones, except for the use of Celtic crosses and the placement in Catholic cemeteries (Clark 1986).

The variation in Jewish cemeteries at first reflects the class position of different Jewish groups, but as most Jews joined the middle and upper classes, a common Jewish form of memorialization appears that defines an ethnic and not a class boundary (Clark 1986). Middle- and upper-class reform Jews of Germanic origin in the late 19th and early 20th century used memorials just like middle- and upper-class Protestants with family plots and the same styles of stones and decorations. Working-class Orthodox Jews from Eastern Europe had tall narrow stones like those of other Eastern European and Italian groups, and they did not use family plots, but buried each individual separately. As these Eastern European Jews became middle class in the third and fourth decades of the 20th century, the memorials of both Reform, Orthodox and the newly created Conservative Jewish communities became similar. This Jewish cemetery form with relatively massive, gray stones arranged in spouse plots continued up until the last decade. Increasingly in the last 10 years Jewish memorials are indistinguishable from the modest memorials of the Protestants and Irish, except for the star of David and frequent use of Hebrew epitaphs.

Eastern Europeans and the Italians first entered Broome County in large numbers in the first half of the 20th century and most of them continue in the working class today. In the 20th century the working class was divided by ethnic boundaries rather than being unified by a common ethnicity as the Irish had been. Ethnic solidarity and group action was, however, utilized to challenge management practices. For example, in the 1930s, when the E-J company laid off Italian workers in the tannery, the local chapter of the Sons of Italy confronted the company president and got the men rehired.

In the first three decades of this century the graves of these groups occur as single interments on the edges of the Catholic cemeteries, with a scattering of very modest monuments engraved in native languages and occasionally of unique form. In the 1920s and 1930s a variety of separate ethnic cemeteries were established and family plots with central markers begin to appear. Following World War II, there is a shift to spouse plots, but contrary to Protestant trends, investment in memorials increases instead of decreasing. These groups tend to use distinctive decorative motifs, such as statues and photos, that separate their memorials from Irish, Jews, and Protestant memorials. The Italians are the only group to erect family mausoleums since World War II. The individuals building these edifices are leaders in the Italian community and are most commonly contractors (Clark 1986).

The material manifestations of elite competition and working-class cultures, such as the cemeteries, took an active role in the negotiation of power relations in the county because they provided a material reality that objectified the divisions between competing groups. The consciousness engendered by this objectification and other processes of interaction was an a priori condition for group action, such as the elite's attempts to stave off the destruction of the rural manufacturing economy and the Irish cigar strike of 1890. The differences discussed in the cemeteries visibly challenged the dominant ideology, but also reinforced it by giving reality to stereotypes of the subordinate groups. For example, middle- and upper-class Protestants and Irish regard the elaborate memorials of the Italians as ostentatious evidence of the Italian's extravagance and lack of good taste.

A focus on the dominant ideologies of 19th- and 20th-century Broome County does provide an understanding of the most prominent changes in the cemeteries of the area, but leaves many anomalies unaccounted for. Close examination of some of these anomalies, including the graves of the rural elite and ethnic cemeteries, reveals that the dominant ideology was fractured and reworked into ideologies of resistance. An instrumentalist notion of ideology would not necessarily have accounted for these practices and could have denied us access to them.

The creation and recreation of Broome County cemeteries as meaningful landscapes involved more than ideological dialogue about power relations. The most obvious meanings in the cemetery concern death. These meanings are not simply the decorations on an ideological veil but are part of a larger cultural structure that includes ideology. The changes in beliefs about death are linked to the changes in the dominant ideology at this broader cultural level.

THE CEMETERY, CULTURE, AND DEATH

I have argued that ideology is but a piece of a larger cultural system of ideas and beliefs that structures thought. Culture by this definition is inherently mystifying because a specific categorization process that gives meaning to the world necessarily masks or hides knowledge that would be revealed through a different process of categorization. Specific elements in this process may or may not become involved in ideology, may or may not be consciously or unconsciously manipulated in power relations. The larger structure of culture, however, continues to link and affect the form of the elements included in ideology.

We can see these linkages in the cemeteries of Broome County and use them to expose underlying structures through a consideration of shifting meanings of death in this context. These shifts parallel the shifts from naturalization to denial in the ideologies of class and family revealing a more fundamental cultural shift from a system of mystification based on naturalization in the late 19th century to one based on denial in the 20th century.

In the mid-to-late 19th century, Victorian Americans dealt with the pain and shock of death by establishing an ongoing relationship with the dead (Stannard 1975:180; Jackson 1977:302; Farrell 1980:107). This was accomplished through a wide variety of practices and material culture (Pike and Armstrong 1980). An extensive literature had appeared by the 1830s that included fictionalized deathbed accounts, extensive mourner's manuals, hymnals, and poems (Douglas 1975). Some examples of this literature discussed what heaven was like down to details such as what was served for breakfast (Douglas 1975:63). Heaven was portrayed as a natural extension of the real world in which the relations and realities of the corporeal life continue but in a purer form. Deathbed scenes (especially of dying mothers or children), gravestones, cemeteries and scenes of heaven were extremely common in popular art, and they would appear on parlor walls, in schoolbooks, and in samplers. Also popular were photos of the deceased in their coffin which the family hung on the walls of their home.

The cemetery represented a bridge that connected the living and the dead. The landscaping and beautification of the rural and lawn-park cemeteries provided a pleasant, perpetual home in which the family could reside. The memorialization of the dead took on new meaning as it represented the physical connection and continuation of the family. For the memory of the person to be lost meant that the connection to the living would be broken; only then would death become a reality. For these reasons the Victorians visited the cemetery often and regarded it as a natural extension of the living world (Fallows 1885: 108).

The glorification of death did not survive the first half of the 20th century. Soon after the turn of the century the Victorian customs were attacked as morbid and wasteful. The competing ideology has been called the "pornography of death" and attempts to deal with death by denying it, removing it from the living (Gorer 1955; Ariès 1974, 1985; Becker 1973). The conflict between these two beliefs continued into the 1930s when the New York Times included articles lauding the advantages of cremation, arguing for understated cemeteries and railing at the outrageous cost of funerals (Roveland 1984:59; Warner 1959). The emphasis on burial shifted to economical and "socially inconspicuous" ways of disposing of the dead (Jackson 1977:147). More recently the attitude is manifest in critiques of the funerary industry that deplore the cost and emotional manipulation of the funeral, while the similar extravagances and emotional manipulations of weddings go unchallenged (Bowman 1964; Mitford 1963; Huntington and Metcalf 1979).

This shift in death ritual was in part allowed by the declining death rate, especially among children, and the increased use of hospitals to house the dying (Huntington and Metcalf 1979). These changes removed the reality of death from normal experience and have been accompanied by ritual denials of death. The deceased is usually embalmed to a lifelike state and laid at rest in a "slumber room" at the mortuary removed from the home (Ariès 1974). Following the funeral, prolonged periods of mourning and the wearing of black in everyday activities are discouraged as morbid and deleterious to recovery from the grief (Huntington and Metcalf 1979).

The Memorial Park cemetery that first appeared in Broome County in the 1930s provides the final expression of the denial of death. The cemetery resembles a golf course except for the fact that the terrain is too steep. Those who pass it are not confronted with the dead through their monuments, but instead observe a verdant well-kept lawn with scattered vases of flowers.

The changes in the cemetery that create the appearance necessary for the denial of death are consistent with the changes that allow the denial of class and gender inequality. The decrease in investment and standardization of monuments serves both ends. This does not have to be the case. In the early 19th century inequalities were denied in Broome County cemeteries through the use of standardized, highly visible, white marble tablets. These tablets created an equality in the graveyard that did not exist in life, but they also affirmed the certainty of death. The finality of death was denied in the symbols and epitaphs on these monuments, which promised a blessed spiritual life for eternity. Over the last 150 years the form of the Broome County cemetery resulted from and justified the existing ideology *and* the beliefs about death. In no case is the cultural landscape of the cemetery explicable solely in terms of only one of these systems of belief. Ideology and death must accommodate each other in the cemetery to maintain a minimal degree of consistency, so that the appearances created by one set of beliefs does not contradict and challenge the other.

I find it difficult to convincingly link the shifts in beliefs surrounding death to changes in the capitalist economy over the last 150 years and/or to the manipulations and renegotiations of power relations that accompanied these shifts. They appear to connect with the shifts in ideology surrounding the family and stratification at a more basic level and in a more general cultural context. The similarities between these belief systems and their expression in the cemeteries of Broome County suggest a shift in the underlying structure of culture and the mystification inherent in culture. This has been a shift from a naturalization of those things that are exploitative, or in the case of death, traumatic, to a denial of those things. This shift derives from and promulgates changes in the nature of the capitalist economy, but does so as part of a larger cultural whole. This conclusion points to the desirability of an even wider cultural and social analysis of the cemetery than that attempted here.

The dead of Broome County engage the living in a dialogue through the monuments they erected and the cultural landscapes they created in the cemeteries. They do not communicate in the simple and direct fashion that many of us as archaeologists have been wont to interpret them. Our assumptions that mortuary display will directly reflect status are not only empirically incorrect in Broome County, but also deny us the ability to ask the truly intriguing questions that allow us to unravel the complexity of the changing discourse with the dead.

Culture and ideology lie at the heart of this discourse, and the fusing of statements concerning family, stratification, and death in the cemetery provides a vehicle to examine change in the underlying structure of culture and ideology. The dead, however, can establish the discourse but not maintain it. The discourse must ultimately go on in the consciousness of the living, and the changes in the material conditions and experiences of the living affect the forms that the discourse will take. In this way the cemetery becomes an active agent in social negotiations and culture change.

ACKNOWLEDGMENTS

This paper is just one product of a larger research project and could not have been completed without the assistance of the other people who have worked on the project, including Lynn Clark, Louann Wurst, Karlene Leeper, and James Gibb. The managers of the cemeteries in Broome County have assisted our work greatly, especially Roger Cooper of Riverhurst Cemetery in Endwell. Conversations with Ted Dethlefsen, Robert Paynter, Catherine Lutz, Eric Wolf, Jane Collins, and Meg Conkey were extremely helpful to my formulation of this study. Numerous individuals read earlier drafts of the paper and provided me with valuable advice, not all of which I followed, including Susan Pollack, Tammy Bray, Andy Black, Jane Collins, Lynn Clark, Cynthia Woodsong, Ian Hodder, Sarah Elbert, George Cotkin, and Mark Leone. Parker Potter deserves special thanks for his input into the revision process. Louann Wurst led me to the insight that dominant and subordinate ideologies could not function in the same way.

REFERENCES CITED

Abercombie, Nicholas, Stephen Hill, Bryan S. Turner
    1980   *The Dominant Ideology Thesis*. London: Allen and Unwin.

Althusser, Louis
    1971   *Lenin and Philosophy*. New York: Monthly Review Press.

Amsden, John
 1979   Introduction. In *100 Years of Labor in the USA,* ed. Daniel Guein,
         pp. 1–30. London: Ink Links.

Ariès, Philippe
 1974   *Western Attitudes towards Death from the Middle Ages to the Present.*
         Baltimore: Johns Hopkins University Press.
 1985   *Images of Man and Death.* Cambridge: Harvard University Press.

Bartel, Brad
 1982   A Historical Review of Ethnological and Archaeological Analyses of
         Mortuary Practices. *Journal of Anthropological Archaeology* 1(1) :
         32–58.

Becker, Ernst
 1973   *The Denial of Death.* New York: Free Press.

Benes, Peter
 1977   *The Mask of Orthodoxy.* Amherst: University of Massachusetts
         Press.

Binford, Lewis R.
 1962   Archaeology as Anthropology. *American Antiquity* 28: 217–25.
 1971   Mortuary Practices: Their Study and Their Potential. *Society for
         American Archaeology, Memoirs* 25: 6–29.

Bloch, Maurice
 1986   *From Blessing to Violence.* Cambridge: University of Cambridge
         Press.

Bowman, Le Roy
 1964   *The American Funeral: A Study in Guilt, Extravagance and Sublimity.*
         New York: Paperback Library.

Carver, Thomas Nixon
 1926   *The Present Economic Revolution in the United States.* London: George
         Allen and Unwin Ltd.

Chandler, Alfred Dupont
 1967   *Giant Enterprise, Ford, General Motors and the Automobile Industry.*
         New York: McGraw-Hill.

Clark, Lynn Marie
 1986   Ethnicity in Binghamton Cemeteries. Master's thesis, State Univer-
         sity of New York, Binghamton.

Conwell, Russell H.
 1905   *Acres of Diamonds.* New York: Random House.

Darnall, Margaretta J.
  1983   The American Cemetery as Picturesque Landscape: Bellefontaine
         Cemetery, St. Louis. *Winterthur Portfolio* 18: 249–70.

Deetz, James, and Edwin J. Dethlefsen
  1978   Death's Heads, Cherub, Urn and Willow. In *Historical Archaeology*,
         ed. R. L. Schuyler, pp. 83–89. Farmingdale, N.Y.: Baywood.

Dethlefsen, Edwin J.
  1977   The Cemetery and Culture Change: Archaeological Focus and Eth-
         nographic Perspective. In *The Archaeology of U.S.*, ed. R. A. Gould
         and M. B. Schiffer, pp. 137–60. New York: Academic Press.

Douglas, Ann
  1975   Heaven Our Home: Consolation Literature in the Northern United
         States, 1830–1880. In *Death in America*, ed. D. E. Stannard, pp.
         49–68, Philadelphia: University of Pennsylvania Press.

Epstein, Barbara Leslie
  1981   *The Politics of Domesticity*. Middletown, Conn.: Wesleyan Univer-
         sity Press.

Ewen, Stuart
  1976   *Captains of Consciousness: Advertising and the Social Roots of the Con-
         sumer Culture*. New York: McGraw-Hill.

Fallows, D. D.
  1885   *The Home Beyond, or Views of Heaven and Its Relation to Earth*. Chi-
         cago: Fairbanks and Palmer.

Farrell, James
  1980   *Inventing the American Way of Death, 1830–1920*. Philadelphia: Tem-
         ple University Press.

Ford, Henry
  1929   *My Philosophy of Industry*. New York: Coward-McCann.

French, Stanley
  1975   The Cemetery as Cultural Institution: The Establishment of Mount
         Auburn and the "Rural Cemetery Movement." In *Death in Amer-
         ica*, ed. D. E. Stannard, pp. 69–91. Philadelphia: University of
         Pennsylvania Press.

Gibb, James G.
  1985   Gravestones and Wakes: Binghamton's Funerary Industry Since
         1860. Paper presented at the 69th annual meeting of the New York
         State Archaeological Association, April 19–21, Oneonta.

Godelier, Maurice
    1982   The Ideal in the Real. In *Culture Ideology and Politics,* ed. Raphael
            Samuel and G. S. Jones, pp. 12–38. London: Routledge and Kegan
            Paul.

Gorer, Geoffrey
    1955   The Pornography of Death. *Encounter* 5: 49–52.

Gramsci, Antonio
    1971   *Selections from the Prison Notebooks.* New York: International Pub-
            lishers.

Guein, Daniel
    1979   *100 Years of Labor in the USA.* London: Ink Links.

Handsman, Russell G.
    1983   Towards Archaeological Histories of Robbins Swamp. *Artifact*
            11(3): 1–20.

Hodder, Ian
    1982   Theoretical Archaeology: A Reactionary View. In *Symbolic and
            Structural Archaeology,* ed. Ian Hodder, pp. 1–16. Cambridge: Cam-
            bridge University Press.

Huntington, Richard, and Peter Metcalf
    1979   *Celebrations of Death: The Anthropology of Mortuary Ritual.* Cam-
            bridge: Cambridge University Press.

Jackson, Charles O.
    1977   *Passing—The Vision of Death in America.* Westport, Conn.: Green-
            wood Press.

Kristiansen, Kristian
    1984   Ideology and Material Culture: An Archaeological Perspective. In
            Marxist Perspectives in Archaeology, ed. Matthew Spriggs, pp.
            72–100. Cambridge: Cambridge University Press.

Larrain, Jorge
    1983   *Marxism and Ideology.* London: Macmillan.

Leone, Mark P.
    1986   Symbolic, Structural, and Critical Archaeology. In *American Archae-
            ology Past and Future*, ed. D. J. Meltzer, D. D. Fowler, and J. A.
            Sabloff, pp. 415–38. Washington, D.C.: Smithsonian Institution
            Press.

Linden, Blanche M. G.
    1980   The Willow Tree and Urn Motif. *Markers* 1: 149–56.

Lukacs, Georg
 1971   *History and Class Conciousness.* Cambridge, Mass.: MIT Press.

Lynd, Robert S., and Helen Merrell Lynd
 1929   *Middletown.* New York: Harcourt Brace Jovanovich.

Mandel, Ernest
 1978   *Late Capitalism.* London: Verso.

Marx, Karl
 1978   *The Eighteenth Brumaire of Louis Bonaparte.* Peking: Foreign Language Press.

Marx, Karl, and Friedrich Engles
 1947   *The German Ideology.* New York: International Publishers.

Matthaei, Julie A.
 1982   *An Economic History of Women in America.* New York: Schocken Books.

Mepham, John
 1979   The Theory of Ideology in Capital. In *Issue in Marxist Philosophy III,* ed. John Mepham and D. H. Ruben, pp. 141–74, Atlantic Highlands: Humanities Press.

Meyer, Stephen III
 1981   *The Five Dollar Day.* Albany: SUNY Press.

Miller, Daniel
 1982   Structures and Strategies: An Aspect of the Relationship between Social Hierarchy and Cultural Change. In *Symbolic and Structural Archaeology,* ed. Ian Hodder, pp. 89–98, Cambridge: Cambridge University Press.

Miller, Daniel, and Christopher Tilley (eds.)
 1984   *Ideology, Power, and History.* Cambridge: Cambridge University Press.

Mitford, Jessica
 1963   *The American Way of Death.* New York: Simon and Schuster.

Nelson, Daniel
 1975   *Managers and Workers: Origins of the New Factory System in the United States 1880–1920.* Madison: University of Wisconsin Press.

O'Shea, John M.
 1984   *Mortuary Variability: An Archaeological Investigation.* Orlando: Academic Press.

Pearson, Michael Parker
    1982   Mortuary Practices, Society and Ideology: An Ethnoarchaeological Study. In *Symbolic and Structural Archaeology,* ed. Ian Hodder, pp. 99–114. Cambridge: Cambridge University Press.

Pike, Martha V., and Janice Gray Armstrong
    1980   *A Time to Mourn: Expressions of Grief in Nineteenth Century America.* Stony Brook: Museum of Stony Brook.

Roveland, Blythe Emily
    1984   Houses of the Dead: A Study of Mausoleums in the Binghamton Area. *Harpur Academic Review* 1: 47–70.

Saum, Lewis O.
    1975   Death in the Popular Mind of Pre-Civil War America. In *Death in America,* ed. D. E. Stannard, pp. 330–48, Philadelphia: University of Pennsylvania Press.

Saxe, A. A.
    1970   Social Dimensions of Mortuary Practices. Ph.D. diss., University of Michigan, Ann Arbor.

Shanks, Michael, and Christopher Tilley
    1982   Ideology, Symbolic Power and Ritual Communication: A Reinterpretation of Neolithic Mortuary Practices. In *Symbolic and Structural Archaeology,* ed. Ian Hodder, pp. 129–54, Cambridge: Cambridge University Press.

Sochen, June
    1981   *Herstory. A Record of the American Women's Past.* Sherman Oaks, Calif.: Alfred Publishing Co.

Stannard, David E.
    1975   *Death in America.* Philadelphia: University of Pennsylvania Press.

Stowe, Harriet Beecher
    1865   *House and Home Papers.* Boston: Ticknor and Fields.

Strasser, Susan M.
    1982   *Never Done: A History of American Housework.* New York: Pantheon Books.

Sumner, William Graham
    1963   *Social Darwinism: Selected Essays.* Englewood Cliffs: Prentice-Hall.

Tainter, Joseph A.
    1978   Mortuary Practice and the Study of Prehistoric Social Systems. *Advances in Archaeological Method and Theory* 1: 106–43.

Tashjian, Dickran, and Ann Tashjian
1974   *Memorials for Children of Change*. Middletown, Conn.: Wesleyan
        University Press.

Veblen, Graham
1899   *The Theory of the Leisure Class*. London: George Allen and Unwin.

Warner, W. Lloyd
1959   *The Living and the Dead*. New Haven, Conn.: Yale University
        Press.

White, Leslie
1959   *The Evolution of Culture*. New York: McGraw-Hill.

Wurst, Lou Ann
1986   A Rope of Sand: Second Great Awakening Symbolism on the
        Gravestones of the Rural Elite in Broome County, New York.
        Master's thesis, State University of New York, Binghamton.

Zahavi, Gerld
1983   Negotiated Loyalty: Welfare Capitalism and the Shoeworkers of
        Endicott-Johnson, 1920–1940. *Journal of American History* 70(3):
        602–20.

Index